1,001 GED® Test Practice Questions

by Stuart Donnelly, PhD

1,001 GED® Test Practice Questions For Dummies®

Published by: **John Wiley & Sons, Inc.,** 111 River Street, Hoboken, NJ 07030-5774, www.wiley.com

For general information on our other products and services, please contact our Customer Care Department within the U.S. at 877-762-2974, outside the U.S. at 317-572-3993, or fax 317-572-4002. For technical support, please visit https://hub.wiley.com/community/support/dummies.

Wiley publishes in a variety of print and electronic formats and by print-on-demand. Some material included with standard print versions of this book may not be included in e-books or in print-on-demand. If this book refers to media such as a CD or DVD that is not included in the version you purchased, you may download this material at http://booksupport.wiley.com. For more information about Wiley products, visit www.wiley.com.

Library of Congress Control Number: 2017940030

ISBN 978-1-119-30098-4 (pbk); ISBN 978-1-119-30099-1 (ebk); ISBN 978-1-119-30100-4 (ebk)

Manufactured in the United States of America

10 9 8 7 6 5 4 3 2 1

Contents at a Glance

Table of Contents

Introduction

Welcome to *1,001 GED Practice Questions For Dummies.* Don't take the book title personally. In fact, I would like to congratulate you on making two very smart decisions. First, you've decided to pursue your high-school equivalency, which is one of the smartest decisions you'll ever make. Second, by purchasing this book, you've decided to put in the time and dedication to practice answering the types of questions that will appear on the GED exam, which will maximize your chances of achieving your goal.

Getting your GED will show that you have the skills and knowledge necessary to handle the rigors of college or professional employment. Many students who have successfully moved on to college, graduate school, or career-level employment consider passing the GED exam the first step in a life-changing process that placed them on the road to success. With that in mind, don't waste any time. Get practicing already!

What You'll Find

One of the best ways to maximize your exam performance is to continually expose yourself to questions that mimic the ones you'll encounter on the GED. The practice problems in this book are divided into four chapters that correspond to the four sections on the test: Reasoning Through Language Arts, Mathematical Reasoning, Social Studies, and Science. I've constructed the questions to closely resemble the actual test in both format and level of difficulty so you know exactly what to expect on the big day.

If you miss a question or guess an answer, be sure to examine the answer explanations for tips on how to improve your approach next time. It's even worth checking out the explanations for those questions you answer correctly. Often, I reveal not only how to answer the problem but also how to answer it most efficiently, which can make all the difference on test day. Be proactive. This book contains hundreds of questions, so after you've taken a bunch of tests and evaluated your performance, review the questions you missed and form your own explanations for why the credited answer is better than yours. Then check my explanations for confirmation. Apply your discoveries to more practice problems. You can benefit from this book all by itself, but it's even better when you pair it with the in-depth reviews and strategies available in latest edition of *The GED For Dummies* (Wiley). Either way, this book helps you solidify your approach and confidence in all subject areas. So keep calm, carry on, and score big on the GED!

About This Book

The first half of this book contains the practice questions for the four sections of the GED exam: Reasoning Through Language Arts, Mathematical Reasoning, Social Studies, and Science. You find the answers and explanations in the second half of the book.

The four sections of the GED exam are detailed for you in the following sections.

Social Studies

The social studies section lasts 70 minutes and is made up of 50 questions from the following content areas:

- History (U.S. or Canada, 25%; World, 15%)
- Geography (15%)
- Civics and government (25%)
- Economics (20%)

Science

The science section lasts 90 minutes and contains 50 questions from the following content areas:

- Physical science (physics and chemistry, 35%)
- Life science (45%)
- Earth and space science (20%)

Mathematics

The mathematics section lasts 115 minutes and contains 50 questions divided into two parts, and it focuses on the following content areas:

- Number operations and number sense (20–30%)
- Measurement and geometry (20–30%)
- Data analysis, statistics, and probability (20–30%)
- Algebra, functions, and patterns (20–30%)

Note that you are not allowed to use a calculator on the first five questions of the GED's mathematics section. Calculators are permitted for the remaining questions.

Reasoning Through Language Arts

The language arts section lasts 150 minutes and is split into two parts: reading and writing.

The reading section consists of 40 questions and contains passages from the following content areas:

- Fictional literature (75%)
- Nonfiction (25%)

The writing section is divided into two parts. The scores are combined and reported as a single score.

The first part contains 50 questions from the following content areas:

- Organization (15%)
- Sentence structure (30%)
- Usage (30%)
- Mechanics (25%)

The second part consists of writing an essay about a familiar subject. You have 45 minutes to plan, write, and revise your essay. The essay topic will require you to present your opinion or explain your views about the assigned topic. Two trained readers will score your essay based on the following criteria:

- Focused main points
- Clear organization
- Specific development of ideas
- Sentence structure control, punctuation, grammar, word choice, and spelling

Each reader will score your essay on a four-point scale, and the scores will be averaged to find your final score. If you earn a final score of less than 2 on the essay, you must retake language arts, writing.

Foolish Assumptions

In writing this book, I assumed several things about you, the reader, including the following:

- You've already made getting your GED a priority in your life because you want to advance in the workplace or move on to college.

- You've already studied the subject matter in depth for each of the four sections of the GED (Reasoning Through Language Arts, Mathematical Reasoning, Social Sciences, and Science) and feel relatively confident with the content of each section.
- You want access to the best GED practice questions available to help sharpen your test-taking skills.
- You have sufficient English language skills to handle the test (***Note:*** The GED is also available in Spanish).
- You've already checked that the state you live in currently offers the GED as a high-school equivalency test.
- You've already checked to make sure that you meet your state's requirements regarding age, residency, and the length of time since leaving school that make you eligible to take the GED exam. (Double-check with your local GED test administrator to find out your state's requirements.)

Beyond the Book

Your purchase of this book gives you so much more than a thousand (and one) problems to work on to improve your GED performance. It also comes with a free, one-year subscription to hundreds of practice questions online. Not only can you access this digital content anytime you want, on whichever device is available to you, but you can also track your progress and view personalized reports that show you which concepts you need to study the most.

The online practice that comes with this book offers you the same questions and answers that are available here. Of course, the real beauty of the online problems is your ability to customize your practice. In other words, you get to choose the types of problems and the number of problems you want to tackle. The online program tracks how many questions you answer correctly versus incorrectly so you get an immediate sense of which topics need more of your attention.

To gain access to practice online, all you have to do is register. Just follow these simple steps:

1. Find your PIN access code:

   Print-book users: If you purchased a print copy of this book, turn to the inside front cover of the book to find your access code.

   E-book users: If you purchased this book as an e-book, you can get your access code by registering your e-book at `www.dummies.com/go/getaccess`. Go to this website, find your book and click it, and answer the security questions to verify your purchase. You'll receive an email with your access code.
2. Go to Dummies.com and click *Activate Now.*
3. Find your product (*1,001 GED Practice Questions For Dummies*) and then follow the on-screen prompts to activate your PIN.

Now you're ready to go! You can come back to the program as often as you want — simply log in with the username and password you created during your initial login. No need to enter the access code a second time.

This product also comes with an online Cheat Sheet that helps you increase your odds of performing well on the GED. To get the Cheat Sheet, go to www.dummies.com and type "1,001 GED Practice Questions For Dummies cheat sheet" in the search box. (No access code required. You can benefit from this info before you even register.)

For Technical Support, please visit http://wiley.custhelp.com or call Wiley at 1-800-762-2974 (U.S.) or +1-317-572-3994 (international).

Where to Go for Additional Help

The solutions to the practice problems in this book are meant to walk you through how to get the right answers; they're not meant to teach the material. If certain concepts are unfamiliar to you, you can find help at www.dummies.com. Just type "GED" into the search box to turn up a wealth of GED-related information.

1 The Questions

IN THIS PART . . .

Practice math questions: number operations, geometry, data analysis, and algebra.

Answer questions on history, geography, government, and economics.

Analyze scientific data to answer questions covering biology, chemistry, and physics.

Tackle reading comprehension questions.

Test your knowledge of sentence structure, organization, usage, and mechanics.

Answer essay questions.

Chapter 1
Mathematical Reasoning

The GED's mathematics section lasts 115 minutes and contains 50 questions divided into two parts: a calculator-allowed part and a no-calculator-allowed part. The no-calculator-allowed questions tend to be less math-heavy and more concept-based, whereas the calculator-allowed questions tend to more challenging and require more calculations. In this chapter, you get 285 questions to practice your math skills.

The Problems You'll Work On

The mathematics section focuses on the following content areas for both the calculator and no-calculator parts:

- Number operations and number sense
- Measurement and geometry
- Data analysis, statistics, and probability
- Algebra, functions, and patterns

What to Watch Out For

To increase your accuracy and improve time management, avoid these snags:

- Making mistakes in simple math, such as improperly subtracting negative numbers
- Spending more than a couple of minutes on any one problem instead of marking time-consuming questions and returning to them later
- Failing to review key formulas and concepts from all math areas
- Engaging in complex calculations when you can instead apply time-saving strategies such as trying answer choices and plugging in values for variables

1. If $f(x) = 2x - 3$, what is the value of $f(x)$ when x is -5?

(A) -13

(B) -7

(C) 7

(D) 11

2. What is the correct way of writing "x is less than 5 but greater than or equal to -3"?

(A) $x - 5 \geq -3$

(B) $5 - x \geq -3$

(C) $-3 \leq x < 5$

(D) $-3 \geq x > 5$

3. If $x^2 + 3x = 10$, which of the following is a possible value of x?

(A) -2

(B) 5

(C) 7

(D) -5

4. Jim rented a lawnmower from 9:00 a.m. until 5:30 p.m. He paid a total of $53.04. What was the hourly rental fee? (*Note:* You may *not* use a calculator for this problem.)

(A) $5.58

(B) $6.24

(C) $6.63

(D) $7.07

5. What is the value of $6x - 3y^2$ when $x = 12$ and $y = -5$?

(A) -153

(B) 297

(C) -3

(D) 147

6. Alex earns a weekly base salary of $650 as a car salesman. He also earns a 9% commission on his monthly sales after the first $10,000. What was his total salary this month if he sold 7 cars whose average price was $4,500 each?

(A) $1,935

(B) $2,585

(C) $2,835

(D) $3,485

7. Simplify the expression completely.

$\sqrt{20} \cdot \sqrt{10}$

(A) $5\sqrt{2}$

(B) $\sqrt{200}$

(C) $2\sqrt{10}$

(D) $10\sqrt{2}$

8. A human hair has an average diameter of 2.5×10^{-5} meters. What is the maximum number of human hairs that could fit side by side (without overlapping) on a microscope slide that is 50 millimeters wide? Write your answer in scientific notation.

(A) 2.0×10^3

(B) 2.0×10^5

(C) 2×10^6

(D) 10^{-3}

9. Bob is planning a birthday party for his son and has a maximum budget of $475 to spend. He intends to rent a party room that costs $125 for the day. He expects a total of 35 people to attend the party and plans to provide them all with lunch. Which of the following inequalities shows how to calculate the amount x that Bob can spend on lunch for each person?

(A) $125x + 35 \geq 475$

(B) $125x + 35 \leq 475$

(C) $125 + 35x \geq 475$

(D) $125 + 35x \leq 475$

10. Four years ago, Jenny's annual salary was $22,625. This year, her salary was $32,433. What will her new salary be in 5 years if it continues to rise at the same linear rate?

(A) $34,885

(B) $42,241

(C) $44,693

(D) $55,058

11. Mr. White's math class has n students. Mrs. Black's math class has 22 students fewer than triple the number of students in Mr. White's class. Which expression shows the number of students in Mrs. Black's class in terms of n?

(A) $22 < 3n$

(B) $3(n-22)$

(C) $22-3n$

(D) $3n-22$

Questions 12 through 14 are based on the following information.

Denise measures the height of a sunflower every other week over a three-month period and records the results in the following table.

Weeks	Height (in cm)
1	3.00
3	4.70
5	6.40
7	8.10
9	9.80
11	11.50
13	13.20

12. Denise plots the data on a coordinate grid. She begins by plotting the data for Week 3 and Week 11.

What are the coordinates of the two points that Denise plots?

(A) (11,3) and (11.5, 4.7)

(B) (3, 11) and (4.7, 11.5)

(C) (3, 4.7) and (11, 11.5)

(D) (4.7, 3) and (11.5, 11)

13. Denise creates an equation that will allow her to predict the height of the sunflower in the future, where x is the week and y is the height. Which of the following gives the correct equation?

(A) $y=0.85x+2.15$

(B) $y=1.7x+2.15$

(C) $y=0.85x+1.3$

(D) $y=1.7x+1.3$

14. If the sunflower continues to grow at the same rate, at what week will it reach a height of 16.6 cm?

(A) Week 15

(B) Week 17

(C) Week 19

(D) Week 21

15. A doctor measured the blood sugar levels of one of her patients shortly after giving the patient a candy bar to eat. The graph below shows the patient's blood sugar level (y) x hours after she ate the candy bar.

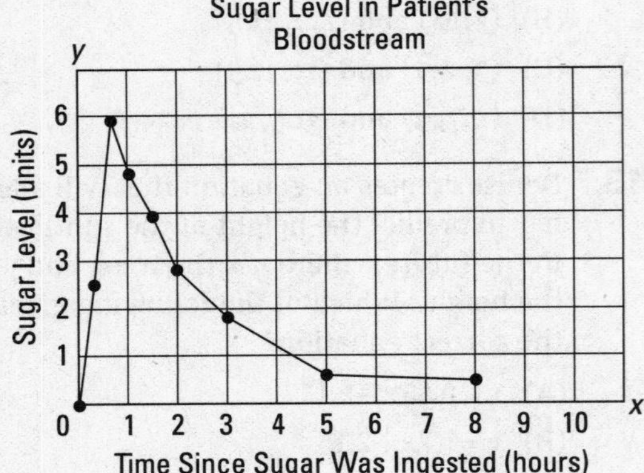

How long after eating the candy bar was the patient's blood sugar level the highest?

(A) 20 minutes

(B) 30 minutes

(C) 40 minutes

(D) 1 hour

16. A candy store sells soda in cone-shaped cups with the dimensions shown here:

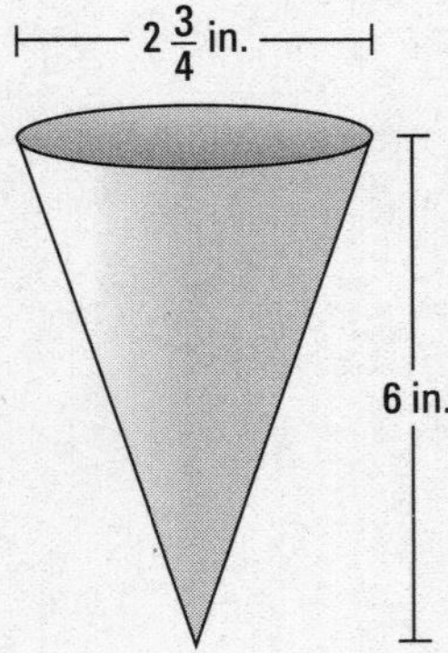

What volume of soda can each cup hold? Give your answer to the nearest tenth of a cubic inch. The formula for the volume V of a cone with radius r and height h is $V = \frac{1}{3}\pi r^2 h$.

(A) 11.8

(B) 11.9

(C) 47.5

(D) 142.5

17. Anne plans to spend no more than \$60 ordering socks for school. The online sock company charges a shipping fee of \$15 for any order. The inequality $15 + 5x \leq 60$ represents the number of pairs of socks Anne can order from the company. What is the maximum number of pairs of socks that Anne can buy?

____

Questions 18 and 19 are based on the following information.

Ten students took a math quiz that consisted of 10 questions. The median score was 5.5. The modal score was 6. The teacher recorded the results of the first nine students in the following line plot.

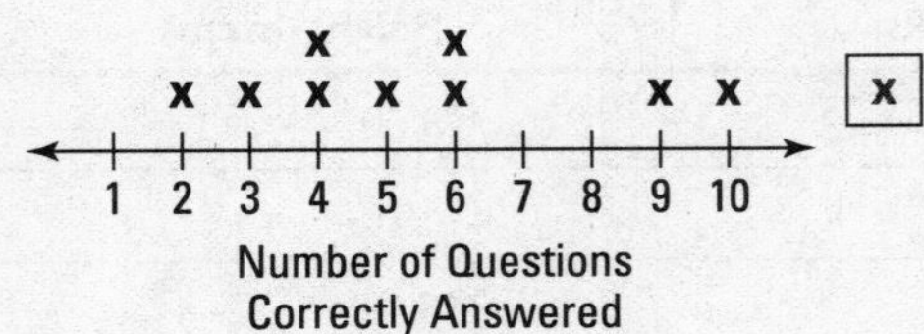

18. What was the average score of the first nine students whose scores were represented on the line plot? Give your answer to one decimal place.

(A) 4.9

(B) 5.4

(C) 5.5

(D) 5.7

19. What score did the tenth student get in the quiz?

(A) 4

(B) 5

(C) 6

(D) 7

Questions 20 through 22 are based on the following information.

The probability that it will snow during the next three days is given in the following table.

Day	Monday	Tuesday	Wednesday
Probability of snow	70%	20%	40%

20. What is the probability that it will *not* snow on Tuesday?

(A) 20%

(B) 40%

(C) 60%

(D) 80%

21. What is the probability that it will snow on all three days?

____

22. What is the probability that it will snow on two out of three days? Round your answer to the nearest whole number.

(A) 33%

(B) 43%

(C) 90%

(D) 130%

23. Using the information in the following chart, estimate to the nearest thousand the total number of tickets sold at the concert hall. (*Note:* You may *not* use a calculator.)

Concert	Tickets Sold
The Ghastly Girls	4,721
Two Directions	5,301
Taylor Speedy	8,783
Maroon 6	270
The Subdominants	11,802

(A) 27,000

(B) 29,000

(C) 31,000

(D) 31,877

24. Egypt's Great Pyramid is 150 m tall and has a square base with a length of 225 m. What is the approximate volume of the pyramid in cubic meters? The formula for the volume V of a pyramid of base area B and height h is given by $V = \frac{1}{3}Bh$.

(A) 500,000

(B) 1,500,000

(C) 2,500,000

(D) 7,500,000

Questions 25 through 27 are based on the following set.

Set A: $\{41, 51, 61, 71, 81, 91, 101\}$

25. What is the range of Set A?

(A) 41

(B) 60

(C) 71

(D) 142

26. What is the median of Set A?

(A) 41
(B) 60
(C) 71
(D) 142

27. What is the arithmetic mean (average) of Set A?

(A) 41
(B) 60
(C) 71
(D) 142

28. Four hundred eighty yards is what fraction of a mile? (1 mile = 1,760 yards)

(A) $\frac{27}{100}$
(B) $3\frac{2}{3}$
(C) $\frac{2}{5}$
(D) $\frac{3}{11}$

29. Tim measures the lengths of four cats' tails and records his results in the following table.

Cat	Tail Length (Inches)
Mrs. Whiskers	$7\frac{3}{4}$
Bootsie	$7\frac{3}{8}$
Mr. Bigglesworth	$7\frac{11}{16}$
Catty McCatface	$7\frac{25}{32}$

Which cat has the longest tail? (*Note:* You may *not* use a calculator.)

(A) Mrs. Whiskers
(B) Bootsie
(C) Mr. Bigglesworth
(D) Catty McCatface

30. The U.S. Senate has 100 senators. In 2015, only 20 senators were female. What is the ratio of female senators to male senators? (*Note:* You may *not* use a calculator.)

(A) 1:5
(B) 1:4
(C) 4:5
(D) 4:1

31. Alex test drives four cars and records the distance traveled and the gallons of gas used in each case in the following table.

Car	Distance Driven (Miles)	Gas Used (Gallons)
A	102.3	11.5
B	78.1	7.9
C	57.8	6.2
D	142.9	15.9

Which car has the best gas mileage (miles per gallon)?

(A) Car A
(B) Car B
(C) Car C
(D) Car D

Questions 32 and 33 are based on the following information.

A fair die has six sides, each marked with a different integer from 1 to 6. Each side is equally likely to land face up when the die is rolled.

32. Suppose you roll the die 66 times. How many times are you likely to roll a 6?

(A) 6
(B) 11
(C) 55
(D) 66

33. Suppose you roll the die three times. What is the probability of not rolling any 1s during the three rolls? Express your answer as a fraction reduced to its lowest terms.

____

34. Monthly sales of a particular brand of smartphone are inversely proportional to the number of occurrences of exploding cellphone batteries during that month. If 88 million phones were sold when there were 2 exploding batteries, how many cell phones would be sold during a month in which 22 batteries exploded?

(A) 4 million

(B) 8 million

(C) 44 million

(D) 176 million

35. The scale on a blueprint for a boat is 2 cm = 5 meters. If the length of the boat on the blueprint measures 7.5 cm, how long is the actual boat?

(A) 12.50 m

(B) 15.25 m

(C) 18.75 m

(D) 20.25 m

36. A New York City taxi charges an initial fee of $2.50 plus $0.50 for every $\frac{1}{5}$ of a mile traveled. If Jim's total fare (not including tip) equals $14.50, how many miles did Jim travel?

(A) 4.8 miles

(B) 5.8 miles

(C) 24 miles

(D) 29 miles

37. Arnold invested $700 in a savings account. After one year, his account balance was $726.25. What percent annual interest did his bank pay?

____

Questions 38 and 39 are based on the following information.

At Becky's Burger Shack, cooks earn an average of $950 per week, whereas waiters earn an average of $725 per week. Let *x* and *y* equal the number of cooks and waiters, respectively, employed by the restaurant.

38. Which of the following functions represents the total payroll *(P)* that Becky's restaurant pays for all of these types of workers?

(A) $P = 950y + 725x$

(B) $P = (950x)(725y)$

(C) $P = 950x + 725y$

(D) $P = (x + y)(950 + 725)$

39. Becky employs 5 cooks and can spend no more than $9,825 per week on the payroll for all her cooks and waiters. What is the maximum number of waiters that she can employ?

(A) 3

(B) 5

(C) 7

(D) 9

40. If $\frac{2}{7}x = 31$, what does $\frac{4}{7}x$ equal?

(A) 15.5

(B) 62

(C) 108.5

(D) 217

Questions 41 and 42 are based on the following information.

A moving company rents small or large vans for a fixed fee of $80 and $125, respectively, plus $3.75 per mile driven. The company also offers professional movers at a rate of $18 per mover per hour.

41. Sid rents a large van with 3 professional movers for 5 hours and drives a total of 42 miles. How much will the company charge him (not including tips or taxes)?

____

42. Jenny's moving bill was $450 before taxes and tips. If taxes are 6% and she also wants to tip her three professional movers $20 each, what does her total bill equal?

(A) $497

(B) 498.20

(C) $537

(D) $540.60

Questions 43 through 45 are based on the following graph.

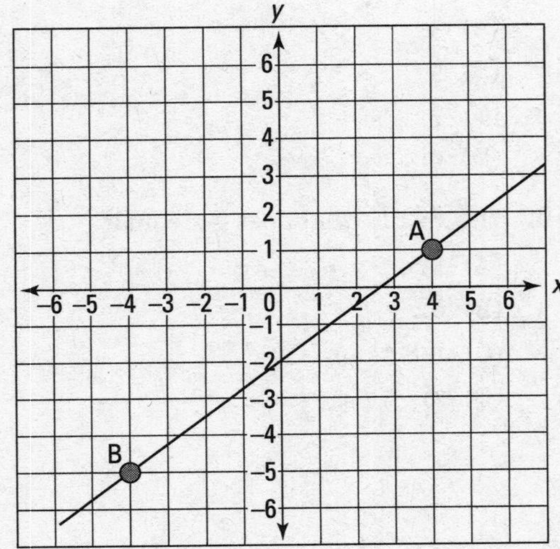

43. What are the coordinates of point *A*?

(A) (4,1)

(B) (1,4)

(C) (−5, −4)

(D) (−4, −5)

44. What is the slope of the line?

(A) $\frac{4}{3}$

(B) $\frac{3}{4}$

(C) $-\frac{3}{4}$

(D) $\frac{2}{3}$

45. What is the equation of the line?

(A) $y = \frac{4}{3}x - 2$

(B) $y = \frac{3}{4}x - 2$

(C) $y = -2x + \frac{3}{4}$

(D) $y = -2x + \frac{4}{3}$

46. A car dealership offers 45% off all its cars during its annual sale. Jessica pays $7,150 for her discounted vehicle. What was the original price of the car? Round your answer to the nearest dollar.

(A) $3,933

(B) $10,368

(C) $13,000

(D) $15,889

47. On a sunny day, a tree casts a shadow that is 33 feet long. At the same time, a nearby 4-foot-tall mailbox casts a shadow that is 5.5 feet long. What is the height of the tree? Round your answer to the nearest foot.

(A) 24 feet

(B) 33 feet

(C) 38 feet

(D) 45 feet

48. The hypotenuse of a right triangle is 17 inches. If one of the legs of the triangle is 8 inches long, what is the length of the other leg?

(A) 8 inches

(B) 12 inches

(C) 15 inches

(D) 19 inches

Questions 49 through 51 are based on the following graph.

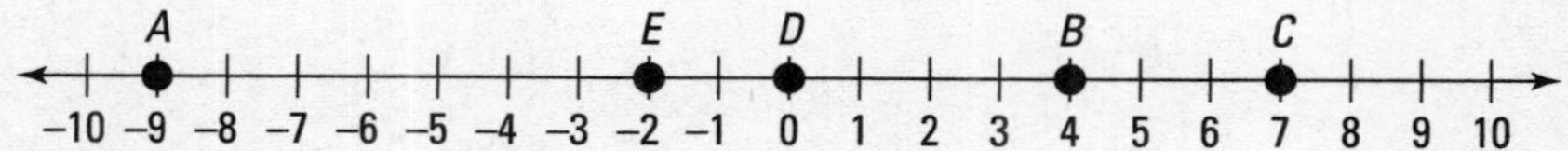

49. What is the value of *A* minus *E*?

(A) −13

(B) −11

(C) −7

(D) 7

50. What is the product of *A* times *C* times *D* times *E*?

(A) −126

(B) 0

(C) 63

(D) 126

51. Which of the following is true?

(A) $|A| < |C|$

(B) $|D| > |E|$

(C) $-|E| < A$

(D) $-A > |E| + |B|$

52. If $x^2 - 5x = 24$, which of the following is a possible value of x?

(A) −8

(B) 3

(C) 8

(D) 24

53. $(x+y)^2$ is equivalent to which of the following?

(A) $x^2 + y^2$

(B) x^2y^2

(C) $x^2 + y^2 + 2xy$

(D) $2x + 2y$

54. A cube has a surface area of 216 square inches. What is its volume in cubic inches?

(A) 6

(B) 36

(C) 108

(D) 216

55. $\sqrt{162}$ is equivalent to which of the following?

(A) $3\sqrt{2}$

(B) $9\sqrt{2}$

(C) $54\sqrt{3}$

(D) $2\sqrt{81}$

56. $\sqrt{129}$ is between which numbers?

(A) 10 and 11

(B) 11 and 12

(C) 14 and 15

(D) 64 and 65

Questions 57 through 59 are based on the following information.

Steven bought a bag of nuts containing 15 almonds, 3 peanuts, 12 cashews, and 10 pistachios.

57. What fraction of the nuts were cashews? Reduce your answer to its lowest terms.

(A) $\frac{12}{40}$

(B) $\frac{3}{40}$

(C) $\frac{3}{10}$

(D) $\frac{5}{20}$

58. Steven takes 2 nuts out of the bag without looking at them or replacing them. What is the probability that both of the nuts are peanuts? Reduce your answer to its lowest terms.

(A) $\frac{1}{20}$

(B) $\frac{3}{40}$

(C) $\frac{5}{79}$

(D) $\frac{1}{260}$

59. If the bag of nuts cost Steven $5.20, what was the average cost per nut?

(A) $0.08

(B) $0.11

(C) $0.13

(D) $0.17

60. Solve the following equation for x:
$19 - 2x = -1$

____

Questions 61 and 62 are based on a line whose equation is given by the following:

$y - 4x = 13$

61. Point A lies on the line. If the y-coordinate of point A is 5, what is the value of the corresponding x-coordinate?

(A) −7

(B) −2

(C) 3

(D) 33

62. Fill in the blanks by choosing the correct values from the brackets:

The value of the slope of the line is ______ [−13, −4, 4, 13], and the value of the y-intercept is ______ [−13, −4, 4, 13].

63. A company manufactures light bulbs. If 1 out of 25 light bulbs produced by the company is found to be defective, how many defective light bulbs will there be in a batch of 3,075 light bulbs?

(A) 25

(B) 123

(C) 500

(D) 76,875

Questions 64 through 66 are based on the following rectangle.

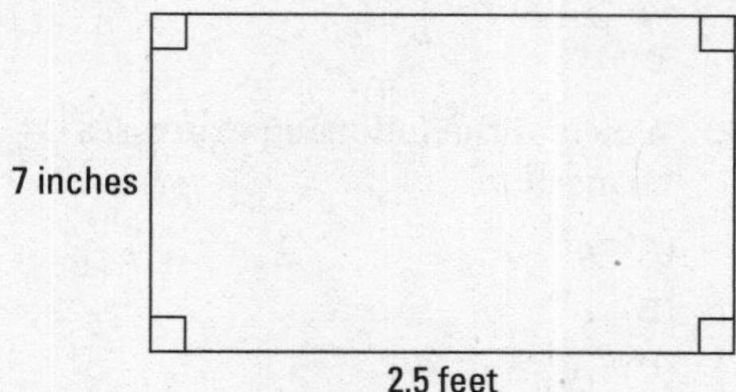

64. What is the area of the rectangle? (Give your answer to the nearest square inch.)

(A) 10

(B) 17

(C) 18

(D) 210

65. If the rectangle were enlarged by a factor of 3 (so that its sides became 3 times as long as they were previously), what would be the ratio of the new perimeter to the old perimeter?

(A) 1:3

(B) 1:9

(C) 3:1

(D) 9:1

66. If rectangle *ABCD* were enlarged by a factor of 3 (so that its sides became 3 times as long as they were previously), what would be the ratio of the new area to the old area?

(A) 1:3

(B) 1:9

(C) 3:1

(D) 9:1

67. What is the decimal equivalent of $\frac{3}{8}$? (*Note:* You may *not* use a calculator.)

____

68. What is the sum of $2.8\times10^5 + 1.7\times10^4$? (*Note:* You may *not* use a calculator.)

(A) 4.5×10^5

(B) 4.5×10^9

(C) 2.97×10^4

(D) 2.97×10^5

69. What is the product of $(8\times10^6)\times(4\times10^{-3})$? Write your answer in scientific notation. (*Note:* You may *not* use a calculator.)

(A) 3.2×10^{-17}

(B) 3.2×10^2

(C) 32×10^3

(D) 3.2×10^4

70. Select from the options to correctly fill in the blanks.

Two lines that never meet are called ________________ lines, and their slopes are ________________. Two lines that meet at right angles are called ________________ lines, and their slopes are ________________.

Options:

parallel

perpendicular

equal

negative reciprocals

Questions 71 through 73 are based on the following information.

The average price of a gallon of gasoline increased in a linear fashion over a 4-week period as shown in the table.

Week	Price ($ per Gallon)
Week 1	$3.29
Week 2	$3.38
Week 3	$3.47
Week 4	$3.56

71. What is the range of the prices in the table? (Round your answer to the nearest cent.)

____

72. What is the average price of a gallon of gasoline during the given 4-week period? (Give your answer to the nearest cent.)

(A) $3.42

(B) $3.43

(C) $3.51

(D) $3.52

73. If the average price of a gallon of gasoline continues to rise at the same rate, what will 3 gallons of gasoline cost during Week 8?

(A) $3.92

(B) $4.24

(C) $7.51

(D) $11.76

Questions 74 through 76 are based on the following information.

$x = p^7$, $y = p^{-3}$, and $z = \frac{1}{p}$

74. Which of the following expresses $\left(\frac{x}{y}\right)^2$ in terms of p?

(A) p^8

(B) p^{10}

(C) p^{20}

(D) p

75. Which of the following expresses $\left(\frac{x^2 \cdot y^4}{z^3}\right)^0$ in terms of p?

(A) 0

(B) 1

(C) p^{-5}

(D) p

76. Which of the following expresses $(x)(y)^2(z)$ in terms of p?

(A) 1

(B) p

(C) p^7

(D) p^9

77. $f(x) = \frac{10 - x^2}{x^2}$

What is the value of $f(x)$ when x is -3?

(A) 9

(B) 10

(C) $\frac{1}{9}$

(D) $\frac{19}{9}$

Questions 78 through 80 are based on the following diagram, which shows a pair of parallel lines crossed by a transversal line.

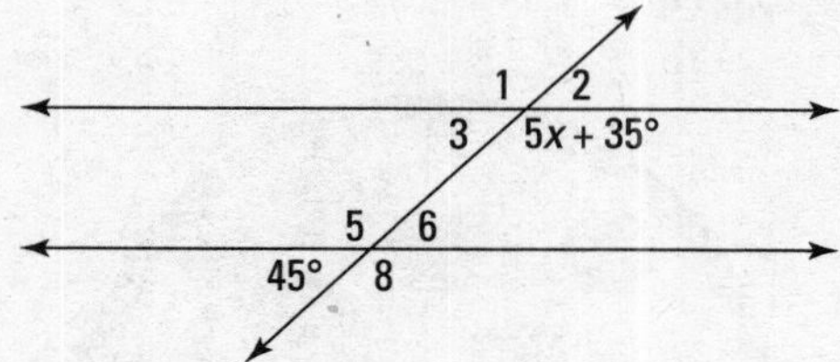

78. Select from the options to correctly fill in the blanks.

Angle 2 is a/an ______________ angle and is ______________ to angle 1. Angle 5 is a/an ______________ angle and is ______________ to angle 8.

Options:

acute

obtuse

reflex

complementary

supplementary

congruent

79. What is the measure of angle 1? (***Note:*** You may *not* use a calculator.)

(A) 45°

(B) 125°

(C) 135°

(D) 145°

80. What is the value of x?

____

81. A boat's sail is in the shape of an isosceles triangle. If the largest angle of the sail is 90°, what is the measure of the smallest angle in degrees?

____

82. The angles of a triangle are in a ratio of 5 : 9 : 14. What is the measure of the largest angle?

(A) 25°

(B) 45°

(C) 90°

(D) 140°

83. A recipe for cookies calls for $\frac{3}{8}$ cup of brown sugar to make 2 dozen cookies. If Sasha has 4.5 cups of brown sugar available and enough of all the other ingredients, how many dozen cookies can he make?

(A) 9 dozen

(B) 12 dozen

(C) 15 dozen

(D) 24 dozen

84. Simplify: $(5x+1)(3x-4)$

(A) $15x^2-17x-4$

(B) $-2x-4$

(C) $8x-3$

(D) $15x^2+23x-4$

85. Which number equals 7 thousandths?

(A) 0.7

(B) 0.07

(C) 0.007

(D) 7,000

86. A newspaper charges advertisers a total of $5.50 for the first ten words and $0.70 for each additional word. What is the cost of a 27-word advert?

(A) $6.20

(B) $17.40

(C) $18.90

(D) $66.90

Questions 87 and 88 are based on the following information.

A sports enthusiast measures the number of calories used per hour per pound of weight for four different sports. He records the results in the following table.

Sport	Calories Used per Hour per Pound of Weight
Cycling	8.8
Running	12.7
Soccer	9.4
Tennis	6.1

87. What is the average number of calories used per hour per pound of weight for the four sports listed in the table? Give your answer to the nearest one hundredth of a calorie.

____

88. Which of the following could be used to calculate how many calories a 170-pound man would use by cycling for 20 minutes?

(A) $\frac{170\times 8.8}{3}$

(B) $\frac{170\times 8.8}{20}$

(C) $\frac{170\times 20}{8.8}$

(D) $\frac{20\times 8.8}{170}$

Questions 89 through 91 are based on the following information.

A large circular pizza has an 18-inch diameter and is cut into 8 equal slices.

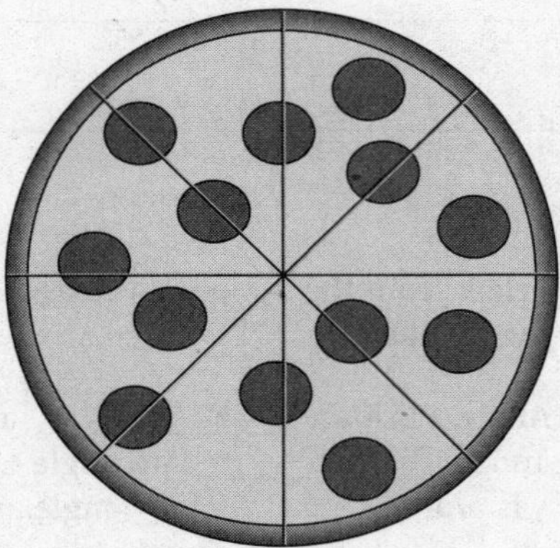

89. What is the innermost angle of one slice of the pizza?

____

90. What is the perimeter of one slice of the pizza?

(A) 2.25π

(B) $2.25\pi+9$

(C) $2.25\pi+18$

(D) 81π

91. What is the total area of two slices of the pizza?

(A) 20.25π

(B) 36π

(C) 41.5π

(D) 81π

Questions 92 and 93 are based on the following information.

Jack needs to put a fence around his lawn. The dimensions of the lawn are shown in the following diagram.

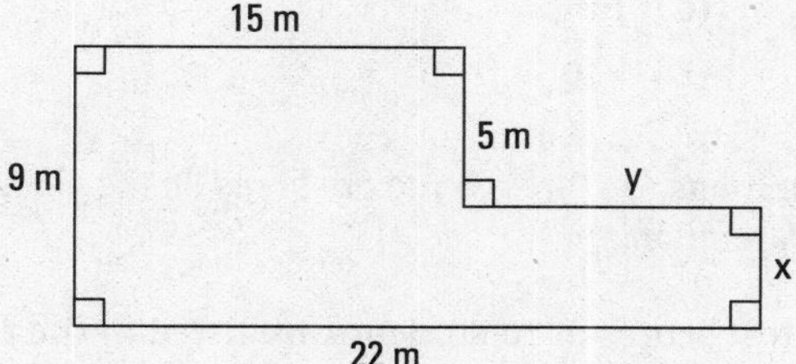

92. Find the values of x and y, respectively.

(A) $x = 7, y = 4$

(B) $x = 4, y = 7$

(C) $x = 5, y = 15$

(D) $x = 15, y = 5$

93. If lawn fertilizer costs $0.15 per square meter, how much will it cost Jack to fertilize his lawn? Round your answer to the nearest dollar.

(A) $24

(B) $25

(C) $30

(D) $163

94. What is the radius (in cm) of a circle whose circumference happens to equal its area (in cm²)?

(A) 2 cm

(B) 3 cm

(C) 5 cm

(D) 10 cm

95. What is the probability of tossing 5 heads in a row when using a fair coin?

(A) $\frac{1}{2}$

(B) $\frac{1}{8}$

(C) $\frac{1}{32}$

(D) $\frac{5}{2}$

96. The temperature at 5:00 a.m. was −11 degrees. By 8:00 a.m., the temperature is −2 degrees. If the temperature continues to rise at the same rate, what will the temperature be at 2:00 p.m.?

(A) 7 degrees

(B) 16 degrees

(C) 21 degrees

(D) 27 degrees

97. If sales tax is 6 percent, what would be the tax on a shirt that cost $68.30? Round your answer to the nearest cent.

(A) $4.09

(B) $4.10

(C) $4.58

(D) $4.59

98. The dimensions of a rectangular prism are 9 inches wide by 18 inches long by 2 feet tall. What is the volume of the prism in cubic feet?

(A) 2.25

(B) 8.75

(C) 36

(D) 324

Questions 99 through 101 are based on the following diagram, which shows a right triangular prism.

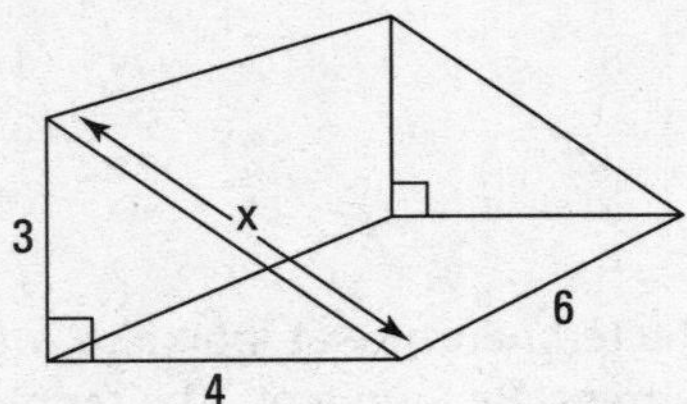

99. What is the length of the hypotenuse of the prism's triangular base?

____

100. What is the area of the triangular base of the prism?

(A) 6

(B) 10

(C) 12

(D) 36

101. What is the volume of the prism?

(A) 36

(B) 45

(C) 72

(D) 90

102. If $a = -3$ and $b = 2$, what is the value of $\frac{a^2 - 3b}{a} + 4$?

(A) 3

(B) 9

(C) 15

(D) 21

103. What is the next term in the following geometric sequence?

810, −270, 90, −30, …

(A) $\frac{10}{3}$

(B) $-\frac{10}{3}$

(C) 10

(D) −10

Questions 104 through 106 are based on the following information.

The test scores of 10 students are listed in the following frequency table.

Score	Number of Students
72	1
85	3
90	4
100	2

104. What is the average score? (Round your answer to the nearest whole number)

(A) 35

(B) 81

(C) 87

(D) 89

105. If the lowest two scores are omitted, what is the new average score? (Round your answer to the nearest whole number)

(A) 73

(B) 89

(C) 91

(D) 92

106. Simplify the expression: $(7x-5y+2z)-(2x-y+3z)$

(A) $5x-6y+5z$

(B) $5x-4y+5z$

(C) $5x-4y-z$

(D) $9x-4y-z$

107. If your daily commute equals 95 minutes, how long, in hours and minutes, do you spend commuting during a 5-day work week?

(A) 1 hour, 35 minutes

(B) 6 hours, 25 minutes

(C) 7 hours, 55 minutes

(D) 8 hours, 45 minutes

108. If the base of a triangle is 6 inches and its area is 60 square inches, what is the height of the triangle?

(A) 5 inches

(B) 10 inches

(C) 20 inches

(D) 180 inches

109. The speed of sound in air is 320 meters per second. If you see a flash of lightning and it takes 8 seconds before you hear the thunder, how many kilometers away was the lightning strike? (Assume that the light reaches you instantly.)

(A) 2.56 kilometers

(B) 4 kilometers

(C) 40 kilometers

(D) 2560 kilometers

110. What is the slope of the line that passes through the coordinates (1, –7) and (8, 5)?

(A) $-\frac{2}{7}$

(B) $-\frac{7}{2}$

(C) $\frac{12}{7}$

(D) $\frac{7}{12}$

111. On Monday, Andrea finished $\frac{1}{4}$ of her homework assignment. On Tuesday, she completed $\frac{1}{2}$ of the remaining work. What fraction of her assignment does Andrea still have left to complete?

(A) $\frac{1}{8}$

(B) $\frac{1}{4}$

(C) $\frac{3}{8}$

(D) $\frac{5}{8}$

112. Norman is determining what his gross pay at the end of the week should be. If he gets paid $13.15 per hour and works 18 hours, what should his gross pay be? (*Note:* You may *not* use a calculator.)

____

Questions 113 and 114 are based on set A listed here.

$A = \{11, 7, 2, 16, 3, 11, 2, 37, 0, 11\}$

113. Fill in the blanks with the correct values to complete the sentence below:

The mode of set *A* equals _______, whereas the median of set *A* equals _______.

114. Find the arithmetic mean (average) of set *A*.

(A) 7

(B) 9

(C) 10

(D) 11

115. Simplify $5\times(91^0+3^2)$.

(A) 35

(B) 45

(C) 50

(D) 500

116. What is the solution to the equation?

$5(x-2)+x=2(3-x)$

(A) 2

(B) $\frac{8}{7}$

(C) 4

(D) $\frac{7}{16}$

117. Children's tickets to the zoo cost $9 each, and adult tickets cost $16 each. On Monday, the zoo sold a total of 95 tickets and made $1,380 on ticket sales. Which of the following systems of equations could be used to find out how many of each ticket type was sold? Let a equal the number of adult tickets, and let c equal the number of child tickets.

(A) $a+c=1{,}380,\ 9c+16a=95$

(B) $a+c=95,\ 9a+16c=1{,}380$

(C) $a+c=95,\ 9c+16a=1{,}380$

(D) $a+c=1{,}380,\ 9a+16c=95$

118. Fred's wallet contains coins with a total worth of $1.45. Suppose he has three times as many dimes as quarters and has exactly 7 nickels and no pennies. How many dimes does he have?

(A) 2

(B) 3

(C) 6

(D) 9

Questions 119 and 120 are based on the following function.

$f(x)=8-4x$

119. What is the value of the function when $x=-1$?

(A) 4

(B) 8

(C) 12

(D) 24

120. For what value of x does $f(x)=-4$?

(A) −8

(B) −1

(C) 3

(D) 24

121. The formula for the volume of a cylinder is $V=\pi r^2 h$, where r is the radius of the base and h is the height of the cylinder. Which formula could be used to find h if you're given V and r?

(A) $h=\frac{\pi r^2}{V}$

(B) $h=V\pi r^2$

(C) $h=\frac{V}{\pi r^2}$

(D) $h=\frac{r^2}{\pi V}$

122. Three friends are going to the theater. They arrive just in time to get the last 3 seats that are available together in a row. How many different seating arrangements can the friends sit in?

123. On a sunny day, a clock tower casts a shadow that is 50 feet long. At the same time, a nearby 3-foot-tall stick casts a shadow that is 2.5 feet long. What is the height of the clock tower? Round your answer to the nearest foot.

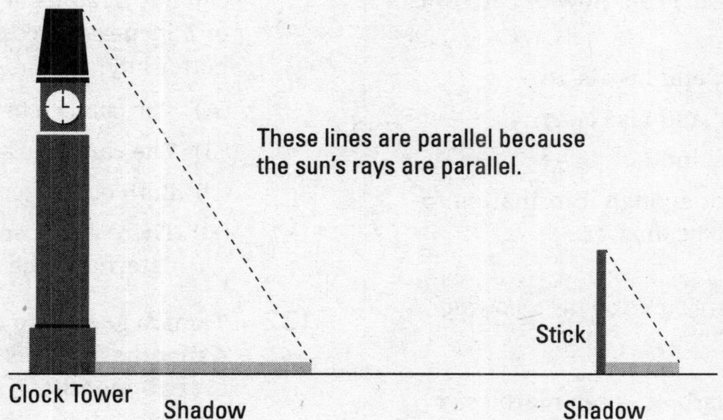

(A) 24 feet

(B) 33 feet

(C) 38 feet

(D) 60 feet

124. The hypotenuse of a right triangle is 10 inches. If one of the legs of the triangle is 8 inches long, what is the length of the other leg?

(A) 2 inches

(B) 6 inches

(C) $\sqrt{188}$ inches

(D) 40 inches

Questions 125 through 127 are based on the following linear equation.

$y = -\frac{3}{7}x - 9$

125. Which line would be parallel to the given line?

(A) $y = \frac{3}{7}x + 9$

(B) $y = -\frac{3}{7}x + \frac{1}{9}$

(C) $y = -\frac{7}{3}x - 9$

(D) $y = \frac{7}{3}x - 9$

126. Which line would be perpendicular to the given line?

(A) $y = \frac{3}{7}x + 9$

(B) $y = -\frac{3}{7}x + \frac{1}{9}$

(C) $y = -\frac{7}{3}x - 9$

(D) $y = \frac{7}{3}x - 9$

127. Which of the following sets of coordinates lies on the given line?

(A) (0, 9)

(B) (7, 6)

(C) (7, −12)

(D) (14, −9)

128. Lisa and Erica were investigating the relationship of their ages. They figured out that Erica's age is currently 5 less than twice Lisa's age. In addition, the sum of their ages is 73. How old are Erica and Lisa?

(A) Erica is 47, and Lisa is 26.

(B) Erica is 26, and Lisa is 47.

(C) Erica is 20, and Lisa is 53.

(D) There is not enough information to determine the answer.

Questions 129 and 130 are based on the following information.

A bag contains 6 blue marbles, 5 red marbles, 3 green marbles, and 2 yellow marbles.

129. What fraction of the marbles is blue?

(A) $\frac{3}{8}$

(B) $\frac{3}{5}$

(C) $\frac{6}{17}$

(D) $\frac{2}{5}$

130. If 2 marbles are removed from the bag one at a time, without being replaced, what is the probability of selecting 2 red marbles in a row?

(A) $\frac{5}{16}$

(B) $\frac{4}{15}$

(C) $\frac{1}{12}$

(D) $\frac{9}{31}$

131. Soup is sold in both rectangular card-board cartons and large cylindrical cans. The carton has dimensions of 3 inches by 4 inches by 7 inches and costs \$4.20. The can has a radius of 3 inches and a height of 4 inches and costs \$6.79. Which is a better buy?

(A) The can is a better value.

(B) The carton is a better value.

(C) Both containers offer the same value.

(D) There is not enough information to determine the answer.

132. Tamara goes for a dental checkup every 6 months and gets her eyesight checked every 8 months. If she visited her dentist and her optician this week, how many months will it be until she visits them both in the same week again?

____

133. Meg can swim 4 laps in 11 minutes. How long should she plan to practice if she needs to swim 10 laps, assuming her speed is constant?

(A) 4.4

(B) 15.7

(C) 22

(D) 27.5

Questions 134 through 136 are based on the following information.

Barney joined a gym to become stronger, and every 4 weeks he notes the maximum amount of weight that he can bench-press. He records his progress over a five-month period in the following table.

Weeks	Weight in Pounds
0	30
4	38
8	46
12	54
16	62
20	70

134. Barney plots the data on a coordinate grid. He begins by plotting the data for Week 4 and Week 16.

What are the coordinates of the two points?

____

135. Which of the following equations allows Barney to predict the maximum weight he will be able to lift in the future?

(A) $y = -2x + 3$

(B) $y = 30x + 2$

(C) $y = -2x + 30$

(D) $y = 2x + 30$

136. If Barney's strength continues to grow at the same rate, at what week will he be able to lift 100 pounds?

(A) Week 25

(B) Week 30

(C) Week 35

(D) Week 50

137. A box has the dimensions shown here:

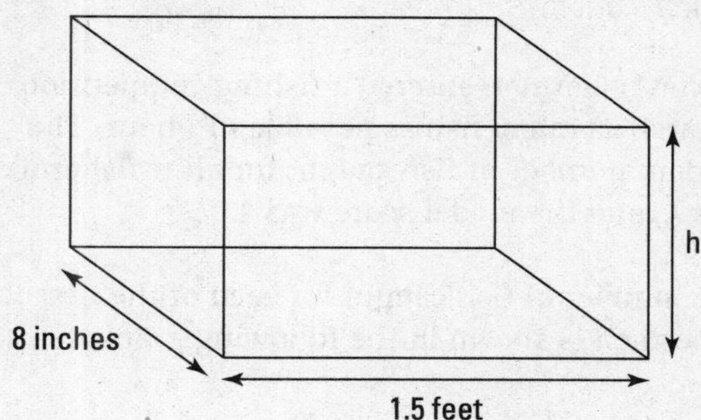

If the volume of the box is 1,368 cubic inches, what is the height of the box? Give your answer to the nearest tenth of an inch.

(A) 7.5

(B) 9.5

(C) 12.0

(D) 114.0

138. Which of the following graphs shows all the possible numbers represented by the inequality $30 < 15x \le 90$.

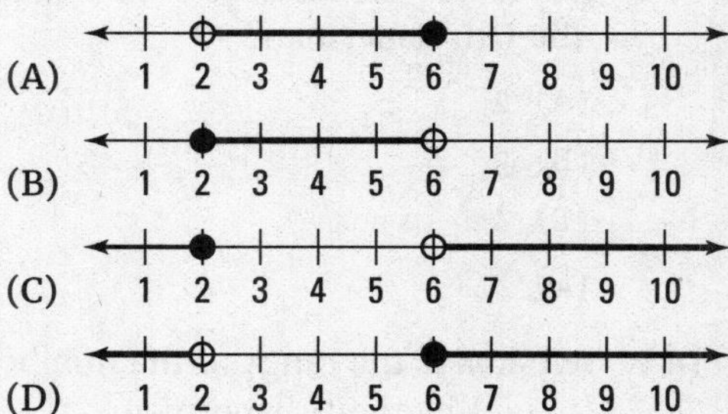

Questions 139 through 141 are based on the following information.

Eleven fishermen entered a fishing competition to catch as many fish as possible in 1 hour. The median number of fish caught for all 11 fishermen was 4, and the modal score was 3.

The number of fish caught for each of the first 10 fishermen is shown in the following graph.

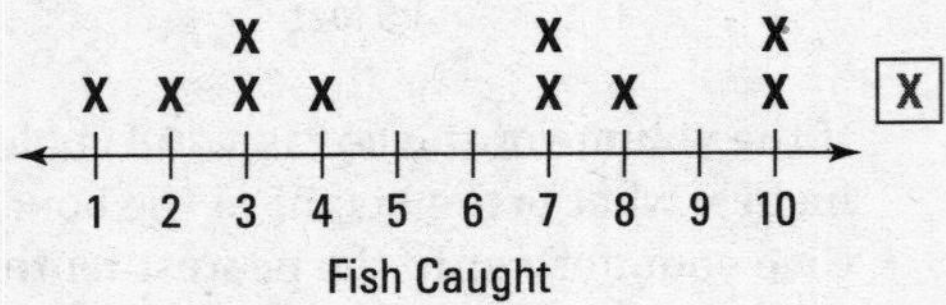

139. What was the average number of fish caught by the first 10 fishermen represented on the line plot?

(A) 4.5
(B) 5.0
(C) 5.5
(D) 6.5

140. What was the number of fish caught by the 11th fisherman?

(A) 2
(B) 3
(C) 4
(D) 5

141. What was the range of the number of fish caught by the 11 fishermen?

____

Questions 142 and 143 are based on the following information.

The probability that Daryl will pass each of three tests is given in the following table.

Test	Math	English	Chemistry
Probability of passing	50%	60%	80%

142. What is the probability that Daryl will not pass his chemistry test?

(A) 20%
(B) 40%
(C) 50%
(D) 80%

143. What is the chance that Daryl will pass all three tests?

____

144. What is the probability that Daryl will pass two out of the three tests? Round your answer to the nearest whole percentage.

(A) 30%
(B) 46%
(C) 52%
(D) 190%

145. Using the information in the following table, estimate to the nearest hundred the total number of tickets sold at the movie theater last week. (*Note:* You may *not* use a calculator.)

Movie	Tickets Sold
The Godmother	721
Moon Wars	391
The Silence of the Goats	813
A Clockwork Lemon	270
Pulp Fake News	602

(A) 2,600

(B) 2,800

(C) 3,000

(D) 3,100

Questions 146 through 148 are based on the following information.

After Halloween, the average price of a pound of candy drops in a linear fashion over a four-week period, as shown in the following table:

Weeks after Halloween	Price ($ per Pound)
Week 1	$5.29
Week 2	$4.58
Week 3	$3.87
Week 4	$3.16

146. What is the range of the prices in the table? Give your answer to the nearest cent.

____

147. What is the average price of a pound of candy during the given four-week period? Give your answer to the nearest cent.

(A) $3.42

(B) $3.43

(C) $4.22

(D) $4.23

148. If the average price of a pound of candy continues to decrease at the same rate, what will 4 pounds of candy cost six weeks after Halloween?

(A) $1.03

(B) $1.74

(C) $4.12

(D) $6.96

Questions 149 and 150 are based on the following information.

$x = p^3$, $y = p^{-2}$, and $z = p^2$

149. Which of the following expresses $(y \cdot z)^x$ in terms of p?

(A) p^3

(B) p^{-12}

(C) p^{20}

(D) 1

150. Which of the following expresses $(x)(y)(z)^3$ in terms of p?

(A) 0

(B) p^{-2}

(C) p^7

(D) p^9

Questions 151 through 153 are based on the following figure, which shows a picture frame for a photo.

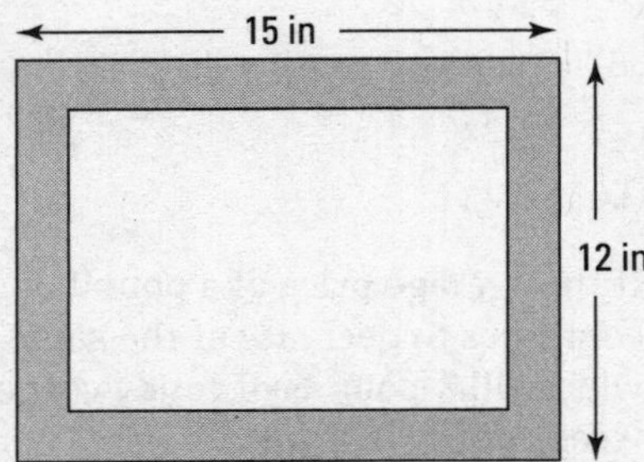

151. What is the perimeter of the rectangular picture frame?

____

152. Sammy has a 12-inch by 9-inch photo that he wants to put in the frame. What is the length of the diagonal of the rectangular photo?

(A) 8

(B) 13

(C) 15

(D) 84

153. Jeff has a different photo that he wants to put in the frame. If the wooden border of the frame (shown by the shaded region in the figure) is *x* inches wide all the way around, which of the following represents the area *A* of Jeff's photo (the non-shaded region)?

(A) $A=(15-x)(12-x)$

(B) $A=(15-2x)(12-2x)$

(C) $A=(15+2x)(12+2x)$

(D) $A=(15+x)(12+x)$

154.

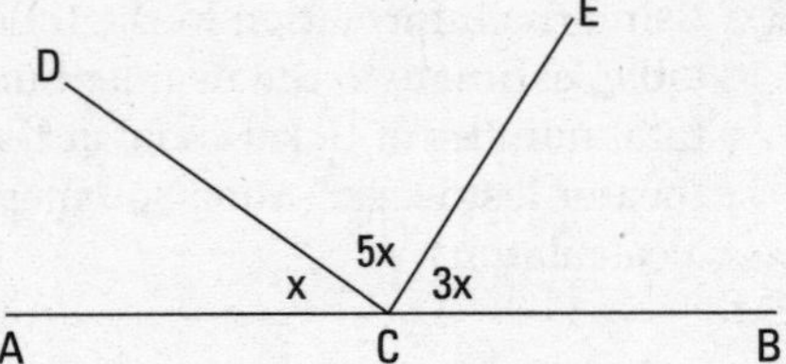

What is the measure of the obtuse angle shown in the figure?

(A) 20°

(B) 60°

(C) 100°

(D) 140°

155. If 3 out of 8 drivers exceed the speed limit on a given stretch of highway, what is the chance that a speed camera will catch a speeder if it photographs a car at random? Give your answer to the nearest tenth of a percent.

(A) 30.0%

(B) 37.5%

(C) 42.5%

(D) 45.0%

156. If the base of a triangle is 8 inches and the area of the triangle is 48 square inches, what is the height of the triangle?

(A) 6 inches

(B) 8 inches

(C) 10 inches

(D) 12 inches

157. Which number equals 2 hundredths?

(A) 0.2

(B) 0.02

(C) 0.002

(D) 200

158. A limo company charges \$25.50 for the first 8 miles plus an additional \$3.50 for each extra mile. What is the cost of a 13-mile limo ride?

(A) \$29.00

(B) \$43.00

(C) \$45.50

(D) \$221.50

Questions 159 and 160 are based on the following information.

The following table shows the time needed to cook a turkey based on the weight of the turkey and the temperature of the oven. After the turkey is removed from the oven, it should be left to rest for 30 minutes before it's carved to ensure that it remains juicy.

Weight of Turkey (Pounds)	Cooking Time at 325°F	Cooking Time at 375°F
8–12 lb.	2.5–3.0 hours	2.0–2.5 hours
12–16 lb.	3.0–3.5 hours	2.5–3.0 hours
16–20 lb.	3.5–4.0 hours	3.0–3.5 hours
20–24 lb.	4.0–4.5 hours	3.5–4.0 hours

159. How long does a 23-pound turkey take to cook at an oven temperature of 375°F?

(A) 2.5–3.0 hours

(B) 3.0–3.5 hours

(C) 3.5–4.0 hours

(D) 4.0–4.5 hours

160. Venus is cooking a Thanksgiving turkey that weighs 16 pounds. Her oven has only two temperature settings: 325°F or 375°F. If she wants to serve a juicy turkey to her family at 2:00 p.m., what is the latest time that she can begin to cook the turkey?

(A) 10:30 a.m.

(B) 11:00 a.m.

(C) 11:30 a.m.

(D) Noon

161. If $\frac{2}{17}x = 15$, what is $\frac{6}{17}x$? (***Note:*** You may *not* use a calculator.)

____

Questions 162 through 164 are based on the following information.

Jack earned \$30,000 per year for two consecutive years. For each of the next three years, Jack earned \$40,000 per year.

162. Fill in the blanks with the appropriate values to complete the sentence below.

During the 5-year period, the mode of Jack's salary equaled ____________, and the range equaled ____________.

163. What was the median value of Jack's salary during the 5-year period?

(A) \$30,000

(B) \$35,000

(C) \$36,000

(D) \$40,000

164. What was the mean value of Jack's salary during the 5-year period?

____

Questions 165 through 167 are based on the following figure.

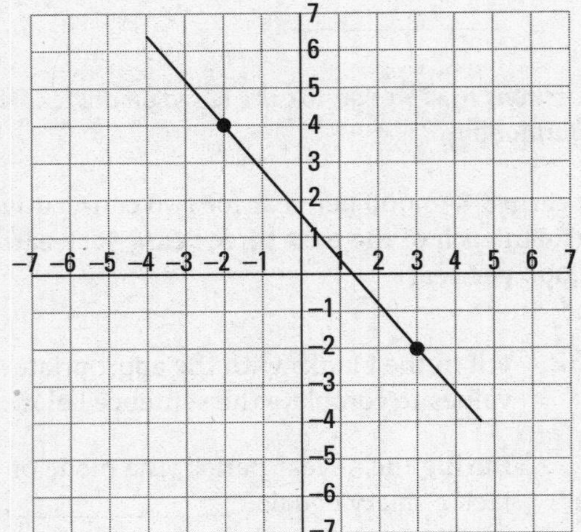

165. What is the slope of the line?

(A) $-\frac{6}{5}$

(B) $-\frac{5}{6}$

(C) $\frac{6}{5}$

(D) $\frac{5}{6}$

166. What is the length of the line segment joining the two data points shown on the figure?

(A) $\sqrt{61}$

(B) $\sqrt{71}$

(C) 11

(D) $\sqrt{17}$

167. What is the location of the midpoint of the segment joining the two data points shown in the figure?

(A) (0,2)

(B) (1.5, 0)

(C) (1.0, 0.25)

(D) (0.5, 1)

168. Anne asks the butcher for $1\frac{3}{4}$ pounds of ham. The butcher places some ham on the digital scale, which reads 1.95. How much ham must the butcher remove to give Anne the amount that she asked for? (***Note:*** You may *not* use a calculator.)

(A) 0.10 pounds

(B) 0.20 pounds

(C) 0.45 pounds

(D) 0.70 pounds

169. Tom's gross weekly salary is $840. His salary is taxed at 17%. What is Tom's net salary? Round your answer to the nearest cent.

(A) $142.80

(B) $672,90

(C) $697.20

(D) $982.80

170. The dimensions of a fish tank are 1 foot, 6 inches wide by 1 foot, 8 inches tall by 4 feet long. What is the volume of the tank in cubic feet?

(A) 10

(B) $11\frac{2}{3}$

(C) 13

(D) $14\frac{1}{12}$

171. The distance between two planets is 4,560,000,000 miles. Express this in scientific notation.

(A) 4.56×10^6

(B) 4.56×10^7

(C) 456×10^7

(D) 4.56×10^9

172. A hiker walks 16 miles due north and then turns and walks 12 miles due west. How many miles is the hiker from his starting point?

173. Jeff currently weighs 214 pounds. He plans to go on a diet and lose 4.5 pounds per month. How many pounds should he weigh after 5 months of dieting? (***Note:*** You may *not* use a calculator.)

(A) 186.4

(B) 191.5

(C) 195.5

(D) 199.5

174. Which of the following lists the solutions to the equation $x^2 - x - 20 = 0$?

(A) 2 and −10

(B) −2 and 10

(C) 4 and −5

(D) −4 and 5

175. Last season, a soccer team won five times as many games as it lost, with 8 games ending in a draw. If there were 38 games in the season, how many games did the team win?

(A) 5

(B) 6

(C) 24

(D) 25

176. What is the next term in the following sequence?

1, 1, 2, 3, 5, 8, 13, 21, …

____

Questions 177 and 178 are based on the following information.

The speeds of 12 cars (rounded to the nearest 10 miles per hour) were recorded and listed in this frequency table.

Speed in Miles per Hour	Number of Cars
30	2
40	3
50	1
60	6

177. What is the average speed of the 12 cars in miles per hour? Round your answer to the nearest whole number.

(A) 36

(B) 45

(C) 49

(D) 51

178. By what percent is the fastest recorded speed greater than the slowest recorded speed?

(A) 30%

(B) 50%

(C) 80%

(D) 100%

179. Simplify the expression:
$2(7x - 5y) - 3(2x - y)$

(A) $8x - 7y$

(B) $8x - 4y$

(C) $8x - 13y$

(D) $9x - 6y$

180. If 2 cookies cost *y* dollars, how many dollars do *x* cookies cost?

(A) $2xy$

(B) $\frac{xy}{2}$

(C) $\frac{2x}{y}$

(D) $\frac{2y}{x}$

181. The square root of 73 lies between which two integers? (***Note:*** You may *not* use a calculator.)

(A) 6 and 7

(B) 7 and 8

(C) 8 and 9

(D) 9 and 10

182. If two sides of a triangle are 10.2 and 5.8 inches long, which of the following cannot be the length of the other side?

(A) 4.3 inches

(B) 5.8 inches

(C) 11.7 inches

(D) 15.2 inches

183. What is the value of $|3-8|-|8-3|$? (***Note:*** You may *not* use a calculator.)

(A) −10

(B) −5

(C) 0

(D) 22

184. Which of the following rectangular metal boxes can hold the most dice if each die has a volume of one cubic inch and the lid of the box fits tightly?

(A) 9 inches x 15 inches x 11 inches

(B) 20 inches x 7.5 inches x 10 inches

(C) 12.5 inches x 7.5 inches x 16.5 inches

(D) 20 inches x 7.5 inches x 10.5 inches

185. In the number line, the vertical marks are equally spaced. What is the value at point *A*?

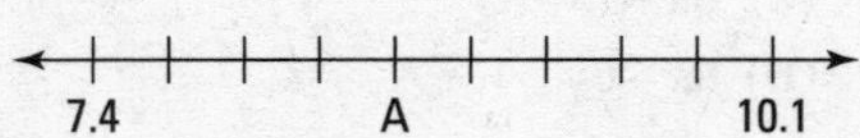

Questions 186 and 187 are based on the figure and information below.

A researcher asked a group of 400 students about what types of pets they preferred. She recorded the results in the following pie chart.

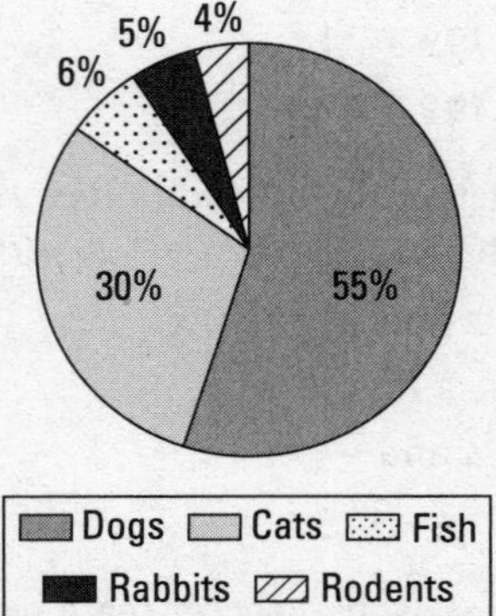

186. What is the ratio of the number of dogs to cats to rabbits that the students prefer? Simplify your answer as much as possible.

(A) 1:6:11

(B) 5:1:6

(C) 11:6:1

(D) 11:5:1

187. How many more students preferred fish than rodents?

____

188. If $\frac{x}{y}\cdot\frac{y}{z}\cdot\frac{z}{w}\cdot p=1$, which of the following represents the value of *p*?

(A) 1

(B) $\frac{x}{w}$

(C) $\frac{w}{x}$

(D) $\frac{1}{p}$

189. If $w = x$ and $y < z$, which of the following is true for all cases?

(A) $w + y > x + z$

(B) $wy < xz$

(C) $w - y > x - z$

(D) $w - x < y - z$

190. Regular tickets to a concert cost $25 each, and VIP tickets cost $45 each. The concert hall sold a total of 270 tickets and made $7,650 on ticket sales.

The number of VIP tickets sold was ____________, and the number of regular tickets sold was ____________.

191. The product of the first six prime numbers is divisible by which of the following?

(A) 16

(B) 18

(C) 22

(D) 24

Questions 192 and 193 are based on the following function.

$f(x) = x^2 - 4x$

192. What is the value of the function when $x = -4$?

(A) −8

(B) 0

(C) 16

(D) 32

193. For what value of x does $f(x) = 12$?

(A) 96

(B) 2 and −6

(C) 6 and −2

(D) 0 and 6

194. Simplify the following expression:
$3^4 + 3^4 + 3^4$

(A) 3^5

(B) 9^{12}

(C) 3^{12}

(D) 3^{64}

195.

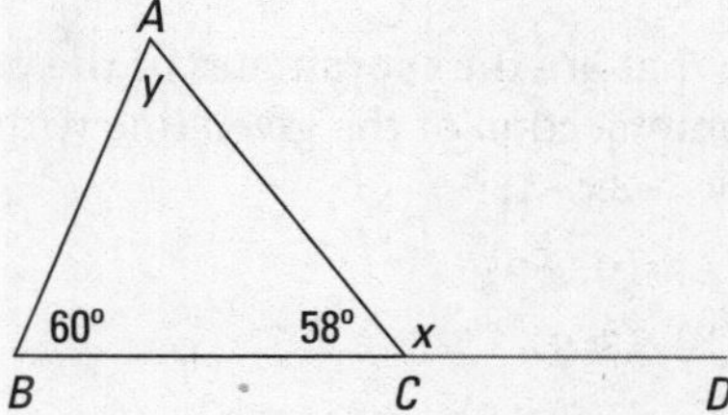

In this triangle, angle x equals ____________ and angle y equals ____________.

196. A cube with 3-inch sides is painted blue and then cut into 27 smaller cubes with 1-inch sides. How many of the new smaller cubes have exactly two faces that are painted blue?

____

197. The lengths of the legs of a right triangle are 4 inches and 5 inches, respectively. What is the length of the hypotenuse?

(A) 3 inches

(B) 9 inches

(C) $\sqrt{41}$ inches

(D) 41 inches

Questions 198 through 200 are based on the following linear equation.

$y = -6x - 9$

198. Which line would be parallel to the given line?

(A) $y = -\frac{1}{6}x + 9$

(B) $y = \frac{1}{6}x + \frac{1}{9}$

(C) $y = -6x - 1$

(D) $y = 6x + 9$

199. Which line would be perpendicular to the given line?

(A) $y=-\frac{1}{6}x+9$

(B) $y=\frac{1}{6}x+\frac{1}{9}$

(C) $y=-6x-1$

(D) $y=6x+9$

200. What are the coordinates of the point of intersection of the given line with the line $y=-3x+18$?

(A) (0, −9)

(B) (3, 9)

(C) (−9, 45)

(D) (−9, −27)

201. Two years ago, Sammy was 5 years younger than Michael is today. If Michael is currently *M* years old, how old will Sammy be 10 years from now?

(A) $M-5$

(B) $M+2$

(C) $M+7$

(D) $M+10$

202. $3\frac{1}{10}+1\frac{11}{100}+2\frac{111}{1{,}000}=$

(***Note:*** You may *not* use a calculator.)

(A) 6.111

(B) 6.123

(C) 6.321

(D) 6.11111

203. Mr. Burke's class has twice as many girls as boys. If half of the boys and a quarter of the girls are in the chess club, what is the ratio of girls to boys who are in the chess club?

(A) 4:1

(B) 2:1

(C) 1:1

(D) 1:2

204. Beans are sold in small or large cylindrical cans. The small can has a diameter of 4 inches and a height of 10 inches and costs $3.50. The big can has a diameter of 8 inches and a height of 5 inches and costs $6.50. Which is a better buy?

(A) The small can

(B) The large can

(C) Both have the same value

(D) Not enough information

205. Two lighthouses flash their lights every 21 seconds and 77 seconds, respectively. If both lighthouses are switched on at the same time so their lights begin by flashing simultaneously, after how many seconds will both lights first flash in synch again?

206. This trapezoid has an area of 38 square feet. What is the length of the unknown base of the trapezoid in feet?

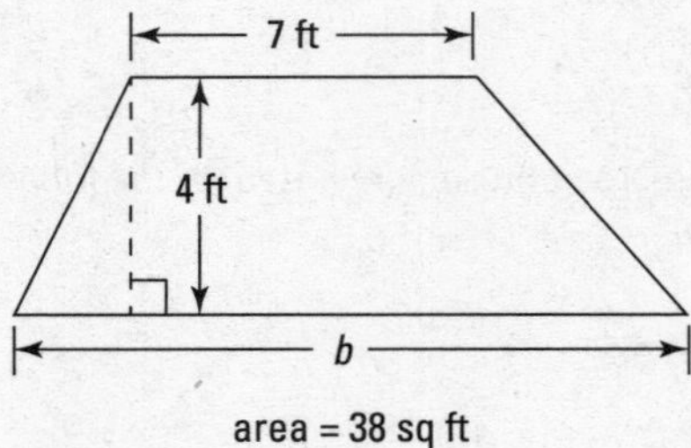

(A) 4

(B) 7

(C) 8

(D) 12

Questions 207 and 208 are based on the following figure.

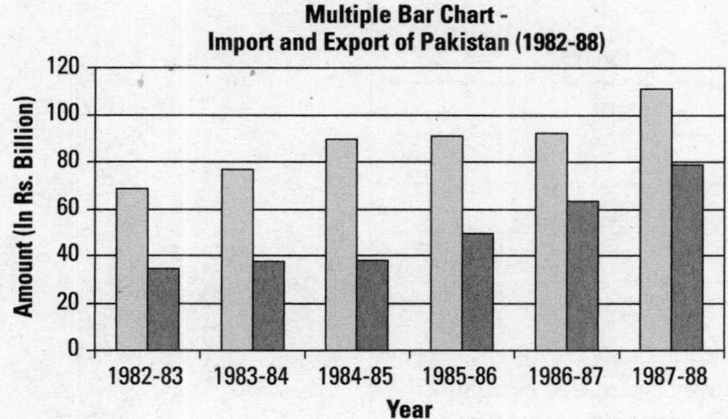

This chart represents the imports and exports of Pakistan during the period 1982–1988 in billions of Pakistani rupees (Rs.). The darker bars represent imports, and the lighter bars are exports.

207. In which year did the value of exports exceed the value of imports by the greatest amount?

(A) 1982–1983

(B) 1983–1984

(C) 1984–1985

(D) 1987–1988

208. What was the average approximate value of the exports (in Rs.) for the six years shown in the chart?

(A) 48 billion

(B) 62 billion

(C) 75 billion

(D) 88 billion

209. What was the average annual increase for imports (in Rs.) for the six years shown in the chart?

(A) 7 billion

(B) 8.4 billion

(C) 11 billion

(D) 42 billion

210. Two square rugs have a combined area of 20 square meters. If the area of the large rug is four times as large as the area of the small rug, what is the perimeter of the smaller rug?

(A) 2 meters

(B) 4 meters

(C) 8 meters

(D) 16 meters

211. Forty percent of the students in Dr. Donnelly's math class received a grade of A. If 10 students received an A, how many students are in Dr. Donnelly's math class?

(A) 4 students

(B) 14 students

(C) 22 students

(D) 25 students

212. What is the acute angle between the hands of a clock when it is exactly 10 p.m.?

(A) 30°

(B) 45°

(C) 60°

(D) 75°

213. What is the missing value in the following table?

x	f(x)
−2	−10
0	−4
2	2
4	?
6	14

214. Janice's car averages 32 miles per gallon (mpg) and holds approximately 13 gallons of gas. If she is driving from Boston to Arizona and the distance between the two locations is 2,220 miles, how many tanks of gas will she need?

(A) 4 tanks
(B) 5 tanks
(C) 6 tanks
(D) 7 tanks

215. Which of the following is equivalent to 45%?

(A) 4.5
(B) 0.045
(C) $\frac{9}{10}$
(D) $\frac{9}{20}$

216. Find the value of x in the figure.

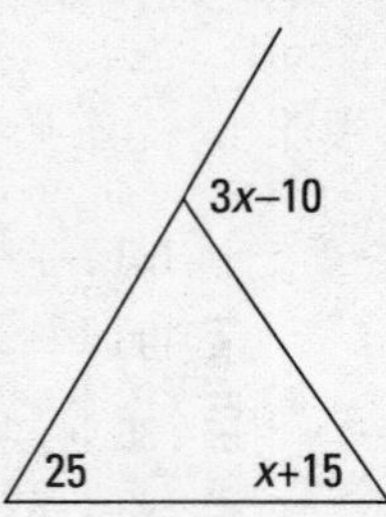

(A) 25
(B) 40
(C) 65
(D) 115

217. Simplify $3\sqrt{5x^6}+6\sqrt{5x^6}$ completely.

(A) $9\sqrt{10x^{12}}$
(B) $9x^2\sqrt{10}$
(C) $9\sqrt{10x^6}$
(D) $9x^3\sqrt{5}$

218. Which of the following is listed in ascending order?

(A) $\frac{1}{3}$, 0.3, $1\frac{2}{5}$, 250%
(B) $\frac{1}{3}$, 250%, 0.3, $1\frac{2}{5}$
(C) 0.3, $\frac{1}{3}$, $1\frac{2}{5}$, 250%
(D) $\frac{1}{3}$, 0.3, $1\frac{2}{5}$, 250%

219. Emily's garden has the same value for its perimeter and its area. Which of the following could be the shape and dimensions of her garden? (*Note:* You may *not* use a calculator.)

(A) rectangle; 2 ft × 8 ft
(B) square; 5 ft × 5 ft
(C) circle; radius = 2 ft
(D) right triangle; 3 ft × 4 ft × 5 ft

220. Ryan works at a coffee shop that sells an average of 107 cups of coffee an hour. If one pot of coffee fills 10 cups, how many pots of coffee will the shop go through on an average day if the shop opens at 7:00 a.m. and closes at 4:00 p.m.?

(A) 96

(B) 97

(C) 963

(D) 1,070

221. Cory likes to ride his hoverboard and can travel at a speed of 11 miles per hour. How fast does Cory go in feet per minute?

____

222. Which of the following is equivalent to 3,888?

(A) $5^2 2^5$

(B) $2^3 3^5$

(C) $3^4 5^3$

(D) $2^4 3^5$

223. The surface area of a cube equals 150 in.^{2}. What is its volume in cubic inches?

(A) 5

(B) 100

(C) 125

(D) 150

224. If $x = p^5$, $y = p^{-4}$, and $z = p$, simplify the following expression, leaving your answer in terms of p.

$$\left(\frac{x \cdot y}{z}\right)^5$$

(A) 0

(B) p^{-50}

(C) p^{-20}

(D) 1

225. In a triangle, the sides have a ratio of 3:7:10. If the perimeter is 210 feet, what is the length of the longest side in feet?

(A) 10.5

(B) 31.5

(C) 73.5

(D) 105

226. If x is a positive integer and $f(x) = \frac{14+x}{2+x}$, then

(A) $f(x) \leq 5$

(B) $f(x) = 5$

(C) $f(x) > 5$

(D) $f(x)$ is sometimes less than 5 and sometimes greater than 5, depending upon the value of x.

Questions 227 and 228 are based on the following image, which shows a rectangle with a semicircular top.

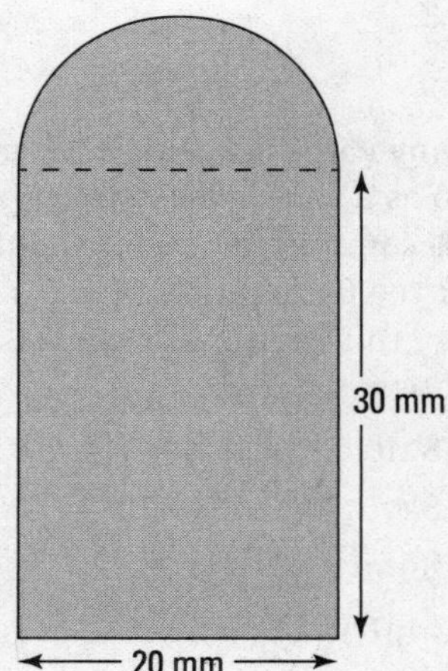

227. What is the perimeter of the shape?

(A) $50 + 20\pi$

(B) $50\pi + 600$

(C) $80 + 10\pi$

(D) $80 + 20\pi$

228. What is the area of the shape?

(A) $20\pi + 600$

(B) $50\pi + 600$

(C) $200\pi + 600$

(D) $400\pi + 600$

229. Harry rents a power drill from 8:30 p.m. until 3:30 p.m. on the same day. He paid a total of $25.06. What was the hourly rental fee, rounded to the nearest penny? (*Note:* You may not use a calculator.)

(A) $3.13

(B) $3.58

(C) $2.23

(D) $2.51

230. What is the value of $\frac{x^2 - 6x + 9}{x^2 - 6x}$ when $x = -3$?

(A) 2

(B) 9

(C) $\frac{4}{3}$

(D) $\frac{2}{3}$

231. Sammy earns a weekly base salary of $750 as a shoe salesman. He also earns a 6% commission on his monthly sales after the first $1,000. What is his total salary this month if he sells $4,500 worth of shoes?

(A) $210

(B) $270

(C) $960

(D) $1,020

232. Solve the following. You may use numbers, symbols, and/or text in your answer.

$\sqrt{64} + \sqrt{36}$

Simplify the expression completely.

____

233. In scientific notation, what would the number 0.0408 be?

(A) 4.08×10^2

(B) 408×10^4

(C) 40.8×10^{-3}

(D) 4.08×10^{-2}

234. Jackson is planning his office's annual party, and he has a maximum budget of $2,825 to spend. He intends to rent a party room that costs $375 per hour from 8:00 p.m. until 11:00 p.m. He expects a total of 250 people to attend the party and plans to provide each person with a bag of party favors. What is the maximum average amount that Jackson can spend on party favors for each person?

____

Questions 235 through 237 are based on the following information.

A plane has a seating capacity of 160 passengers, 40 in first class and the rest in economy class. The average first-class ticket costs $1,200, and the average ticket in economy class is $400.

235. How much revenue does the airline gross if the plane is full?

____

236. If all the first-class tickets are sold but only half of the economy tickets are sold, what is the ratio of the total revenue from the first-class passengers to that of the economy-class passengers?

(A) 1:1

(B) 3:1

(C) 2:1

(D) 1:3

237. The price of each first-class ticket used to be $1,500. What percent decrease does the current price represent?

(A) 20%

(B) 25%

(C) 75%

(D) 80%

Questions 238 and 239 are based on the following information.

The details of Janet's paycheck are shown here.

Salary Details	Amount in Dollars
Gross salary	$1,012
Federal taxes	$234
State taxes	$128
Social Security	$27

238. What is Janet's take-home (net) salary? (***Note:*** You may *not* use a calculator.)

____

239. What percentage of her gross salary does Janet pay toward Social Security? Round your answer to the nearest tenth of a percent.

(A) 0.03%

(B) 2.7%

(C) 0.3%

(D) 26.7%

Questions 240 and 241 are based on the following figure.

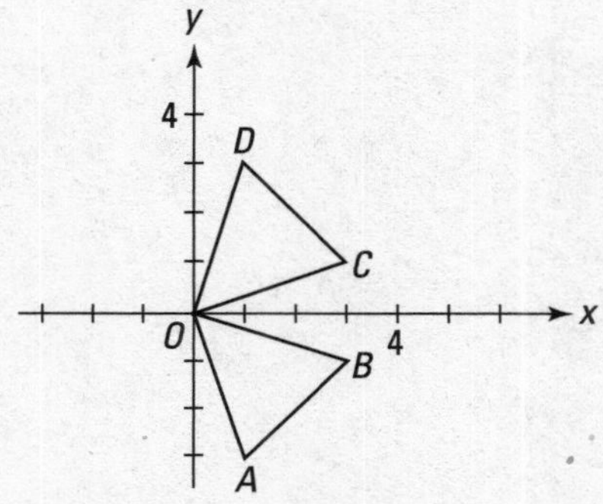

240. What transformation maps triangle ODC onto triangle OBA?

(A) Reflection in the y-axis

(B) Reflection in the line $y = x$

(C) Rotation 90° clockwise about the origin

(D) Translation

241. Which of the following line segments has a slope of −1?

(A) $\overline{OA}$

(B) $\overline{OB}$

(C) $\overline{AB}$

(D) $\overline{DC}$

242. If $x^3 = y^{12}$, what is x in terms of y?

(A) y^{-9}

(B) y^4

(C) y^9

(D) y^{36}

Questions 243 through 245 are based on the following information.

Rachel, Brooke, and Steve love reading novels. The graph shows the number of books that each of them read last year.

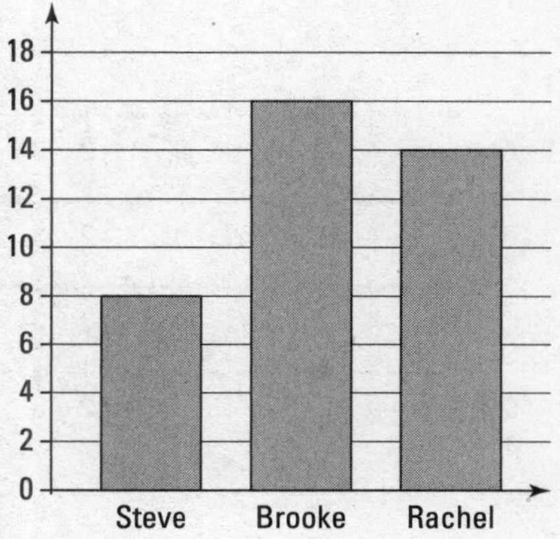

243. What is the ratio of the number of books Brooke read to those Rachel read?

(A) 2:1

(B) 16:13

(C) 8:7

(D) 7:8

244. If Steve wants to read the same number of books that Rachel read, by what percentage would he need to increase his current number of books read?

(A) 6%

(B) 75%

(C) 100%

(D) 175%

245. Based on the graph, which of the following statements must be true?

(A) Brooke can read more words per minute than either Steve or Rachel.

(B) Steve read only half the number of books that Rachel read.

(C) Brooke read 100% more books than Steve read.

(D) The total number of books read equals 40.

246. Which of the following represents the inequality?

$2 \leq x + 5 < 6$

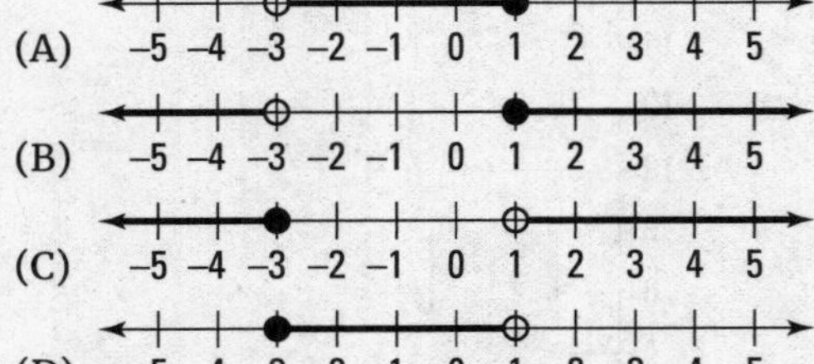

247. If these two boxes have the same volume, what is the height of the second box?

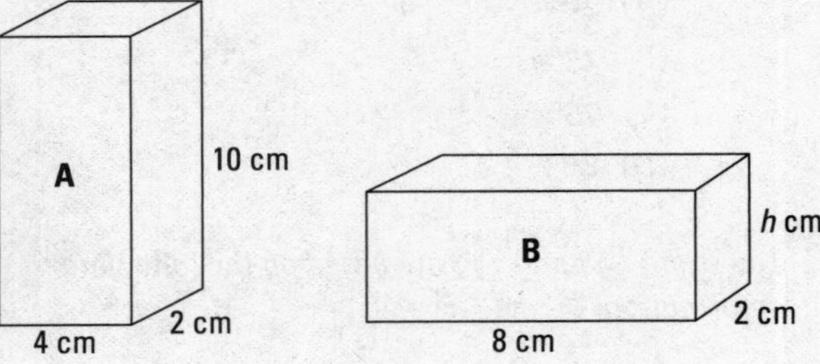

(A) 4

(B) 5

(C) 8

(D) 10

248. Which of the following numbers has the most unique prime factors?

(A) 15

(B) 19

(C) 27

(D) 31

249. The following figure shows a piece of paper that is 15 inches long. Peter folds it in half (along the dotted line) and then makes one cut so that when he unfolds the paper, a perfect circle has been cut out. If the circle's diameter equals one-third of the length of the paper, what was the length of the cut that Peter made?

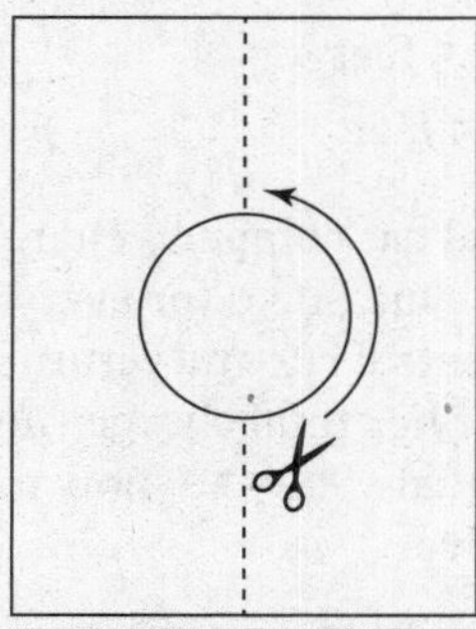

(A) 2.5π

(B) 5π

(C) 10π

(D) 25π

250. Four frogs were entered in the annual charity High-Hop Contest. The highest jump of each frog is recorded in the table.

Frog	Jump Height (Inches)
Mrs. Croak	$5\frac{4}{5}$
Kermit	$5\frac{3}{8}$
Mr. Hopswell	$5\frac{11}{20}$
Froggy McFrogface	$5\frac{7}{10}$

Which frog hopped the highest? (*Note:* You may *not* use a calculator.)

(A) Mrs. Croak

(B) Kermit

(C) Mr. Hopswell

(D) Froggy McFrogface

251. This irregular polygon has sides of unequal lengths. If the polygon has a perimeter equal to 52 inches, what is the value of *x*?

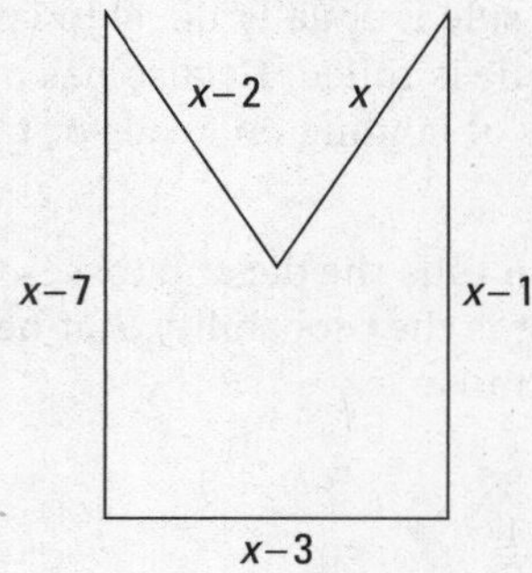

(A) 3

(B) 5

(C) 10

(D) 13

252. The top four runners to finish a 100-meter race had the following times.

Runner	Time (Seconds)
Tom	10.9192
Kenneth	11.0021
Rupert	10.9289
Usain	10.9191

Based on the above information, which of the following is a true statement?

(A) Tom was the slowest runner, and Usain was the fastest.

(B) Kenneth was the slowest runner, and Usain was the fastest.

(C) Rupert was the slowest runner, and Tom was the fastest.

(D) Usain was the slowest runner, and Kenneth was the fastest.

Questions 253 and 254 are based on the following information.

Ian has a die that has six sides, each marked with a different integer from 1 to 6. It's a fair die, meaning that each side is equally likely to land face up when the die is rolled. He also has a coin with equal chances of landing on heads or tails.

253. If Ian rolls the die and tosses the coin, what is the probability that he will get a 6 and tails?

(A) $\frac{2}{3}$

(B) $\frac{1}{8}$

(C) $\frac{1}{12}$

(D) $6\frac{1}{2}$

254. Suppose Ian rolled the die ten times and got ten consecutive 6s. What is the probability of rolling a 6 on the next roll?

(A) Less than $\frac{1}{6}$

(B) More than $\frac{1}{6}$

(C) $\frac{1}{6}$

(D) Impossible to predict

255. When an unbalanced force is applied to a body, the acceleration of the body is inversely proportional to its mass. If a force applied to a 5 kg body gives it an acceleration of 6 m/s^2, what acceleration would the same force produce when applied to a 15 kg body?

(A) 1 m/s^2

(B) 2 m/s^2

(C) 12 m/s^2

(D) 18 m/s^2

256. The scale on Blackbeard's treasure map is 2 inches = 15 feet. According to the map, the treasure is buried 13 inches away from the old hanging tree. If Blackbeard is currently standing under the tree, how many feet away from the treasure is he? (***Note:*** You may *not* use a calculator.)

(A) 26 feet

(B) 30 feet

(C) 97.5 feet

(D) 195 feet

257. A rental car company charges a daily fee of $50 plus $0.50 for every mile traveled. Jane rents a car and returns it after three days. If her total charge (not including tax) equals $225.50, how many miles did she drive?

(A) 15.1 miles

(B) 151 miles

(C) 351 miles

(D) 451 miles

258. Amy invested $500 in a savings account that pays a fixed simple interest rate. After three years, her account balance is $552.50. What percent annual interest did her bank pay?

(A) 3.5%

(B) 5.5%

(C) 10.5%

(D) 17.5%

259. If $\frac{2}{11}x = 50$, what does $\frac{6}{11}x$ equal? (***Note:*** You may *not* use a calculator.)

(A) 25

(B) 150

(C) 275

(D) 1,100

Questions 260 through 262 are based on the following graph.

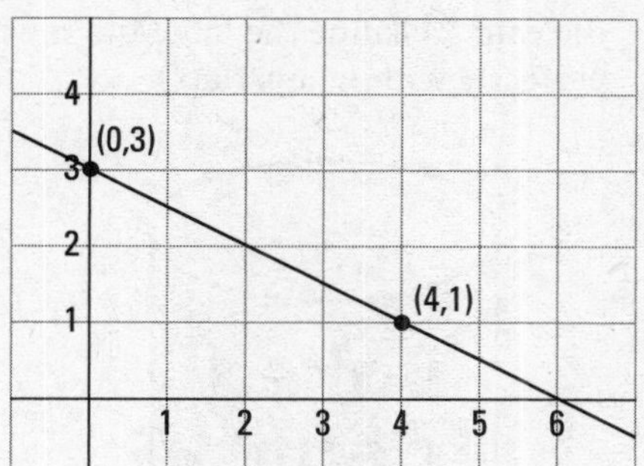

260. What are the coordinates of the midpoint of the two points marked on the graph?

(A) (6, 0)

(B) (2, 2)

(C) (0, 3)

(D) (3, 1.5)

261. What is the slope of the line?

(A) −2

(B) 2

(C) $-\frac{1}{2}$

(D) $\frac{1}{2}$

262. What is the equation of the line?

(A) $y = \frac{1}{2}x + 3$

(B) $y = 3x - \frac{1}{2}$

(C) $y = -\frac{1}{2}x + 3$

(D) $y = +3x + \frac{1}{2}$

263. A clothing store has a 20% off sale. If the sale price of a sweater is $64, what was the original price of the sweater?

(A) $64

(B) $76.80

(C) $80

(D) $96

264. The figure shows two similar triangles: the smaller triangle has a base length of 8 feet and a height of 5 feet (the height of the boy), whereas the second triangle has a base length of 24 feet and a height equal to that of the tree.

How tall is the tree?

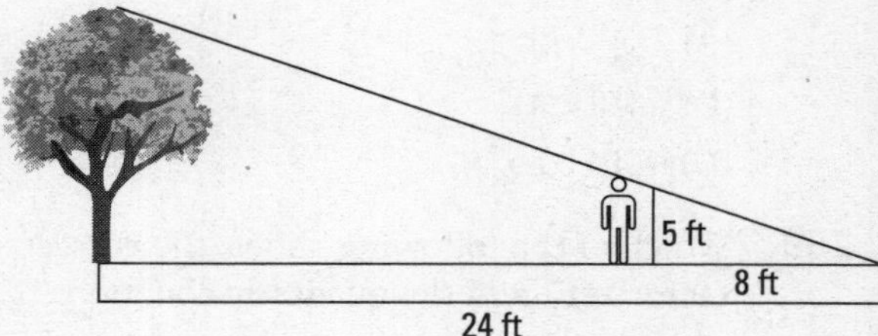

(A) 15 feet

(B) 27 feet

(C) 38.4 feet

(D) 45 feet

265. An isosceles triangle has an obtuse angle equal to 110°. What is the value of each of the other two angles?

(A) 25°

(B) 35°

(C) 45°

(D) 70°

Questions 266 through 268 are based on the following graph.

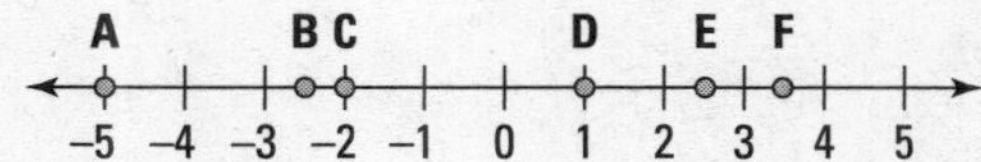

266. What is the value of *E* minus *A*?

(A) −7.5

(B) −2.5

(C) 2.5

(D) 7.5

267. What is the product of *A* times *B* times *C*?

(A) −25

(B) −0.5

(C) 0

(D) 25

268. Which of the following is true?

(A) $|A|<|C|$

(B) $|D|>|E|$

(C) $-|E|<A$

(D) $-A<|B|+|F|$

269. Which of the following shows the correct factorization of the quadratic equation $x^2-2x-24=0$?

(A) $(x-4)(x+6)=0$

(B) $(x+4)(x-6)=0$

(C) $(x+2)(x-12)=0$

(D) $(x+3)(x-8)=0$

270. $(x-y)^2$ is equivalent to which of the following?

(A) x^2-y^2

(B) $-x^2y^2$

(C) x^2+y^2-2xy

(D) x^2-y^2-2xy

271. A can of beans has a circular base whose area is 16π square inches. If the height of the can is 8 inches, what is the area of the label that covers the entire side of the can? (Assume the label fits the can perfectly with no overlap.)

(A) 16

(B) 32π

(C) 64

(D) 64π

Questions 272 through 274 are based on the following information.

Every year, starting on his 10th birthday, Jacob measured the height of a bush in his garden. The results for 5 years are listed in the table.

Age	Height (in inches)
10	52
11	55
12	58
13	61
14	64

272. Based on the results shown in the table, which of the following is true?

(A) The median value is 8 inches, and the range is 58 inches.

(B) The median value is 58 inches, and the range is 12 inches.

(C) The median value is 48 inches, and the range is 12 inches.

(D) The median value is 38 inches, and the range is 8 inches.

273. What was the bush's average height during the five-year period?

(A) 56 inches

(B) 57 inches

(C) 58 inches

(D) 59 inches

274. If Jacob's bush continues to grow at the same rate, how tall will the bush be when Jacob is 17 years old?

(A) 5 feet, 9 inches

(B) 5 feet, 11 inches

(C) 6 feet, 1 inch

(D) 6 feet, 3 inches

275. A company manufactures widgets. If 3 out of every 50 widgets produced by the company are found to be defective, how many defective widgets will there be in a batch of 2,050 widgets?

(A) 14

(B) 41

(C) 123

(D) 246

Questions 276 and 277 are based on this figure of a donut:

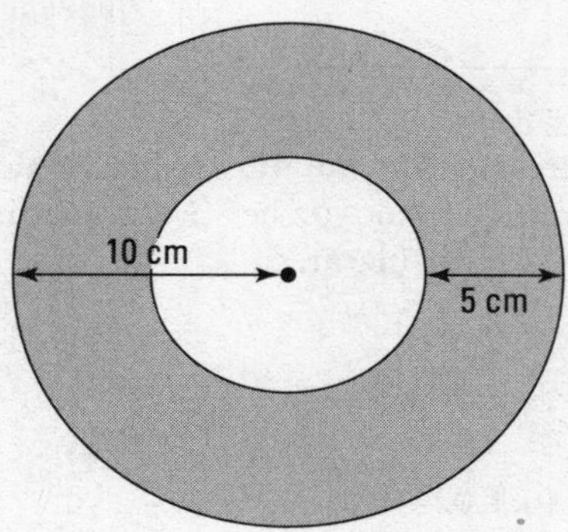

276. What is the outer circumference of the donut?

(A) 10

(B) 10π

(C) 20π

(D) 100π

277. What is the ratio of the area of the donut (the shaded area) to the area of the hole?

(A) 1:1

(B) 2:1

(C) 1:3

(D) 3:1

278. How many square yards of carpet would it take to completely cover a rectangular floor that has dimensions of 12 feet wide by 21 feet long?

(A) 28

(B) 74

(C) 84

(D) 252

279. What is the maximum safe weight w for a person entering a crowded elevator if $\frac{3{,}412+w}{11} \leq 330$?

____

280. In scientific notation, what would the number 0.00502 be? (*Note:* You may *not* use a calculator.)

(A) 50.2×10^{-4}

(B) 5.02×10^{-3}

(C) 5.02

(D) 5.02×10^{3}

Questions 281 through 283 are based on this graph.

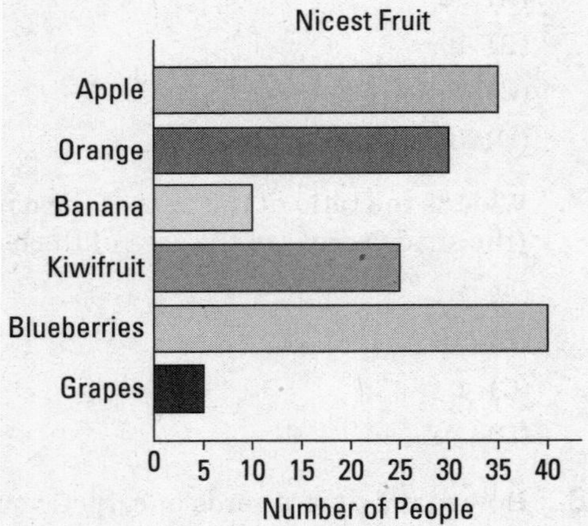

281. Fill in the blanks to complete the sentence.

The most popular fruit is ______________, whereas the least popular fruit is ______________.

282. How many more people prefer oranges than bananas?

(A) 5

(B) 12

(C) 18

(D) 30

283. What is the ratio of the number of people who prefer apples to those who prefer oranges?

(A) 5:4

(B) 4:5

(C) 6:7

(D) 7:6

284. What is the decimal equivalent to $\frac{5}{16}$? (*Note:* You may *not* use a calculator.)

____

285. If $f(x)=15-2x$, for what value of x does $f(x)=x$?

(A) −2

(B) 0

(C) 5

(D) 7.5

Chapter 2

Social Studies

The Social Studies section of the GED lasts 70 minutes and is made up of 50 questions. This chapter offers you 220 chances to test your knowledge.

The Problems You'll Work On

The social studies questions are from the following content areas:

- History (U.S. and world)
- Geography
- Civics and government
- Economics

What to Watch Out For

To maximize your score, avoid these counterproductive and time-sucking activities:

- Not reading the question stems carefully and failing to relate the questions to the information given in passages
- Neglecting to identify the column headings on tables and the axis designations on graphs
- Spending more than a minute on any one question instead of marking it for later and moving on
- Failing to quickly eliminate answers that contain irrelevant data or blatantly contradict information in the passage

Questions 286 through 288 are based on the following excerpts from Abigail Adams and John Adams in 1776. Abigail Adams took the rather bold step of expressing the desire of women to gain representation in the new government.

I long to hear that you have declared an independency. And, by the way, in the new code of laws which I suppose it will be necessary for you to make, I desire you would remember the ladies and be more generous and favorable to them than your ancestors. Do not put such unlimited power into the hands of the husbands. Remember, all men would be tyrants if they could. If particular care and attention is not paid to the ladies, we are determined to foment a rebellion, and will not hold ourselves bound by any laws in which we have no voice or representation. *—Abigail Adams, March 31, 1776*

As to your extraordinary code of laws, I cannot but laugh. We have been told that our struggle has loosened the bonds of government everywhere; that children and apprentices were disobedient; that schools and colleges were grown turbulent; that Indians slighted their guardians, and negroes grew insolent to their masters. But your letter was the first intimation that another tribe, more numerous and powerful than all the rest, were grown discontented. *—John Adams, April 14, 1776*

286. What did Abigail mean when she asked her husband to "remember the ladies"?

(A) She wanted to make sure husbands did not forget their wives' birthdays.

(B) She wanted to make sure women were given proper representation in the new government.

(C) She wanted to make sure men remembered to make all the important decisions for their wives so the ladies would not have to worry about such things.

(D) She wanted women to have more power than their husbands.

287. How best could you describe John Adams's reply to his wife's request?

(A) joyful and appreciative

(B) alarmed but resigned

(C) angry and disbelieving

(D) surprised and condescending

288. Which amendment finally resulted in the fulfillment of Abigail Adams's request when it was passed in 1920?

(A) the Second Amendment

(B) the Thirteenth Amendment

(C) the Eighteenth Amendment

(D) the Nineteenth Amendment

289. The early colonists of North America sought out settlements that had easy access by ship and adequate water supplies. This helps explain why many of the early North American towns were built near

(A) mountains.

(B) glaciers.

(C) rivers.

(D) prairies.

290. Why did President Truman decide that the United States should use atomic weapons against Japan on August 6, 1945?

(A) The United States wanted to launch a preemptive strike to prevent the Japanese from attacking Pearl Harbor.

(B) He wanted to force an immediate Japanese surrender to bring about an end to the war.

(C) He wanted to see whether the newly developed atomic weapons actually worked.

(D) He wanted to convince the German forces to surrender to the Allied forces in Europe.

Use the following information for Questions 291 through 294.

When the Founding Fathers designed the new government under the Constitution, they divided the power of the federal government into three distinct branches as described in the following table.

Branch of Government	Consists Of	Powers
Executive branch	President Vice President Cabinet	Enforces the laws
Judicial branch	Supreme Court (usually 9 justices given lifetime appointments) Federal courts	Evaluates laws according to the Constitution
Legislative branch (Congress)	House of Representatives (435 representatives) Senate (100 senators)	Proposes bills that could become law

291. Which choice correctly completes the following sentence?

Congress has ________ members, including ________ senators and ________ representatives.

(A) Congress has 100 members, including 535 senators and 435 representatives.

(B) Congress has 435 members, including 100 senators and 535 representatives.

(C) Congress has 535 members, including 100 senators and 435 representatives.

(D) Congress has 535 members, including 435 senators and 100 representatives.

292. Which branch of government is responsible for deciding whether a law is constitutional?

____

293. Why did the Founding Fathers divide the federal government into three distinct branches?

(A) They wanted to make sure that the president would have unlimited power.

(B) They wanted to encourage competition among the members of the federal government.

(C) They wanted to base their system of government on the British monarchy.

(D) They wanted to ensure that there were checks and balances to prevent any one part of the government from becoming too powerful.

294. All of the following are reasons the Supreme Court justices are given lifetime appointments EXCEPT

(A) to insulate the justices from politics so they're free to make decisions without fear of losing their jobs.

(B) to ensure that the president doesn't gain too much power by replacing each member of the court with justices who will vote in his favor.

(C) to ensure that no modern ideas are allowed to pollute the Supreme Court's decision-making.

(D) to provide a certain level of judicial stability when the country transitions from one political party to another.

Questions 295 through 297 are based on the following excerpts from two landmark Supreme Court decisions. The first excerpt is from Plessy v. Ferguson *(1896), which sustained the constitutionality of Louisiana's racist Jim Crow law. The second excerpt is from* Brown v. Board of Education of Topeka, Kansas *(1954), which overturned the court's previous ruling.*

We consider the underlying fallacy of the plaintiff's argument to consist in the assumption that the enforced separation of the two races stamps the colored race with a badge of inferiority. If this be so, it is not by reason of anything found in the act, but solely because the colored race chooses to put that construction upon it. . . . The argument also assumes that social prejudice may be overcome by legislation, and that equal rights cannot be secured except by an enforced commingling of the two races. . . . If the civil and political rights of both races be equal, one cannot be inferior to the other civilly or politically. If one race be inferior to the other socially, the Constitution of the United States cannot put them upon the same plane.
—*Plessy v. Ferguson*

To separate them from others of similar age and qualifications solely because of their race generates a feeling of inferiority as to their status in the community that may affect their hearts and minds in a way unlikely ever to be undone. We conclude that, in the field of public education, the doctrine of "separate but equal" has no place. Separate educational facilities are inherently unequal.
—*Brown v. Board of Education of Topeka, Kansas*

295. What was the result of the 1896 Supreme Court decision *Plessy v. Ferguson*?

(A) It upheld state racial segregation laws for public facilities under the doctrine of "separate but equal."

(B) It led to the desegregation of all U.S. public buildings.

(C) It undermined the validity of the Supreme Court.

(D) It led to the desegregation of the U.S. public school system.

296. What was the impact of the *Brown v. Board of Education* decision?

(A) It upheld state racial segregation laws for public facilities under the doctrine of "separate but equal."

(B) It prevented racial segregation in all public places.

(C) It undermined the validity of the Supreme Court.

(D) It led to the desegregation of the U.S. public school system.

297. Which of the following is a factual statement rather than an opinion regarding the *Brown v. Board of Education* decision?

(A) The Court was afraid of antagonizing the African-American population.

(B) The Court considered that segregation was traumatic and unfair to African-American children.

(C) The Court was racist against the African-American population.

(D) The Court was biased against the Board of Education of Topeka, Kansas.

298. What can you conclude about these two landmark Supreme Court decisions?

(A) Once the Supreme Court has made a decision, it can never be overturned.

(B) Supreme Court decisions can be overturned by the president.

(C) The Supreme Court can reverse its previous decisions if the justices feel that a mistake has been made.

(D) Supreme Court decisions can be overturned by state courts.

Questions 299 through 302 are based on the following excerpt from the First Amendment to the U.S. Constitution.

Congress shall make no law respecting an establishment of religion, or prohibiting the free exercise thereof; or abridging the freedom of speech, or of the press; or the right of the people peaceably to assemble, and to petition the Government for a redress of grievances.

299. Which of the following is not guaranteed by the First Amendment?

(A) freedom of the press

(B) freedom of petition

(C) freedom of speech

(D) freedom of life, liberty, and the pursuit of happiness

300. The First Amendment

(A) prohibits Congress from making laws.

(B) increases Congress's power to place restrictions on individual freedoms, such as freedom of religion, freedom of speech, and freedom of the press.

(C) protects the right to bear arms.

(D) protects the general public from the government placing restrictions on individual freedoms, such as freedom of religion, freedom of speech, and freedom of the press.

301. Which of the following laws would be permitted by the First Amendment?

(A) a law that prevents a national newspaper from printing a true article about government incompetence and corruption

(B) a law that prevents the public from peacefully protesting against a president

(C) a law that allocates federal funds to Christian missionary programs

(D) a law that creates guidelines for the public to petition the government to keep a popular act that may soon be abolished

302. What overall effect has the First Amendment had on the United States?

(A) It has had minimal impact on the general public.

(B) It was quickly overturned by the Second Amendment.

(C) It has played an essential role in protecting individual freedoms.

(D) It undermined the Constitution by amending the original document.

Use the following information for Questions 303 through 305.

Beginning at the end of the 15th century, many European countries began exploring and conquering territories in the New World. Driven by the desire for increased economic wealth, access to natural resources, and the wish to spread Christianity to new parts of the world, many European nations formed permanent settlements in the New World.

The following map shows the New World during this period and labels the European countries that controlled each territory at that time.

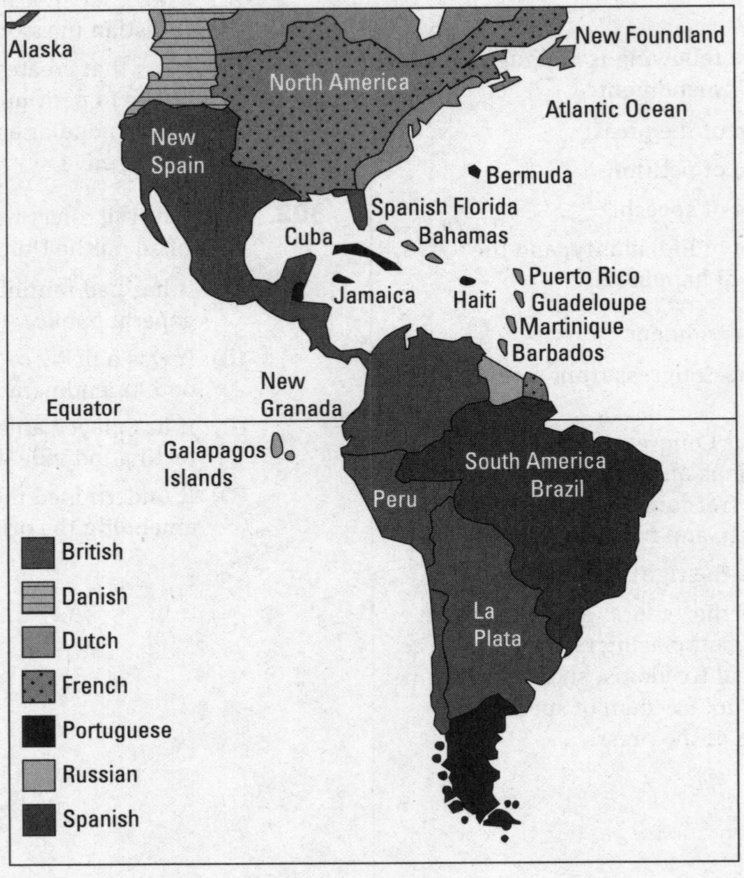

303. According to the map, which European country controlled the largest amount of territory?

(A) Portugal
(B) Great Britain
(C) Spain
(D) The Netherlands

304. According to the passage, all of the following reasons provided motivation to European counties to gain control of more territories in the New World EXCEPT

(A) they wanted to help the natives of the New World.
(B) they wanted to gain access to the natural resources that were available in the New World.
(C) they wanted to spread Christianity throughout the New World.
(D) they wanted to increase their own economic wealth by exploiting the New World.

305. Why did the European nations eventually give up control of their newly gained territories and leave the New World?

(A) They had already used up all the natural resources of the region.
(B) They had finished successfully converting all the natives to Christianity.
(C) They realized that it was morally wrong to exploit the natives and the natural resources of a region that didn't really belong to them.
(D) They were forced out by rebellions, war, and revolutions.

306. What languages are the most commonly spoken in North America, South America, and Central America today?

(A) Dutch, French, and German
(B) German, English, and Portuguese
(C) German, Spanish, and Portuguese
(D) Spanish, English, and Portuguese

Use the following information for Questions 307 through 311.

The United States trades with many countries. When the U.S. sells goods and services to other countries, the value of the goods is recorded as exports. When the U.S. buys goods and services from other countries, the value of those goods is recorded as imports. The *trade balance* is the value of each country's total exports to the United States minus the value of each country's total imports from the United States. A negative trade balance is called a *trade deficit*.

This table shows the value of the exports, imports, and trade balances for the top five largest trade partners of the United States in 2015. Values are given in billions of dollars

Country	Exports (from U.S.)	Imports (to U.S.)	Trade Balance
Canada	312	348	–35
China	124	467	–343
Mexico	240	294	–54
Japan	67	134	–67
Germany	49	123	–74

307. With which country does the United States have the smallest trade deficit?

(A) Canada
(B) China
(C) Mexico
(D) Germany

308. According to the table, which of the following is a true statement?

(A) The United States buys the most goods and services from China and sells the most goods and services to Canada.

(B) The United States buys the most goods and services from Mexico and sells the most goods and services to China.

(C) The United States buys the most goods and services from Canada and sells the most goods and services to China.

(D) The United States buys the most goods and services from Germany and sells the most goods and services to Japan.

309. The value of Japan's trade deficit is what percentage of the value of the U.S. exports to Japan?

(A) 0%

(B) 50%

(C) 67%

(D) 100%

310. Based on the given information, which of the following is a true statement?

(A) The trading partner that buys the least goods and services from the U.S. has the largest trade balance.

(B) The trade deficits for each country will continue to increase each year.

(C) All of the top five trading partners with the United States have negative values for their trade balances.

(D) Of the top five partners, China buys the second largest amount of goods and services from the U.S.

311. Based on the given information, which of the following is an opinion rather than a factual statement?

(A) Of the top five partners, Germany buys the least amount of goods and services from the United States.

(B) China has the largest trade deficit with the United States.

(C) The United States should impose tariffs on Chinese goods in order to reduce the large trade deficit.

(D) Of the top five partners, Mexico has the second smallest trade deficit.

To answer Questions 312 through 316, use the following excerpt from Dr. Martin Luther King Jr.'s famous "I Have a Dream" speech, which he delivered during the March on Washington for Jobs and Freedom on August 28, 1963.

As we walk, we must make the pledge that we shall always march ahead. We cannot turn back. There are those who are asking the devotees of civil rights, "When will you be satisfied?" We can never be satisfied as long as the Negro is the victim of the unspeakable horrors of police brutality. We can never be satisfied, as long as our bodies, heavy with the fatigue of travel, cannot gain lodging in the motels of the highways and the hotels of the cities. We cannot be satisfied as long as the Negro's basic mobility is from a smaller ghetto to a larger one. We can never be satisfied as long as our children are stripped of their selfhood and robbed of their dignity by signs stating "For Whites Only." We cannot be satisfied as long as a Negro in Mississippi cannot vote and a Negro in New York believes he has nothing for which to vote. No, no, we are not satisfied, and we will not be satisfied until justice rolls down like waters and righteousness like a mighty stream. . . .

I say to you today, my friends, so even though we face the difficulties of today and tomorrow, I still have a dream. It is a dream deeply rooted in the American dream. I have a dream that one day this nation will rise up and live out the true meaning of its creed: "We hold these truths to be self-evident: that all men are created equal."

312. What problem was Dr. Martin Luther King Jr. trying to highlight?

(A) the problem of sexual harassment for females in the United States

(B) the problem of racial inequality for African Americans in the United States

(C) the problem of income inequality for the very poor compared to the top 1 percent

(D) the problem of having unrealistic dreams and how to eliminate them

313. According to Dr. King's speech in 1963, African Americans were discriminated against in each of the following ways EXCEPT

(A) they were often victims of police brutality.

(B) they were not allowed to stay in 'White Only' hotels.

(C) they could not get good reception for their mobile phones in the large ghettos.

(D) they were still denied the right to vote in some parts of the country.

314. Toward the end of his speech, Dr. King used the quote "We hold these truths to be self-evident: that all men are created equal," taken from the Declaration of Independence. Why did Dr. King include this quote in his speech?

(A) He was pointing out the differences between the rights of men and the rights of women.

(B) He was trying to convince the audience that African Americans are superior to white Americans and should be treated as such.

(C) He wanted African Americans to declare their independence from the United States.

(D) He wanted to point out the hypocrisy of people who agree with the Declaration of Independence but don't agree with equal rights for African Americans.

315. Dr. Martin Luther King Jr. also led many protests for civil rights during this period of history. What does the term "civil rights" mean in this context?

(A) the rights and freedoms that every citizen has always enjoyed equally

(B) the rights and freedoms that only African Americans have always benefited from

(C) the rights and freedoms that ensure every citizen's ability to participate equally in social and political life

(D) the rights and freedoms required by state law but not federal law

316. Dr. Martin Luther King Jr. was eventually successful in helping to bring an end to racial segregation in the United States. Which of the following best describes racial segregation?

(A) the separation of different races in public institutions and daily life

(B) a belief that the United States Constitution should apply only to "the right kind of people"

(C) the system that helps include more minorities in everyday events

(D) a scientific theory that supports the ideas and beliefs of white supremacists

317. Every decade, the United States Census Bureau takes a census of the population. Which of the following best describes the U.S. Census?

(A) calculations based on global warming

(B) an unconstitutional practice that should be stopped immediately

(C) demographic information (such as age, ethnicity, and level of education) taken every ten years

(D) a tax that every citizen needs to pay every ten years

Use the following information for Questions 318 through 321.

When America entered the war in 1917, Congress passed a law called the Espionage Act, which said that during wartime it was illegal to obstruct the draft (forcing civilians to join the armed forces). Charles Schenck was against the war, so he mailed thousands of pamphlets to men who had been drafted, telling them that the government had no right to send American citizens to other countries to kill people. The government accused Schenck of violating the Espionage Act and brought Schenck to trial. The case was decided by the Supreme Court, in 1919, in favor of the United States.

Justice Holmes admitted that "in many places and in ordinary times," Schenck would have had a right to say everything that he said in his pamphlets. However, Holmes said, how far a person's freedom of speech extends depends on the circumstances. "The question in every case," he said, "is whether the words are used in such circumstances and are of such a nature as to create a clear and present danger that they will bring about the substantive evils that Congress has a right to prevent. . . . The most stringent protection of free speech would not protect a man in falsely shouting fire in a theatre and causing a panic."

318. Which important amendment did the case refer to?

(A) First Amendment
(B) Second Amendment
(C) Eighteenth Amendment
(D) Nineteenth Amendment

319. Under which special circumstances did the Supreme Court state that limits to freedom of speech would apply?

(A) when an individual says something that the president disagrees with
(B) when an individual says something that the Supreme Court disagrees with
(C) when the United States is at war and an individual's speech may cause a clear and present danger to national security
(D) when the United States presents a clear and present danger to an individual

320. Based upon the outcome of this Supreme Court decision, would you have the right to falsely shout, "Fire!" in a crowded cinema?

(A) Yes, because freedom of speech is protected by the First Amendment.
(B) Yes, because freedom of speech is protected by the Second Amendment.
(C) No, because the First Amendment doesn't protect false speech that can cause panic.
(D) No, because the Second Amendment doesn't protect false speech that can cause panic.

321. Which war did the United States enter in 1917?

(A) World War I
(B) World War II
(C) U.S. Civil War
(D) Cold War

322. What was the name of the period from 1917 until 1933 during which the sale or consumption of alcohol was illegal in the United States?

(A) the Great Depression

(B) Prohibition

(C) the Cold War

(D) the Dust Bowl

Use the following information for Questions 323 and 324.

This graph shows the change in the Native-American population of Mexico during the 16th century.

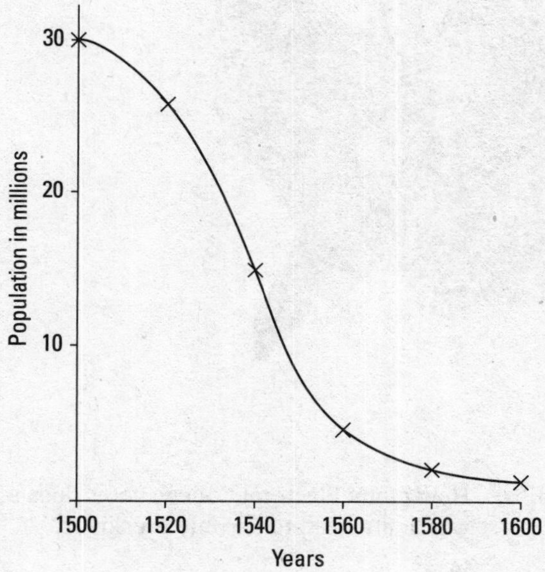

323. The graph suggests that which of the following statements is true?

(A) More Native Americans died during the second half of the century than during the first half of the century.

(B) Most Native Americans immigrated to other countries during the 16th century.

(C) Approximately 20 million Native Americans died during the first half of the century.

(D) The suicide rate among Native Americans rose sharply during the 16th century.

324. What caused the sharp decline in the Native-American population during the 16th century?

(A) Native Americans were executed by the Spanish conquistadors.

(B) Most of the Native Americans emigrated to escape from the Spanish invaders.

(C) Native Americans were killed off by diseases brought by the Europeans invaders.

(D) The suicide rate among Native American rose sharply during the 16th century.

Use the following information for Questions 325 through 329.

The Electoral College system consists of 538 electors. A majority, or 270 electoral votes, is required to elect the president. Each state is allotted one elector for each of its members in the House of Representatives (which is based on the state's population) plus two additional electors to account for the state's two senators. The following figure shows the results of the 2016 presidential election. Senators are elected to six-year terms, and members of the House are elected to two-year terms.

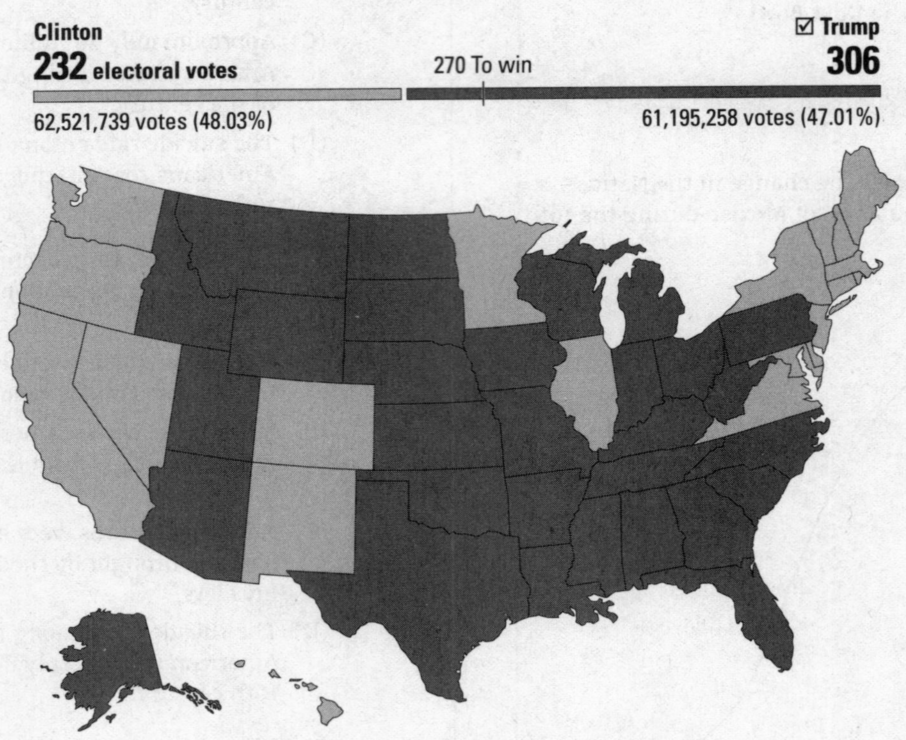

325. Which candidate did most Americans vote for?

(A) Donald Trump

(B) Hillary Clinton

(C) Jill Stein

(D) Gary Johnson

326. How many Electoral College votes does a candidate need to become president?

(A) 232

(B) 270

(C) 306

(D) 538

327. Which of the following statements is FALSE?

(A) The United States is a both a republic and a democracy.

(B) The outcome of the Electoral College system is always in agreement with the outcome of the popular vote.

(C) Each state has two senators.

(D) The number of electors that each state has is based primarily on the state's population.

328. Based on the information in the passage, which of the following is a true statement?

(A) The number of members that a state has in the U.S. Senate is based on the state's population, whereas each state always has two members in the U.S. House of Representatives.

(B) The number of members that a state has in the U.S. House of Representatives is based on the state's population, whereas each state always has two members in the U.S. Senate.

(C) The number of members that a state has in both the U.S. House of Representatives and the U.S. Senate is based on the state's population.

(D) Each state always has two members in both the U.S. Senate and the U.S. House of Representatives.

329. When a senator is elected, how long is his or her term in office?

(A) 2 years

(B) 8 years

(C) 4 years

(D) 6 years

Use the following information for Questions 330 through 334.

Over the years, several changes or amendments have been made to the U.S. Constitution. There have been a total of 27 amendments. The first ten amendments are collectively known as the Bill of Rights. This table summarizes a few of these amendments.

Amendment	Date	Summary
First	1791	Freedom of speech, religion, press, assembly, and petition
Second	1791	Right to bear arms
Fifth	1791	Right to avoid self-incrimination, right to trial, due process
Tenth	1791	Rights that are reserved to the states (issues that are not the responsibility of the federal government)
Eighteenth	1919	Prohibition
Nineteenth	1920	Women's right to vote
Twenty-first	1933	Repeal of the Eighteenth Amendment
Twenty-second	1951	Two-term limit on the president

330. Which amendment prohibits the President of the United States from running for a third term during an election?

(A) First Amendment

(B) Second Amendment

(C) Eighteenth Amendment

(D) Twenty-second Amendment

331. Which of the following is a true statement regarding the U.S. Constitution and its amendments?

(A) The U.S. Constitution can never be changed.

(B) Amendments are merely suggestions, so they aren't legally binding.

(C) An amendment can never be changed once it becomes the law of the land.

(D) An amendment can be changed later if necessary.

332. The first ten amendments were collectively known as the Bill of Rights. What was the main purpose of the Bill of Rights?

(A) to protect the federal government from the people by placing limits on their individual rights

(B) to protect the people and the states from the federal government by guaranteeing their basic individual rights

(C) to protect the president from the states by placing limits on state rights

(D) to replace the original Constitution

333. The National Rifle Association (NRA) strongly supports which amendment?

(A) First Amendment

(B) Second Amendment

(C) Fifth Amendment

(D) Tenth Amendment

334. Which amendment allows a defendant to remain silent when they are being questioned about an issue that might incriminate them?

(A) First Amendment

(B) Fifth Amendment

(C) Eighteenth Amendment

(D) Twenty-first Amendment

Use the following information for Questions 335 through 338.

The following figure shows the percentage of the gross domestic product (GDP) that each country spends on healthcare and social care each year.

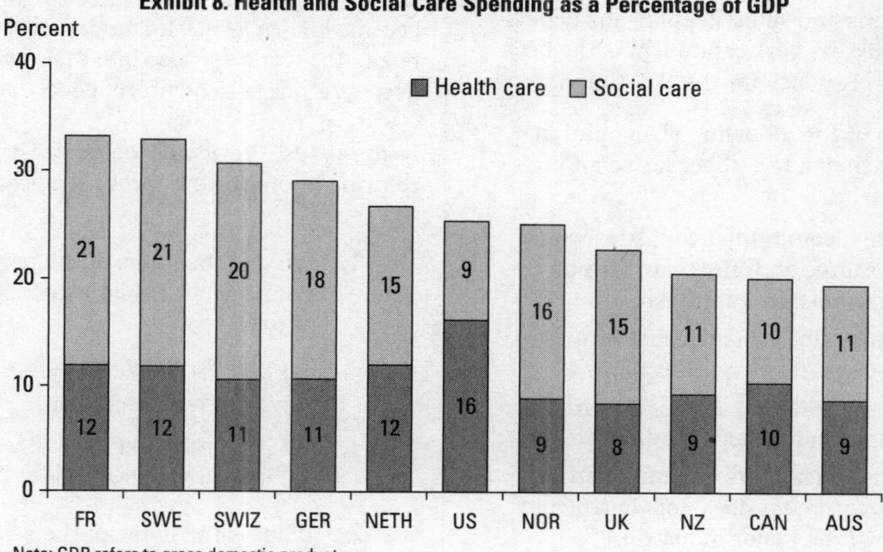

335. Which of the following best describes gross domestic product (GDP)?

(A) the total value of all the repulsive or unattractive household products that each country makes

(B) the total value of all the services provided and goods produced in a country in one year

(C) the total value of all the tax revenue that a country collects in one year

(D) the total value spent on health and social care by each country in one year

336. Which country spends the highest percentage of its GDP on healthcare?

(A) France (FRA)

(B) the United Kingdom (UK)

(C) the United States (US)

(D) New Zealand (NZ)

337. Which country spends the smallest percentage of its GDP on social care?

(A) France (FRA)

(B) the United Kingdom (UK)

(C) the United States (US)

(D) New Zealand (NZ)

338. Regarding the 11 countries listed, which of the following is a true statement?

(A) The United States spends the median total dollar amount on social and health services.

(B) Canada spends approximately the same amount on healthcare as it does on social care.

(C) The United States spends more than 30 percent of its GDP on health and social care.

(D) New Zealand (NZ) cares less about its people than France (FRA).

339. *Laissez-faire capitalism* is defined as the separation of the state and the economy. This economic policy leaves individuals and businesses alone and allows economic events to occur without interference from the government. Most Libertarians and some Republicans believe that laissez-faire capitalism is the best economic policy for the U.S. to follow.

Which of the following is an opinion rather than a fact about laissez-faire capitalism?

(A) Most communist countries would disagree with the main idea of laissez-faire capitalism.

(B) Most Libertarians believe in laissez-faire capitalism.

(C) Laissez-faire capitalism is irresponsible and should be outlawed.

(D) In laissez-faire capitalism, the government does not control and own the major industries.

340. Fossil fuels, such as coal and natural gas, consist of hydrocarbons that are derived from the remains of organisms. Many countries obtain most of their energy needs by burning fossil fuels. The combustion of fossil fuels produces heat, carbon dioxide, and water. Carbon dioxide is a greenhouse gas that contributes to global warming when present in excess in the atmosphere.

Which of the following is a fact rather than an opinion about fossil fuels?

(A) Fossil fuels should be banned because they are too dirty and expensive.

(B) Many countries rely on fossil fuels as their major source of energy.

(C) The United States should bury its fossil fuels so they don't contribute to global warming.

(D) Fossil fuels are more economical than alternative sources of energy.

Use the following information for Questions 341 through 343.

On October 29, 1929, the New York Stock Exchange suffered its worst day ever, wiping out billions of dollars of investors' money in a single day that became known as Black Tuesday. America and the rest of the world spiraled into their longest and deepest economic downturn, which lasted until 1939.

In the 1930s, President Roosevelt issued a series of reforms intended to improve the economy.

341. What is the name of the period of economic decline that lasted from 1929 until 1939?

(A) the Great Repression

(B) the Great Recession

(C) the Great Depression

(D) the Great Obsession

342. What is the name of the series of reforms issued by President Roosevelt in the 1930s that were intended to improve the economy?

(A) the New Deal

(B) the Square Meal

(C) the Raw Deal

(D) Reconstruction

343. What global event in 1939 helped the United States finally recover from its economic decline?

(A) the start of World War I

(B) the start of World War II

(C) the end of World War II

(D) the end of the Vietnam War

Use the following excerpt from the First Amendment for Questions 344 through 346.

Congress shall make no law respecting an establishment of religion, or prohibiting the free exercise thereof, or abridging the freedom of speech, or the press; or the right of the people peaceably to assemble and to petition the Government . . .

344. What is the main purpose of the First Amendment?

(A) to protect the federal government from the people by placing limits on their individual rights

(B) to prevent Congress from making laws

(C) to protect essential freedoms, including the freedom of religion and the freedom to petition the government

(D) to protect the right to bear arms against Congress

345. Which of the following laws would NOT be permitted by the First Amendment?

(A) a law protecting a news website that is printing stories that the government does not approve of

(B) a law guaranteeing the right to complain about the president

(C) a law that establishes a state-run church

(D) a law making it illegal to ban a protest march against an unpopular decision made by the Supreme Court

346. Which choice correctly completes the following sentence?

The First Amendment guarantees _______________, _______________, _______________, and _______________.

(A) freedom of voting, freedom of religion, freedom of speech, freedom of petition

(B) freedom of voting, freedom of religion, freedom of taxation, freedom of petition

(C) freedom of the press, freedom of religion, freedom of speech, freedom of petition

(D) freedom of the press, freedom of religion, freedom of speech, freedom of taxation

347. Which of the following is the riskiest investment?

(A) buying stock in a single startup company

(B) putting your money in a savings account at the bank

(C) buying stock in several large established corporations

(D) putting your money in U.S. Government bonds

348. The Emancipation Proclamation of 1863

(A) ended the presidency of Abraham Lincoln.

(B) established a policy of "separate but equal."

(C) freed slaves in Southern states.

(D) ended the Civil War.

349. All of the following are valid reasons monopolies are not allowed to exist in the United States EXCEPT

(A) monopolies are too efficient.

(B) monopolies prevent healthy competition.

(C) monopolies often give consumers fewer choices.

(D) monopolies give too much power to one company.

350. The slave trade from Africa to the New World from the mid-1500s to the mid-1800s resulted in

(A) a Spanish monopoly of the slave trade business.

(B) virtually no impact on South America.

(C) more opportunities for the immigrants who decided to move to the New World.

(D) the largest forced migration of a group of people in world history.

351. A worker's total compensation usually consists of which components?

(A) wages only

(B) wages and benefits

(C) unemployment benefits

(D) wages plus whatever office supplies he or she can sneak home

352. When workers are trying to gain higher wages or improvements in their working conditions, why is the threat of going on strike such an effective bargaining tool for the workers?

(A) It's usually best to strike while the iron is hot.

(B) Strikes usually shut down all production, which harms the company financially.

(C) The general public usually takes the side of the company in the strike.

(D) A strike allows a company to hire new workers.

353. All of the following are examples of essential infrastructure that supports economic activity EXCEPT

(A) the national highway system.

(B) bridges and tunnels.

(C) the annual U.S. budget.

(D) airports and ports.

354. All the following are features of a communist economy EXCEPT

(A) all the factories are owned by the government, which controls all industries.

(B) the prices of all goods and services are controlled by the government.

(C) the government encourages entrepreneurs to start, own, and operate their own companies.

(D) the government makes all economic decisions.

355. Inflation generally occurs when wages remain stagnant while the prices of goods and services continue to rise. During times of high inflation, which of the following is likely to happen?

(A) Demand for most goods and services increases sharply.

(B) Shortages of goods occur, and prices decline.

(C) Consumers reduce their spending on nonessential items.

(D) Unemployment decreases as jobs are created.

356. When it is discovered that a particular company is engaged in unethical behavior, many people decide to boycott the company by refusing to buy their services or products. How does boycotting a company put pressure on it to change its ways?

(A) Workers go on strike, bringing production to a halt.

(B) Workers demand higher wages.

(C) It damages the company's reputation with its customers.

(D) The sudden increase in demand for the company's products helps drive up the prices.

357. Why would American automobile workers generally support tariffs being placed on foreign imported cars?

(A) Tariffs lower the prices of American-made cars.

(B) Tariffs make the imported cars more expensive, increasing the demand for American-made cars.

(C) Tariffs can help mend strained relationships between hostile nations.

(D) Tariffs can promote free trade among competing nations.

358. The Cold War began at the end of World War II due to mistrust between the democratic United States and the communist Soviet Union. Each nation feared each other's style of government and began to build an arsenal of nuclear weapons to intimidate the other. Which of the following statements is NOT true about the early part of the Cold War?

(A) The Warsaw Pact was created as a response to the formation of NATO.

(B) NATO and the Warsaw Pact were created to work together to promote world peace.

(C) The United States and Western European nations felt threatened by communist actions in Eastern Europe and formed an alliance to confront those threats.

(D) The United Nations was formed primarily to promote world peace after two devastating world wars.

359. During the Industrial Revolution, Great Britain quickly became the world's top producer of goods. Which of the following was NOT a factor in Britain's rise to dominance in world trade during the 1800s?

(A) Great Britain had made advances in the steam train and had developed a rail network, making the transport of goods relatively easy.

(B) Great Britain had lots of coal available to power the machines needed for the mass production of goods.

(C) Great Britain imposed tariffs on goods imported from other countries.

(D) Great Britain's extensive colonization gave it access to raw materials.

360. During World War II, women on the U.S. home front made a significant contribution to the war effort by

(A) taking a reduction in work hours to allow minorities to work longer hours.

(B) not openly protesting the war effort.

(C) filling jobs that were needed for the war effort because so many men were away fighting the war.

(D) taking a reduction in pay so that the working men could still support their families.

361. During the Cold War, the United States' fear of the spread of communism was expressed in its foreign policy known as the Domino Theory. This fear was heightened when China became communist in 1949 and the Korean War broke out in 1950, followed by the U.S. entering the conflict in Vietnam in 1964.

Which of the following statements best summarizes the Domino Theory as it applied to actions in Asia from 1945 through 1975?

(A) The United States was afraid that the popularity of the game of dominos would fade and be overtaken by Chinese checkers.

(B) The United States was concerned only about the Soviet Union becoming communist.

(C) The United States was afraid that communism would fade from the region unless they intervened in Vietnam.

(D) The generalized fear was that if one country fell to communism, all the other countries in the region would also fall to communism.

362. In October 1963, the United States and the Soviet Union faced a 13-day standoff known as the Cuban Missile Crisis after the United States discovered Soviet nuclear missiles in Cuba, just 90 miles away from the continental United States. President Kennedy ordered an immediate naval blockade of Cuba and warned the American people that he was willing to use whatever force necessary to neutralize this threat to national security.

The standoff ended when

(A) the USSR revealed that the "nuclear missiles" in Cuba were actually fakes.

(B) the United States backed down and decided to allow the missiles to remain in Cuba.

(C) President JFK was able to get the Soviet Union to withdraw its missiles from Cuba while the United States agreed to remove nuclear missiles from Turkey.

(D) the USSR negotiated a treaty with the United States to keep the missiles in place without the threat of them ever being used.

Questions 363 through 365 are based on the following two excerpts from speeches made by John Adams and George Washington.

There is nothing which I dread so much as a division of the republic into two great parties, each arranged under its leader, and concerting measures in opposition to each other. This, in my humble apprehension, is to be dreaded as the greatest political evil under our Constitution.
—*John Adams*

The alternate domination of one faction over another, sharpened by the spirit of revenge, natural to party dissension, which in different ages and countries has perpetrated the most horrid enormities, is itself a frightful despotism. But this leads at length to a more formal and permanent despotism. The disorders and miseries, which result, gradually incline the minds of men to seek security and repose in the absolute power of an individual; and sooner or later the chief of some prevailing faction, more able or more fortunate than his competitors, turns this disposition to the purposes of his own elevation, on the ruins of Public Liberty. Without looking forward to an extremity of this kind, (which nevertheless ought not to be entirely out of sight,) the common and continual mischiefs of the spirit of party are sufficient to make it the interest and duty of a wise people to discourage and restrain it. —*George Washington*

363. What danger did John Adams foresee with regard to the American political system?

(A) He warned Americans that they would have to fight for their right to party.

(B) He warned that only a two-party system could protect Americans from turning against each other.

(C) He warned that a two-party system could lead to Americans turning against each other.

(D) He warned that the two-party system may lead to a multiple-party system.

364. Based on the two quotes, were John Adams and George Washington in agreement regarding this issue?

(A) No. Adams was in favor of a two-party system, whereas Washington was against the two-party system.

(B) No. Washington was in favor of the two-party system, whereas Adams was against a two-party system.

(C) Yes. Both Adams and Washington were in favor of a two-party system.

(D) Yes. Both Adams and Washington were against a two-party system.

365. Based on the two quotes and the current prevailing attitudes of many Republicans and Democrats with regard to each other's party, were Washington and Adams right to worry about the possible dangers of the two-party system?

(A) No. Republicans and Democrats have the greatest respect for each other and always work together for the good of the country.

(B) No. Without the two-party system, the American government would become gridlocked and would never get anything done.

(C) Yes. Both Republicans and Democrats appear to detest each other and sometimes put their party's needs above the needs of the country.

(D) The evidence is inconclusive.

366. In 1917, some women, who became known as *suffragettes*, began protesting outside the White House. What were these women trying to achieve?

(A) the right to serve in the armed forces

(B) the right for women to vote

(C) the right to host tea parties on the White House lawn

(D) equal pay with men

367. After the United States won the Spanish-American War in 1898, President Teddy Roosevelt began taking a more aggressive approach to his foreign policy regarding the countries in Latin America. In an effort to extend U.S. influence in the area,

(A) the U.S. adopted a more laid-back attitude toward its involvement in Latin America.

(B) Panama forced the U.S. to build a canal across the region.

(C) the U.S. exerted its force and growing influence in Latin America by "persuading" Panama to let it build the Panama Canal.

(D) the U.S. negotiated successfully with Columbia for access to build a canal across Columbia.

368. During 1965, support for America's involvement in the war in Vietnam was strong, but in less than two years, the war became unpopular at home, leading to student protests across the country. All the following would be a valid reason for students to protest the war EXCEPT

(A) more and more young people were being drafted to fight in Vietnam.

(B) the students believed that America's involvement in the war in Vietnam was a necessary evil.

(C) graphic photos showing atrocities against Vietnamese women and children stoked outrage among the American public.

(D) the numbers of American soldier casualties were increasing each year, and more and more troops were being sent over to fight in the war.

369. Which amendment to the Constitution stated that the powers not delegated to the federal government or prohibited to the states were "reserved to the states"?

(A) Tenth Amendment

(B) Nineteenth Amendment

(C) Twenty-fifth Amendment

(D) Thirty-second Amendment

370. What trend in the media has NOT been a major factor in the U.S. presidential elections since 1960?

(A) The convenience of online news has challenged the dominance of major newspapers as the primary source of information about candidates and elections.

(B) The growth of fake news websites has blurred the lines between fictional and factual information about candidates and elections.

(C) The televised presidential debates continue to command large audiences.

(D) People now rely more on mainstream news than ever for reliable information about candidates and elections.

371. Which of the following is an example of capital?

(A) the owner of a startup company

(B) a deposit of copper

(C) a skilled plumber

(D) a factory

372. Which of the following statements describes a result of the increase in globalization over the past half century?

(A) Terrorist attacks have begun to decrease as more countries are working in cooperation with one another.

(B) Many counties are more dependent on each other for their economic growth.

(C) Human rights have declined sharply around the world.

(D) The number of refugees around the world has declined.

373. The continued reliance of the world's leading economies (the United States and China) upon fossil fuels such as coal and petroleum could lead to all of the following result EXCEPT

(A) an increased need for environmental restrictions on power plants and automobiles.

(B) an increase in global warming due to the production of greenhouse gases.

(C) an increased focus on alternative energy such as wind power and solar energy in China and the United States.

(D) an increase in pollution in large cities such as Hong Kong and New York City.

374. President Roosevelt issued Executive Order 9066 in 1942, just over two months after the Japanese attacked Pearl Harbor. The executive order had serious consequences for over 120,000 people of Japanese ancestry who were living in the United States. What was the intent of this order?

(A) to remove the right of citizenship from all Japanese Americans

(B) to relocate people of Japanese ancestry living in America to ten different internment camps away from the western American coastlines for the duration of the war

(C) to encourage people of Japanese ancestry in America to issue a formal apology and take responsibility for the Japanese attack on Pearl Harbor

(D) to force people of Japanese ancestry living in America to emigrate to Japan

375. In the late 1800s, J. D. Rockefeller, the owner of Standard Oil, incorporated vertical and horizontal business practices into his business model by controlling the drilling, production, transportation, and sale of his products. As a result, he was able to

(A) prevent monopolies from forming in the oil business.

(B) allow smaller competitors easier entry into the oil business.

(C) create a monopoly by controlling nearly 90 percent of the oil production in the U.S.

(D) compete with his competition with only minimal success.

Use the following information for Questions 376 through 378.

This graph shows the immigration rate to the United States throughout the 20th century.

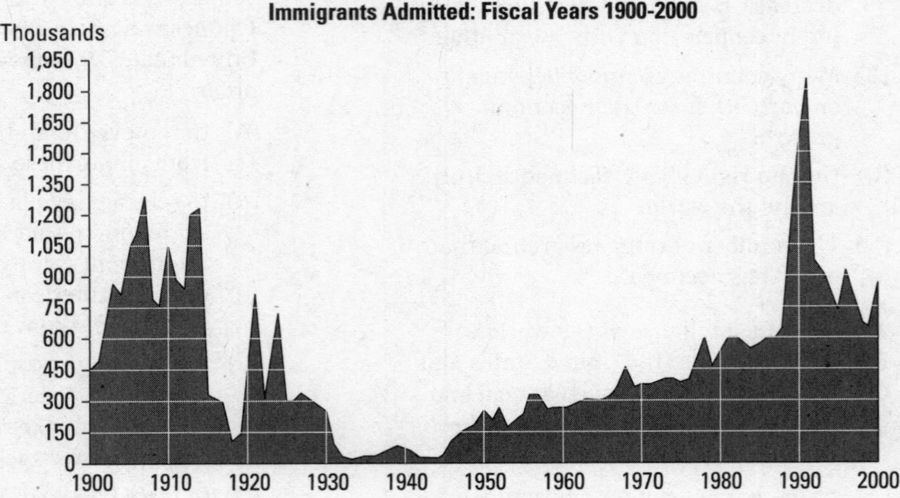

376. Which of the following statements best describes the rate of immigration into the United Stated throughout the 20th century?

(A) The immigration rate remained fairly consistent throughout the 20th century.

(B) The immigration rate increased steadily throughout the 20th century.

(C) The immigration rate decreased steadily throughout the 20th century.

(D) The immigration rate increased steadily throughout the second half of the 20th century and then spiked in the 1990s.

377. Which of the following best explains why the immigration rate fell sharply between 1914 and 1918?

(A) Immigration declined sharply due to World War I.

(B) Immigration declined sharply due to World War II.

(C) Immigration declined sharply due to the Cold War.

(D) Immigration declined sharply due to the U.S. Civil War.

378. Which of the following statements, if true, would best explain why the immigration rate began to rise in the second half of the 20th century?

(A) In 1965, the U.S. established a strict quota system, making it harder to move to the United States.

(B) In 1965, the U.S. passed a law banning all immigration to the United States.

(C) In 1965, the Immigration and Naturalization Act established a new immigration policy aimed at attracting skilled labor to the United States.

(D) In 1965, the U.S. lowered its quota system to permit fewer immigrants into the United States each year.

Use the following two excerpts for Questions 379 through 384. The first excerpt is from the Declaration of Independence, July 4, 1776. The second except is from the Declaration of Sentiments, from the Seneca Falls Convention for women's rights, 1848 (organized by Elizabeth Cady Stanton and Susan B. Anthony).

We hold these truths to be self-evident: That all men are created equal; that they are endowed by their Creator with certain unalienable rights; that among these are life, liberty, and the pursuit of happiness; that, to secure these rights, governments are instituted among men, deriving their just powers from the consent of the governed; that whenever any form of government becomes destructive of these ends, it is the right of the people to alter or to abolish it, and to institute new government, laying its foundation on such principles, and organizing its powers in such form, as to them shall seem most likely to effect their safety and happiness. The history of the present King of Great Britain is a history of repeated injuries and usurpations, all having in direct object the establishment of an absolute tyranny over these states. To prove this, let facts be submitted to a candid world. . . . For quartering large bodies of armed troops among us. . . For cutting off our trade with all parts of the world. . . For imposing taxes on us without our consent. . . For depriving us, in many cases, of the benefits of trial by jury. —*Declaration of Independence, July 4, 1776*

We hold these truths to be self-evident: that all men and women are created equal. . . . The history of mankind is a history of repeated injuries and usurpations on the part of man toward woman, having in direct object the establishment of an absolute tyranny over her. To prove this, let facts be submitted to a candid world. . . . He has never permitted her to exercise her inalienable right to the elective franchise. . . . He has compelled her to submit to laws, in the formation of which she had no voice. —*Declaration of Sentiments, Elizabeth Cady Stanton, Seneca Falls Convention, 1848*

379. Who did the Founding Fathers declare independence from in 1776?

(A) Portugal
(B) Great Britain
(C) Spain
(D) The Netherlands

380. All of the following reasons provided motivation for the American colonies to declare independence from the king in 1776 EXCEPT

(A) he had forced the colonies to pay taxes but did not give them any say in how they would be governed.
(B) he had deprived the people of their right to a fair trial.
(C) he had cut off the colonies' trade to other countries.
(D) he had allowed the American colonists to form a large army.

381. What is the best meaning of the phrase "we hold these truths to be self-evident"?

(A) "You might not be right, but we think we are."
(B) "Only a fool would believe what we are saying."
(C) "Any reasonable, intelligent person would obviously agree with us."
(D) "This isn't obvious, but it could be true."

382. Why did Elizabeth Cady Stanton model her document after the Declaration of Independence?

(A) to highlight the fact that their fight for equality was baseless

(B) to acknowledge that women would soon be accepted as superior to men

(C) to highlight the hypocrisy of not allowing women to vote and participate in making laws that they will be governed by

(D) to celebrate women's achievement of equal rights nearly 70 years after the signing of the Declaration of Independence

383. Why did Elizabeth Cady Stanton change the first few lines from the Declaration of Independence to "we hold these truths to be self-evident: that all men and women are created equal"?

(A) to show that it should be obvious that men and women should have equal rights

(B) to show that the Founding Fathers obviously didn't want women to have any rights

(C) to show that men and women should be treated differently with regard to voting

(D) to point out the horrors of slavery

384. What ultimate goal did Elizabeth Cady Stanton and Susan B. Anthony hope to achieve?

(A) Their goal was to persuade the U.S. government to abolish slavery.

(B) Their goal was to persuade the U.S. government to allow women the right to vote.

(C) Their goal was to each find a husband who would make all their decisions for them.

(D) Their goal was to point out the horrors of slavery.

For Questions 385 through 389, use the following information and the excerpt from President Lyndon B. Johnson's address to Congress on March 15, 1965.

Although the Fifteenth Amendment to the U.S. Constitution, which granted African American men the right to vote, was ratified on February 3, 1870, the promise of the law would not be fully realized for almost a century. Many southern states continued to prevent African Americans from voting by the use of poll taxes, literacy tests and other means. In the 1960's African Americans began a series of peaceful protests to fight for their constitutional rights.

During March 1965, African Americans were staging a peaceful march from Selma to Montgomery when they were brutally attacked by Alabama state troopers and other white racists who tried to prevent them from speaking out for voting rights for African Americans. This atrocity became known as Bloody Sunday. Alabama Governor George Wallace, a notorious segregationist, refused to protect the peaceful protesters, and in response, President Johnson gave this address to Congress one week later:

"I speak tonight for the dignity of man and the destiny of democracy. I urge every member of both parties, Americans of all religions and of all colors, from every section of this country, to join me in that cause. At times history and fate meet at a single time in a single place to shape a turning point in man's unending search for freedom. So it was at Lexington and Concord. So it was a century ago at Appomattox. So it was last week in Selma, Alabama. There, long-suffering men and women peacefully protested the denial of their rights as Americans. Many were brutally assaulted. One good man, a man of God, was killed.

"There is no cause for pride in what has happened in Selma. There is no cause for self-satisfaction in the long denial of equal rights of millions of Americans. But there is cause for hope and for faith in our democracy in what is happening here tonight. . . .

"The bill that I am presenting to you will be known as a civil rights bill. But, in a larger sense, most of the program I am recommending is a civil rights program. Its object is to open the city of hope to all people of all races. Because all Americans just must have the right to vote. And we are going to give them that right. . . .

"Their cause must be our cause too, because it is not just Negroes but really it is all of us, who must overcome the crippling legacy of bigotry and injustice. And we shall overcome."

385. What were the African-American protestors hoping to achieve?

(A) They wanted to violently overthrow the U.S. government.

(B) They wanted equal basic human rights, including the right to vote.

(C) They wanted to provoke the police into using as much violence as possible to make Bloody Sunday famous.

(D) They wanted to help Governor Wallace fight back against President Johnson's speech.

386. Why did Alabama state police violently attack the peaceful protestors during Bloody Sunday?

(A) The state troopers were part of the racist establishment in Alabama who were trying to prevent African Americans from speaking out for their right to vote.

(B) The state troopers were trying to prevent African Americans from taking away white Americans' right to vote.

(C) They had read about Bloody Sunday and knew that it was expected of them.

(D) They had disobeyed Governor Wallace's orders to protect the peaceful protestors.

387. Who was George Wallace?

(A) He was one of the leading African-American protestors in 1965.

(B) He was the president of the United States.

(C) He was the governor of Alabama.

(D) He was the police chief of the Alabama state troopers.

388. Why did President Johnson address Congress one week after Bloody Sunday?

(A) to ask African Americans to stop protesting for their basic human rights

(B) to urge Congress to help Governor Wallace violently put down any further peaceful protests by African Americans

(C) to urge Congress to immediately pass the civil rights bill that would give African Americans the right to vote

(D) to urge Congress to delay passing any legislation until a full inquiry into Bloody Sunday had been carried out

389. What is the most likely reason that President Johnson decided to end his speech to Congress with the phrase "And we shall overcome"?

(A) "We Shall Overcome" was a protest song that was a key anthem of the Civil Rights movement.

(B) He meant that we (the government) would come over to Alabama to set things right.

(C) He meant that African Americans would soon get over their desire to gain the right to vote.

(D) He meant that Governor Wallace would soon achieve victory.

390. Based on the passage, which of the following is a true statement regarding the voting rights of African Americans?

(A) All African Americans were able to vote without any difficulties as soon as the Fifteenth Amendment was ratified in 1870.

(B) In 1870, the Fifteenth Amendment took away voting rights from African Americans until they fought to get them restored in 1965.

(C) Despite the passage of the Fifteenth Amendment in 1870, many African Americans could still not vote in the South until the passage of civil rights legislation in 1965.

(D) All African Americans were able to vote without any difficulties as soon as the Fifteenth Amendment was ratified in 1870, until the passage of civil rights legislation in 1965 took away their voting rights.

Use the following information for Questions 391 and 392.

Every bill that is intended to become part of the law in the United States must be presented to the president for approval. When the president receives the bill, he can sign it into law or return the unsigned bill to Congress with his objections to the bill. The latter case is known as a presidential veto. Congress can overturn a presidential veto with a two-thirds vote of both houses, whereupon the bill becomes law.

Alternatively, if the president doesn't want the bill to become law but doesn't want to be seen as vetoing the law directly, he can use a pocket veto. Whenever Congress is not in session, the president can simply decide not to sign the bill and say that he was unable to return the bill to Congress within 10 days because Congress was 'on vacation.' At that point, the bill is automatically rejected without the president having to do anything.

391. What can Congress do to pass a bill that has been vetoed by the president?

(A) If the president vetoes a bill, preventing it from becoming law, there is nothing Congress can do at that point.

(B) Congress can overturn a presidential veto with a two-thirds majority vote in both the House of Representatives and the Senate.

(C) Congress can ask the Supreme Court to force the bill to become a law.

(D) Nobody knows, because no president has ever used the power of the veto.

392. What happens if the president tries to return an unsigned bill to Congress while its members are on a month-long vacation?

(A) The bill automatically becomes law after 10 days.

(B) The bill is automatically rejected after 10 days.

(C) Congress can still pass the bill into law with a two-thirds majority vote in both houses when they return from vacation.

(D) The president has to try again when Congress returns from vacation.

393. The U.S. Constitution has little to say about reasons for impeachment and removal from office: "treason, bribery, or other high crimes and misdemeanors," including bribery, intimidation, refusal to obey a lawful order, dereliction of duty, perjury, abuse of authority, failure to supervise, conduct unbecoming, and misuse of assets. Which of the following would be grounds for presidential impeachment?

(A) vetoing legislation that Congress wishes to pass

(B) proposing universal healthcare coverage for the millions of uninsured Americans

(C) committing perjury (lying under oath)

(D) signing a law that prevents Wall Street banks from cheating their customers

394. The free market system depends on entrepreneurship. Entrepreneurs start businesses to produce goods and services that are in short supply and then sell those goods and services at a profit. Which of the following is NOT true about the free market system?

(A) Entrepreneurs often develop new technologies or methods of production and marketing to maximize profits.

(B) Natural resources have no impact on the profit margin of a business, as these costs are fixed over time.

(C) Managing human capital (education, training, wages, hours worked, and so on) can help businesses increase profit margins.

(D) Physical capital (buildings and tools) can help businesses increase their profit margins.

Use the following information for Questions 395 and 396.

The Berlin Wall, constructed in 1961, divided capitalist West Germany from impoverished communist East Germany and was a visible symbol of the Cold War. During the three decades that the wall stood, more than 100 people were killed by East German guards as they tried to escape from East Germany. In June 1987, President Ronald Reagan visited Berlin and urged Mikhail Gorbachev, the USSR leader, "If you seek peace, if you seek prosperity for the Soviet Union and Eastern Europe, if you seek liberalization: Come here to this gate! Mr. Gorbachev, open this gate! Mr. Gorbachev, tear down this wall!"

395. This speech is historically significant for all these reasons EXCEPT

(A) the speech helped Reagan urge Gorbachev to become more involved in European foreign affairs.

(B) the speech helped Reagan and Gorbachev start a series of negotiations that led to the dismantling of the Berlin Wall.

(C) within two years of the speech, reforms that had been sweeping across Eastern Europe helped bring about the removal of the wall, beginning on November 11, 1989.

(D) the speech was a challenge to Gorbachev to continue his reform policies of *glasnost* (openness) and *perestroika* (restructuring).

396. Why did so many people risk their lives trying to escape from East Germany to West Germany (but not the other way around)?

(A) East Germany was communist (and impoverished), and therefore the economic and social conditions there were much worse than in capitalist West Germany.

(B) West Germany was communist, and therefore the economic and social conditions there were much worse than in capitalist East Germany.

(C) East Germany was capitalist, and therefore the economic and social conditions there were much worse than in communist West Germany.

(D) West Germany was capitalist, and therefore the economic and social conditions there were much worse than in communist East Germany.

397. Which war did the United States enter in 1941 shortly after the bombing of Pearl Harbor?

(A) World War I

(B) World War II

(C) U.S. Civil War

(D) Cold War

398. Which of the following is likely to be highly valued in a free-market economy?

(A) redistribution of wealth

(B) job security

(C) cooperation

(D) individualism

Read the following information and excerpt from Abraham Lincoln's Gettysburg Address (November 19, 1863), and use this information for Questions 399 through 401.

The Gettysburg Address was delivered by Lincoln during the Dedication of the Soldiers' National Cemetery in Pennsylvania, four and half months after the Battle of Gettysburg. Here's an excerpt:

"It is for us the living, rather, to be dedicated here to the unfinished work which they who fought here have thus far so nobly advanced. It is rather for us to be here dedicated to the great task remaining before us — that from these honored dead we take increased devotion to that cause for which they gave the last full measure of devotion — that we here highly resolve that these dead shall not have died in vain — that this nation, under God, shall have a new birth of freedom — and that government of the people, by the people, for the people, shall not perish from the earth."

399. In what war did the Battle of Gettysburg take place?

(A) the Revolutionary War

(B) the American Civil War

(C) the Spanish-American War

(D) the Cold War

400. The Battle of Gettysburg was fought on July 1–3, 1863, by the Union and Confederate forces, resulting in the largest number of casualties of the war. Which of the following correctly describes how the battle ended?

(A) The battle ended when the Confederate armies defeated the Union armies.

(B) The battle ended when the Union armies defeated the Confederate armies.

(C) The battle ended after both sides completely wiped each other out and there was no one left to fight.

(D) The battle ended in a stalemate.

401. Based on the excerpt, what was the main purpose of Lincoln's speech?

(A) to gloat about how his army had defeated the other side

(B) to bring the American people together so they could finish the work needed to rebuild the nation

(C) to call for severe punishment for those who had fought against him

(D) to beg for mercy from the generals who had just defeated him in battle

402. The repeal of the Eighteenth Amendment, known as Prohibition, meant that alcohol could once again be legally bought and sold. What was the main economic reason the federal government favored its repeal?

(A) so the members of the government could get drunk once in a while

(B) so the government could stop spending money investigating alcohol smuggling

(C) freedom of individual choice

(D) so the government could gain revenue from the sales taxes on alcoholic beverages

403. Which of the following is a true statement?

(A) Each state always has two members in the U.S. Senate and two members in the U.S. House of Representatives.

(B) The number of members that a state has in both the U.S. House of Representatives and the U.S. Senate is based on the state's population.

(C) The number of members that a state has in the U.S. House of Representatives is based on the state's population, whereas each state always has two members in the U.S. Senate.

(D) The number of members that a state has in the U.S. Senate is based on the state's population, whereas each state always has two members in the U.S. House of Representatives.

404. The First Amendment protects freedom of speech and is one of the most important rights needed in a true democracy. Which of the following Supreme Court decisions is one of the best examples of protecting freedom of speech?

(A) *New York Times Co. v. United States* in 1971 prohibited the newspaper for one year from printing an article containing damaging evidence about the government's actions in the Vietnam War.

(B) The Fifth Amendment allows people accused of a crime to remain silent so as not to incriminate themselves.

(C) The Supreme Court ruled in *Tinker v. Des Moines* in 1969 that high school students could not wear black armbands to protest the Vietnam War.

(D) In *Texas v. Johnson* in 1989, the Supreme Court ruled to protect the right to burn the U.S. flag as a form of symbolic speech.

405. Which of the following is most likely to be studied by a macroeconomist?

(A) how much a car salesman saves each month for his retirement

(B) how a computer manufacturer prices its laptops

(C) how a company turns raw materials into a finished product

(D) the main causes of inflation

Use the following information for Questions 406 through 408.

This graph shows the residential electricity consumption per capita by country in 2010.

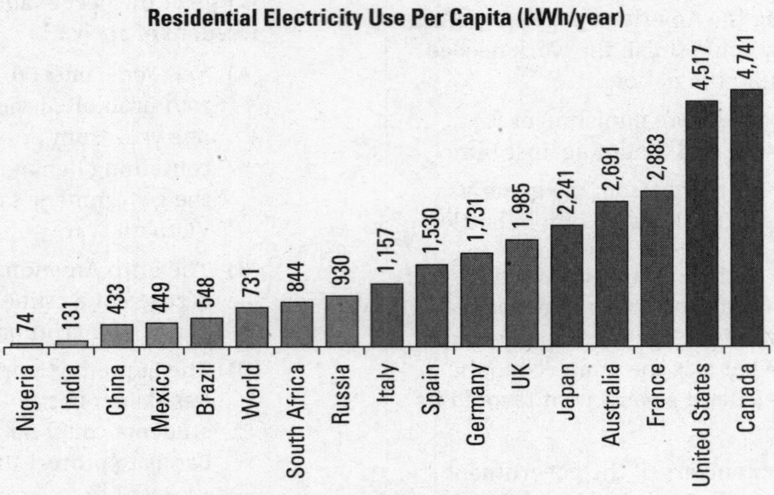

Note: Figures are 2010 residential use divided by population.

406. Based on the graph, which of the following statements is accurate?

(A) Canada consumes more electricity than the United States does.

(B) Factories in the United Kingdom burn more fossil fuels than factories in China do.

(C) Compared to residents of the United States, Japanese residents consume approximately half the amount of electricity per person.

(D) The rate of electricity consumption is rising each year.

407. Which of the following provides the best explanation for the higher electricity consumption rate in Canada compared to the rate in Australia?

(A) Canada's climate is much colder than Australia's.

(B) Australia has a poor economy and has a primitive national electricity grid.

(C) Canadian factories are not as efficient as Australian factories.

(D) Electricity is more expensive in Canada than it is in Australia.

Use the following information for Questions 408 through 413.

The Great Depression, which began with the Stock Market Crash of 1929, was caused partially by the conservative economic philosophy of laissez-faire ("leave it alone"), which had allowed markets to operate without government interference. Before the crash, the government had done nothing to regulate banking, investments, or other basic aspects of the economy. The government had also failed to gather adequate data that could have been analyzed to highlight growing problems in stock market investing, agriculture, or other vital sectors of the economy, leading up to the crash.

In 1933, in response to record unemployment brought about by the Great Depression, newly elected President Roosevelt introduced a domestic program (enacted between 1933 and 1939) that vastly increased the scope of the federal government's activities in the economy. The new program, known as the New Deal, took action to bring about immediate relief to reduce the suffering of unemployed workers and imposed reforms in industry, agriculture, finance, water power, labor, and housing. Perhaps the most far-reaching programs of the entire New Deal were those associated with Social Security, which provided old-age and widows' benefits, unemployment compensation, and disability insurance.

The following figure shows the unemployment rate from 1930 through 1945.

408. What is meant by laissez-faire economics?

(A) The government plays a significant role in the economy by imposing restrictions on odious business practices.

(B) The government controls every aspect of the economy and owns all major industries.

(C) The government allows the free market to determine economic outcomes without interfering.

(D) Laissez-faire economics was the name of one of the programs in Roosevelt's New Deal.

409. According to the passage, what was at least partially responsible for causing the Stock Market Crash of 1929?

(A) laissez-faire economics

(B) too many government restrictions

(C) the Great Depression

(D) Roosevelt's New Deal

410. The Social Security programs of the New Deal provided all of the following EXCEPT

(A) unemployment compensation.

(B) disability insurance.

(C) free housing.

(D) old-age and widows' benefits.

411. According to the graph, what year did unemployment reach a maximum in the United States?

(A) 1932

(B) 1933

(C) 1938

(D) 1939

412. According to the graph, what effect did the New Deal have on the unemployment rate between 1933 and 1937?

(A) The unemployment rate rose steadily until it reached a peak at 25 percent.

(B) The unemployment rate remained constant.

(C) The unemployment rate fell, then rose, and then fell again.

(D) The unemployment rate fell steadily, although it still remained above 14 percent.

413. The United States' involvement in which war during the early 1940s finally helped bring the unemployment rate back down to below 5 percent?

(A) World War II

(B) Vietnam War

(C) Cold War

(D) Korean War

414. Which of the following concepts is NOT related to the American concept of liberty as protected by the First Amendment?

(A) freedom to place limits on the press

(B) freedom of religion

(C) freedom to petition the government

(D) freedom of speech

415. What does the systems of "checks and balances" do with regard to the federal government?

(A) It gives the majority of the power to the executive branch.

(B) It gives the majority of the power to the legislative branch.

(C) It gives the majority of the power to the judicial branch.

(D) It divides the power among the three branches by giving them distinctive roles to prevent any one branch from becoming too powerful.

Use the following information for Questions 416 through 419.

The second paragraph of the United States Declaration of Independence starts as follows: "We hold these truths to be self-evident, that all men are created equal, that they are endowed by their Creator with certain unalienable Rights, that among these are Life, Liberty and the Pursuit of Happiness."

This table summarizes the constitutional amendments and an act regarding voting rights in the United States:

Amendment/Act	Date	Summary
15th Amendment	1870	Allowed all men to vote regardless of race or color
19th Amendment	1920	Granted women the right to vote
24th Amendment	1964	Banned the poll tax for voting privileges
Voting Rights Act	1965	Prohibited racial discrimination in voting and banned literacy tests
26th Amendment	1972	Lowered the voting age from 21 to 18

416. In what year were African-American women first allowed to legally vote?

(A) 1870
(B) 1920
(C) 1964
(D) 1965

417. Why was there a need to pass the Twenty-Fourth Amendment and the Voting Rights Act when the rights of American men and women of all races were already protected by the Fifteenth Amendment and Nineteenth Amendment, respectively?

(A) Even though the right to vote was protected by the Constitution, many states still tried to make it almost impossible for minorities to exercise that right.
(B) The laws were needed to make sure the "wrong type of people" couldn't vote.
(C) The new laws were needed to make sure that minorities could read and write before they would be allowed to vote.
(D) The new laws were needed to prevent people from voting twice.

418. Based on the information in the passage, what conclusion can be made regarding the implementation of the U.S. Constitution and the ideals described by the Declaration of Independence?

(A) The United States has always lived up to the ideal that "all men are created equal."
(B) The United States has not always lived up to the ideal that "all men are created equal."
(C) The United States abandoned its earlier ideal that "all men are created equal."
(D) The United States never believed in its earlier ideal that "all men are created equal."

419. What spurred the debate about lowering the voting age that led to the passing of the Twenty-Sixth Amendment in 1972?

(A) Conscription during the Vietnam War meant than many 18-to 20-year-olds were angry that they were considered old enough to fight for their country but not old enough to vote.
(B) Many 18- to 20-year-olds were angry that they were considered old enough to drink alcohol but not old enough to vote.
(C) Many 18- to 20-year-olds were angry that they were considered old enough to drive but not old enough to drink alcohol.
(D) Many 18- to 20-year-olds were angry that they were considered old enough to vote but not old enough to fight for their country.

Use the following information for Questions 420 through 422.

The Fifth and Sixth Amendments were part of the Bill of Rights (1791), which protects individual freedoms from the powers of federal government. The Fifth Amendment focuses on procedural safeguards designed to protect the rights of the criminally accused and includes the phrase "no person shall be compelled in any criminal case to be a witness against himself." The Sixth Amendment guarantees a citizen a speedy trial, a fair jury, an attorney if the accused person wants one, and the chance to confront the witnesses accusing the defendant of a crime.

In *Miranda v. Arizona* (1966), the Supreme Court ruled that detained criminal suspects, prior to police questioning, must be informed of their constitutional right to an attorney and against self-incrimination.

420. The Sixth Amendment guarantees a citizen all of the following EXCEPT

(A) a speedy trial.

(B) and the chance to confront witnesses.

(C) the right to remain silent.

(D) a fair jury.

421. Based on the passage information, which of the following is a true statement regarding the Fifth and Sixth Amendments?

(A) The Fifth Amendment guarantees the criminally accused the right to remain silent, whereas the Sixth Amendment guarantees the right to a lawyer.

(B) The Fifth Amendment guarantees the right to a lawyer, whereas the Sixth Amendment guarantees the criminally accused the right to remain silent.

(C) The Fifth Amendment and the Sixth Amendment are both more important than the First Amendment.

(D) The Fifth Amendment guarantees the criminally accused a speedy trial, whereas the Sixth Amendment guarantees the right to a lawyer.

422. The outcome of the *Miranda v. Arizona* Supreme Court case in 1964 is significant for those under arrest because now, once someone is both in police custody and about to be interrogated, police are required to

(A) uphold only the Fifth Amendments.

(B) uphold only the Sixth Amendments.

(C) uphold both the Fifth and Sixth Amendments.

(D) uphold neither the Fifth Amendment nor the Sixth Amendment.

423. How do the president's Supreme Court justice selections help secure his own legacy even after he is out of office?

(A) The Supreme Court has a minimal role in helping establish a president's legacy after he leaves office.

(B) A president serves only eight years at the most and has insufficient time to build a lasting legacy.

(C) The president helps secure his own legacy by appointing Supreme Court justices, who will serve long after he's gone.

(D) The Supreme Court can reinstate the president even after he is voted out of office.

424. Taxes at local, state, and federal levels allow the government to provide goods and services for the general population. Which of the following is NOT true about taxation?

(A) Once a tax rate has been set, it can't be challenged or changed.

(B) Sales taxes, property taxes, income taxes, and corporation or business taxes have different rates and purposes.

(C) Federal taxes are the same in each state, but state taxes may vary from state to state.

(D) Both federal and state governments depend upon the collection of taxes to fund various programs.

425. Globalization, which occurs whenever companies shift their focus from a local or regional basis to an international basis, can lead to the outsourcing of jobs overseas. Which of the following is an example of globalization?

(A) A car manufacturer invests in robots to assemble its cars and then lays off hundreds of workers who used to do that job.

(B) A computer manufacturer finds it cheaper to outsource its customer service call center to workers in India instead of employing local workers.

(C) A sales rep goes on vacation to Europe instead of going to California.

(D) A Chinese company hires local Chinese workers for its factory in Beijing.

426. Based on the map, which of the following statements is true?

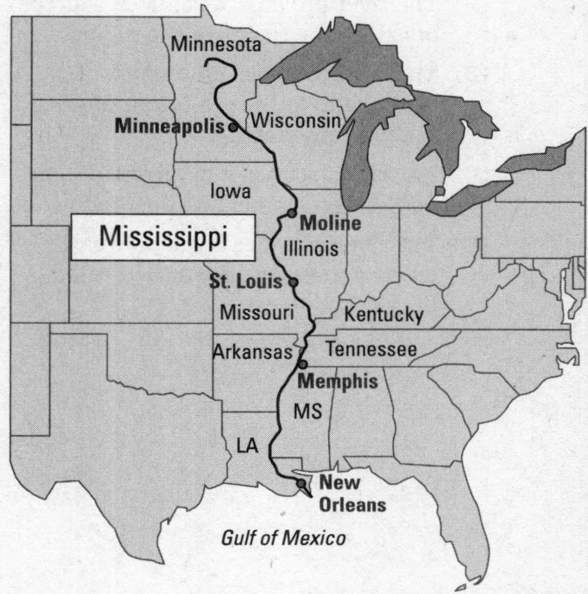

(A) major cities tend to be built up in the mountains.

(B) The American South is home to some of the largest cities in America.

(C) Most American states border the Atlantic Ocean.

(D) Major cities tend to develop along major rivers.

427. What effect has the Mississippi River had on the development of the American Midwest?

(A) The river provides a valuable source of salt to the towns in the region.

(B) The river provides an important connection to the sea for landlocked Midwestern states.

(C) The river has had a negligible impact on the development of the region.

(D) The river provides a valuable east–west connection across the United States.

428. A tariff is a special tax that is imposed on imported goods and services to restrict trade and increase the price of imported goods and services. The United States occasionally imposes tariffs in an attempt to persuade Americans to buy American-made goods and services.

According to the given information, which of the following is an example of a tariff?

(A) Congress imposes a tax on beer that is manufactured in California but sold in New York.

(B) Congress increases the price of all gasoline to fund clean energy research.

(C) Congress imposes a tax on imported Japanese cars in order to protect domestic car sales.

(D) Congress creates a flat-tax rate for all income levels.

Use the following graph and information for Questions 429 through 431.

The gross domestic product (GDP) per capita is the average value of all the goods and services produced by the workers of a particular country in one year. GDPs can be used to compare the relative wealth of different countries.

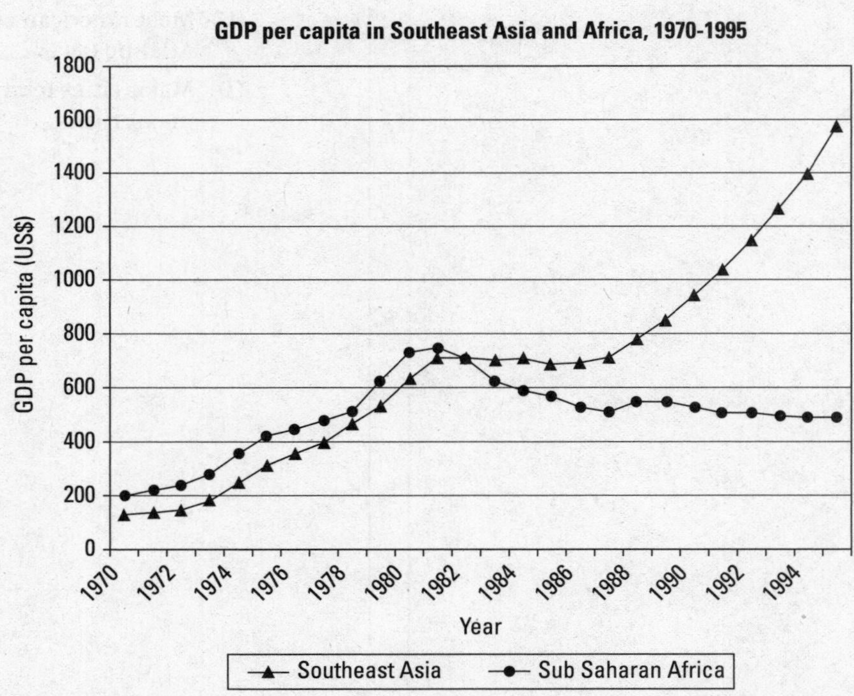

429. According to the graph, which year were the GDPs of each region the most similar?

(A) 1975

(B) 1983

(C) 1985

(D) 1995

430. According to the graph, which of the following is a true statement?

(A) The GDP of Southeast Asia has always been greater than the GDP of Sub-Saharan Africa.

(B) The GDP of Southeast Asia has always been less than the GDP of Sub-Saharan Africa.

(C) The GDP of both regions grew at approximately the same rate during the 1970s.

(D) The GDP of both regions grew at approximately the same rate during the 1980s.

431. Based on the graph, which of the following is an opinion rather than a factual statement?

(A) Sub-Saharan Africa no longer has the resources it needs in order to grow its GDP.

(B) The GDP of Sub-Saharan Africa has declined since the early 1980s.

(C) The GDP of Southeast Asia was approximately $400 per capita in 1978.

(D) The GDP of Southeast Asia increased dramatically in the early 1990s.

Use the following graph and information for Questions 432 through 434.

The graph shows the energy consumption by source in the United States in 2015.

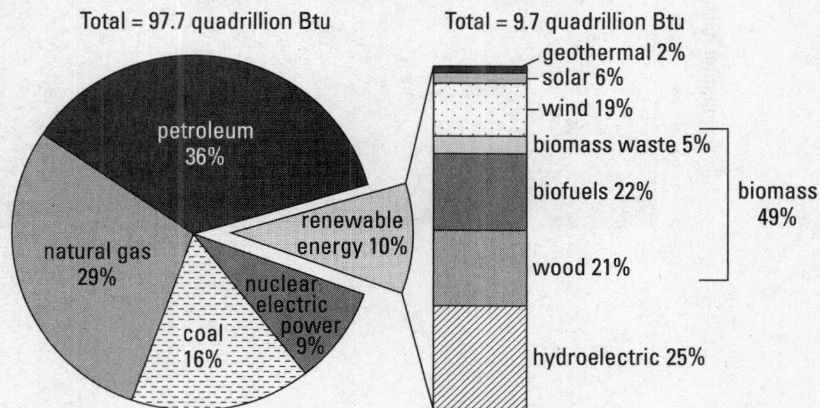

432. What percentage of the total U.S. energy consumption comes from fossil fuels?

(A) 16%

(B) 36%

(C) 52%

(D) 81%

433. What percentage of the total U.S. energy consumption comes from hydroelectric power?

(A) 2.5%

(B) 5%

(C) 10%

(D) 25%

434. Which of the following is a factual statement that is supported by the graph?

(A) Renewable energy will soon become a larger source of energy than coal.

(B) Geothermal energy provides less than 1% of the total U.S. energy consumption.

(C) Nuclear power is dangerous and produces harmful radioactive waste.

(D) The United States should focus more on renewable energy.

435. Which war resulted in the United States gaining control of Texas?

(A) the Spanish-American War

(B) the Mexican-American War

(C) the Texas-American War

(D) the Civil War

Questions 436 through 440 are based on the following graph and tables, which show the projected growth in world population and list the top 10 most populous countries in 2015 and 2050.

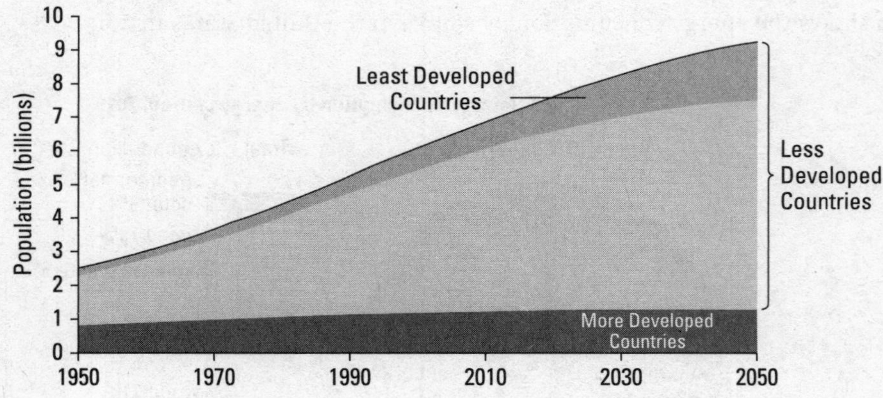

2015

Country	Population (Millions)
China	1,357
India	1,277
United States	316
Indonesia	249
Brazil	196
Pakistan	191
Nigeria	174
Bangladesh	157
Russia	143
Japan	127

2050

Country	Population (Millions)
India	1,652
China	1,314
Nigeria	440
United States	400
Indonesia	366
Pakistan	363
Brazil	227
Bangladesh	202
Congo Dem Rep	182
Ethiopia	178

436. Based on the graph, in what year will the world population reach 8 billion people?

(A) 2015
(B) 2018
(C) 2022
(D) 2028

437. Based on the tables, which country's population is expected to grow by the biggest percentage by 2050?

(A) China
(B) India
(C) Nigeria
(D) United States

438. Based on the graph, which of the following is a true statement regarding the predicted global population growth?

(A) Most of the population growth is expected to come from less developed countries.
(B) Most of the population growth is expected to come from more developed countries.
(C) Both developed and less developed countries contribute equally to the predicted population growth.
(D) The global population is expected to remain relatively steady until 2050.

439. Based on the given information, which of the following is a factual statement?

(A) China's population is expected to rise steadily by 2050.
(B) All of the top 10 most populous countries in 2013 will still be in the top 10 most populous countries in 2050.
(C) The world population appears to be doubling in size every 40 to 60 years.
(D) Russia's population will fall by 2050.

440. Based on the given information, which of the following is an opinion rather than a factual statement?

(A) China's population is expected to fall slightly by 2050.

(B) Nigeria should encourage birth control measures to prevent its population from growing too quickly.

(C) The United States population is expected to grow by less than 30% by 2050.

(D) India is expected to become the most populous country in the world by 2050.

441. Cities that lie along the Gulf of Mexico or along the coast of the Atlantic Ocean face a serious threat from hurricanes. Based on this information, which city would you NOT expect to be seriously threatened by hurricanes?

(A) Los Angeles

(B) Houston

(C) Miami

(D) New Orleans

Questions 442 through 446 are based on the following figure, which shows the life expectancy and illiteracy rates for China, India, and Nepal.

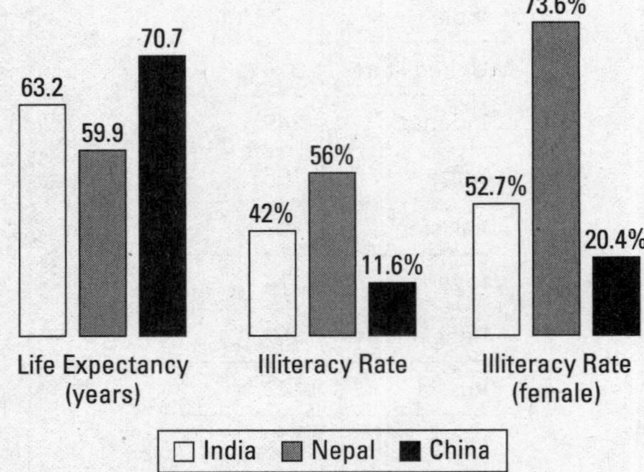

442. According to the chart, approximately how many years longer does a person born in India live compared to a person born in Nepal?

(A) 3 years

(B) 7 years

(C) 11 years

(D) 63 years

443. According to the chart, which of the following is a true statement?

(A) A higher percentage of the population of Nepal knows how to read and write compared with the populations of China and India.

(B) China has the longest life expectancy in the world.

(C) The majority of women in Nepal do not know how to read or write.

(D) All three countries are ruled by repressive regimes.

444. Which of the following statements would best explain the high level of illiteracy among women compared to men in Nepal?

(A) Nepalese women are not given the same educational opportunities as men.

(B) Nepalese women are simply not as smart as Nepalese men.

(C) Nepalese women tend to read more books and magazines per week than Nepalese men do.

(D) All three countries are ruled by female leaders who spend more on women's educational programs than on men's.

445. According to the table, what general trend appears to be true regarding life expectancy and illiteracy rates in these three countries?

(A) The higher the illiteracy rate, the longer the life expectancy.

(B) The lower the illiteracy rate, the shorter the life expectancy.

(C) The lower the illiteracy rate, the longer the life expectancy.

(D) There is no correlation between illiteracy rate and life expectancy.

446. Based on the chart, all of the following statements are opinions rather factual statements EXCEPT

(A) most Indian women prefer watching soap operas on television to reading novels.

(B) most Chinese women are able to read and write properly.

(C) although the Nepalese people may not live as long as Chinese people do, they usually live happier lives.

(D) women in India and Nepal should band together to form pressure groups to fight for more educational opportunities.

447. In 1803, the United States vastly increased its territory when Thomas Jefferson paid 50 million francs to France for the land that now includes North Dakota, South Dakota, Arkansas, Iowa, Kansas, Oklahoma, Nebraska, Montana, Wyoming, northern Texas, and Louisiana.

What was the name of this transaction?

(A) the Louisiana Purchase

(B) the California Purchase

(C) the New York Purchase

(D) the Gadsden Purchase

Questions 448 through 450 are based on the following information.

When he was a young boy, Theodore Roosevelt wanted to be a scientist who studied nature. As an adult, President Roosevelt passed legislation that preserved vast regions of the U.S. for future generations. Here are his words:

"It is also vandalism wantonly to destroy or to permit the destruction of what is beautiful in nature, whether it be a cliff, a forest, or a species of mammal or bird. Here in the United States we turn our rivers and streams into sewers and dumping-grounds, we pollute the air, we destroy forests, and exterminate fishes, birds and mammals — not to speak of vulgarizing charming landscapes with hideous advertisements. But at last it looks as if our people were awakening."

448. Based on the given information, which of the following was likely set up by President Roosevelt between 1901 and 1909 to preserve the United States natural treasures for future generations?

(A) transportation system

(B) National Parks system

(C) Wall Street

(D) United States Treasury

449. What is the practice of preserving natural resources known as?

(A) environmental alarmism
(B) conservation
(C) global warming
(D) accelerated consumption

450. Which current U.S. agency plays an important role in ensuring that U.S. companies do not pollute the country's natural environment?

(A) NRA (National Rifle Association)
(B) DOE (Department of Energy)
(C) FBI (Federal Bureau of Investigation)
(D) EPA (Environmental Protection Agency)

451. In 1794, inventor Eli Whitney patented the modern cotton gin, which made it much easier to separate cotton fibers from their seeds. Why was the cotton gin such an important invention during that period of American history?

(A) It ended the need for slavery in the United States.
(B) It caused the economic destruction of farmland, leading to the Great Depression.
(C) It greatly expanded the cotton industry in the Southern states.
(D) It helped protect the American cotton industry from imported synthetic fabrics from China.

452. The quote below is from Alexander Hamilton, one of the Founding Fathers.

"Constitutions should consist only of general provisions; the reason is that they must necessarily be permanent, and that they cannot calculate for the possible change of things."

How does the Constitution of the United States "calculate for the possible change of things"?

(A) It does not contain any provisions that allow for change.
(B) It protects the Supreme Court from having to explain their decisions.
(C) It states that the powers of the president will not be questioned.
(D) It allows for amendments to be made when necessary.

Use the following information and the quote from President John Quincy Adams for Questions 453 through 455.

During the 19th century, it was believed that the United States should continue its westward expansion and that it was destined to stretch from coast to coast. This prevailing attitude, known as Manifest Destiny, helped fuel both the forcible removal of Native American from their homeland and the war with Mexico. Here are Adams's words:

"The whole continent of North America appears to be destined by Divine Providence to be peopled by one nation, speaking one language, professing one general system of religious and political principles, and accustomed to one general tenor of social usages and customs."

453. What was the main message President John Quincy Adams was trying to convey to the American colonists?

(A) American colonists should respect the rights of the Native American people.

(B) American colonists should seize the land from Native Americans, even though they know what they'll be doing is immoral and against God.

(C) America should become a "melting pot" where all cultures can live together in harmony.

(D) American colonists should seize the land from Native Americans because doing so is part of God's plan.

454. What is the meaning of Manifest Destiny?

(A) the belief that the expansion of the U.S. throughout the American continents was both justified and inevitable

(B) the belief that the American colonists should stay on the East Coast to avoid confrontation with the natives

(C) the belief that the expansion of the U.S. throughout the American continents was a crime against humanity

(D) the belief that God was destined to punish the colonists for their immoral behavior

455. Based on the information in the passage, the attitude of Manifest Destiny helped to encourage which two atrocities?

(A) the Boston Massacre and the Declaration of Independence from Great Britain

(B) the beginning of slavery and the war against France

(C) the forcible removal of Native Americans and the war with Mexico

(D) the forcible removal of Native Americans and the beginning of slavery

456. Which of the following statements is true regarding the Bill of Rights?

(A) It abolished slavery throughout the United States.

(B) It gave women the right to vote.

(C) It was added to the Constitution shortly after ratification.

(D) It was never added to the Constitution.

Use the following information for Questions 457 through 459.

On the evening of March 5, 1770 in Boston, a crowd of American workmen began throwing snowballs and rocks at British soldiers. A shot rang out, and then several soldiers fired their weapons, resulting in the deaths of five civilians. This event became known as the Boston Massacre.

The following figure shows an engraving by Paul Revere produced three weeks later, titled *The Bloody Massacre Perpetrated in King-Street.* The engraving depicts an orderly line of smiling British soldiers firing calmly into a peaceful, unarmed American crowd. It is considered one of the most effective pieces of war propaganda in American history.

The BLOODY MASSACRE perpetrated in King Street BOSTON on March 5th 1770, by a party of the 29th REG
BUTCHER'S HALL
Engrav'd Printed & Sold by PAUL REVERE BOSTON
Unhappy BOSTON! see thy Sons deplore,
Thy hallow'd Walks besmear'd with guiltless Gore
While faithless P—n and his savage Bands
With murd'rous Rancour stretch their bloody Hands
Like fierce Barbarians grinning o'er their Prey,
Approve the Carnage, and enjoy the Day.
If scalding drops from Rage from Anguish Wrung
If speechless Sorrows lab'ring for a Tongue,
a weeping World can ought appease
plaintive Ghosts of Victims such as these;
The Patriot's copious Tears for each are shed,
A glorious Tribute which embalms the Dead.
But know, FATE summons to that awful Goal,
Where JUSTICE strips the Murd'rer of his Soul:
Should venal C—ts the scandal of the Land,
Snatch the relentless Villain from her Hand,
Keen Execrations on this Plate inscrib'd,
Shall reach a JUDGE who never can be brib'd.
SAML GRAY, SAML MAVERICK, JAMS CALDWELL, CRISPUS ATTUCKS & PATK CARR
two of them (CHRISTR MONK & JOHN CLARK) Mortally

457. Which of the following is a true statement regarding the Boston Massacre?

(A) British troops attacked the peaceful, unarmed crowd without provocation.

(B) Paul Revere's engraving is an accurate depiction of the actual events of the Boston Massacre.

(C) More people were killed during the Boston Massacre than during the entire Civil War.

(D) British troops were attacked by an unruly crowd, and shots were fired during the ensuing chaos, leading to the death of several civilians.

458. All of the following features of Paul Revere's engraving help explain why it's considered propaganda rather than a true depiction of events EXCEPT

(A) some of the British troops are smiling as they shoot into the unarmed crowd.

(B) the American colonists are dressed as members of the upper class rather than as workmen, giving them a perceived higher social status.

(C) several American colonists are shown lying on the floor, either dead or dying.

(D) the British troops are shown lined up in an orderly fashion as they shoot into the crowd.

459. What effect did the Boston Massacre and Paul Revere's engraving have on the American colonists?

(A) They helped ease tensions between the colonists and the British Empire.

(B) They helped ignite tensions between the colonists and the British Empire, eventually leading to the American Revolution.

(C) They helped break the fighting spirit of the colonists, effectively ending the American Revolution.

(D) They made the colonists proud to be part of the powerful British Empire.

Use the following information for Questions 460 through 462.

The Founding Fathers introduced a system of checks and balances to the Constitution and split the federal government into three separate branches: the legislative branch, the executive branch, and the judicial branch. The goal of this separation of power was to prevent any one branch from becoming too powerful.

460. Which of the following is one of the provisions of this system of checks and balances?

(A) The president cannot be removed from office by the other branches of government under any circumstances.

(B) The decisions of the Supreme Court can be vetoed by the president.

(C) The president does not need the approval of the other branches of government to declare war on other nations.

(D) New Supreme Court Justices must be appointed by the president and confirmed by the Senate.

461. To which branch of government does the president belong?

(A) executive branch

(B) legislative branch

(C) judicial branch

(D) the president belongs to all three branches

462. Which branch of government is responsible for introducing and passing new laws?

(A) executive branch

(B) legislative branch

(C) judicial branch

(D) The Constitution does not allow new laws to be made.

Use the following information for Questions 463 through 466.

This map shows the global exploration attempts made by European explorers during the 30-year period from 1492 to 1522.

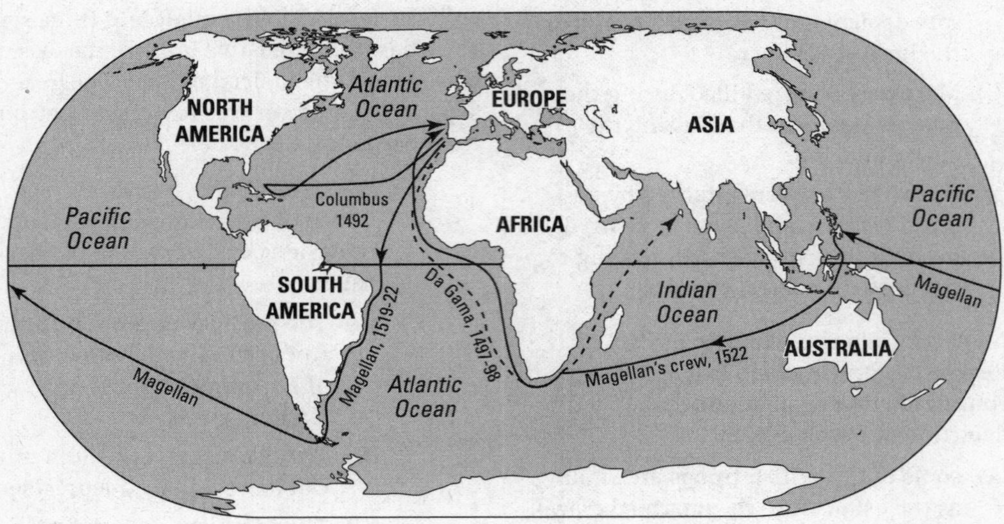

463. European explorers traveled around the world for all of the following reasons EXCEPT

(A) to find a shorter route to the East Indies

(B) to satisfy their taste for adventure and proudly go where no man had gone before

(C) to discover new lands and secure natural resources

(D) to win first place in an official global exploration contest held in 1522

464. Based on the map, which of the following statements is true regarding Christopher Columbus?

(A) He returned to the mainland of the United States several times during this period.

(B) He traveled much farther than Magellan did during this period.

(C) His voyage took over three years to complete.

(D) He didn't actually step foot on the mainland of the United States during this period.

465. Based on the map, which of the following statements is true regarding Magellan's circumnavigation of the world?

(A) His voyage took over five years to complete.

(B) He followed the same route that da Gama had taken almost 20 years earlier.

(C) Magellan did not actually return home with his ship in 1522.

(D) He had originally intended to circumnavigate the world by sailing from the North Pole to South Pole and back again.

466. Based on the map, which of the following is a true statement rather than an opinion regarding European exploration during the 30-year period from 1492 to 1522.

(A) Magellan was clearly the best European explorer during this period.

(B) Da Gama was afraid to sail to America, so he decided to head over to Asia instead.

(C) Columbus was the worst explorer and must have become dizzy from sailing in circles.

(D) Da Gama was the first of the three explorers to reach Asia by ship.

For Questions 467 through 471, use the following excerpt from President Franklin D. Roosevelt's famous "Day of Infamy" speech to Congress in 1941.

December 7, 1941 — a date which will live in infamy — the United States of America was suddenly and deliberately attacked by naval and air forces of the Empire of Japan. The United States was at peace with that nation and, at the solicitation of Japan, was still in conversation with its Government and its Emperor looking toward the maintenance of peace in the Pacific. . . . It will be recorded that the distance of Hawaii from Japan makes it obvious that the attack was deliberately planned many days or even weeks ago. During the intervening time the Japanese Government has deliberately sought to deceive the United States by false statements and expressions of hope for continued peace. The attack yesterday on the Hawaiian Islands has caused severe damage to American naval and military forces. . . . As Commander-in-Chief of the Army and Navy, I have directed that all measures be taken for our defense. . . . Hostilities exist. There is no blinking at the fact that our people, our territory and our interests are in grave danger. With confidence in our armed forces, with the unbounded determination of our people, we will gain the inevitable triumph — so help us God. I ask that the Congress declare that because the unprovoked and dastardly attack by Japan on Sunday, December 7th, a state of war has existed between the United States and the Japanese Empire. —*President Franklin D. Roosevelt*

467. Based on the excerpt, what had just happened the day before Roosevelt's speech to Congress?

(A) The United States had launched an unprovoked attack on the Japanese at Pearl Harbor.

(B) The Japanese had launched an unprovoked attack on the United States at Pearl Harbor.

(C) The ongoing war between the United States and Japan had suddenly intensified.

(D) The Japanese invaded the continental United States.

468. Based on the excerpt, why was the attack on Pearl Harbor so surprising?

(A) Pearl Harbor was a peaceful place with no strategic significance in the war.

(B) The United States and Japan were in the process of discussing a peace treaty at the time of the attack.

(C) The Japanese had warned the United States about the dangers of an imminent attack, but Roosevelt had ignored their warning.

(D) Pearl Harbor is so close to Washington, DC, that Roosevelt had thought it was safe from attack.

469. Which war was the attack on Pearl Harbor part of?

(A) World War I

(B) World War II

(C) the Korean War

(D) the Vietnam War

470. Based on the excerpt, what was President Roosevelt trying to convince Congress to do?

(A) surrender to the Japanese army immediately

(B) declare war on Hawaii

(C) declare war on Japan

(D) negotiate with Japan for better weapons to fight the Hawaiians

471. Based on the excerpt, why was Pearl Harbor chosen as the location for the surprise attack?

(A) Pearl Harbor was an important U.S. naval base.

(B) Hawaii had already declared war on Japan.

(C) Pearl Harbor was very close to Japan and easy to reach.

(D) Pearl Harbor had lots of beaches for the soldiers to relax on after the attack was over.

472. The United Nations (UN) is an international organization based in New York City. Its member countries include 193 out of the 195 countries in the world. The UN was founded at the end of World War II and is dedicated to global peace, human rights, and international law.

Which of the following is a fact rather than an opinion regarding the United Nations?

(A) The United Nations should do more to protect the rights of minorities around the world.

(B) The United States is clearly the most important member of the United Nations.

(C) Most countries in the world are members of the United Nations.

(D) The United Nations is no longer needed to secure global peace.

Use the following information for Questions 473 through 476.

The following figures show the average precipitation and the average temperature range for Tampa, Florida.

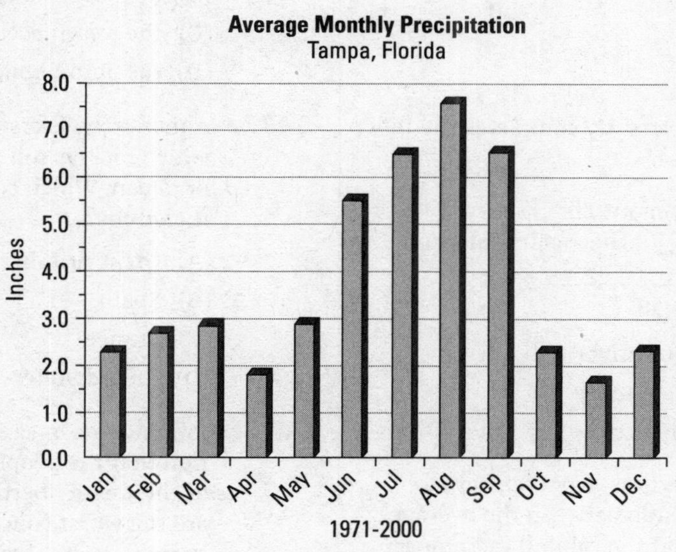

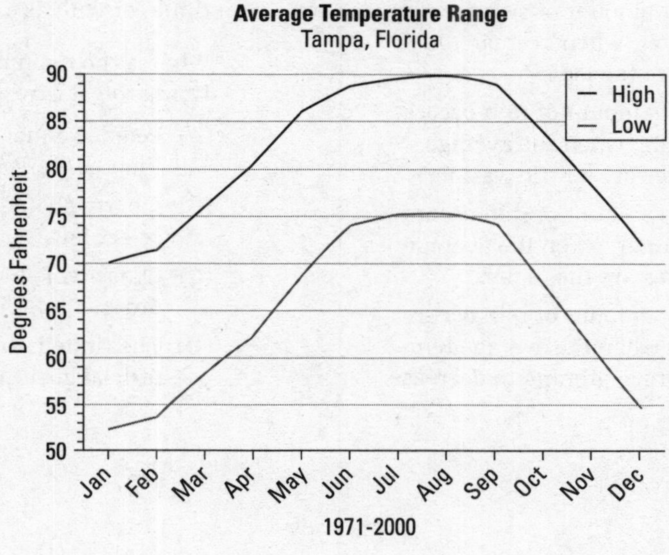

473. Based on the figures, during which month does Tampa experience the highest average temperature?

(A) January

(B) June

(C) August

(D) November

474. Which choice correctly completes the following sentence?

Tampa's driest month is _______________, whereas its coldest month is _______________.

(A) January, April

(B) January, November

(C) November, January

(D) August, January

475. Based on the figures, what appears to be the relationship between the average temperature and the rainfall in Tampa?

(A) The highest amount of snow occurs during winter, when average temperatures are the lowest.

(B) The highest amount of rain occurs during spring, when the average temperatures are a little warmer.

(C) The highest amount of rain occurs during summer, when the average temperatures are the highest.

(D) The highest amount of rain occurs during fall, when the average temperatures are beginning to decrease.

476. Which segment of the economy would be affected the most by an unusually long spell of dry weather?

(A) the banking industry

(B) farming and agriculture

(C) the pharmaceutical industry

(D) the automobile industry

477. A monarchy is a system of government in which one person reigns, usually a king or queen. Which country has never had a monarchy?

(A) Great Britain

(B) Spain

(C) France

(D) United States

478. John Adams once said, "The proposition that the people are the best keepers of their own liberties is not true. They are the worst conceivable, they are no keepers at all; they can neither judge, act, think, or will, as a political body."

What is the main point the Adams was trying to get across?

(A) People cannot be trusted to defend their own freedoms and liberties.

(B) Liberty should be given only to a select few.

(C) Chaos will always be better than order.

(D) The United States should have no official government.

Use the following information for Questions 479 and 480.

This figure shows the unemployment rate from 1890 until 1923.

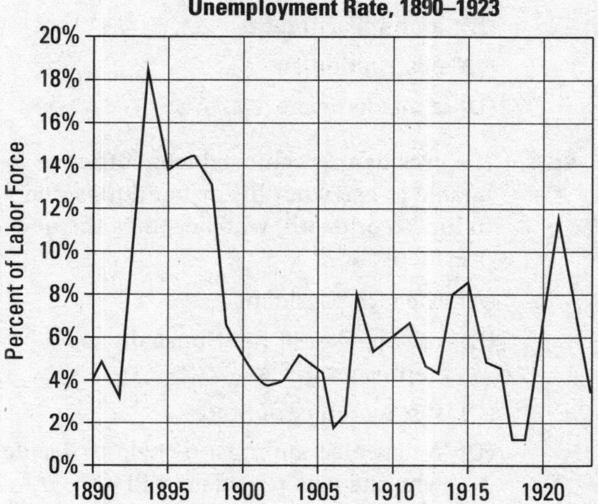

479. Which of the following explains the sudden drop in unemployment during 1917 and 1918?

(A) the abolishment of slavery

(B) the stock market crash known as Black Tuesday

(C) the United States' entrance into World War I

(D) the outbreak of World War II

480. Which of the following is an opinion rather than factual statement regarding the graph?

(A) The unemployment rate more than quadrupled from 1890 until 1894.

(B) The sharp increase in unemployment in the early 1890s was due to the actions of incompetent leaders.

(C) The unemployment rate remained below 10% during the first two decades of the 20th century.

(D) The unemployment rate never equaled zero during the indicated time frame.

For Questions 481 through 484, use the following excerpt from Article II, Sections 1 and 4 of the U.S. Constitution.

The executive power shall be vested in a President of the United States of America. He shall hold his office during the term of four years, and, together with the Vice President, chosen for the same term, be elected, as follows: . . .

No person except a natural born citizen, or a citizen of the United States, at the time of the adoption of this Constitution, shall be eligible to the office of President; neither shall any person be eligible to that office who shall not have attained to the age of thirty five years, and been fourteen Years a resident within the United States.

In case of the removal of the President from office, or of his death, resignation, or inability to discharge the powers and duties of the said office, the same shall devolve on the Vice President, and the Congress may by law provide for the case of removal, death, resignation or inability, both of the President and Vice President, declaring what officer shall then act as President, and such officer shall act accordingly, until the disability be removed, or a President shall be elected. . . .

Before he enter on the execution of his office, he shall take the following oath or affirmation:—"I do solemnly swear (or affirm) that I will faithfully execute the office of President of the United States, and will to the best of my ability, preserve, protect and defend the Constitution of the United States." . . .

The President, Vice President and all civil officers of the United States, shall be removed from office on impeachment for, and conviction of, treason, bribery, or other high crimes and misdemeanors.

481. According to the excerpt, before a new president officially becomes the President of the United States, he must swear an oath to do what?

(A) protect and defend the United States

(B) protect and defend his family

(C) protect and defend the Constitution of the United States

(D) protect and defend himself from his political enemies

482. According to the excerpt, to be eligible to be President of the United States, a person must meet all of the following criteria EXCEPT

(A) be a natural born citizen of the United States

(B) be at least 35 years old

(C) be a white male

(D) have lived in the United States for at least 14 years

483. What is the term for the filing charges by the House of Representatives that accuse either the president or vice president of committing offenses that could lead to his legal removal from office before the official end of his term?

(A) a coup

(B) an impeachment

(C) obstructionism

(D) a misdemeanor

484. If a president is removed from office or is unable to carry out his or her duties due to illness or death, who becomes the new president?

(A) the vice president

(B) the Speaker of the House of Representatives

(C) the Secretary of State

(D) A new election must be held to decide who the new president will be.

Use the following information for Questions 485 and 486.

This map shows the average annual precipitation for the continental United States.

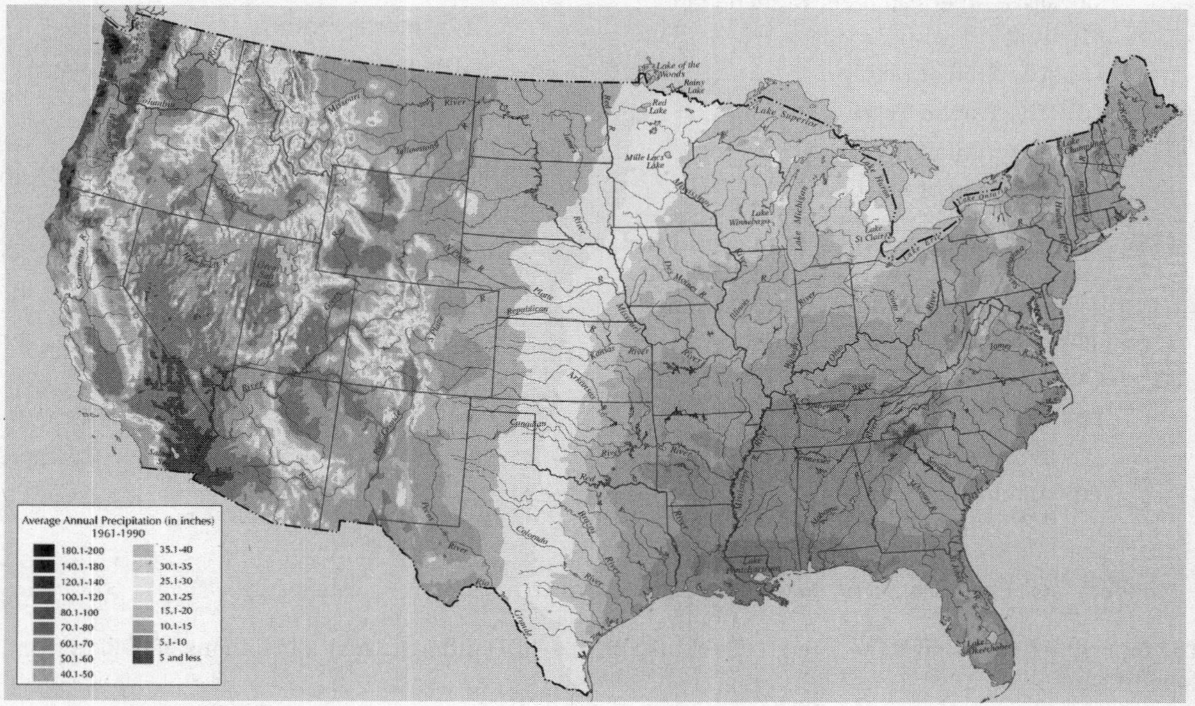

485. Some areas of the United States receive less than 10 inches of precipitation per year. What are these areas known as?

(A) prairies

(B) tundras

(C) savannas

(D) deserts

486. Which states receive the most precipitation per year?

(A) Oregon and Washington

(B) California and Arizona

(C) New York and New Jersey

(D) North Dakota and South Dakota

487. Why were Native-American tribes forcibly relocated from their tribal lands in the 1830s?

(A) White settlers wanted to steal the lands in the eastern states that belonged to the Indians for themselves.

(B) Native Americans left their native lands in the eastern states to search for gold in the West.

(C) Whites were concerned for the health of the Native Americans and felt that the climate west of the Mississippi River would be better for them.

(D) The land had originally belonged to the Founding Fathers.

488. What was the name of the forced relocation of Native Americans in the 1830s, ordered by President Jackson, that resulted in the deaths of thousands of Native American men, women, and children?

(A) The Trail of Death

(B) The Trail of Tears

(C) The Trail of the Lonesome Pine

(D) The Trail of Eviction

489. Which Supreme Court decision overturned the doctrine of "separate but equal" and led to the desegregation of United States public schools?

(A) *Plessy v. Ferguson*

(B) *Roe v. Wade*

(C) *Brown v. Board of Education*

(D) *Miranda v. Arizona*

490. Which branch of government is the Senate part of?

(A) executive branch

(B) legislative branch

(C) judicial branch

(D) obstructionist branch

Use the following information for Questions 491 through 493.

The following figure shows the foreign direct investment (FDI) inflow to Africa in billions of dollars from 1990 to 2010.

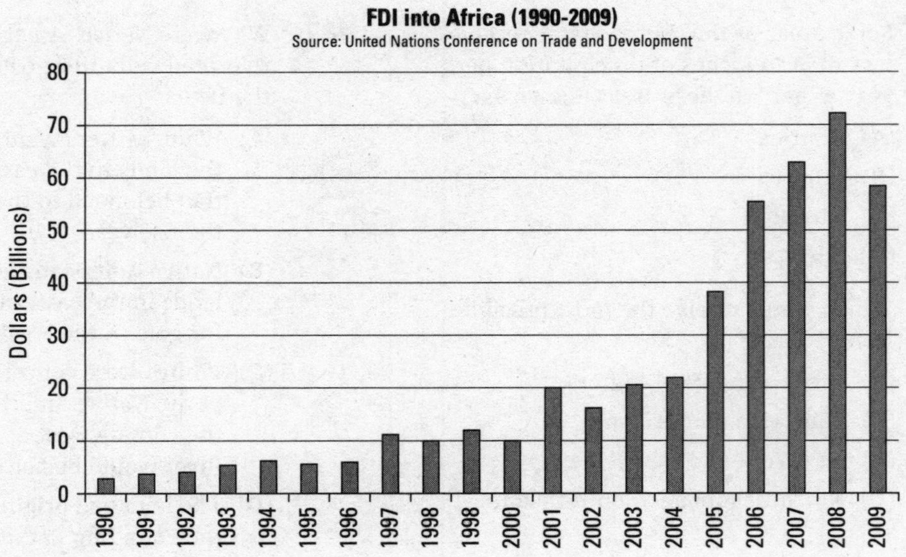

491. Based on the chart, which of the following best describes the general trend of foreign direct investment inflow to Africa during the indicated time period?

(A) It has remained steady.

(B) It decreased sharply during the first decade of the new millennium.

(C) It increased at a steady rate throughout the indicated time period.

(D) It grew slowly during the 1990s and then grew rapidly after the year 2000.

492. Why would some American companies want to invest in various African nations?

(A) All American companies are run by philanthropists who simply want to help their fellow man.

(B) African nations provide valuable resources that the American companies need.

(C) African countries have some of the world's strongest economies.

(D) African leaders are blackmailing American companies into giving them money.

493. Based on the figure, which of the following is an opinion rather than a factual statement regarding foreign direct investment inflow to Africa?

(A) The highest level of foreign investment occurred in 2008.

(B) Foreign investment in Africa remained below 10 billion dollars before 1996.

(C) Foreign investments in Africa should be increased to relieve the suffering of millions of Africans.

(D) African economies have been boosted by foreign investment.

Use the following information for Questions 494 through 499.

To become president of the United States, a candidate must win at least 270 electoral votes. This map shows the electoral votes by state for the presidential election.

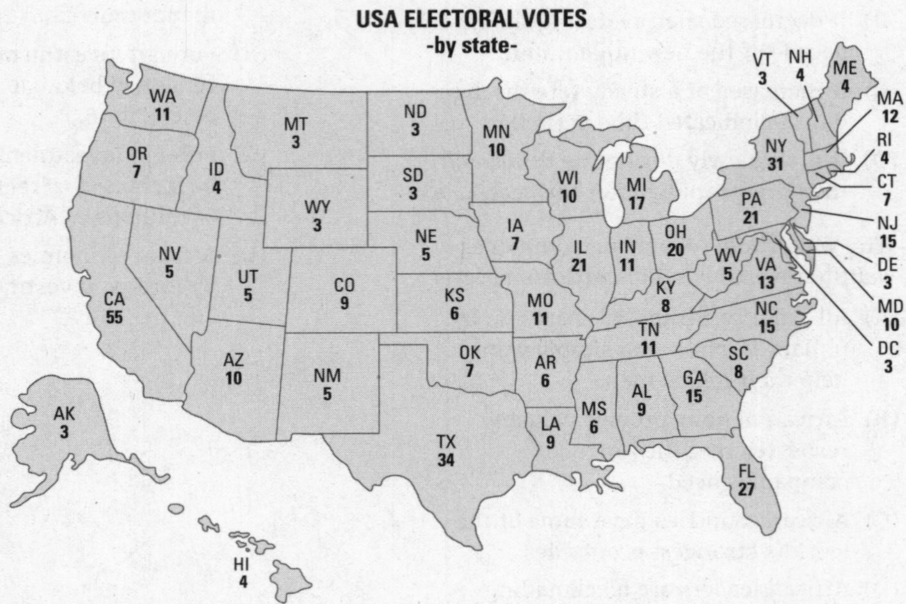

The Twelfth Amendment requires that each elector cast one vote for president. In each state, electors are chosen every four years on the Tuesday after the first Monday in November. Congress certifies the Electoral College vote in January, which allows the new president to take office on January 20. There are a total of 538 electors, corresponding to the 435 representatives and 100 senators, plus the three electors of the District of Columbia. The number of representatives per state depends on the population of that state, whereas each state is given two senators.

The Electoral College has elected the candidate who received the most popular votes nationwide, except in five elections: 1824, 1876, 1888, 2000, and 2016.

If no person receives an absolute majority of electoral votes for president, the Twelfth Amendment provides that the House of Representatives will select the president, with each of the 50 state delegations casting one vote. If no person receives a majority of electoral votes for vice president, then the Senate will select the vice president, with each of the 100 senators having one vote.

494. What does a candidate need to do before he or she becomes president of the United States?

(A) win the televised debates

(B) win the popular vote

(C) win the electoral vote

(D) have the most Americans vote for him or her

495. Why do some states like California (with 55 electors) and Texas (34) have a lot more electors than states like Utah (5) or Montana (3)?

(A) California and Texas are simply better states than Utah or Montana.

(B) The electoral vote is biased against states like Utah and Montana.

(C) People from California and Texas are more important and deserve more say in who becomes president.

(D) The number of electors that a state has depends on the population of that state.

496. Which of the following is a true statement?

(A) Each state always has two senators and two representatives.

(B) The number of senators and representatives for each state depends on the state's population.

(C) The number of representatives per state depends on the population of that state, whereas each state is given two senators.

(D) The number of senators per state depends on the population of that state, whereas each state is given two representatives.

497. When does the winning candidate officially become president of the United States?

(A) January 20 following the election

(B) on the Tuesday after the first Monday in November

(C) as soon as a winner of the popular vote has been determined

(D) as soon as a winner of the electoral vote has been determined

498. Which amendment to the U.S. Constitution determines the rules for electing a new president?

(A) First Amendment

(B) Ninth Amendment

(C) Twelfth Amendment

(D) Twentieth Amendment

499. According to the passage, if no candidate receives an absolute majority of the electoral vote, who will select the next president?

(A) The House of Representatives will select the new president.

(B) The current president will select the new president.

(C) The American people will vote again to select the new president.

(D) The current president remains president for the next four years.

Use the preamble to the U.S. Constitution, reproduced here, for Questions 500 and 501.

We the People of the United States, in Order to form a more perfect Union, establish Justice, insure domestic Tranquility, provide for the common defence, promote the general Welfare, and secure the Blessings of Liberty to ourselves and our Posterity, do ordain and establish this Constitution for the United States of America.

500. Why does the Constitution have a preamble?

(A) to negate the meaning of the Constitution

(B) to reject the notion of universal human rights

(C) to warn people against taking the wording of the Constitution too seriously

(D) to explain the purpose of the Constitution

501. The preamble mentions that in order to form a more perfect union, the people must do all of the following EXCEPT

(A) establish justice.

(B) promote the general welfare.

(C) eliminate all the Native Americans.

(D) insure domestic tranquility.

502. What does NAFTA stand for?

(A) North Atlantic Free Trade Agreement

(B) North American Free Trade Agreement

(C) New Association for Traffic Assessment

(D) New Association for Traders' Agents

503. The Jim Crow laws sought to

(A) protect the rights of African Americans

(B) limit the rights of African Americans

(C) protect the rights of Native Americans

(D) limit the rights of Native Americans

504. Fill in the blank to correctly complete the sentence:

A ____________ is a market containing a single firm that has almost total control of the market.

505. Which of the following statements correctly summarizes communism and capitalism?

(A) Communism is associated with state-owned industries, income redistribution, and classless society, whereas capitalism is associated with private ownership, profit motive, and competitive markets.

(B) Communism is associated with private ownership, profit motive, and competitive markets, whereas capitalism is associated with state-owned industries, income redistribution, and classless society.

(C) Communism is associated with state-owned industries, income redistribution, and competitive markets, whereas capitalism is associated with private ownership, profit motive, and classless society.

(D) Communism is associated with private ownership, income redistribution, and classless society, whereas capitalism is associated with state-owned industries, profit motive, and competitive markets.

Chapter 3
Science

The Science section of the GED lasts 90 minutes and contains 50 questions. This section tests your ability to work with science information from life science, physical science, and earth and space science. In this chapter, you can try your hand at 225 science questions.

The Problems You'll Work On

When working through the questions in this chapter, be prepared to do the following:

- » Analyze data represented in tables and graphs.
- » Sift through text for information on experiment procedure and setup.
- » Consider science topics from all areas of biology, chemistry, and physics.

What to Watch Out For

To maximize your score, avoid these counterproductive and time-sucking activities:

- » Not reading the question stem carefully and failing to relate it to the information given in charts, diagrams, or passages
- » Neglecting to identify the column headings on tables and the axis designations on graphs
- » Believing you need to know a bunch of science concepts to answer the questions
- » Spending more than a minute on any one question instead of marking it for later and moving on
- » Failing to quickly eliminate answers that contain irrelevant data or blatantly contradict information in the passage

Questions 506 and 507 are based on the following figure.

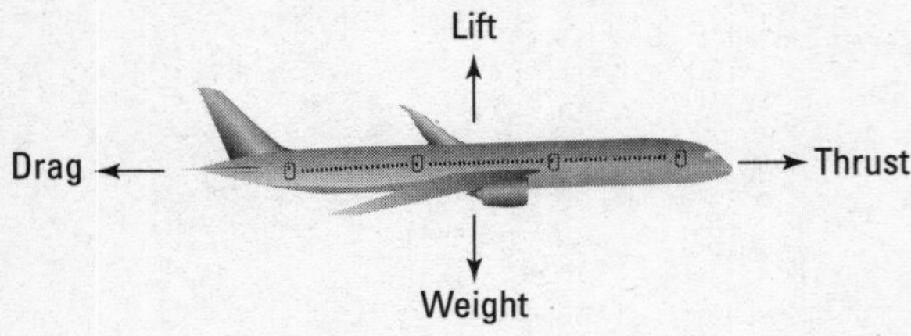

506. Which force is responsible for keeping the plane in the air?

(A) drag
(B) lift
(C) weight
(D) thrust

507. If the plane maintains a constant speed and altitude and travels in a straight line, which of the following must be true according to Newton's law of inertia?

(A) The plane is weightless.
(B) There are no unbalanced forces acting on the plane.
(C) The lift must be greater than the weight to keep the plane from falling to the ground.
(D) The thrust must be greater than the drag to keep the plane moving forward.

508. Complete the sentence by filling in the blanks.

As an object falls from a table to the floor, it loses its stored (______________) energy and gains ______________ energy as it begins to speed up. When the object hits the ground, it loses its energy of motion, which is converted into ______________ energy.

509. Which organelle is found only in plant cells and helps the plant to produce its own food via photosynthesis?

(A) cell wall
(B) vacuoles
(C) mitochondria
(D) chloroplasts

Questions 510 through 512 are based on the following information.

A gardener is interested in growing pea plants of a particular height. He draws a Punnett square to display all the possible combinations of alleles when two hybrid pea plants are crossed to help him determine the possible genotypes of the offspring. *T* represents the dominant allele for tall plants, and *t* represents the recessive allele for short plants. The genotype of one parent plant is shown on the top of the square, and the other parent's genotype is shown on the left of the square. The genotypes of the offspring are shown in the boxes. The Punnett square is shown here:

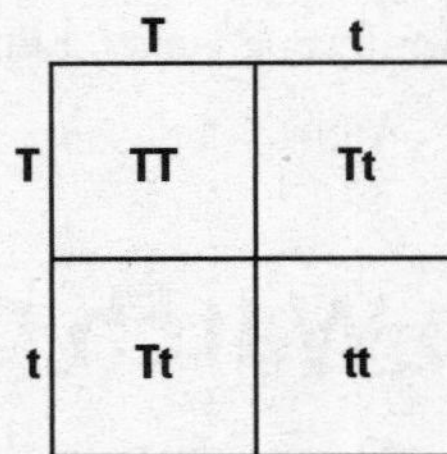

	T	t
T	TT	Tt
t	Tt	tt

510. What is the probability that an offspring will be tall?

(A) 0%
(B) 25%
(C) 75%
(D) 100%

511. Fill in the blanks to correctly complete the sentence:

The genotype of both parent plants is ______________, which means that both parents will be ______________.

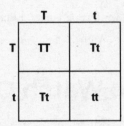

512. The gardener now chooses two new parent plants, both with the genotype TT. What is the probability that one of their offspring, chosen at random, will be short?

(A) 0%

(B) 25%

(C) 75%

(D) 100%

513. What causes a solar eclipse?

(A) the moon passing between the Earth and the sun

(B) the sun passing between the Earth and the moon

(C) clouds

(D) the Earth passing between the sun and the moon

514. Fill in the blanks to correctly complete the sentence:

An astronaut standing on the moon weighs ____________ [more than, less than, the same as] she does on Earth but has ____________ [more, less, the same] mass than/as she has on Earth.

Use the following information for Questions 515 through 517.

Plants produce their own food by using the energy from the sun as shown in the following equation:

$$\text{sunlight} + 6CO_2 + 6HO_2 \rightarrow 6O_2 + C_6H_{12}O_6$$

515. What biochemical process does the equation show?

(A) synthesis of ATP

(B) cellular respiration

(C) photoelectric effect

(D) photosynthesis

516. What type of chemical reaction does the equation show?

(A) nuclear fission reaction

(B) nuclear fusion reaction

(C) endothermic reaction

(D) exothermic reaction

517. Fill in the blanks to correctly complete the sentence:

Plants use the energy from ____________ to convert ____________ and ____________ into ____________ and ____________.

518. Which element is the basis of all living organisms on Earth?

(A) carbon dioxide

(B) oxygen

(C) water

(D) carbon

519. Why is the light that the Hubble telescope detects from distant galaxies red-shifted?

(A) Greenhouse gases in the atmosphere filter out green light so that only red light remains.

(B) The distant galaxies are moving away from Earth.

(C) The distant galaxies are moving toward Earth.

(D) The light bounces off the surface of the red planet Mars before reaching us.

520. Which type of particle is emitted in the nuclear decay reaction shown here?

$${}^{222}_{88}Ra \rightarrow {}^{218}_{86}Rn + {}^{4}_{2}He$$

(A) alpha decay

(B) beta decay

(C) gamma decay

(D) nuclear fusion

521. Fill in the blanks to correctly complete the sentence:

The nuclei of two isotopes of an element contains the same number of ________________ but a different number of ________________.

Use the following information for Questions 522 through 525.

Light travels at 300,000 km per second in the vacuum of space. The sun produces an enormous amount of energy. Some of that energy reaches Earth in the form of sunlight and affects Earth's systems.

522. The light from the sun takes approximately 8 minutes to reach us. Approximately how far away is the sun from the Earth?

(A) 150 million kilometers

(B) 150 billion kilometers

(C) 150 trillion kilometers

(D) 150 gazillion kilometers

523. Which statement best explains how the energy from the sun reaches Earth?

(A) The sun's energy reaches Earth via conduction because heat flows from the hot sun to the cooler Earth.

(B) The sun's energy reaches Earth via convection currents.

(C) The sun's energy reaches Earth via thermal radiation in the form of electromagnetic waves.

(D) The sun's energy reaches Earth via all of the above methods.

524. How does the sun produce its energy?

(A) The sun produces energy via nuclear fission reactions at its core.

(B) The sun produces energy via nuclear fusion reactions at its core.

(C) The sun produces energy via combustion reactions on its surface.

(D) The sun produces energy via exothermic chemical reactions on its surface.

525. Why is it usually much colder at the North Pole and the South Pole compared to places nearer the equator?

(A) The snow and ice at the North Pole and South Pole cool down the air, causing the temperature to drop.

(B) There's no atmosphere at the North Pole and the South Pole, so all the heat escapes, causing the temperature to drop.

(C) The poles are farther away from the sun than most other places on Earth.

(D) The curvature of the Earth causes the sun's rays to spread out over a larger surface area at the poles compared to at the equator.

526. Which of the following statements describes the role of DNA in a cell?

(A) DNA is the material that the cell wall is constructed from.

(B) DNA provides the energy that fuels the cell's activities.

(C) DNA provides information to make proteins for the cell.

(D) DNA is the building block for proteins in the cell.

527. Which of the following is a way to combat global warming?

(A) Ban gardeners and farmers from using greenhouses because carbon dioxide is a greenhouse gas.

(B) Use renewable energy sources such as wind or solar power.

(C) Cut down more trees in the rainforests to stop them from producing carbon dioxide during photosynthesis.

(D) Burn more fossil fuels to get rid of these carbon-containing compounds.

528. The number of which subatomic particle determines the identity of an element?

(A) neutrons

(B) protons

(C) electrons

(D) alpha particles

Use the following information for Questions 529 and 530.

Scientists believe that Earth's continents were once joined together into a single landmass called *Pangaea.* This supercontinent began to break up 175 million years ago and slowly drifted apart in a process known as *continental drift* to form the separate continents we see today. This diagram shows what Pangaea is believed to have looked like and how the continents drifted apart to appear as they do today.

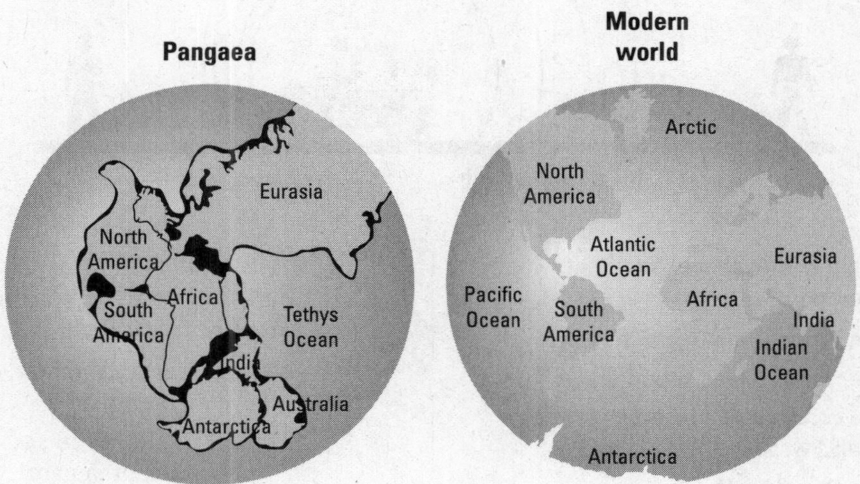

529. What was the main cause of continental drift?

(A) Convection currents within the Earth's fluid mantle caused the tectonic plates floating on the mantle to move relative to each other and separate

(B) Thermal expansion of the rock due to human-caused global warming

(C) The meteorite that killed off the dinosaurs smashed into Pangaea 65 million years ago, causing it to split and drift apart

(D) Tremors left over from the Big Bang that created the universe

530. Which of the following statements does NOT support the Pangaea theory?

(A) Identical deposits of minerals have been found at corresponding locations along both the African and South American coasts.

(B) The shape of the west coast of Africa seems to fit perfectly with the shape of the east coast of South America.

(C) Paleontologists have discovered matching fossils from identical species of land animals at corresponding locations along both the African and South American coasts.

(D) The Big Bang theory states that all matter in the universe expanded outward from the same point in space.

Use the following information for Questions 531 and 532.

This figure shows how the sound waves from the siren of an ambulance appear to change as the ambulance moves toward or away from a stationary observer.

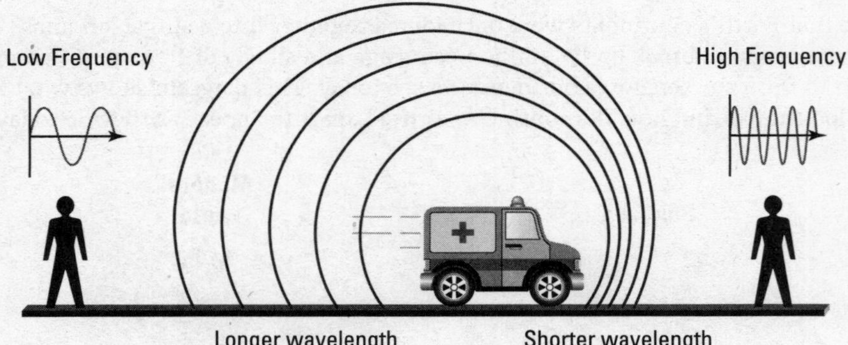

531. This figure shows an example of which phenomenon?

(A) the reflection of sounds waves

(B) the refraction of sound waves

(C) the constructive interference of sound waves

(D) the Doppler effect

532. Fill in the blanks to correctly complete the sentence.

As the ambulance moves *away from* the stationary observer, the frequency of the siren appears to _______________.
As the ambulance moves *toward* the stationary observer, the frequency of the siren appears to _______________.

533. Which of the following correctly represents the hierarchy in living organisms, classified from smallest to the largest?

(A) cell, organelle, tissue, organ system, organ, organism

(B) cell, tissue, organ system, organ, organelle, organism

(C) organism, organ system, organ, tissue, cell, organelle

(D) organelle, cell, tissue, organ, organ system, organism

534. Which of the following always stays the same when a chemical reaction takes place?

(A) the amount of gas

(B) the number of molecules

(C) the number of atoms

(D) the temperature

535. Which of the following correctly represents the progression of life on Earth according to the fossil record, from earliest life forms to the most recent?

(A) fish, amphibians, birds, reptiles, mammals

(B) amphibians, fish, reptiles, mammals, birds

(C) fish, amphibians, reptiles, birds, mammals

(D) fish, reptiles, amphibians, mammals, birds

Use the following information for Questions 536 and 537.

The carbon cycle describes the circulation and transformation of carbon between living things and the environment as it moves through Earth's systems. The carbon cycle is shown in the following figure.

The Carbon Cycle

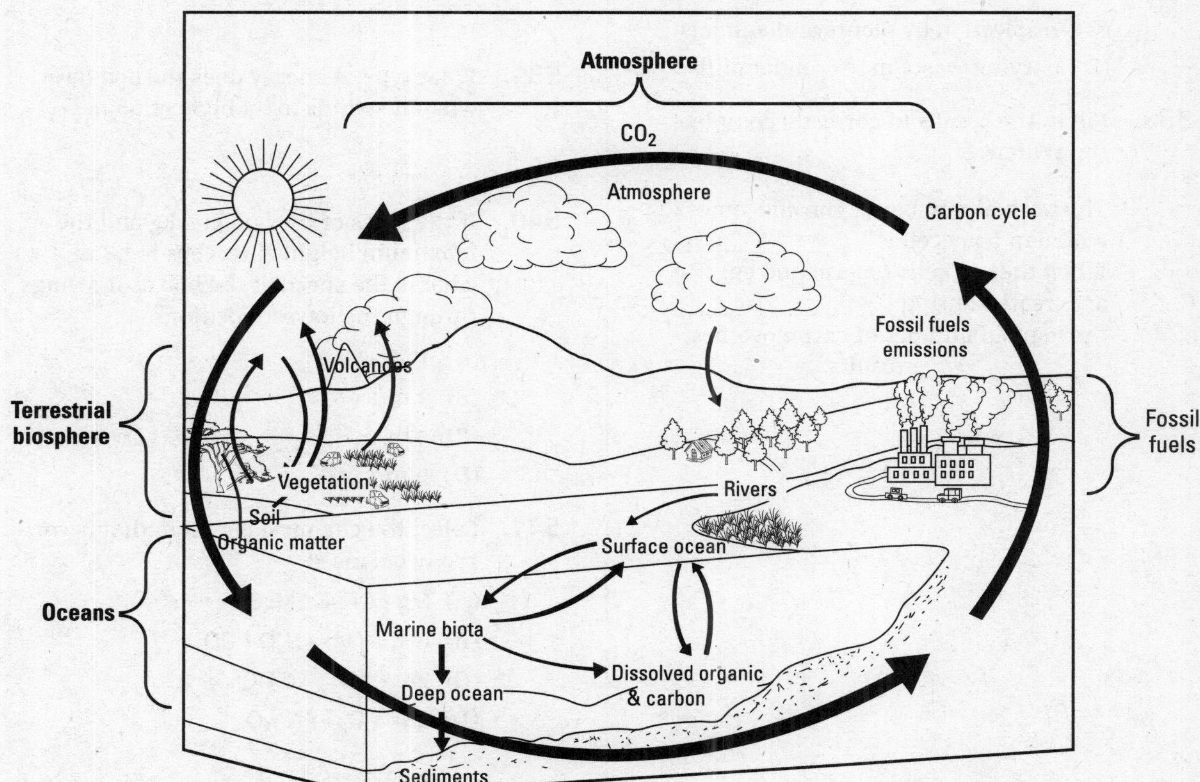

536. Which recent event led to a sharp increase in the amount of carbon dioxide released into the atmosphere, contributing to global warming?

(A) The invention of renewable energy sources such as solar power

(B) The recent increase in the human population, because humans breathe out carbon dioxide during respiration

(C) Sending astronauts to the moon, which produced greenhouse gases as the rocket fuel was consumed

(D) The Industrial Revolution, which led to a sharp increase in the rate of combustion of fossil fuels.

537. Which of the following processes releases carbon dioxide to the atmosphere?

(A) photosynthesis

(B) the formation of fossils and fossil fuels

(C) respiration by plants and animals

(D) burying waste matter in landfills

538. Fill in the blanks to correctly complete the sentence:

The normal number of chromosomes in a human body cell is _____________. When the sex cells (sperm and egg) are created during _____________, the haploid number of chromosomes, _____________, results.

Use the following information for Questions 539 and 540.

The conservation of energy states that the mechanical energy of an isolated system is always conserved. Energy cannot be created or destroyed; it can only be converted from one form to another. When a pendulum bob is released from its highest point, it swings down through the lowest position before swinging back up to the same height on the other side, as shown in the following diagram.

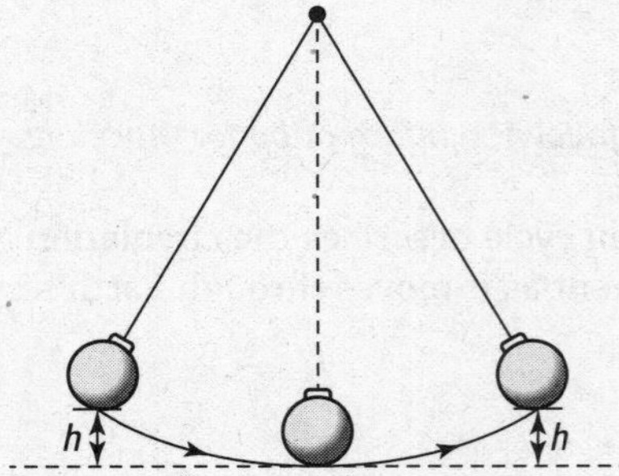

539. What type of energy does the bob have when it swings to its highest point?

____

540. If the mass of the bob is 4 kg and the maximum height it reaches is 1.8 m, what is the speed of the bob as it swings through the lowest position?

(A) 1 m/s

(B) 3 m/s

(C) 5 m/s

(D) 6 m/s

541. Select the chemical equation that is correctly balanced.

(A) $Mg + Cl_2 \rightarrow 2MgCl$

(B) $CH_4 + O_2 \rightarrow H_2O + CO_2$

(C) $2Al + 3Cl_2 \rightarrow 2AlCl_3$

(D) $2Na + O_2 \rightarrow Na_2O$

Use the following information to help answer Questions 542 through 545.

The periodic table organizes elements based on their atomic structure. The periodic table has rows (called *periods*) and columns (called *groups*). The group tells you how many valence electrons the element possesses, whereas the period tells you how many energy levels the atom has. Here is a simplified period table showing the first three periods of the Group A elements:

1A	2A	3A	4A	5A	6A	7A	8A
1 H 1.01							2 He 4.00
3 Li 6.94	4 Be 9.01	5 B 10.8	6 C 12.0	7 N 14.0	8 O 16.0	9 F 19.0	10 Ne 20.2
11 Na 23.0	12 Mg 24.3	13 Al 27.0	14 Si 28.1	15 P 30.1	16 S 32.1	17 Cl 35.5	18 Ar 39.9

542. How many valence electrons does a carbon atom (symbol C) have?

(A) 4

(B) 6

(C) 12

(D) 18

543. Which of the following elements is the least chemically reactive?

(A) fluorine, based on its seven valence electrons

(B) neon, based on its Group 8 status

(C) lithium, based on its one valence electron

(D) sulfur, based on its six valence electrons

544. Which of the following statements about sodium (symbol Na) is NOT true?

(A) Sodium has 11 electrons.

(B) Sodium has 23 neutrons.

(C) Sodium has 3 electron shells.

(D) Sodium's first energy shell can hold a maximum of 2 electrons.

545. Which of the following statements is true?

(A) Hydrogen bonds to itself, forming hydrogen bonds.

(B) Carbon reacts with hydrogen by sharing valence electrons to form covalent bonds.

(C) Potassium reacts with chlorine by sharing valence electrons to form a covalent bond.

(D) Magnesium reacts with argon to form ionic bonds.

546. Which of the following statements is FALSE?

(A) Mercury is the closest planet to the sun.

(B) Saturn is a giant gas planet.

(C) Pluto is no longer considered to be a proper planet.

(D) Jupiter is about half the size of the sun.

Use the following information for Questions 547 through 550.

A student is testing out Newton's laws of motion by applying different forces for 3 seconds to different-colored toy cars of the same mass (2 kg each). The cars start at rest. She records the data for the toy cars in the following chart.

Car Color	Car Acceleration (m/s^2)	Final Velocity (m/s)
Red	4.0.	12
Orange	2.0.	6
Green	0.0	0
Blue	3.0.	9

547. What is the value of the unbalanced force acting on the green car?

(A) 0 N

(B) 4 N

(C) 6 N

(D) 10 N

548. Which car has the greatest unbalanced force acting on it?

(A) red

(B) orange

(C) green

(D) blue

549. Which of the following statements is true?

(A) All the cars have the same final momentum, but the green car has the smallest inertia.

(B) All the cars have the same final momentum, but the red car has the smallest inertia.

(C) All the cars have the same inertia, but the green car has the smallest final momentum.

(D) All the cars have the same inertia, but the red car has the smallest final momentum.

550. At the end of the 3-second period, the red car collides with the green car, causing the red car to stop suddenly. What speed does the green car move off at?

(A) 2 m/s

(B) 8 m/s

(C) 12 m/s

(D) 24 m/s

551. The year can be split into four seasons (spring, summer, autumn, and winter), which are marked by particular weather patterns and daylight hours. What is the main factor that causes the change in the seasons?

(A) the distance of the Earth from the sun

(B) global warming

(C) the tilt of the Earth's axis of rotation

(D) movement of tectonic plates

552. According to the best scientific estimates, approximately how old is the Earth?

(A) 6,000 years old

(B) 5 million years old

(C) 5 billion years old

(D) 15 billion years old

Use the following information for Questions 553 through 555.

The rock cycle describes the processes by which the Earth recycles rocks by transforming them from one type to another. The rock cycle is shown in the following diagram.

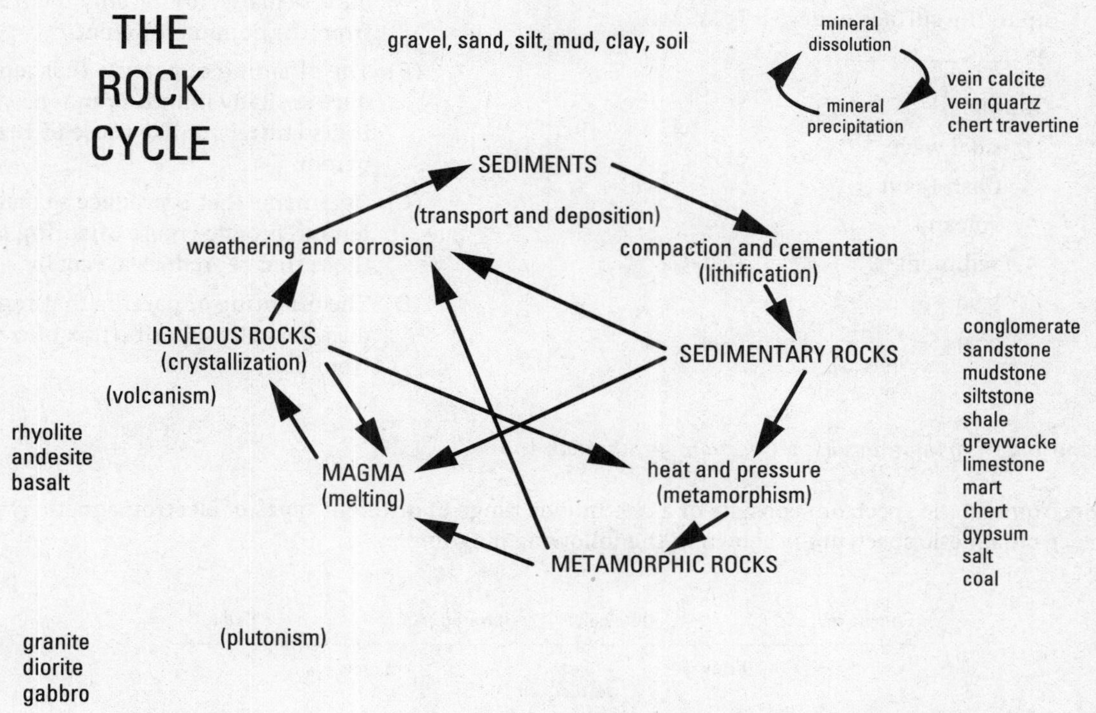

553. Fossils are produced when a plant or animal dies and its remains become buried in mud, silt, or sand, which then gets compacted and compressed into rock. Which of the following types of rock is most likely to contain fossils?

(A) sedimentary rock

(B) igneous rock

(C) metamorphic rock

(D) magma

554. Which of the following statements does this figure support?

(A) Magma forms directly from all three types of rocks.

(B) Sediment forms only from the weathering and erosion of sedimentary rocks.

(C) Each type of rock is continuously transformed into the other types.

(D) Metamorphic rock is produced from sediment.

555. Select the correct words from the given options to fill in the blanks:

Magma is molten rock beneath the Earth's surface. Magma is sometimes expelled via a ______________ up to the surface, where it is known as ______________.

Options:

tidal wave

flash flood

volcano

sediment

lava

coal

556. Why is there a greater level of genetic diversity for species that reproduce sexually compared to those that reproduce asexually?

(A) The offspring of parents that reproduce sexually inherit only the traits from the dominant parent.

(B) The offspring of parents that reproduce sexually inherit brand-new traits entirely unlike those of either parent.

(C) Organisms that reproduce sexually tend to produce more offspring than those that reproduce asexually.

(D) The offspring of parents that reproduce sexually inherit a mix of traits from both parents.

Use the following information for Questions 557 through 560.

The electromagnetic spectrum consists of a continuous range of different types of electromagnetic waves. The electromagnetic spectrum is shown in the following diagram.

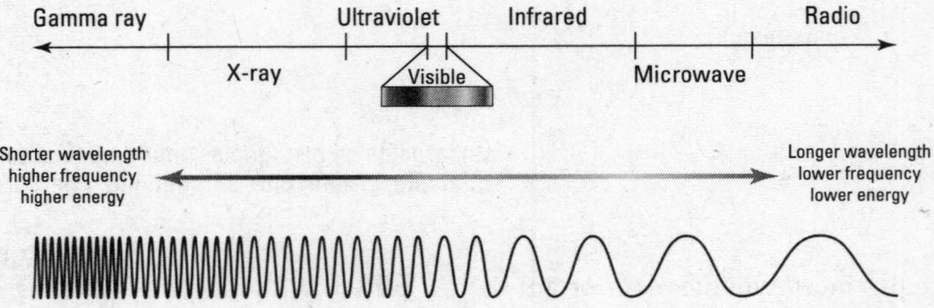

557. Which of the following statements is supported by the diagram of the electromagnetic spectrum?

(A) Microwaves can be used to cook food.

(B) The human eye can see only a small fraction of the electromagnetic spectrum.

(C) X-rays have longer wavelengths than visible light.

(D) Some insects, such as butterflies, can see ultraviolet light.

558. Which of the following colors in the visible part of the spectrum has the lowest energy?

(A) red light

(B) green light

(C) purple light

(D) blue light

559. Select the correct words from the given options to fill in the blanks:

Gamma rays have ____________ wavelengths and ____________ frequencies, whereas radio waves have ____________ wavelengths and ____________ frequencies.

Options:

long

short

high

low

560. Which of the following best explains why we use radio waves for our communications applications?

(A) Radio waves have short wavelengths and are low-energy waves.

(B) Radio waves have short wavelengths and are high-energy waves.

(C) Radio waves have long wavelengths and are low-energy waves.

(D) Radio waves have long wavelengths and are high-energy waves.

561. Which of the following systems includes the surface of the Earth?

(A) lithosphere

(B) biosphere

(C) hydrosphere

(D) atmosphere

562. Which *two* events listed are highly predictable?

[A] lunar eclipses

[B] hurricanes

[C] earthquakes

[D] the appearance of Haley's comet

Use the following information for Questions 563 through 566.

Food chains are used to represent the flow of energy in an ecosystem. An expanded food chain is called a *food web.* The arrows in a food chain or food web go in the direction of the energy flow, or rather, to the organism that is doing the eating. An example of a food web is shown here.

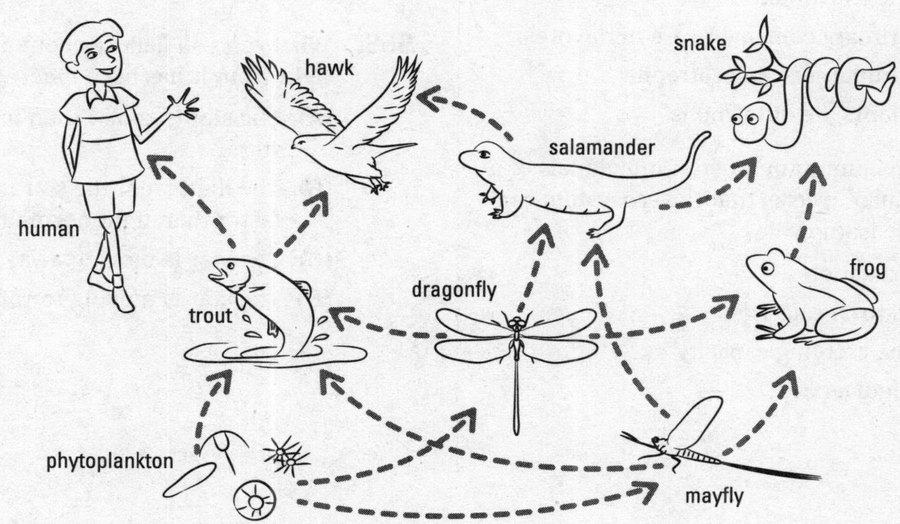

563. Which of the following is a true statement?

(A) The dragonflies are producers, the phytoplankton are primary consumers, and the snakes are tertiary consumers.

(B) The phytoplankton are producers, the dragonflies are primary consumers, and the snakes are tertiary consumers.

(C) The phytoplankton are producers, the snakes are primary consumers, and the dragonflies are tertiary consumers.

(D) The snakes are producers, the dragonflies are primary consumers, and the phytoplankton are tertiary consumers.

564. If a virus were to suddenly wipe out most of the frog population, which species in the food web would increase in number?

(A) snakes

(B) mayflies and dragonflies

(C) humans and fish

(D) hawks

565. Which of the following statements regarding a food web is NOT true?

(A) When an organism is eaten, most of the energy stored in its body is transferred to the biomass (flesh) of the consumer.

(B) Primary consumers are herbivores.

(C) Animals are heterotrophs.

(D) Plants are autotrophs.

566. The maximum number of individuals of a particular species that the ecosystem can handle is known as

(A) predation

(B) natural selection

(C) the carrying capacity

(D) biodiversity

567. Which of the following did not play a significant part in Charles Darwin's theories of evolution?

(A) survival of the fittest.

(B) natural selection.

(C) DNA.

(D) adaptation.

Use the following information for Questions 568 through 571.

Some of the stars you see in the night sky are so far away from Earth that the light from them has taken millions of years to reach you. So what you are really seeing is what those stars looked like millions of years ago. You are actually seeing into the past. To help us handle these huge distances, we use a special unit of measurement called a light-year to describe them. As its name suggests, a light-year is equal to the distance that light travels in one year. Light travels at 300,000 km per second in the vacuum of space.

568. Sirius is the name of a star that is approximately 86 trillion kilometers (8.6 light-years) away from the Earth. How long does the light from Sirius take to reach the Earth?

(A) 86 trillion seconds

(B) 300,000 seconds

(C) 8.6 seconds

(D) 8.6 years

569. What can you deduce about a star if the light from it has been blue-shifted?

(A) The star is cooler than most other stars.

(B) The light from the star is traveling faster than light normally travels.

(C) The star is moving away from Earth.

(D) The star is moving toward Earth.

570. All the following statements provide evidence supporting the Big Bang theory EXCEPT

(A) the discovery of cosmic microwave background radiation.

(B) the Doppler effect showing that starlight is red-shifted.

(C) spectral analysis of starlight showing a relative abundance of hydrogen and helium.

(D) sound waves left over from the Big Bang.

571. Select the correct order from smallest to largest.

(A) universe, galaxy, solar system, star

(B) solar system, star, galaxy, universe

(C) star, solar system, galaxy, universe

(D) star, galaxy, universe, solar system

572. Which of the following statements does NOT provide evidence supporting the common ancestry theory?

(A) Scientists believe that of all the species on Earth that have ever existed, 99 percent of them are now extinct.

(B) Many different animals have similar anatomical structures.

(C) All organisms on Earth have a large percentage of their DNA identical to that of other species.

(D) A lot of different animal species, including humans, start out looking the same as embryos.

573. What name is given to a substance that speeds up the rate of a reaction by decreasing the activation energy needed for the reactants to turn into products?

(A) a noble gas

(B) a compound

(C) an alloy

(D) a catalyst

574. Which of the following is an example of a positive feedback mechanism in the climate system of Earth?

(A) Global warming causes extreme weather, including severe thunderstorms.

(B) Higher global temperatures cause sea levels to rise.

(C) Higher ocean temperatures lead to an increase in the numbers of tropical fish found off the coast of Florida.

(D) Higher global temperatures cause the polar ice caps, which reflect sunlight back into space, to melt, leading to further global warming.

Use the following information for Questions 575 through 578.

Jenny is investigating magnetic fields and forces. She has the following equipment available to her: two strong bar magnets and a plotting compass.

Circuit 1: This consists of a coil of wire wrapped around an iron bar. There is a battery in this circuit and a switch but no light bulb present.

Circuit 2: This consists of a coil of wire attached to a light bulb. There is no battery in this circuit.

575. What happens when the student closes the switch in Circuit 1?

(A) The light bulb lights up.

(B) The iron bar becomes magnetized.

(C) Nothing, because iron does not conduct electricity.

(D) The iron bar becomes hot and begins to melt.

576. What happens when the student positions the two strong magnets near each other with one north pole and one south pole facing each other?

(A) The first magnet will be attracted to the second magnet, but the second magnet will be repelled by the first magnet.

(B) The magnets will become warm due to electromagnetic radiation given off by their north poles.

(C) The magnets will attract each other.

(D) The magnets will repel each other.

577. What happens when the student moves one of the magnets into and out of the coil in Circuit 2?

(A) The light bulb remains unlit because there is no battery to power the circuit.

(B) The light bulb lights up because electricity is created.

(C) An electromagnet is generated.

(D) The magnet becomes demagnetized.

578. Which direction will the plotting compass point when the student places it at the north pole of one of the bar magnets?

(A) Toward the magnet's north pole

(B) Away from the magnet's north pole

(C) Away from Earth's North Pole

(D) Toward Earth's North Pole

579. What is the name of the human body system consisting of the skin, hair, and nails that serves to protect the body from various kinds of damage, such as loss of water or abrasion, from the outside?

(A) digestive system

(B) integumentary system

(C) circulatory system

(D) muscular system

580. Groundwater often drips from the ceilings of underground caves, leaving behind tiny deposits of minerals (such as calcium carbonate) that were dissolved in the water. Over millions of years, these tiny deposits build up to form stalactites.

Which of the following questions can be answered using this information?

(A) What is the difference between stalactites and stalagmites?

(B) How tall can stalactites become?

(C) What causes the formation of stalactites in underground caverns?

(D) How are stalagmites formed?

581. Daisy was conducting an investigation using two liquids. Both liquids were clear and were at the same temperature, 25°C. When she combined the liquids in a large beaker, gas bubbles were produced and the liquid turned blue. The student took the temperature of the beaker, which now measured 27°C. All of the following show that a chemical reaction may have occurred EXCEPT

(A) a temperature change occurred.

(B) a color change occurred.

(C) the two liquids mixed together.

(D) a gas was produced.

Questions 582 through 585 are based on the following figure, which shows a block being dragged across the floor.

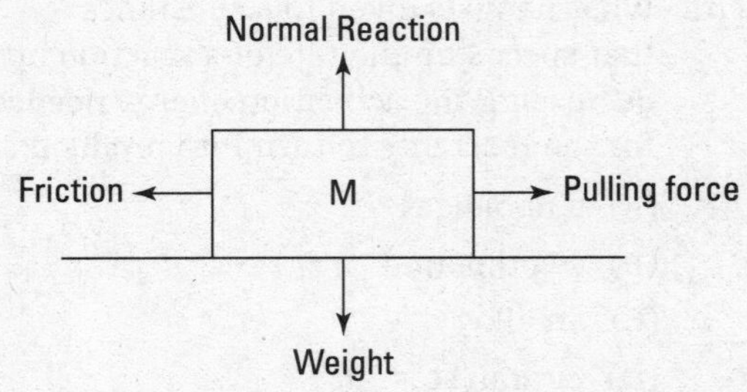

582. If the block has a mass of 2 kg, what is the approximate force on it due to gravity?

(A) 2 N

(B) 10 N

(C) 20 N

(D) 40 N

583. If the block has a mass of 2 kg and the pulling force and the frictional force acting on the block both equal 20 N, what is the acceleration of the block?

(A) $0\,m/s^2$

(B) $10\,m/s^2$

(C) $40\,m/s^2$

(D) The acceleration cannot be determined without additional information.

584. If the block is moving at a constant velocity, then which of the following is a true statement?

(A) The pulling force must be greater than the frictional force, but the weight of the object is equal to the normal reaction force.

(B) The pulling force must be greater than the frictional force, and the weight of the object is greater than the normal reaction force.

(C) The pulling force must be equal to the frictional force, and the weight of the object is equal to the normal reaction force.

(D) The pulling force must be equal to the frictional force, but the weight of the object is less than the normal reaction force.

585. If the block has a mass of 2 kg, and a pulling force of 20 N acting on the block causes it to accelerate at $4\,m/s^2$, what is the value of the frictional force acting on the block?

(A) 10 N

(B) 12 N

(C) 20 N

(D) 40 N

Questions 586 through 589 are based on the following information.

Pea plants produce two types of seeds: round seeds or wrinkled seeds. A gardener cross-breeds two pea plants and draws a Punnett square (shown in the figure below) where (R) represents the dominant allele for round seeds and (r) represents the allele for wrinkly seeds. The outside of the square displays the genes of the parents, whereas the inside of the square shows the genes of the potential offspring.

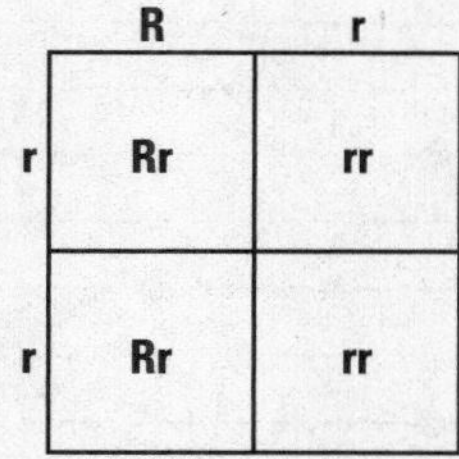

586. What is the probability that their offspring will have wrinkled seeds?

(A) 0%

(B) 25%

(C) 50%

(D) 100%

587. Based on the given Punnett square, which of the following is a true statement?

(A) Both parent plants are homozygous.

(B) Both parent plants are heterozygous.

(C) One parent plant is heterozygous, and the other is homozygous.

(D) Neither parent plant is heterozygous or homozygous.

588. If the gardener cross-breeds two pea plants that have wrinkly seeds, what is the probability that their offspring will have round seeds?

(A) 0%

(B) 25%

(C) 75%

(D) 100%

589. If the gardener cross-breeds two pea plants that are heterozygous, what is the probability that their offspring will have round seeds?

(A) 0%

(B) 25%

(C) 75%

(D) 100%

590. Which of the following arranges the units in ascending order (from smallest to largest)?

(A) microgram, milligram, gram, kilogram

(B) milligram, microgram, gram, kilogram

(C) microgram, gram, milligram, kilogram

(D) microgram, milligram, kilogram, gram

Use the following graphs for Questions 591 through 593.

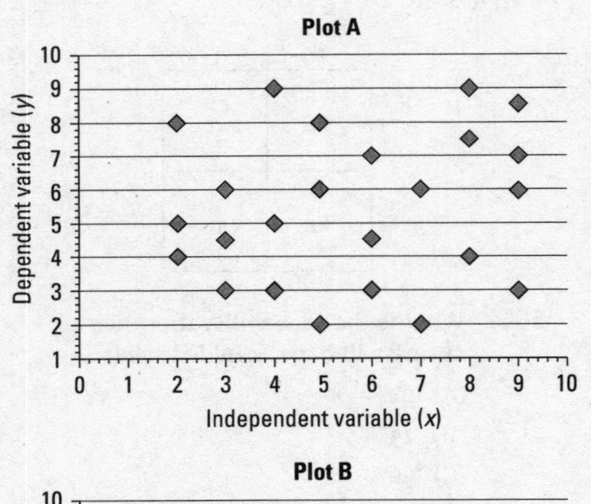

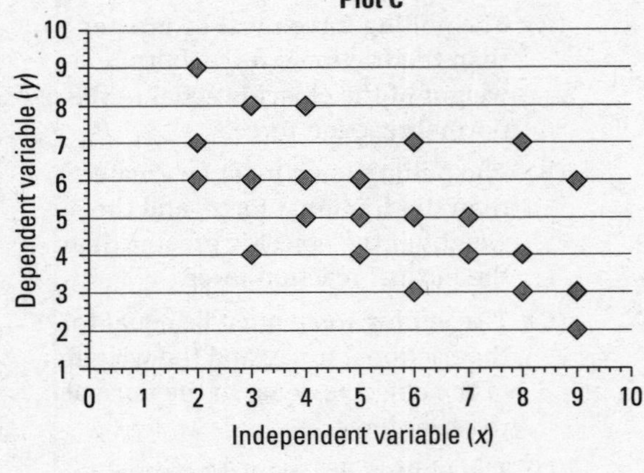

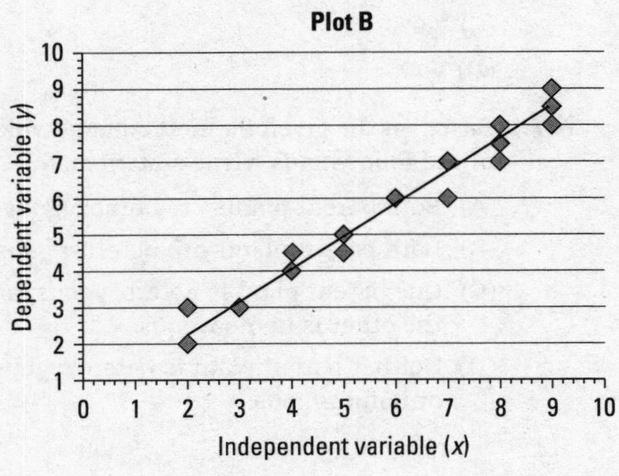

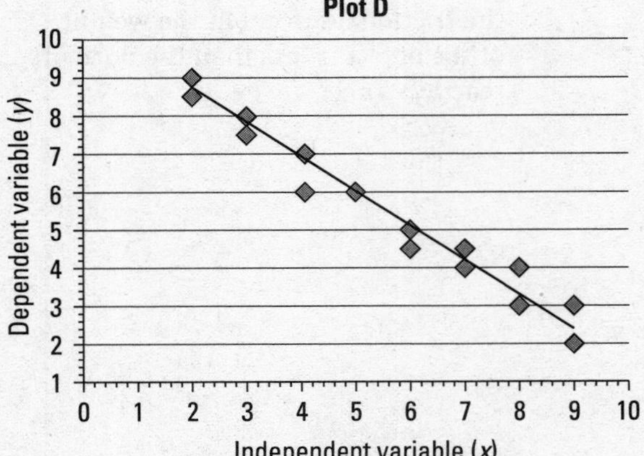

591. Which graph shows strong positive correlation between the variables?

(A) Plot A

(B) Plot B

(C) Plot C

(D) Plot D

592. Which graph shows strong negative correlation between the variables?

(A) Plot A

(B) Plot B

(C) Plot C

(D) Plot D

593. Which graph shows no correlation between the variables?

(A) Plot A

(B) Plot B

(C) Plot C

(D) Plot D

594. Which of the following statements is correct?

(A) Two variables that are correlated must always increase together or decrease together.

(B) If two variables are correlated, causation always exists between them.

(C) Correlation exists between two variables that happen together and may be related.

(D) Causation is an inferred cause-and-effect relationship that cannot be proved.

595. Which of the following correctly lists the atoms in the following compounds?

(A) CO_2 has 1 chlorine atom and 2 oxygen atoms.

(B) H_2O has 1 hydrogen atom and 2 oxygen atoms.

(C) $C_6H_{12}O_6$ has 6 chlorine atoms, 12 hydrogen atoms, and 6 oxygen atoms.

(D) CH_4 has 1 carbon atom and 4 hydrogen atoms.

596. Which type of particle is emitted in the nuclear decay reaction shown here?

$^{214}_{82}\text{Pb} \rightarrow {}^{214}_{83}\text{Bi} + {}^{0}_{-1}\text{e}$

(A) alpha decay

(B) beta decay

(C) gamma decay

(D) nuclear fusion

597. The mass number of an element is the sum of the number of ____________ within the nucleus of the atom.

(A) protons and electrons

(B) electrons and neutrons

(C) alpha particles

(D) protons and neutrons

Use the following information for Questions 598 through 600.

Arctic foxes have a thick layer of fat and dense, white fur to help protect them from the freezing temperatures of the Arctic habitat where they live. Natural selection is thought to be involved in the evolution of the Arctic fox's thick coat of fur.

598. Which of the following best explains how natural selection is involved in the evolution of the Arctic fox's thick fur coat?

(A) Arctic foxes with thinner coats migrated south for the winter.

(B) Arctic foxes with thinner coats did not survive because they were not well-suited to the harsh conditions of their environment.

(C) Arctic foxes with thick coats preferred to mate only with other Arctic foxes who had thick fur coats.

(D) Arctic foxes with thick fur coats killed off all the Arctic foxes thinner coats.

599. How does the Arctic fox's thick fur coat help to keep the animal warm in the frigid Arctic conditions?

(A) Fur is a good conductor of heat, so the fox absorbs heat from the surroundings.

(B) The thick fur helps convection currents direct heat from the surroundings into the animal's skin.

(C) Fur traps a layer of air next to the animal's body, which keeps it warm because air is a poor conductor of heat.

(D) The white color of the fur reflects thermal radiation from the sun.

600. Black fur emits more body heat to the colder surroundings than white fur does. Which of the following does NOT help explain why the Arctic fox has white fur rather than black fur?

(A) Black fur emits heat more than white fur does, so an animal with black fur would lose its body heat more quickly than an animal with white fur.

(B) Black fur would make it easier for the fox's prey to spot the fox coming and escape.

(C) Black fur provides an excellent contrast with the white background of the Arctic snow.

(D) White fur blends in with the fox's snowy surroundings better than black fur, helping the fox hide from predators.

601. Which of the following is the best example of Newton's first law (the law of inertia), which states that an object at rest stays at rest and an object in motion stays in motion at the same speed in the same direction unless acted upon by an unbalanced force?

(A) a train slowing to a stop as it enters the station

(B) the recoil of a cannon when a cannonball is fired into the air

(C) a skydiver who has already reached terminal velocity and is falling at a constant speed toward the ground

(D) a rocket blasting off on its way to the moon

602. What will happen if an atom gains an electron?

(A) Its charge would become negative.

(B) Its charge would become positive.

(C) Its charge would remain neutral.

(D) The charge is impossible to determine without further information.

603. Which of the following places each type of chemical bond in ascending order from weakest to strongest?

(A) hydrogen bonds, ionic bonds, London dispersion bonds, dipole-dipole bonds

(B) dipole-dipole bonds, hydrogen bonds, ionic bonds, London dispersion bonds

(C) London dispersion bonds, dipole-dipole bonds, hydrogen bonds, ionic bonds

(D) ionic bonds, London dispersion bonds, dipole-dipole bonds, hydrogen bonds

604. Which of the following is NOT a unit of weight or mass?

(A) ton

(B) gram

(C) kilowatt

(D) ounce

Use the following information for Questions 605 through 608.

A pharmaceutical company was testing out a new drug that was intended to lower blood pressure in diabetic patients. Two groups of volunteers were assembled. Group 1 consisted of 200 men, whereas Group 2 consisted of 200 women. All of the trial's participants were diabetics between the ages of 20 and 50 with similar lifestyles, diet, and general health. Group 2 was given the trial drug, while Group 1 was given a sugar pill as a placebo (fake pill).

605. Which of the following is true about the experimental drug trial?

(A) Both groups were control groups.

(B) Both groups were experimental groups.

(C) Group 2 was the experimental group, and Group 1 was the control group.

(D) Group 1 was the experimental group, and Group 2 was the control group.

606. If the results of the experiment showed no change in the blood pressure for the members of either group, what conclusion can be made?

(A) The drug does not lower blood pressure in either men or women.

(B) The drug does not lower blood pressure in men.

(C) The drug does not lower blood pressure in women.

(D) The drug may lower blood pressure in men.

607. Which of the following could lead to an error in this experiment?

(A) One of the groups was not given any real medication.

(B) All of the participants had diabetes.

(C) There were too many participants in each group.

(D) The members of the experimental group and the control group were not similar enough.

608. How could the design of the experiment be improved to eliminate this potential source of error?

(A) Give the members of both groups the medication.

(B) Choose only participants who do not have diabetes.

(C) Reduce the number of participants in each group to 20 each.

(D) Swap 100 of the males from Group 1 with 100 of the females from Group 2.

Use the following information to for Questions 609 through 611.

High levels of dissolved carbon dioxide can increase the acidity of water and potentially harm the marine life living there. Scientists conducted an experiment to see whether increased acidity affects hearing in fish. One hundred fertilized eggs from the same parent fish were placed in three separate tanks of water. Tank A contained water with the usual atmospheric pressure of carbon dioxide (400 microatmospheres). The carbon dioxide pressure levels in Tanks B and C were 800 microatmospheres and 1,200 micro atmospheres, respectively. Once the fish reached maturity, underwater speakers placed at one end of each tank played the sounds of the fish's natural predators (these sounds could be heard only when the fish were near the speaker). The positions of the fish in each tank were recorded throughout the experiment. It was found that the fish raised in elevated carbon dioxide levels did not avoid the sound of the predators. However, the fish raised in regular carbon dioxide levels did avoid the end of the tank that had the speaker.

609. Scientists inferred that the fish raised in elevated carbon dioxide levels suffered from a loss of hearing. What evidence suggests this?

(A) High levels of dissolved carbon dioxide can increase the acidity of water and potentially harm the marine life living there.

(B) The positions of the fish in each tank were recorded throughout the experiment.

(C) One hundred fertilized eggs from the same parent fish were placed in three separate tanks of water.

(D) It was found that the fish raised in elevated carbon dioxide levels did not avoid the sound of the predators.

610. Which of the following statements is the best hypothesis for this experiment?

(A) An increase in ocean acidity causes a decrease in predator avoidance in fish.

(B) Fish lose their hearing when greenhouse gases are dissolved in the ocean.

(C) Increasing ocean acidity impedes the transfer of sound through the water.

(D) Fish hearing improves with increasing ocean acidity.

611. Which of the following is a true statement?

(A) The independent variable of the experiment was the temperature of the water in each tank, and the dependent variable was the hearing ability of the fish.

(B) The independent variable of the experiment was the carbon dioxide level in each tank, and the dependent variable was the position of the fish in the tank.

(C) The independent variable of the experiment was hearing ability of the fish in each tank, and the dependent variable was the position of the fish in the tank.

(D) The independent variable of the experiment was the position of the fish in the tank, and the dependent variable was the carbon dioxide level in each tank.

Use the following equation to answer Questions 612 through 615.

$$C_6H_{12}O_6 + 6O_2 \rightarrow 6CO_2 + 6H_2O + \text{energy}$$

612. Which is the name of the compound whose formula is $C_6H_{12}O_6$?

(A) chlorophyll

(B) propane gas

(C) glucose

(D) cellulose

613. Which is the name of the compound whose formula is H_2O?

(A) hydrogen peroxide

(B) water

(C) oxygen dihydride

(D) glucose

614. Which is the name of the compound whose formula is CO_2?

(A) carbon

(B) carbon monoxide

(C) carbon dioxide

(D) glucose

615. Which reaction is shown by the earlier equation?

(A) photosynthesis

(B) anaerobic respiration

(C) aerobic respiration

(D) combustion of fossil fuel

616. Select the chemical equation that is NOT correctly balanced.

(A) $2Mg + 2Cl_2 \rightarrow 2MgCl_2$

(B) $CH_4 + 2O_2 \rightarrow 2H_2O + CO_2$

(C) $2Al + 3O_2 \rightarrow 2Al_2O_3$

(D) $2Ca + O_2 \rightarrow 2CaO$

617. According to the best scientific estimates, approximately how old is the universe?

(A) 15 thousand years old

(B) 15 million years old

(C) 15 billion years old

(D) 15 trillion years old

Use the following information for Questions 618 through 620.

White light consists of seven colors: red, orange, yellow, green, blue, indigo, and violet. When white light shines upon an object, some colors are reflected and some are absorbed. The color of the object is determined by the colors that are reflected back.

618. Which of the following statements is true?

(A) A black shirt reflects all colors except black, which is absorbed.

(B) A black shirt absorbs all colors except black, which is reflected back.

(C) A blue shirt reflects blue light.

(D) A red shirt reflects all colors except red light, which is absorbed.

619. On a hot, sunny day, why does wearing a white shirt keep you cooler than wearing a black shirt made from the same material?

(A) The material of the black shirt is thicker and makes the person feel hotter.

(B) The black shirt absorbs more of the sun's energy, helping the person to feel cooler.

(C) The white shirt reflects more of the sun's energy, helping the person to stay cooler.

(D) Only "cool" people wear white shirts.

620. Compared to red light, blue light has

(A) a higher frequency and a shorter wavelength and carries more energy

(B) a lower frequency and a longer wavelength and carries more energy

(C) a lower frequency and a longer wavelength and carries less energy

(D) a higher frequency and a shorter wavelength and carries less energy

621. Which method can be used to determine whether two sisters are identical twins?

(A) Check to see whether their blood glucose levels are identical.

(B) Compare their physical appearances to see whether they look alike.

(C) Check their family history.

(D) Do a DNA analysis.

622. Sammy was boiling some brine (seawater) but forgot that he left the heat on. When he returned to the pan 40 minutes later, he noticed a white residue left at the bottom of the pan.

Which of the following best explains the white residue?

(A) The metal pan rusted due to the presence of the water.

(B) The water evaporated, leaving salt behind.

(C) The water burned and left ashes behind.

(D) The pan must have been dirty before Sammy put the brine in.

Use the following information for Questions 623 through 626.

Angela steps onto an elevator on the 40th floor of a New York City skyscraper. She stands on a scale that she brought with her to measure her weight. She then presses the button for the ground floor, and the elevator begins to accelerate downward until it reaches a constant speed of 6 m/s. Shortly before the elevator reaches the ground floor, it begins to decelerate; its speed is zero as it reaches the ground floor.

623. In which direction is the unbalanced force acting as the elevator begins to accelerate downward?

(A) downward

(B) upward

(C) toward the entrance of the elevator

(D) There is no unbalanced force.

624. In which direction is the unbalanced force acting during the part of the trip where the elevator is traveling at 6 m/s?

(A) downward

(B) upward

(C) toward the entrance of the elevator

(D) There is no unbalanced force.

625. As the elevator is accelerating downward, the reading of Angela's weight according to the scale will be

(A) equal to her actual weight.

(B) less to her actual weight.

(C) more than her actual weight.

(D) possibly more or possibly less than her actual weight.

626. If Angela usually weighs 750 N, what will the reading on the scale be during the part of the trip when the elevator is traveling down at 6 m/s?

____

627. Which of the following is an example of an organism?

(A) river

(B) mountain

(C) tree

(D) sunlight

628. The acceleration due to gravity on the moon is much smaller than it is on Earth. There is also no air resistance on the moon (because there is no air on the moon).

If an astronaut hits a golf ball on the moon, how will the ball's path differ compared to its path if the ball had been hit here on Earth?

(A) the ball on the moon would travel farther and reach a greater height

(B) the ball on the Earth would travel farther and reach a greater height

(C) the ball on the moon would travel farther but would not go as high

(D) the ball on the Earth would travel farther but would not go as high

Use the following information for Questions 629 through 632.

This graph shows an experiment in which a block of ice at −20 degrees Celsius was heated continuously until it melted and turned to water and then eventually turned into steam.

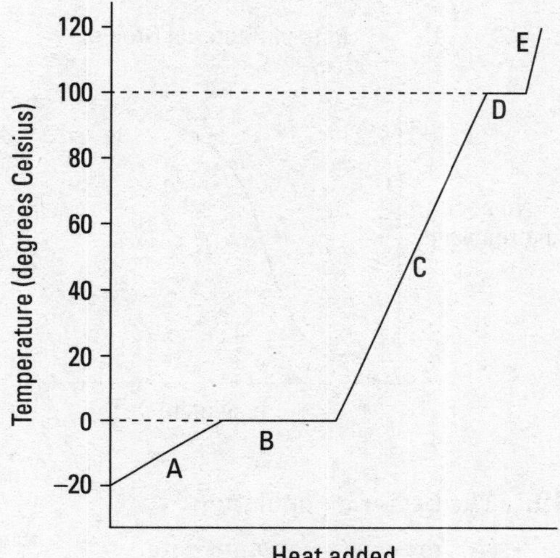

629. Why did the temperature remain constant during the period marked by the letter B on the graph?

(A) The heat had been switched off during this time.

(B) The ice was melting and was using the heat to break the bonds between its molecules.

(C) All of the heat was escaping into the surroundings.

(D) The water was boiling and using the heat to break the remaining bonds between its molecules.

630. What was happening during the period marked with the letter D on the graph?

(A) The ice was melting.

(B) The water was freezing, turning back into ice.

(C) The water was boiling.

(D) The steam was condensing, turning back to water.

631. Which letter represents the part of the experiment in which the entire sample was in the liquid phase?

(A) A

(B) B

(C) C

(D) D

632. Compared to either a liquid or a solid, a typical gas has

(A) a higher density and contains molecules that are closer together.

(B) a higher density and contains molecules that are father apart.

(C) a lower density and contains molecules that are father apart.

(D) a lower density and contains molecules that are closer together.

633. Which of the following explains why, every fourth year, we have a leap year that has 366 days rather than the usual 365 days?

(A) An extra day is added so that people born on February 29 can celebrate their birthday every four years.

(B) An extra day is added to make February more interesting because February is usually the most boring month of the year.

(C) An extra day is added to keep the calendars accurate because the moon actually takes 365.25 days to orbit the Earth.

(D) An extra day is added to keep the calendars accurate because the Earth actually takes 365.25 days to orbit the sun.

634. Jim likes to make fruit jelly. He uses a pressure cooker as part of the process. If he follows the correct procedure, the jelly will be properly sterilized and will be good to eat at a later date.

Why does Jim use the pressure cooker?

(A) to prevent unpleasant odors

(B) to kill bacteria

(C) to enhance the flavor of the jelly

(D) to preserve the color of the jelly

635. What is the force that keeps a roller coaster moving in a circular path when the track makes a vertical circular loop?

(A) the force due to gravity

(B) the magnetic force of attraction between the roller coaster and the track

(C) centripetal force

(D) electrostatic force between the roller coaster and the track

636. Which of the following is found in the nucleus of a hydrogen atom?

(A) proton

(B) neutron

(C) electron

(D) positron

637. Which of the following systems includes the plants and animals of Earth?

(A) lithosphere

(B) biosphere

(C) hydrosphere

(D) atmosphere

638. Which of the following is a simple machine?

(A) airplane

(B) tiger

(C) pulley

(D) computer

Use the following information for Questions 639 and 640.

Jamel cultures some bacteria on a petri dish to study the rate of its growth. He observes the bacteria under a microscope at regular intervals and records the results in the following graph.

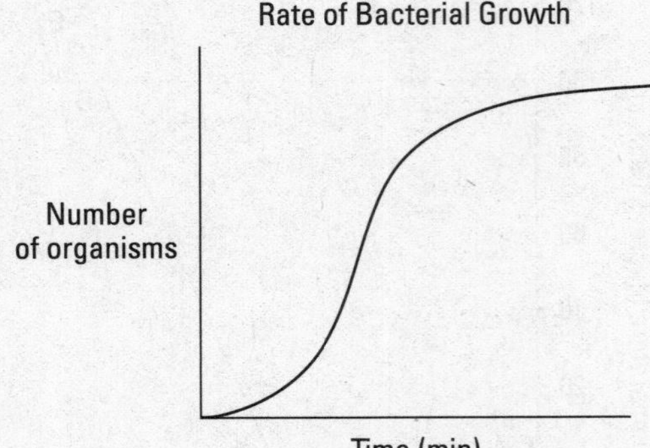

639. The bacteria population

(A) grew at a constant rate.

(B) started small, then increased exponentially.

(C) started at zero, then increased rapidly before it became constant.

(D) started small, then increased rapidly before it became constant.

640. What is a reasonable explanation for why the bacteria population did not continue to grow exponentially?

(A) The population had reached the environment's carrying capacity.

(B) Predators were killing the bacteria.

(C) There were too many nutrients available on the petri dish.

(D) The bacteria's offspring had mutated into a different organism.

641. The following table shows the pH of several substances.

Substance	pH
Water	7
Vinegar	2
Baking soda	8
Lime juice	3

Which of the substances is/are acidic?

(A) water

(B) baking soda

(C) vinegar and baking soda

(D) lime juice and vinegar

Use the following information for Questions 642 through 645.

The following graph shows how the solubility of three different substances in water varies as the temperature of the water varies. Substances A and B are gases. Substance C is a solid.

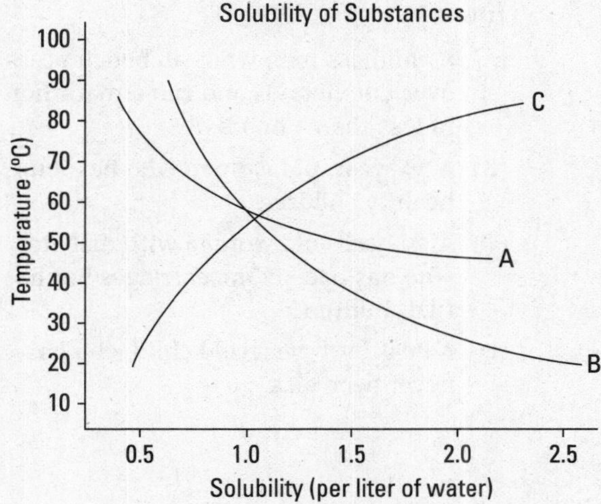

642. What is the solubility of substance B at 20 degrees Celsius?

(A) 0.5 grams per liter

(B) 1.0 grams per liter

(C) 1.5 grams per liter

(D) 2.0 grams per liter

643. Based upon the graph, as the temperature of the water increases, the solubility of

(A) both gases and solids appears to increase.

(B) both gases and solids appears to decrease.

(C) gases appears to increase, but the solubility of solids appears to decrease.

(D) gases appears to decrease, but the solubility of solids appears to increase.

644. If you place a cold glass of water on your bedside table before going to sleep on a warm night, why do you see small bubbles on the inside of the glass when you wake up the next morning? Write a sentence or two to explain this phenomenon with reference to the graph.

____

____

____

645. Which of the following statements is supported by the information given in the graph?

(A) Most gases dissolve at the same rate in water.

(B) The temperature of the water appears to have a large effect on the solubility of some substances.

(C) Pressure has no effect on the solubility of most substances in water.

(D) Water is the best solvent for dissolving any substance.

646. A parasite is an organism that relies on another organism, called the *host*, to survive. The parasite always causes harm to the host organism.

Which of the following is an example of a parasite?

(A) hummingbirds that drink nectar from flowers and spread the pollen from one flower to another

(B) natural bacteria in the human intestines that produce vitamin K

(C) a dog that relies on its owner for food and shelter

(D) a hookworm that lives in the intestines of a human and drinks blood, depriving the human of nutrients

Use the following information for Questions 647 through 649.

During a chemical reaction, the reactants are changed into the products. The following graph shows the potential energy stored in the chemical bonds at various stages of the reaction.

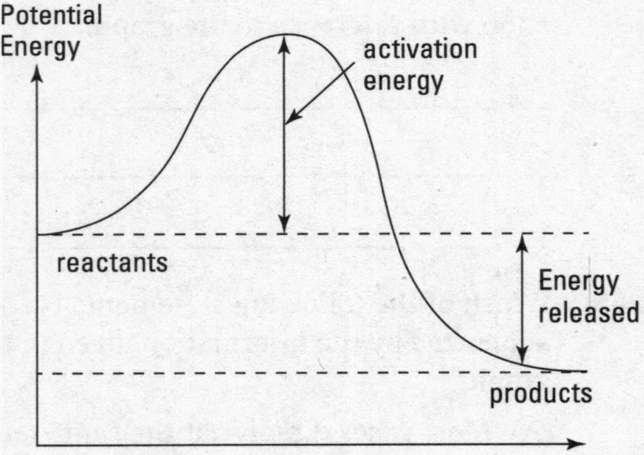

647. Which of the following statements correctly interprets the graph?

(A) The kinetic energy is initially high.

(B) The amount of potential energy drops midway through the reaction.

(C) The products have less potential energy than the reactants.

(D) The products have more potential energy than the reactants.

648. What type of reaction is this?

(A) endothermic reaction

(B) exothermic reaction

(C) fission reaction

(D) fusion reaction

649. How does a catalyst speed up the reaction?

(A) It decreases the activation energy, making it easier for the reactants to turn into products.

(B) It increases the activation energy, making it harder for the reactants to turn into products.

(C) It increases the activation energy, making it easier for the products to turn back into reactants.

(D) It makes the reaction go backward.

650. Evolutionary fitness is determined by how much an individual contributes to the gene pool of the next generation. The more living offspring an individual produces, the fitter that individual is. According to this definition, which of the following individuals is currently the fittest?

(A) A childless man who can bench press over 400 pounds and run a marathon in less than 3 hours.

(B) A 29-year-old woman who has four healthy children.

(C) A 59-year-old woman with diabetes who has had six miscarriages but has five children.

(D) A healthy 5-year-old child who has never been sick.

651. Sometimes, as different species evolve, they adapt in similar ways to their environment. This occasionally results in different animals developing different body parts that perform the same function, even though they may look very different from each other. These body parts are known as *analogous structures.*

Which of the following are analogous structures?

(A) the hive of a bee colony and the ant hill of an ant colony

(B) the wing of an eagle and the wing of a bee

(C) the foot of a baby and the foot of an adult

(D) the tail of a fish and the stomach of a cow

652. The following table shows the typical composition of human blood.

Component	Percentage
Water	52%
Red blood cells	42%
Vitamins and nutrients	3%
White blood cells	2%
Dissolved gases	1%

What percentage of human blood consists of cells?

(A) 2%

(B) 42%

(C) 44%

(D) 100%

653. When a young bird is born, it learns to recognize its parent, which is usually the first object that the baby bird sees when it first opens its eyes. However, during this critical phase of the young bird's development, if the baby is exposed to a different object (other than its real parent), it will learn to recognize this object as its mother. This type of learned behavior during this critical period of the bird's development is called *imprinting.*

Which of the following is an example of imprinting?

(A) A monkey learns to use a stick as a tool to get ants out of an anthill.

(B) A duck learns to wait by the side of the pond during lunchtime so it can eat the scraps from people's sandwiches.

(C) A 3-year-old dog is given a chew toy that it now carries with it everywhere it goes.

(D) A newly hatched goose follows a balloon that it saw shortly after it was born.

654. On a particular island, lions prey on zebras. If a deadly virus that affects only zebras were to spread through the island, what effect would that have on the lion population?

(A) It will increase because the lions will no longer have to compete with the zebras for food.

(B) It will increase because the lions will evolve to resist the deadly virus.

(C) It will decrease because the virus will kill off some of the lions.

(D) It will decrease because there will not be enough food to feed the lions.

655. Bees serve as pollinators for many flowers and play an important role in the ecosystem. Approximately one-third of the human food supply consists of plants that bees pollinate. Recently, the global population of bees began sharply declining. What is the most important consequence of the declining bee population to humans?

(A) Fewer plants will be eaten by the bees, leaving more available for humans to eat.

(B) Fewer plants will be available for humans to eat because plants depend upon the bees to reproduce.

(C) Fewer people will be stung by the bees.

(D) There will be less honey available for humans to eat.

656. If one side of a stemmed plant receives more sunlight than the other side, a growth hormone called auxin will concentrate on the shady side of the stem in order to stimulate more growth there.

As a result, the plant will

(A) bend toward the ground

(B) bend toward the light

(C) grow a thicker stem and increase in girth

(D) produce a flower

657. What type of intramolecular bonding occurs when carbon reacts with hydrogen to make methane gas?

(A) ionic bonding

(B) hydrogen bonding

(C) carbon bonding

(D) covalent bonding

Questions 658 through 661 are based on the following information.

A scientist who is interested in genetics cross-pollinates some foxglove plants to investigate what color the flowers of their offspring will be. She draws a Punnett square to display all the possible combinations of alleles when two hybrid foxglove plants are crossed to help her determine the possible genotypes of the offspring. *P* represents the dominant allele for purple flowers, and *p* represents the recessive allele for white flowers. The genotype of one parent plant is shown on the top of the square, and the other parent's genotype is shown on the left of the square. The genotypes of the offspring are shown in the boxes. The Punnett square is shown here:

	P	p
P	PP	Pp
p	Pp	pp

658. What is the probability that the flowers of an offspring chosen at random will be white?

(A) 0%

(B) 25%

(C) 75%

(D) 100%

659. Which of the following is a true statement?

(A) The genotype of the offspring with white flowers and the genotype of the parent plants are both homogeneous.

(B) The genotype of the offspring with white flowers and the genotype of the parent plants are both heterogeneous.

(C) The genotype of the offspring with white flowers is homogeneous, whereas the parent plants are heterogeneous.

(D) The genotype of the offspring with white flowers is heterogeneous, whereas the parent plants are homogeneous.

660. The scientist now cross-breeds two plants with white flowers. What is the probability that one of their offspring, chosen at random, will have purple flowers?

(A) 0%

(B) 25%

(C) 75%

(D) 100%

661. The scientist now cross-breeds a plant with white flowers with a plant that has purple flowers. What is the probability that the flowers of an offspring chosen at random will be pink?

(A) 0%

(B) 25%

(C) 50%

(D) 100%

662. The Earth's magnetic field is caused by the rotation of the liquid magma around the Earth's iron core. Over the years, changes in this rotation have caused the Earth's magnetic North Pole to shift position from its earliest recorded position in northern Canada to its current position today.

What can you infer from this information?

(A) Earth's magnetic core is shifting toward the plant's surface.

(B) All magnets are made of iron.

(C) Earth's magnetic poles are at different locations than the geographic poles.

(D) A compass will no longer be affected by the Earth's magnetic field.

663. What is the main genetic advantage that sexual reproduction has over asexual reproduction?

(A) Sexual reproduction produces a greater variety of offspring.

(B) Sexual reproduction produces offspring that are genetically identical to each other.

(C) Sexual reproduction results in more offspring per parent.

(D) Sexual reproduction is easier to accomplish.

664. Which of the following would you use to best view the features of the moon's surface?

(A) an electron microscope

(B) a lens with a short focal length

(C) a telescope

(D) the naked eye

Use the following information for Questions 665 through 670.

There were three finalists in a soapbox car race. Contestant 1 built his car out of aluminum, Contestant 2 built his car from steel, and Contestant 3 built his car from wood. Each car was the same size. The contestants all started from rest at the top of a hill that is 20 meters higher than the finish line at the bottom of the hill.

If friction and air resistance are ignored, the conservation of energy states that the loss in potential energy equals the gain in kinetic energy (motion energy).

In order to calculate each contestant's potential energy and gained kinetic energy, the mass of each car, the mass of each driver, and the final velocity reached by each contestant were recorded in this table.

Contestant	Car Mass (kg)	Driver Mass (kg)	Final Velocity (m/s)
Contestant 1	20	40	20
Contestant 2	25	35	15
Contestant 3	15	45	18

The equations for potential energy *(PE)* and kinetic energy *(KE)* are given here:

$$PE = mgh$$

$$KE = \frac{1}{2}mv^2$$

Both potential energy and kinetic energy are measured in joules (J). Use $g = 10\ \text{m/s}^2$ for the acceleration due to gravity.

665. Which material is the heaviest?

(A) wood

(B) steel

(C) aluminum

(D) The materials all weigh the same.

666. Which contestant had the most potential energy at the beginning of the race?

(A) Contestant 1

(B) Contestant 2

(C) Contestant 3

(D) Each contestant began with the same potential energy.

667. Which of the following statements is true?

(A) Contestant 3 has the greatest ratio of car mass to driver mass, and Contestant 2 has the smallest ratio of car mass to driver mass.

(B) Contestant 1 has the greatest ratio of car mass to driver mass, and Contestant 3 has the smallest ratio of car mass to driver mass.

(C) Contestant 2 has the greatest ratio of car mass to driver mass, and Contestant 1 has the smallest ratio of car mass to driver mass.

(D) Contestant 2 has the greatest ratio of car mass to driver mass, and Contestant 3 has the smallest ratio of car mass to driver mass.

668. What is the gained kinetic energy of Contestant 1 at the end of the race?

(A) 60 J

(B) 600 J

(C) 6,000 J

(D) 12,000 J

669. Which of the following is a true statement?

(A) The car driven by Contestant 1 was the most efficient because it converted more of its kinetic energy into potential energy.

(B) The car driven by Contestant 1 was the most efficient because it converted more of its potential energy into kinetic energy.

(C) The car driven by Contestant 2 was the most efficient because it converted more of its kinetic energy into potential energy.

(D) The car driven by Contestant 3 was the most efficient because it converted more of its potential energy into kinetic energy.

670. The conservation of energy states that energy is never created or destroyed; however, some of the contestants in the soapbox car race ended up with less kinetic energy than the potential energy they began with. Write a sentence or two that explains what might have happened to this "missing energy."

____

____

____

671. A scientist measured the life spans of five fruit flies (labeled A to E) and recorded her data in the following table; however, her data for fruit fly E was lost.

Fruit Fly	Life Span (Days)
A	18
B	12
C	17
D	11
E	?

Luckily, she remembered that the mean of the five life spans was 15 days. What must the missing value for the life span of fruit fly E have been? ________

Use the following information for Questions 672 through 677.

The nucleus of an atom consists of protons (which are positively charged) and neutrons (which are neutral). The atomic number of an atom is equal to the number of protons. Each element has a unique atomic number. The sum of the number of protons and neutrons in the nucleus is known as the *atomic mass number.*

Atoms also contain electrons, which are found in energy shells that surround the nucleus of the atom. Because the number of electrons (which are negatively charged) is equal to the number of positively charged protons, the atom has zero charge.

The first energy shell holds a maximum of 2 electrons. The second energy shell can hold a maximum of 8 electrons. The number of electrons found in the outermost shell is known as the number of *valence electrons.* Only the valance electrons are involved in chemical reactions.

The atomic structures of three elements, sodium (Na), hydrogen (H), and fluorine (F), are shown in the following table.

Element	Number of Protons	Number of Neutrons	Number of Electrons
Sodium (Na)	11	12	11
Hydrogen (H)	1	0	1
Fluorine (F)	9	10	9

672. What is the atomic number of fluorine?

(A) 9

(B) 10

(C) 19

(D) 28

673. What is the atomic mass number of sodium?

(A) 11

(B) 22

(C) 23

(D) 34

674. A scientist is trying to determine the identity of an unknown element whose atoms contain 9 protons, 9 electrons, and 12 neutrons. Which of the following correctly determines the element's identity and gives the appropriate reasoning behind the determination?

(A) sodium, because the atom contains 12 neutrons

(B) fluorine, because the atom contains 9 electrons

(C) hydrogen, because the atom contains the same number of electrons and protons

(D) fluorine, because the atom contains 9 protons

675. Which element has the same value for its atomic number and atomic mass number?

(A) sodium

(B) hydrogen

(C) fluorine

(D) No element has the same value for its atomic number and atomic mass number.

676. Which of the following is a true statement?

(A) Sodium contains 1 valence electron, whereas fluorine contains 7 valence electrons.

(B) Sodium contains 11 valence electrons, whereas fluorine contains 9 valence electrons.

(C) Sodium contains 1 valence electron, whereas fluorine contains 9 valence electrons.

(D) Sodium contains 9 valence electrons, whereas fluorine contains 7 valence electrons.

677. What will happen if a sodium atom loses an electron?

(A) Its charge would become negative.

(B) Its charge would become positive.

(C) Its charge would remain neutral.

(D) The charge is impossible to determine without further information.

678. A comet is a small celestial body made of ice and dust that orbits the sun in an elliptical or oval path. Because the path is not perfectly circular, sometimes the comet is closer to the sun, and sometimes it is farther away from the sun. As the comet approaches the sun, the comet begins to warm up, and some of the dust and ice begins to stream away, forming the long, distinctive comet tail. Some scientists consider comets to be the most interesting of the celestial bodies.

Based on this information, which of the following statements is an opinion rather than a fact?

(A) The tail of a comet is made of ice and dust.

(B) Comets orbit around the sun in elliptical paths.

(C) Comets are much more interesting than other celestial bodies.

(D) Comets are small celestial bodies made of ice and dust.

679. Earthworms help to break down the bodies of dead organisms such as leaves, returning nutrients to the soil in the process.

Based on this information, what role do earthworms play in the food chain?

(A) They are producers.

(B) They are primary consumers.

(C) They are tertiary consumers.

(D) They are decomposers.

680. The hydrosphere consists of all Earth's water, including the oceans, lakes, and rivers. The atmosphere consists of all Earth's air, such as the nitrogen and oxygen that surround the planet.

Which of the following scientists would be most likely to apply his or her knowledge of the hydrosphere and the atmosphere while at work?

(A) an astronaut who is preparing to live on the moon for 3 months

(B) a zoologist who is studying hereditary patterns of primates

(C) a meteorologist who is studying weather patterns to predict the weather

(D) a chemist who is studying the chemical reaction of water and fluorine gas in the laboratory

681. Which of the following contains true statements?

(A) The planet nearest the sun is called Jupiter. The planet that is the third closest to the sun is called Earth. The largest planet in the solar system is called Mercury.

(B) The planet nearest the sun is called Mercury. The planet that is the third closest to the sun is called Jupiter. The largest planet in the solar system is called Earth.

(C) The planet nearest the sun is called Mercury. The planet that is the third closest to the sun is called Earth. The largest planet in the solar system is called Jupiter.

(D) The planet nearest the sun is called Mercury. The planet that is the third closest to the sun is called Earth. The largest planet in the solar system is called Saturn.

682. Which of the following places the events in the correct order (from the earliest to the most recent)?

(A) *Homo sapiens* (modern humans) first appeared > extinction of the dinosaurs > life first appeared on Earth > Big Bang > formation of planet Earth

(B) formation of planet Earth > Big Bang > life first appeared on Earth > extinction of the dinosaurs > *Homo sapiens* (modern humans) first appeared

(C) Big Bang > formation of planet Earth > life first appeared on Earth > *Homo sapiens* (modern humans) first appeared > extinction of the dinosaurs

(D) Big Bang > formation of planet Earth > life first appeared on Earth > extinction of the dinosaurs > *Homo sapiens* (modern humans) first appeared

Use the following information for Questions 683 through 685.

The nitrogen cycle describes the circulation and transformation of nitrogen between living things and the environment as it moves through Earth's different systems. The nitrogen cycle is shown in the following figure.

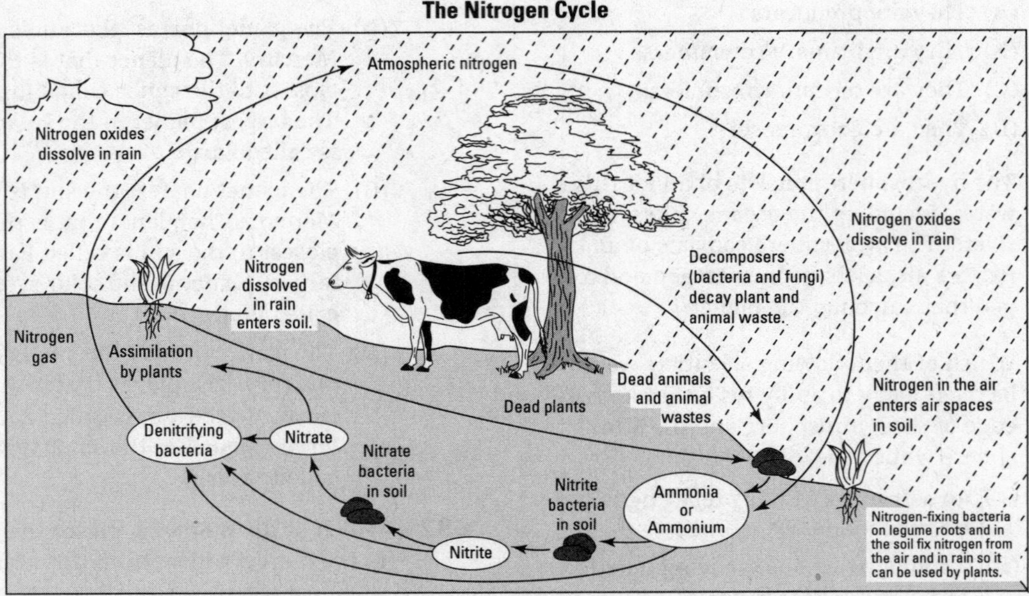

683. Nitrogen accounts for approximately what percent of the air in the atmosphere?

(A) 1%

(B) 21%

(C) 57%

(D) 78%

684. Many farmers who grow organic produce are against the use of artificial fertilizers that contain synthetic nitrogen-containing compounds. Which of the following is an alternative method that an organic famer might use to increase the nitrogen content of the soil?

(A) use compost made from animal and plant waste matter

(B) place the artificial fertilizer in water-tight containers so none of it escapes to the soil

(C) switch to crops that require more nitrogen

(D) switch to crops that require more sodium

685. When a farmer has grown corn in the same field for several years, the nitrogen content of the soil can become severely depleted. Nitrogen is necessary for healthy plant growth, so in order to combat this problem, a farmer who grows organic produce may also grow legumes such as soybeans in the same field, next to the corn. How does the use of legumes help the farmer solve the problem?

(A) Legumes contain denitrifying bacteria that help release nitrogen back into the atmosphere.

(B) Legumes contain nitrogen-fixing bacteria that return nitrogen to the soil.

(C) The money from selling legumes can be used to buy artificial fertilizers.

(D) Cows prefer the taste of the legumes, so the cows will eat the legumes instead of the crop the farmer wants to sell.

Use the following information for Questions 686 through 689.

In 1911, a British scientist called Ernest Rutherford directed a series of experiments that greatly increased our understanding of atomic structure. During the experiment, his students fired positively charged alpha particles (helium nuclei, each of which contains two protons and two neutrons) at an extremely thin sheet of gold. (Gold is a very malleable metal that can be beaten into a foil that's only a few atoms thick.) Rutherford expected all the alpha particles to go through the gold foil with minimal deflection, but to his surprise, a few alpha particles bounced straight back. Rutherford concluded that atoms consisted mostly of empty space with a dense nucleus at the center and electrons orbiting the nucleus.

686. What charge does an alpha particle have?

(A) −2

(B) 0

(C) +2

(D) +4

687. What charge does a gold nucleus have?

(A) negative

(B) positive

(C) neutral

(D) It is impossible to determine based on the information given.

688. Why did Rutherford prefer gold rather than a different metal such as lead?

(A) Rutherford wanted to impress the other scientists by showing off some of his bling.

(B) Gold was very cheap in 1911 and easy to obtain.

(C) Gold is more malleable and can be beaten into a foil that is only a few atoms thick, which reduces the chance of multiple collisions with the alpha particles.

(D) Gold is the only atom that consists mainly of empty space.

689. Which of the following statements provides evidence that an atom has a nucleus that contains most of the atom's mass and all of its positive charge?

(A) Most of the alpha particles passed straight through the gold foil.

(B) Some alpha particles bounced straight back off the gold foil.

(C) Gold is very expensive, so the gold sheet was very thin.

(D) Alpha particles are very small.

690. Which of the following physical changes involves the release of heat?

(A) evaporating and condensing

(B) melting and boiling

(C) freezing and condensing

(D) subliming and boiling

691. When Alex works out at the gym, he sometimes lifts weights. As he lifts the barbell to its highest point, several energy transitions take place. Which of the following lists these energy transitions in the correct order?

(A) chemical energy to gravitational potential energy to kinetic energy

(B) chemical energy to kinetic energy to gravitational potential energy

(C) kinetic energy to gravitational potential energy to chemical energy

(D) gravitational potential energy to chemical energy to kinetic energy

692. Why is copper used for electrical wiring in electric circuits?

(A) Copper is a good insulator.

(B) Copper is a good conductor.

(C) Copper is easily magnetized.

(D) Copper has a low melting point.

693. If the south poles of two strong magnets are placed close together on a smooth table, what will happen?

(A) The magnets will move together because the two south poles will attract each other.

(B) The magnets will move apart because the two south poles will attract each other.

(C) The magnets will move together because the two south poles will repel each other.

(D) The magnets will move apart because the two south poles will repel each other.

694. Ohm's law tells you that the electric current is inversely proportional to the resistance within the circuit if the voltage remains constant.

What will happen to the current in a circuit with a fixed voltage if the resistance of a circuit is suddenly doubled?

(A) The current will be halved.

(B) The current will stay the same.

(C) The current will be doubled.

(D) The current will change direction.

Use the following information for Questions 695 and 696.

Earth's atmosphere can be divided into several layers, including the troposphere, the stratosphere, the mesosphere and ionosphere, and the thermosphere. The temperature and altitude of each layer is listed in the following table.

Layer	Altitude	Temperature (Degrees Fahrenheit)
Troposphere	0 to 5 miles	Average 60 degrees
Stratosphere	6 to 30 miles	–75 to 32 degrees
Mesosphere and ionosphere	31 to 50 miles	–212 to 32 degrees
Thermosphere	51 to 43 miles	Thousands of degrees

695. In which layer of the atmosphere do most humans live?

(A) troposphere

(B) stratosphere

(C) mesosphere and ionosphere

(D) thermosphere

696. Which layer has the coldest average temperature?

(A) troposphere
(B) stratosphere
(C) mesosphere and ionosphere
(D) thermosphere

Use the following information for answer Questions 697 through 701.

The solar system consists of the sun, eight planets and their moons, asteroids, and comets. Because the sun is much bigger than any of the planets (it contains more than 99% of the mass of the solar system!), the planets orbit the sun. The time taken for one complete revolution around the sun determines how long one year is on that planet. In addition to orbiting the sun, the planets also rotate around their own axes. The time a planet takes to complete one rotation about its axis determines the length of one day on the planet. This table shows some detail regarding the movement of the planets in the solar system.

Planet	Distance from Sun	Number of Moons	Rotation Period (Day)	Revolution Period (Year)
Mercury	36 million miles	0	59 Earth days	88 Earth days
Venus	67 million miles	0	243 Earth days	225 Earth days
Earth	93 million miles	1	23 hours, 56 minutes, 4.1 seconds	365 days, 5 hours, 48 minutes, 46 seconds
Mars	142 million miles	2	24 hours, 37 minutes	687 Earth days
Jupiter	484 million miles	50	9 hours, 51 minutes	11.86 Earth years
Saturn	0.9 billion miles	53	10 hours, 14 minutes	29.46 Earth years
Uranus	1.8 billion miles	27	17 hours, 12 minutes	84 Earth years
Neptune	2.8 billion miles	13	16 hours, 7 minutes	165 Earth years

697. Which planet is farthest from the sun?

(A) Mercury
(B) Venus
(C) Mars
(D) Neptune

698. Which planet is closest to Earth?

(A) Venus
(B) Mars
(C) Saturn
(D) Uranus

699. A day on which planet takes approximately the same amount of time as a day on Earth?

____

700. According to the table and the given information, which of the following is a true statement?

(A) The planet with the shortest day is Mars, and the planet with the longest year is Jupiter.

(B) The planet with the shortest day is Mercury, and the planet with the longest year is Earth.

(C) The planet with the shortest day is Jupiter, and the planet with the longest year is Neptune.

(D) The planet with the shortest day is Earth, and the planet with the longest year is Saturn.

701. According to the table and the given information, which of the following is a true statement?

(A) A day on Venus takes longer than a year on Venus.

(B) All planets have at least one moon.

(C) All planets take approximately one Earth year to orbit the sun.

(D) The sum of the masses of all of the planets is greater than the mass of the sun.

Use the following information for Questions 702 and 703.

This figure shows how the two leading causes of death have changed between 1950 and 2014.

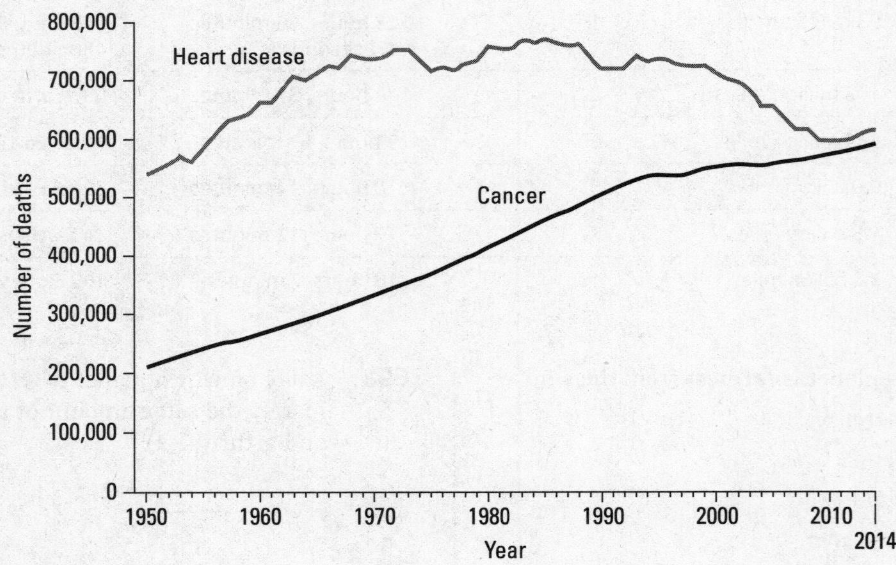

702. According to the figure and the given information, which of the following is a true statement?

(A) Cancer is now the leading cause of death.

(B) The number of deaths due to heart disease has more than doubled since 1950.

(C) Although heart disease is still the leading cause of death, the number of deaths due to cancer has increased steadily since 1950.

(D) The number of deaths via cancer was approximately the same in 2014 as it was in 1960.

703. By approximately what percent did the number of deaths due to cancer increase since 1950?

(A) 0%

(B) 50%

(C) 100%

(D) 200%

Use the following information for Questions 704 through 707.

Metabolism describes the rate of the chemical reactions that take place within the body of an organism. An example of a metabolic process is breaking down food for the energy needs of the organism. The metabolic rate of each organism varies from species to species. Several animals' relative metabolic rates compared to body weight are shown in the figure:

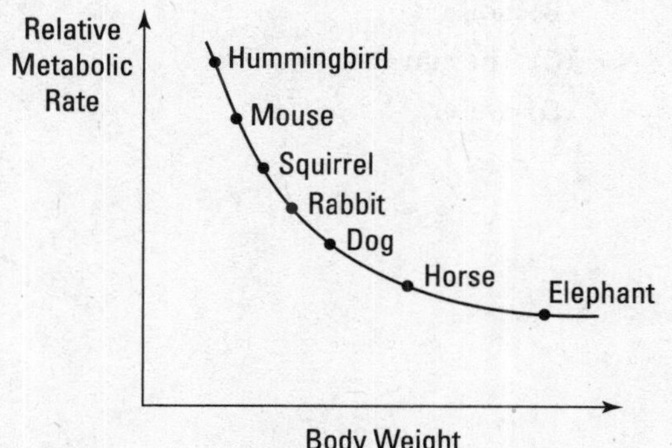

704. Based on the given information, which organism has the fastest metabolism?

(A) hummingbird

(B) squirrel

(C) dog

(D) elephant

705. Calculating the median metabolic rate gives scientists a way to compare the basal or baseline metabolic rate of each species. Based on the given information, which organism has the median body weight?

(A) hummingbird

(B) squirrel

(C) rabbit

(D) horse

706. Which of the following is a true statement?

(A) There is no relationship between the animal's weight and its metabolic rate.

(B) The faster the metabolic rate, the more the animal weighs, whereas the slower its metabolic rate, the less the animal weighs.

(C) The more the animal weighs, the slower its metabolic rate, whereas the less the animal weighs, the faster its metabolic rate.

(D) The more the animal weighs, the faster its metabolic rate, whereas the less the animal weighs, the slower its metabolic rate.

707. A scientist calculated the average metabolic rate of the seven types of animals shown on the graph. He then removed the data related to the elephant and calculated the new average. How does the new average compare to the old average?

(A) The new average is greater than the old average.

(B) The new average is less than the old average.

(C) The new average is the same as the old average.

(D) It is impossible to tell unless we know the weight of the elephant.

Use the following information to help answer Questions 708 through 711.

The complex pattern of how energy flows from organism to organism through an ecosystem is called a food web. Plants are called producers because they produce their own food using the energy of the sun. Other organisms that cannot produce their own food are called consumers because they rely on eating plants or other animals in order to achieve their energy requirements. The arrows in a food chain or food web go in the direction of the energy flow or, rather, to the organism that is doing the eating. An example of a food web is shown here.

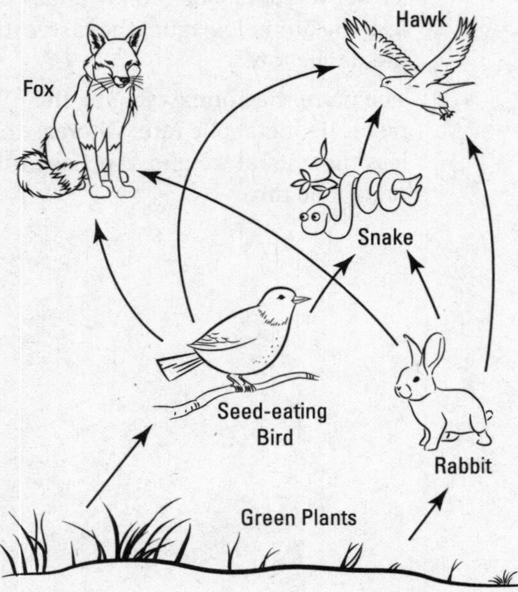

708. Choose the correct words to correctly complete the sentence:

Grass and plants are ____________, whereas rabbits are ____________.

(A) primary consumers, tertiary consumers

(B) producers, tertiary consumers

(C) primary consumers, carnivores

(D) producers, primary consumers

709. If a virus were to suddenly wipe out most of the fox population, what effect would this have on the food web?

(A) The population of rabbits and birds would decrease.

(B) The population of rabbits and birds would increase.

(C) The hawks and snakes would decrease.

(D) The amount of grass and plants would increase.

710. Approximately what percentage of the energy stored in a plant is transferred to the biomass (flesh) of a primary consumer when the plant is eaten?

(A) 100%

(B) 50%

(C) 10%

(D) 1%

711. What is the ultimate source of energy of a food web?

(A) plants

(B) soil

(C) the sun

(D) water

712. What does the theory of plate tectonics help explain?

(A) changes in the atmosphere

(B) changes in the mantle

(C) changes in the Earth's crust

(D) changes in the Earth's core

713. Which of the following is a theory rather than a fact about tectonic plates?

(A) Earthquakes often occur along the boundaries of tectonic plates.

(B) About 200 million years ago, all the continents were joined in a single landmass known as Pangaea.

(C) The San Andreas fault lies on the boundary between the Pacific and North American plates.

(D) The continents of North America and Europe are slowly drifting apart.

714. When a gas is released into a container, it tends to expand until it fills the entire container. This process is known as diffusion. Which of the following shows an example of the diffusion of a gas?

(A) When electricity flows through a resister, the resister gets warm.

(B) When a bar of iron is heated, it expands.

(C) When oil and water are placed in the same sealed container and shaken, the oil eventually moves to the top, forming a separate layer from the water.

(D) A student sitting at the back of class breaks wind. The unpleasant odor quickly spreads through the room, forcing the teacher to open all the windows.

Use the following information for Questions 715 through 718.

Blood consists of a liquid called plasma with red and white blood cells and proteins suspended in it. Red blood cells carry oxygen from the lungs to all the cells of the body, where it is used during cellular respiration. White blood cells produce antibodies that help protect the body from infectious diseases. The plasma consists mainly of water and surrounds the blood cells. It helps maintain blood pressure and body temperature and helps transport nutrients around the body and remove waste products. The percentage of each major component of blood is shown in the table.

Blood Component	Percentage
Plasma	55%
Red blood cells	44%
White blood cells	1%
Platelets	<1%

715. What is the main function of the white blood cells?

(A) They carry oxygen to all the cells of the body, where it is used during cellular respiration.

(B) They help transport nutrients around the body.

(C) They produce antibodies that help protect the body from infectious diseases.

(D) They help remove waste products from the body

716. What is the main function of the red blood cells?

(A) They carry oxygen to all the cells of the body, where it is used during photosynthesis.

(B) They carry oxygen to all the cells of the body, where it is used during cellular respiration.

(C) They produce antibodies that help protect the body from infectious diseases.

(D) They make the blood appear red.

717. According to the information in the passage, all of the following statements are true statements regarding plasma EXCEPT

(A) plasma consists mainly of water.

(B) plasma helps maintain blood pressure.

(C) plasma helps maintain body temperature.

(D) plasma carries dissolved oxygen around the body.

718. What percentage of the blood consists of cells?

(A) 1%

(B) 44%

(C) 45%

(D) 100%

Use the following information for Questions 719 through 722.

The nuclei of radioactive elements spontaneously decay into different, more stable daughter elements by emitting radioactive particles. The amount of time needed for half of a sample of radioactive material to decay into its more stable product is called the *half-life.*

This table shows the half-life of several radioactive materials, along with their typical uses.

Radioactive Isotope	Half-life	Typical Uses
Uranium-238	4.5×10^{9} years	Determining the age of Earth's crust
Carbon-14	5,750 years	Determining the age of artifacts
Carbon-11	20 minutes	Biomedical imaging
Americium-241	430 years	Smoke detectors

719. Which of the following is a true statement?

(A) The isotope with the longest half-life is uranium-238, and the isotope with the shortest half-life is carbon-14.

(B) The isotope with the longest half-life is carbon-11, and the isotope with the shortest half-life is uranium-238.

(C) The isotope with the longest half-life is uranium-238, and the isotope with the shortest half-life is Americium-241.

(D) The isotope with the longest half-life is uranium-238, and the isotope with the shortest half-life is carbon-11.

720. What is the most likely reason that carbon-14 is not used for biomedical imaging, whereas carbon-11 is used for this purpose?

(A) The element carbon is deadly to all living creatures.

(B) The half-life of carbon-14 is too short to be used in biomedical imaging.

(C) The half-life of carbon-14 is too long, so the radiation it emits could be harmful to the patient if it remained in the body.

(D) If carbon-14 were used in biomedical imaging, there would not be enough left to use in the carbon dating of artifacts.

721. In what way does the nucleus of an atom of carbon-14 differ from the nucleus of an atom of carbon-11?

(A) Carbon-14 contains 14 protons, whereas carbon-11 contains only 11 protons.

(B) Carbon-14 contains 14 neutrons, whereas carbon-11 contains only 11 neutrons.

(C) Carbon-14 contains 8 protons, whereas carbon-11 contains only 5 protons.

(D) Carbon-14 contains 8 neutrons, whereas carbon-11 contains only 5 neutrons.

722. A biomedical researcher prepared 2 kilograms of carbon-11 and then went out to lunch. How many grams of carbon-11 would remain by the time she returned from lunch an hour later?

(A) 2,000 grams

(B) 1,000 grams

(C) 500 grams

(D) 250 grams

723. The human body system that transports nutrients dissolved in the blood to all the cells of the body is called the

(A) digestive system.

(B) integumentary system.

(C) circulatory system.

(D) muscular system.

724. Which of the following is an example of a chemical change?

(A) A block of ice melts and becomes water.

(B) Steam from a hot shower condenses and forms droplets of water on the shower curtain.

(C) The gunpowder in a cannon explodes, sending a cannonball high into the air.

(D) A block of "dry ice" sublimes to become gaseous carbon dioxide.

Use the following information for Questions 725 through 727.

The record high temperatures were recorded for four major Australian cities this year. This chart compares these temperatures to the previous record high temperatures in each city.

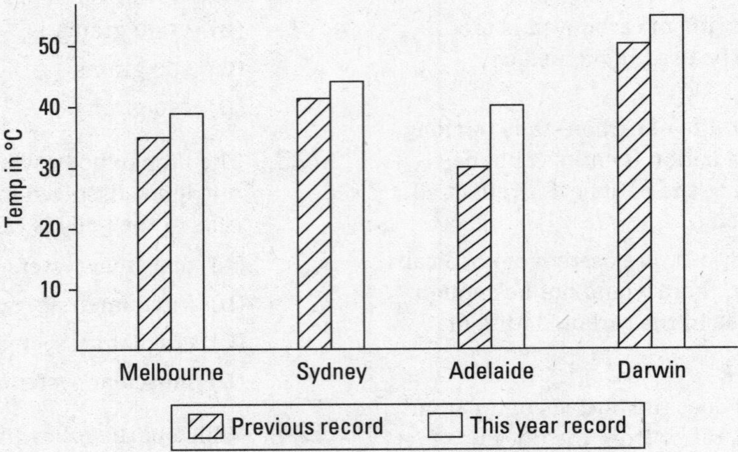

725. Which city experienced the smallest increase in its record temperature?

(A) Melbourne

(B) Sydney

(C) Adelaide

(D) Darwin

726. According to the chart, which of the following statements is true?

(A) Next year's temperatures will be higher than the current record highs.

(B) This year's record temperatures were higher than the previous record temperatures in all four cities.

(C) The record temperature increased by less than 5 degrees in all four cities.

(D) Each of the cities also experienced a major drought this year.

727. By approximately what percentage did Adelaide's record temperature increase this year?

(A) 10%

(B) 25%

(C) 33%

(D) 50%

Use the following information for Questions 728 and 729.

Newton's law of gravitation states that the gravitational force of attraction (F) acting on two objects of mass m_1 and mass m_2 is directly proportional to the product of the masses and inversely proportional to the square of the distance r between them. This relationship can be represented by the following equation:

$$F = \frac{Gm_1m_2}{r^2}$$

where G is the gravitational constant.

728. Which statement is accurate concerning the forces acting on each mass?

(A) A repulsive force acts on each mass, pushing the masses apart.

(B) An attractive force acts on each mass, pushing the masses apart.

(C) A repulsive force acts on each mass, pulling the masses together.

(D) An attractive force acts on each mass, pulling the masses together.

729. Which of the following is a true statement?

(A) Increasing the masses decreases the gravitational force acting on them, whereas increasing the distance decreases the gravitational force acting on the objects.

(B) Increasing the masses increases the gravitational force acting on them, whereas increasing the distance decreases the gravitational force acting on the objects.

(C) Increasing the masses increases the gravitational force acting on them, and increasing the distance increases the gravitational force acting on the objects.

(D) Increasing the masses decreases the gravitational force acting on them, and increasing the distance increases the gravitational force acting on the objects.

730. If the distance between the two objects is doubled, what effect will this have on the gravitational force between them?

(A) The force will be decreased by a factor of 4.

(B) The force will be halved.

(C) The force will be doubled.

(D) The force will be quadrupled.

Chapter 4

Reasoning Through Language Arts

The Reasoning Through Language Arts section of the GED exam lasts 150 minutes and consists of two parts: a reading section and a writing section. This chapter gives you 271 practice questions, including three essays.

The Problems You'll Work On

Language Arts, Reading: The reading comprehension component of the GED consists of 40 questions and contains both fictional and nonfictional passages, which you will need to analyze in order to answer the questions that follow. You will be asked to determine the main idea, the point of view, the meaning of words and phrases, and inferences and claims based on texts that span a range of complexity.

Language Arts, Writing: The writing section is divided into two parts: sentence corrections and an essay. The first part consists of 50 questions and contains passages that are not complete. You have to select the best sentence or completion of a sentence from among the four choices, testing your knowledge of organization, sentence structure, usage, and mechanics.

The second part of the writing section consists of writing an essay about a familiar subject. You will have 45 minutes to plan, write, and revise your essay. The essay topic will require you to present your opinion or explain your views about the assigned topic. Your essay will be scored on the basis of the following features: focused main points, clear organization, specific development of ideas, sentence structure control, and correct punctuation, grammar, word choice, and spelling.

What to Watch Out For

Trap answers include the following:

- Phrasings that seem correct until you read them within the context of the entire sentence
- Misused alternatives to proper phrasing, such improperly using *effect* instead *affect*
- Enticements to rely on your own knowledge or opinion
- Ideas that aren't directly supported by the passage
- Facts that are true but don't answer the question
- Words and phrases that suggest value judgments, such as *too much* or *not enough*
- Terms that leave no room for exception, such as *never* or *all*

Multiple-Choice and Fill-in-the-Blank Questions

Questions 731 through 735 are based on the following passage.

This excerpt is from A Christmas Carol *by Charles Dickens.*

"A merry Christmas, uncle! God save you!" cried a cheerful voice. It was the voice of Scrooge's nephew, who came upon him so quickly that this was the first intimation he had of his approach.

"Bah!" said Scrooge, "Humbug!"

He had so heated himself with rapid walking in the fog and frost, this nephew of Scrooge's that he was all in a glow; his face was ruddy and handsome; his eyes sparkled, and his breath smoked again.

"Christmas a humbug, uncle!" said Scrooge's nephew. "You don't mean that, I am sure?"

"I do," said Scrooge. "Merry Christmas! What right have you to be merry? What reason have you to be merry? You're poor enough."

"Come, then," returned the nephew gaily. "What right have you to be dismal? What reason have you to be morose? You're rich enough."

Scrooge having no better answer ready on the spur of the moment, said, "Bah!" again; and followed it up with "Humbug."

"Don't be cross, uncle!" said the nephew.

"What else can I be," returned the uncle, "when I live in such a world of fools as this? Merry Christmas! Out upon merry Christmas! What's Christmas time to you but a time for paying bills without money; a time for finding yourself a year older, but not an hour richer; a time for balancing your books and having every item in 'em through a round dozen of months presented dead against you? If I could work my will," said Scrooge indignantly, "every idiot who goes about with 'Merry Christmas' on his lips, should be boiled with his own pudding, and buried with a stake of holly through his heart. He should!"

"Uncle!" pleaded the nephew.

"Nephew!" returned the uncle, sternly, "keep Christmas in your own way, and let me keep it in mine."

"Keep it!" repeated Scrooge's nephew. "But you don't keep it."

"Let me leave it alone, then," said Scrooge. "Much good may it do you! Much good it has ever done you!"

"There are many things from which I might have derived good, by which I have not profited, I dare say," returned the nephew. "Christmas among the rest. But I am sure I have always thought of Christmas time, when it has come round—apart from the veneration due to its sacred name and origin, if anything belonging to it can be apart from that—as a good time; a kind, forgiving, charitable, pleasant time; the only time I know of, in the long calendar of the year, when men and women seem by one consent to open their shut-up hearts freely, and to think of people below them as if they really were fellow-passengers to the grave, and not another race of creatures bound on other journeys. And therefore, uncle, though it has never put a scrap of gold or silver in my pocket, I believe that it has done me good, and will do me good; and I say, God bless it!"

The clerk in the tank involuntarily applauded. Becoming immediately sensible of the impropriety, he poked the fire, and extinguished the last frail spark for ever.

"Let me hear another sound from you," said Scrooge, "and you'll keep your Christmas by losing your situation! You're quite a powerful speaker, sir," he added, turning to his nephew. "I wonder you don't go into Parliament."

"Don't be angry, uncle. Come! Dine with us tomorrow." Scrooge said that he would see him—yes, indeed he did. He went the whole length of the expression, and said that he would see him in that extremity first.

"But why?" cried Scrooge's nephew. "Why?"

"Why did you get married?" said Scrooge.

"Because I fell in love."

"Because you fell in love!" growled Scrooge, as if that were the only one thing in the world more ridiculous than a merry Christmas. "Good afternoon!"

"Nay, uncle, but you never came to see me before that happened. Why give it as a reason for not coming now?"

"Good afternoon," said Scrooge.

"I want nothing from you; I ask nothing of you; why cannot we be friends?"

"Good afternoon," said Scrooge.

"I am sorry, with all my heart, to find you so resolute. We have never had any quarrel, to which I have been a party. But I have made the trial in homage to Christmas, and I'll keep my Christmas humour to the last. So A Merry Christmas, uncle!"

"Good afternoon!" said Scrooge.

"And a Happy New Year!"

"Good afternoon!" said Scrooge.

His nephew left the room without an angry word, notwithstanding. He stopped at the outer door to bestow the greetings of the season on the clerk, who, cold as he was, was warmer than Scrooge; for he returned them cordially.

731. Based on the excerpt, what does Scrooge think about Christmas?

(A) He thinks Christmas is the best time of the year.
(B) He hates Christmas.
(C) He likes to spend Christmas with his family.
(D) He likes to celebrate Christmas by eating his favorite humbug candies.

732. Based on the passage, which of the following is an accurate description of Scrooge and his nephew?

(A) Scrooge is miserable and wealthy, whereas Scrooge's nephew is amicable and forgiving.
(B) Scrooge is amicable and forgiving, whereas Scrooge's nephew is miserable and wealthy.
(C) Scrooge is miserable and poor, whereas Scrooge's nephew is amicable and wealthy.
(D) Scrooge is amicable and wealthy, whereas Scrooge's nephew is arrogant and cynical.

733. What does Scrooge mean when he turns to his employee and says, "Let me hear another sound from you, and you'll keep your Christmas by losing your situation"?

(A) Scrooge is warning his employee not to get so drunk over Christmas that he loses his senses.

(B) Scrooge wants to hear more about his employee's family situation during the Christmas holidays.

(C) Scrooge is worried that his employee is going insane.

(D) Scrooge is threatening to sack his employee if he says another word.

734. What is Scrooge doing when he tells his nephew, "You're quite a powerful speaker, sir. I wonder you don't go into Parliament"?

(A) Scrooge is praising his nephew's excellent speech.

(B) Scrooge thinks his nephew should go into politics and is offering valuable career advice.

(C) Scrooge is being sarcastic.

(D) Scrooge thinks that his nephew would make a great partner and is offering him a job.

735. Why does Scrooge repeat the phrase "good afternoon" several times toward the end of the excerpt?

(A) Scrooge knows that his nephew has a hearing problem, so he wants to make sure his nephew heard him.

(B) Scrooge wants to end the conversation.

(C) Scrooge is full of Christmas spirit and is having a very good afternoon.

(D) Scrooge is getting old and often repeats himself.

Questions 736 through 738 are based on the following poem.

"A Poison Tree" by William Blake

I was angry with my friend;
I told my wrath, my wrath did end.
I was angry with my foe:
I told it not, my wrath did grow.

And I waterd it in fears,
Night & morning with my tears:
And I sunned it with smiles,
And with soft deceitful wiles.

And it grew both day and night.
Till it bore an apple bright.
And my foe beheld it shine,
And he knew that it was mine.

And into my garden stole,
When the night had veild the pole;
In the morning glad I see;
My foe outstretched beneath the tree.

736. What does the apple in the poem represent?

(A) friendship

(B) poisonous hatred

(C) forgiveness

(D) nothing — it is just an apple

737. What are the main themes of the poem?

(A) hope and forgiveness

(B) life and death

(C) gardening and avoiding dangerous fruits

(D) anger, revenge, and death

738. What advice would the author give to you if you were angry at a friend's actions?

(A) Keep your angry feelings to yourself, and they will eventually fade away.

(B) Tell your friend why you are angry, and your anger will fade away.

(C) Grow your angry until you can use it to eliminate your friend.

(D) Avoid eating any apples that your friend might give you.

Questions 739 through 746 are based on the following passage.

This excerpt is from Cooking Basics For Dummies *by Bryan Miller and Maria Rama (Wiley).*

Cooking is fun and interesting and can be relaxing, exciting, and even therapeutic. Cooking is a life skill, but it can also be a hobby and a passion. When you cook at home, you can eat for less money than you'd spend ordering take-out or dining in a restaurant every night, and you control the ingredients, flavors, and health profile of your food so you know exactly what you're eating.

Cooking gives you options, allowing you to adapt your meals to suit your own nutritional and taste preferences. When you cook, you can always get exactly the food you want. Plus, cooking the food you eat makes you more aware of your food, your health, and your environment.

Whether you have a cramped apartment kitchen with counter space the size of a cereal box or a sprawling country kitchen with a commercial stove and a work island, this chapter helps you set up an efficient and comfortable environment. Knowing how to use what you have efficiently is even more important than square footage. You'd be surprised to see how small some restaurant kitchens are; they work, however, because everything is in its place and is easily accessible.

In this chapter, we give you a broad overview of what you need to know to be an effective cook. We talk about how to set up your cooking space and introduce you to the major appliances of a kitchen. Then we discuss kitchen safety and help you get started with a nice, easy, practical recipe.

You don't need a fabulous kitchen to prepare fabulous food, but a well-designed workspace sure makes cooking easier and more pleasurable. Chances are, you aren't in the process of remodeling your kitchen, and you have to make do with the basic kitchen design you have. However, if you are at liberty to shift some things around or you're designing your cooking space, consider the concept of access. If you want to spend the day running, join a health club. If you want to enjoy an efficient and pleasurable cooking experience, consider where your main appliances are located and where you store the equipment and ingredients you use the most. Do you have to walk 10 feet from the stove to get the salt? That's not efficient. Although nothing is wrong with a large, eat-in kitchen, the design of the cooking area in particular should be practical.

You should be able to move from your working counter space to the stove/oven, refrigerator, and sink in a smooth, unobstructed fashion. This working space actually has a name: the kitchen triangle. It applies whether you have a long narrow kitchen, a U-shaped kitchen, or an L-shaped kitchen. Consider the positioning of these three major appliances and jettison any obstacles — if a table, plant, or small child is blocking the way, move it. Even if you can't redesign your kitchen space or move your refrigerator to another wall, you can arrange what you need in a way that works for you.

739. Based on the excerpt, cooking can be all of the following EXCEPT

(A) exciting.

(B) therapeutic.

(C) fun.

(D) frustrating.

740. Based on the excerpt, cooking allows you to control all of the following EXCEPT

(A) how much a meal at your favorite restaurant costs.

(B) the ingredients that go into the meal.

(C) the flavors of the food.

(D) the health profile of the food.

741. Based on the passage, which of the following is a true statement?

(A) The ideal kitchen is a sprawling environment with a fabulous working space.

(B) The ideal kitchen is a comfortable environment with an efficient working space.

(C) The ideal kitchen is a cramped environment with an efficient working space.

(D) The ideal kitchen is an efficient environment with comfortable working space.

742. Why does the passage state, "If you want to spend the day running, join a health club"?

(A) to show how important exercise is for your health

(B) to show that jogging is the most efficient type of exercise

(C) to show how important it is to set up an efficient working space

(D) to show that you can combine cooking and exercise in an efficient way

743. Fill in the blank to correctly complete the sentence:

The working space in a kitchen is also known as the _____________.

744. The triangular-shaped working space in a kitchen is formed by which three items?

(A) the sink, the stove, and the refrigerator

(B) the table, the refrigerator, and the stove

(C) a table, a plant, and a small child

(D) the back door, the stove, and the dishwasher

745. The working space described in the passage should be suitable for all kitchen shapes EXCEPT

(A) a long, narrow kitchen.

(B) a short, wide kitchen.

(C) a U-shaped kitchen.

(D) an L-shaped kitchen.

746. The author's tone in the passage can best be described as

(A) sarcastic

(B) informative

(C) ambivalent

(D) belligerent

Questions 747 through 752 are based on the following passage.

This excerpt is from Drones For Dummies *by Mark LaFay (Wiley).*

Before you buy a drone, you need to know how you will use it. The reason for this is simple: Every drone has its own set of features and options, some better-suited for certain applications than others. If you plan to use your drone strictly for hobby flying, you want to look for a drone with a built-in camera or no camera at all. Conversely, if you want to use your drone to take pictures and video, you want to look for a drone that comes with a high- quality camera or a mount for your own camera. Whatever scenario you can think of, the important thing to understand is that the way you intend to use your drone should determine which drone you buy.

Here are some questions and explanations to help you think through how you intend to use your drone.

- *Do you intend to fly for hobby purposes only?* If you intend to fly your drone for hobby purposes only, you may not need camera support, internal or add-on.
- *Do you intend to fly for extended periods of time?* If you intend to fly for extended periods of time, you want to make sure that you have the right balance of motor power and battery life. You also want to consider

whether you need the ability to swap out batteries or add additional batteries.

- *How do you want to fly? Do you want to fly fast in a straight line?* If you want to fly fast in a straight line, an airplane or other fixed wing drone may be the right fit. If you want to be able to hover, vertically take off and land, and go in any direction what-so-ever, then a multi-copter may be a good option for you.
- *Do you intend to use your drone for aerial pictures or video?* If you intend to use your drone for aerial pictures or video, you may want to consider camera support. This opens up a **litany** of additional questions.
- *How important are picture and video quality?* If picture or video quality is of high importance, you may need to consider a drone that can support an add-on camera device.
- *How important is streaming video support?* If streaming video support is of high importance, you need to select a drone with a built-in camera that supports video streaming, or you need to be prepared to make an add-on camera purchase that supports this functionality.
- *How far do you want to be able to fly your drone?* Communication with your controls is a big deal, so you will want to make sure you look at communication methods and distance.

Of course, the age old question that must always be answered is: "What is your budget?" It almost always comes down to this, right? The spectrum of drone pricing is vast. You can spend as little as $100 for a drone and as much as hundreds of thousands of dollars (although pricing in this range is for drones that are intended for more than hobby, personal, or small business uses). Establishing a budget can help you whittle down your options. When contemplating budget, take into consideration how much money you can spend on replacement parts and repairs. It doesn't take much to render a propeller unusable. One serious crash and, depending on the drone, you may have a pricey replacement on your hands. Whether you are a hobby flyer, photographer, videographer, or maybe you have a use within your business, diving deep into how you intend to use your drone will help you select the right drone.

747. According to the passage, what is the first thing you need to know before you buy a drone?

(A) what your budget is

(B) what you intend to use the drone for

(C) how fast the drone can fly

(D) what type of camera it has

748. According to the passage, which type of drone should you consider if you intend to fly it fast in a straight line?

(A) a helicopter

(B) a multi-copter

(C) an airplane or other fixed-wing drone

(D) a drone with excellent battery life

749. Based on the information in the passage, if you intend to fly a drone for extended periods, you need to find the right balance of

(A) cost and quality

(B) speed and stability

(C) camera quality and streaming video support

(D) motor power and battery life

750. According to the passage, a drone that costs hundreds of thousands of dollars would be used for

(A) hobbies.

(B) personal use.

(C) business use.

(D) The passage does not specify.

751. In addition to the cost of buying the drone itself, what other factors should you consider when working out your budget?

(A) the cost of fuel for the drone

(B) the cost of a license for the drone

(C) the cost of replacement parts and repairs

(D) the cost of customizing the drone to make it look cool

752. As used in the passage, what is the best meaning of the word *litany*?

(A) couple

(B) technology

(C) lawsuit

(D) long list

Questions 753 through 760 are based on the following passage.

This excerpt is from Nanotechnology For Dummies *by Earl Boysen and Nancy Muir (Wiley).*

Nanotechnology has been around as a recognized branch of science for only about fifty years, so it's a baby compared to physics or biology, whose roots go back more than a thousand years. Because of the young age of nanotechnology and our still-evolving understanding of it, defining it is an ongoing process, as you find in this chapter.

Finally, the promise nanotechnology holds for the human race ranges from extending our lives by centuries to providing cheap energy and cleaning our air and water. In this chapter, you explore the broad reach that nanotechnology has across several scientific disciplines and many industries.

To help you understand exactly what nanotechnology is, we start by providing a definition — or two. Then we explore how nano-sized particles compare with atoms.

Nanotechnology is still evolving, and there doesn't seem to be one definition that everybody agrees on. We know that nano deals with matter on a very small scale: larger than atoms but smaller than a breadcrumb. We know that matter at the nano scale can behave differently than bulk matter. Beyond that, individuals and groups focus on different aspects of nanotechnology as a discipline. Here are a few definitions of nanotechnology for your consideration.

The following definition is probably the most barebones and generally agreed upon:

Nanotechnology is the study and use of structures between 1 nanometer (nm) and 100 nanometers in size.

To put these measurements in perspective, you would have to stack 1 billion nanometer-sized particles on top of each other to reach the height of a 1-meter- high (about 3-feet 3-inches-high) hall table. Another popular comparison is that you can fit about 80,000 nanometers in the width of a single human hair.

The word *nano* is a scientific prefix that stands for 10^{-9} or 1 billionth; the word itself comes from the Greek word *nanos*, meaning dwarf.

The next definition is from the Foresight Institute and adds a mention of the various fields of science that come into play with nanotechnology:

Structures, devices, and systems having novel properties and functions due to the arrangement of their atoms on the 1 to 100 nanometer scale. Many fields of endeavor contribute to nanotechnology, including molecular physics, materials science, chemistry, biology, computer science, electrical engineering, and mechanical engineering.

The European Commission offers the following definition, which both repeats the fact mentioned in the previous definition that materials at the nanoscale have novel properties, and positions nano vis-à-vis its potential in the economic marketplace:

Nanotechnology is the study of phenomena and fine-tuning of materials at atomic, molecular and macromolecular scales, where properties differ significantly from those at a larger scale. Products based on nanotechnology are already in use and analysts expect markets to grow by hundreds of billions of euros during this decade.

This next definition from the National Nanotechnology Initiative adds the fact that nanotechnology involves certain activities, such as measuring and manipulating nanoscale matter:

Nanotechnology is the understanding and control of matter at dimensions between approximately 1 and 100 nanometers, where unique phenomena enable novel applications. Encompassing nanoscale science, engineering, and technology, nanotechnology involves imaging, measuring, modeling, and manipulating matter at this length scale.

The last definition is from Thomas Theis, director of physical sciences at the IBM Watson Research Center. It offers a broader and interesting perspective of the role and value of nanotechnology in our world:

[Nanotechnology is] an upcoming economic, business, and social phenomenon. Nano-advocates argue it will revolutionize the way we live, work, and communicate.

753. According to the passage, how does nanotechnology differ compared to other sciences like biology or physics?

(A) Nanotechnology is much older than the other sciences.

(B) Nanotechnology is much younger than the other sciences.

(C) Nanotechnology deals with much larger particles than the other sciences.

(D) Nanotechnology is not a real science.

754. According to the passage, there is no single agreed upon definition of *nanotechnology* because

(A) nobody really knows what nanotechnology is.

(B) nanotechnology is indefinable.

(C) nanotechnology is too complex to have a precise definition.

(D) nanotechnology is still evolving, so its definition keeps changing.

755. According to the passage, the word *nano* means all of the following EXCEPT

(A) dwarf.

(B) 1 billionth.

(C) 10^9.

(D) larger than atoms but smaller than a breadcrumb.

756. According to the passage, about how wide is a human hair?

(A) 1 nanometer

(B) 100 nanometers

(C) 10^{-9} nanometers

(D) 80,000 nanometers

757. According to the passage, nanotechnology will help to extend our lifespans by doing all of the following EXCEPT

(A) providing cheap energy.

(B) cleaning our air.

(C) cleaning our water.

(D) providing jobs.

758. According to the passage, how much will the market for nanotechnology products grow during the current decade?

(A) thousands of euros

(B) millions of euros

(C) billions of euros

(D) trillions of euros

759. According to the passage, what appears to be the upper size limit for structures, devices, and systems to be considered nanotechnology?

(A) 1 nanometer

(B) 100 nanometers

(C) 10^{-9} nanometers

(D) 80,000 nanometers

760. What makes Thomas Theis's definition of nanotechnology different from the other definitions given in the passage?

(A) It focuses on the size of the particles involved.

(B) It focuses on the different sciences that are contributing to the field.

(C) It focuses on the potential economic growth of nanotechnology markets.

(D) It focuses on the potential impact on the way we live.

Questions 761 through 768 are based on the following passage.

This excerpt is from Animal Farm *by George Orwell.*

Early in October, when the corn was cut and stacked and some of it was already threshed, a flight of pigeons came whirling through the air and alighted in the yard of Animal Farm in the wildest excitement. Jones and all his men, with half a dozen others from Foxwood and Pinchfield, had entered the five-barred gate and were coming up the cart-track that led to the farm. They were all carrying sticks, except Jones, who was marching ahead with a gun in his hands. Obviously they were going to attempt the recapture of the farm.

This had long been expected, and all preparations had been made. Snowball, who had studied an old book of Julius Caesar's campaigns which he had found in the farmhouse, was in charge of the defensive operations. He gave his orders quickly, and in a couple of minutes every animal was at his post.

As the human beings approached the farm buildings, Snowball launched his first attack. All the pigeons, to the number of thirty-five, flew to and fro over the men's heads and muted upon them from mid-air; and while the men were dealing with this, the geese, who had been hiding behind the hedge, rushed out and pecked viciously at the calves of their legs. However, this was only a light skirmishing manoeuvre, intended to create a little disorder, and the men easily drove the geese off with their sticks. Snowball now launched his second line of attack. Muriel, Benjamin, and all the sheep, with Snowball at the head of them, rushed forward and prodded and butted the men from every side, while Benjamin turned around and lashed at them with his small hoofs. But once again the men, with their sticks and their hobnailed boots, were too strong for them; and suddenly, at a squeal from Snowball, which was the signal for retreat, all the animals turned and fled through the gateway into the yard.

The men gave a shout of triumph. They saw, as they imagined, their enemies in flight, and they rushed after them in disorder. This was just what Snowball had intended. As soon as they were well inside the yard, the three horses, the three cows, and the rest of the pigs, who had been lying in ambush in the cowshed, suddenly emerged in their rear, cutting them off. Snowball now gave the signal for the charge. He himself dashed straight for Jones. Jones saw him coming, raised his gun and fired. The pellets scored bloody streaks along Snowball's back, and a sheep dropped dead. Without halting for an instant, Snowball flung his fifteen stone against Jones's legs. Jones was hurled into a pile of dung and his gun flew out of his hands. But the most terrifying spectacle of all was Boxer, rearing up on his hind legs and striking out with his great iron-shod hoofs like a stallion. His very first blow took a stable-lad from Foxwood on the skull and stretched him lifeless in the mud. At the sight, several men dropped their sticks and tried to run. Panic overtook them, and the next moment all the animals together were chasing them round and round the yard. They were gored, kicked, bitten, trampled on. There was not an animal on the farm that did not take vengeance on them after his own fashion. Even the cat suddenly leapt off a roof onto a cowman's shoulders and sank her claws in his neck, at which he yelled horribly. At a moment when the opening was clear, the men were glad enough to rush out of the yard and make a bolt for the main road. And so within five minutes of their invasion they were in **ignominious** retreat by the same way as they had come, with a flock of geese hissing after them and pecking at their calves all the way.

All the men were gone except one. Back in the yard Boxer was pawing with his hoof at the stable-lad who lay face down in the mud, trying to turn him over. The boy did not stir.

"He is dead," said Boxer sorrowfully. "I had no intention of doing that. I forgot that I was wearing iron shoes. Who will believe that I did not do this on purpose?"

"No sentimentality, comrade!" cried Snowball from whose wounds the blood was still dripping. "War is war. The only good human being is a dead one."

761. What appears to have happened on the farm shortly before the events detailed in the excerpt take place?

(A) Jones sold the farm to another farmer called Snowball.

(B) The animals rebelled and took over the farm.

(C) Pinchfield and Foxwood stole the farm from Mr. Jones.

(D) Mr. Jones became partners with Foxwood and Pinchfield.

762. Who was in charge of coordinating the animals' defenses?

(A) Pinchfield

(B) Snowball

(C) Boxer

(D) Jones

763. What is the first line of defense that the animals employ against Jones and his men?

(A) The sheep rush forward and prod and butt the men from every side.

(B) The pigeons fly over the men's heads while the geese peck at the men's legs.

(C) Boxer and the cows attack the men.

(D) Snowball and the pigs attack the men.

764. How do the animals manage to ambush the men in the yard during the attack?

(A) The animals pretend to retreat but then cut the men off from the rear when they enter the yard.

(B) The pigeons and geese drive the men into the yard.

(C) The men run into the yard to attack the animals' ringleader.

(D) It is a complete accident that the men enter the yard where the pigs are hiding.

765. What is the best meaning of the word *ignominious* as used in the passage?

(A) ignorant

(B) anonymous

(C) shameful

(D) honorable

766. What type of animal is Boxer?

(A) a pig

(B) a sheep

(C) a cow

(D) a horse

767. How do Boxer and Snowball react to the death of the stable lad?

(A) They are both sad about the boy's death.

(B) They are both happy that the boy is dead.

(C) Snowball shows no remorse, but Boxer is upset.

(D) Boxer shows no remorse, but Snowball is upset.

768. Which three words best describe Snowball's personality?

(A) sympathetic, resourceful, and kind

(B) cunning, sympathetic, and kind

(C) timid, resourceful, and kind

(D) cunning, resourceful, and brave

Questions 769 through 776 are based on the following passage.

This excerpt is from Prediabetes For Dummies *by Alan L. Rubin, MD (Wiley).*

About 60 million people in the United States have prediabetes. That means if you are in a room with three other adult U.S. citizens, one of you will probably have prediabetes, and chances are that person won't know it. The purpose of this book is to radically change that situation. Anyone who reads this book will know whether he or she has prediabetes. Anyone who follows the recommendations in this book will *not* proceed to diabetes and will probably return to normal health.

This book will not make you younger, but it will help you continue to get older.

Diagnosing prediabetes is crucial because prediabetes is the critical step before developing diabetes. As you find out in this book, diabetes is associated with complications that may cause considerable physical and mental discomfort at best and be life-threatening at worst. So you don't want to go there.

Even if you go on to develop diabetes, all is not lost. You can use the suggestions found here to avoid further complications. You can't get rid of the diagnosis, but you can get rid of the problems.

In this chapter, you discover how to differentiate among three physical states: normal health, prediabetes, and diabetes. I explain that prediabetes is a recent phenomenon, which parallels the epidemic of obesity and lack of exercise in the United States and around the world.

Next, you discover who is affected by prediabetes and which groups of people are at the highest risk. I also touch on special considerations for children and the elderly at risk for prediabetes.

Finally, I focus on the costs of prediabetes, which are not only monetary. I explain that even though prediabetes is often considered a benign condition and not a disease, changes occur in the body of a person with prediabetes that may not be benign after all.

Jane Johnson is a 48-year-old woman. She is postmenopausal and has gained about 15 pounds since her twenties, when her weight was normal. She complains of some fatigue. She goes to Dr. Sugarfeld, who discovers that Jane has family members with diabetes. Jane mentions that she used to be physically active but doesn't have the time to do much exercise these days. A physical examination reveals only that Jane is overweight and has mild high blood pressure, so Dr. Sugarfeld sends her for blood tests. One of the blood tests the doctor orders is called a *fasting blood glucose,* and it discovers the level of sugar in someone's blood in the morning after that person has fasted through the night.

When Jane returns a week later, Dr. Sugarfeld informs her that her fasting blood glucose was 114 mg/dl (6.3 mmol/L). The doctor asks Jane to have one more fasting blood glucose test. This value is 108 mg/dl (6 mmol/L). Dr Sugarfeld informs Jane that she has prediabetes.

This **anecdote** describes one of the most common ways that prediabetes is discovered. Another common occurrence is simply the discovery that the *blood glucose* — the amount of sugar in the blood — is higher than it should be in a routine blood test.

The diagnosis of prediabetes is made the same way that a diagnosis of diabetes is made: by doing a blood glucose test in the laboratory.

769. Using the information in the passage, if you were in a room with 39 other typical adult U.S. citizens, how many of the people in the room would have prediabetes?

(A) 1

(B) 9.75

(C) 10

(D) 60 million

770. What is the purpose of the first paragraph of the passage?

(A) to warn the reader about the dangers of prediabetes

(B) to give a definition of prediabetes

(C) to convince the reader to read the rest of the book

(D) to explain how diabetes was discovered

771. In the second paragraph, what point is the author trying to make when he says, "This book will not make you younger, but it will help you continue to get older"?

(A) He knows that many people like to look older than they actually are.

(B) He is warning that people with prediabetes often age faster than normal people.

(C) He is suggesting that older people can look younger by reading his book.

(D) He is suggesting that reading this book could prevent you from dying of diabetes.

772. According to the passage, there are three physical states of health. They include each of the following EXCEPT

(A) normal health.

(B) prediabetes.

(C) diabetes.

(D) postdiabetes.

773. The passage warns that the United States is facing major health epidemics, including each of the following EXCEPT

(A) obesity.

(B) AIDS.

(C) lack of exercise.

(D) prediabetes.

774. What is the best meaning of the word *anecdote* as used in the passage?

(A) a medicine taken to counteract a particular poison

(B) a method of diagnosing prediabetes

(C) a brief, revealing account of an individual person's experience

(D) an amusing tale

775. In the paragraphs that describe how Jane Johnson discovered that she was prediabetic, what is the most likely reason the author chose the name Dr. Sugarfeld as the name of Jane's doctor?

(A) The author wants to emphasize that prediabetes is caused by too much blood sugar.

(B) The author probably chose the name at random.

(C) Sugarfeld is the name of the author's own doctor.

(D) Sugarfeld means prediabetes in German.

776. How is prediabetes diagnosed?

(A) by measuring how much sugar a person eats per week

(B) by measuring the fasting blood glucose level

(C) by noting the many symptoms that the person with prediabetes experiences

(D) prediabetes cannot be diagnosed

Questions 777 through 786 are based on the following passage.

This excerpt is from Stress Management For Dummies *by Allen Elkin (Wiley).*

Are you feeling more tired lately than you used to? Is your fuse a little shorter than normal? Are you worrying more? Enjoying life less? If you feel more stress in your life these days, you aren't alone. Count yourself among the ranks of the overstressed. Most people feel that their lives have too much stress. Your stress may come from your job or lack thereof, your money worries, your personal life, or simply not having enough time to do everything you have to do — or want to do. You could use some help. Thankfully, you can eliminate or at least minimize much of the stress in your life and better manage the stress that remains. This chapter helps you get started.

You probably can't make it through a single day without seeing or hearing the word *stress* someplace. Just glance at any magazine stand and you'll find numerous cover stories all about stress. In most larger bookstores, an entire section is devoted to books on stress. TV and radio talk shows regularly feature stories documenting the negative effects of stress in our lives. Why all the fuss? Hasn't stress been around forever? Wasn't it stress that Adam felt when he was caught red-handed with little bits of apple stuck between his teeth? Is all of this just media hype, or are people really experiencing more stress today?

In her insightful book *The Overworked American: The Unexpected Decline of Leisure*, economist Juliet Schor points out that, in spite of all the new innovations and contraptions that could make our lives easier, we still need about the same amount of time to do what has to be done at home. In the 1910s, a full-time housewife spent about 52 hours a week on housework. Sixty years later, in the 1970s, the figure was about the same. Yes, some activities did become less time consuming. Food preparation fell almost 10 hours a week, but this was offset by an increase in the time spent shopping and taking care of the home and kids. Contrary to everyone's predicted expectations, we have less leisure time now than we did 50 years ago . . .

A 2010 study published by the American Psychological Association shows an America still recovering from the recession. Americans report that money (76 percent) and the economy (65 percent) are their most common sources of stress. A difficult and uncertain economy has become *the* major source of stress in our lives. The recession and its aftermath have resulted in prolonged financial and emotional distress for too many of us.

Money may or may not be the root of all evil, but worrying about it certainly is a major source of stress. Balancing your checkbook at the end of the month (if you bother) reminds you that living is expensive. You remember that your parents bought their house for a pittance and now realize that today you couldn't afford to buy that same house if you wanted to. The mortgage, college tuition, braces for the kids' teeth, camp, travel, taxes, savings for retirement — it all adds up. And so does the stress.

Having a job may mean avoiding the stress that comes with unemployment, but it certainly doesn't guarantee a stress-free existence. For many people, jobs and careers are the biggest source of stress. Concerns about job security, killer hours, long commutes, unrealistic deadlines, bosses from hell, office politics, toxic coworkers, and testy clients are just a few of the many job-related stresses people experience. Workloads are heavier today than they were in the past, leaving less and less time for family and the rest of your life.

777. What is the most likely reason that the author began the passage with a series of questions?

(A) He wants to gather information from the reader.

(B) He knows the reader will probably answer yes to these questions and will be interested in reading more.

(C) He knows that the questions will probably stress out the reader.

(D) He couldn't think of a proper way to start the passage, so he just wrote the first thing he thought of.

778. According to the first paragraph, all of the following are causes of stress EXCEPT

(A) your job.

(B) being unemployed.

(C) having too much money.

(D) your personal life.

779. What incident is the author referring to when he says, "Wasn't it stress that Adam felt when he was caught red-handed with little bits of apple stuck between his teeth?"

(A) an embarrassing dinner where the author's date pointed out that he had food stuck between his teeth

(B) a stressful apple-eating competition

(C) the time his nephew, Adam, went to the dentist without cleaning his teeth

(D) the Bible story in which God confronts Adam in the Garden of Eden about eating from the Tree of Knowledge

780. According to the first paragraph, all of the following are symptoms of stress EXCEPT

(A) being more short-tempered.

(B) having suicidal thoughts.

(C) worrying more.

(D) feeling tired.

781. According to the economist Juliet Schor, why haven't all the new time-saving inventions that make our lives easier helped relieve the stresses of doing household chores?

(A) We still need about the same amount of time to do what has to be done at home.

(B) In the past, people used to relieve stress by doing more chores.

(C) It now takes longer to prepare meals than it did in the past.

(D) We have more leisure time now than we did 50 years ago.

782. According to the American Psychological Association, what is the number one cause of stress for most Americans?

(A) the relationship with their partners

(B) work

(C) money

(D) the economy

783. For some people, jobs and careers are a major source of stress. Which of the following contains only the work-related potential sources of stress listed in the passage?

(A) office parties and insufficient salaries

(B) office politics, traveling to and from work, and unpleasant bosses

(C) having dinner with clients, and fears about not being promoted

(D) office seating arrangements and giving presentations

784. According to the passage, why is work-related stress more of a problem today than it used to be?

(A) Workloads were much heavier before robots were invented.

(B) Many people love their jobs and prefer to work longer hours than they did in the past.

(C) People now spend more time at work to deal with today's larger workloads.

(D) The economy has improved recently, making it easier to change jobs.

785. According to the author, what is the best thing that you can do to learn how to reduce your stress level?

(A) earn more money

(B) get a better job

(C) exercise more and get a better night's sleep

(D) read his book

786. Which of the following best describes the author's tone throughout the passage?

(A) belligerent

(B) serious

(C) playful but informative

(D) capricious

Questions 787 through 794 are based on the following passage.

This excerpt is from Day Trading For Dummies *by Ann C. Logue (Wiley).*

Day trading is a crazy business. Traders work in front of their computer screens, reacting to blips, each of which represents real dollars. They make quick decisions because their ability to make money depends on successfully executing a large number of trades that generate small profits. They close out their positions in the stocks, options, and futures contracts they own at the end of the day, which limits some of the risks — nothing can happen overnight to disturb an existing profit position — but those limits on risk can limit profits. After all, a lot can happen in a year, increasing the likelihood that your trade idea will work out, but in a day? You have to be patient and work fast. Some days offer nothing good to buy. Other days, every trade seems to lose money.

The individual human-being day trader is up against a tough opponent: high- frequency algorithms programmed and operated by brokerage firms and hedge funds that have no emotion and can make trades in less time than it takes to blink your eye. If you're not prepared for that competition, you will be crushed.

The definition of day trading is that day traders hold their securities for only one day. They close out their positions at the end of every day and then start all over again the next day. By contrast, *swing traders* hold securities for days and sometimes even months; *investors* sometimes hold for years. The short-term nature of day trading reduces some risks, because nothing can happen overnight to cause big losses. Meanwhile, many other types of investors go to bed thinking their position is in great shape only to wake up the next morning to find that the company has announced terrible earnings or that its CEO is being indicted on fraud charges.

But there's a flip side (there's always a flip side, isn't there?): The day trader's choice of securities and positions has to work out in a day, or it's gone. Tomorrow doesn't exist for any specific position. Meanwhile, the swing trader or the investor has the luxury of time, because it sometimes takes a while for a position to work out the way your research shows it should. In the long run, markets are efficient, and prices reflect all information about a security. Unfortunately, a few days of short runs may need to occur for this efficiency to kick in.

Day traders are speculators working in zero-sum markets one day at a time. A zero-sum game has exactly as many winners as losers. And options and futures markets, which are popular with day traders, are zero-sum markets. If the person who holds an option makes a profit, then the person who *wrote* (which is option-speak for *sold*) that option loses the same amount. There's no net gain or net loss in the market as a whole. That makes the dynamics different from other types of financial activities you may have been involved in. When you take up day trading, the rules that may have helped you pick good stocks or find great mutual funds over the years no longer apply. Day trading is a different game with different rules.

Professional traders fall into two categories: speculators and hedgers. *Speculators* look to make a profit from price changes. *Hedgers* look to protect against a price change. They make their buy and sell choices as insurance, not as a way to make a profit, so they choose positions that offset their exposure in another market.

787. According to the passage, day traders make money by executing

(A) their rivals.

(B) a transaction and holding onto a stock for as long as it takes for its value to increase.

(C) a small number of trades that generate huge profits.

(D) a large number of trades that generate small profits.

788. According to the passage, how do day traders limit some of their risks?

(A) by closing out their positions at the end of each day

(B) by holding each stock for a year to increase the likelihood that the trade will be profitable

(C) by investing only in stocks that are guaranteed to increase in value

(D) by not trading at all

789. According to the passage, high-frequency algorithms have all of the following advantages over individual human day traders EXCEPT

(A) their decisions are not clouded by emotions.

(B) they can make trades in a fraction of a second.

(C) they are charged cheaper fees for each trade they perform.

(D) they are operated by powerful brokerage firms and hedge funds.

790. According to the passage, why might a successful long-term investor make a terrible day trader?

(A) Unlike long-term investing, day trading does not involve zero-sum markets.

(B) Long-term investors make their trading decisions too quickly.

(C) The rules that may have helped the investor pick good long-term investments do not apply to day trading.

(D) Many long-term investors are nocturnal and sleep during the day.

791. According to the passage, which of the following would be an example of a zero-sum game?

(A) Three friends start a successful business together, and they all become rich.

(B) Three friends start an unsuccessful business together, and they lose all of their money.

(C) A mobile phone provider takes market share away from its main rival.

(D) A drug company invents a cure for cancer that saves thousands of lives each day.

792. Based on the information in the passage, which of the following accurately describes the trading habits of day traders, swing traders, and investors?

(A) *Investors* hold their securities for only one day, *swing traders* hold securities for days and sometimes even months, and *day traders* sometimes hold securities for years.

(B) *Day traders* hold their securities for only one day, *swing traders* hold securities for days and sometimes even months, and *investors* sometimes hold securities for years.

(C) *Swing traders* hold their securities for only one day, *day traders* hold securities for days and sometimes even months, and *investors* sometimes hold securities for years.

(D) *Day traders* hold their securities for only one day, *investors* hold securities for days and sometimes even months, and *swing traders* sometimes hold securities for years.

793. According to the passage, what is the main difference between hedgers and speculators?

(A) Speculators try to profit from price changes, whereas hedgers try to protect themselves from price changes.

(B) Speculators try to protect themselves from price changes, whereas hedgers try to profit from price changes.

(C) Speculators are amateur traders, whereas hedgers are professional traders.

(D) Hedgers are amateur traders, whereas speculators are professional traders.

794. According to the passage, which of the following would probably have the best personality fit to be a successful day trader?

(A) a professional gambler

(B) a successful long-term investor

(C) a patient, quick-thinking risk-taker who possesses self-discipline

(D) anyone can be a good day trader

Questions 795 through 802 are based on the following passage. The passage is not complete. You have to select the best sentence or completion of a sentence from among the given choices.

The following excerpt is from Business Plans Kit For Dummies *by Steven D. Peterson (Wiley).*

Almost all successful businesses begin with a good idea. The idea may be based on a brand new product or service. Or, it may introduce an existing product or service into a new niche. Great business ideas are born when someone figures out a better way to make something or to provide customers what they need or want. Successful business ideas don't have to be world-shaking. But no matter how modest or extensive they are, they have to appeal to customers in order to succeed.

SEE QUESTION 795 The process of writing a business plan can help you identify both the strengths and weaknesses of your idea. Doing so can enable you to tweak your idea to make it as strong as possible.

Facebook started with a good idea. So did Whole Foods. Toyota had a pretty good idea when it developed a hybrid engine. *SEE QUESTION 796* Today, Tesla is an engine of innovative ideas. So is Google. Even simple ideas — like creating a website where people with accommodations to rent connect with people who want to rent them — can grow into billion-dollar businesses.

Good ideas aren't limited to major companies. *SEE QUESTION 797* Or, there's the home brewer who realizes that a small-town ale can make it big. Even the local caterer who decides to take her business on the road in the form of a fleet of food trucks may be able to turn that idea into profit.

SEE QUESTION 798 After all, when you're building something from the ground up, you definitely need a concept and a plan for turning it into reality. But a well-developed idea is just as essential for an established business aiming to grow or planning to pivot in a new strategic direction.

SEE QUESTION 799 A business plan for a start-up has to cover all the bases. A plan for growing your business may zero in specifically on customer analysis and marketing strategy. On the other hand, a plan for pivoting a business may focus on how to leverage current resources to make the turn in a new direction. But whether you're aiming to launch, grow, or pivot your business, you need to be clear about the business idea upon which you can build your goals and strategies.

Don't assume that defining the idea behind the business plan for growing or pivoting your company is easier than for a start-up. In some ways, it's tougher. An established company with an entrenched way of doing business often has trouble changing its corporate culture quickly and thoroughly enough to make a fleet change in direction. It has to overcome a lot of inertia. A business plan for pivoting to a whole new product or service line, or a new business model, needs to address the obstacles that the business must overcome. *SEE QUESTION 800* Ask these questions:

Plenty of profitable businesses owe their success to a personal passion. A baker who starts a successful bakery, a musician who opens a recording studio, a teacher who starts a nonprofit tutoring service all have passion in common. That's great. Excitement and confidence are crucial to making a business a success.

So is a good dose of reality.

SEE QUESTION 801 Businesses that begin with passionate optimism sometimes go belly-up. Personal passion can carry you away, blinding you to the hard realities that any business faces in making it in today's highly competitive world. The bottom line of all for-profit businesses is ultimately — you guessed it — profit. *SEE QUESTION 802*

The question may be simple. Answering it isn't always so easy.

795. Select the best sentence from among the given choices.

(A) Writing a business plan is one of the most important steps in shaping an idea and putting it to it's first test.

(B) Writing a business plan is one of the most important steps in shaping an idea and putting it to its first test.

(C) Write a business plan is one of the most important steps in shaping an idea and putting it to it's first test.

(D) Writing a business plan is one of the most important steps in shaping an idea and putting them to their first test.

796. Select the best sentence from among the given choices.

(A) Apple did too, when the company decides to build a touch screen device big enough to read, draw, and right on.

(B) Apple did too, when the company decided to build a touch screen device big enough to read, draw, and right on.

(C) Apple did too, when the company decides to build a touch screen device big enough to read, draw, and write on.

(D) Apple did too, when the company decided to build a touch screen device big enough to read, draw, and write on.

797. Select the best sentence from among the given choices.

(A) The young couple who decides to open a doggy day care in a town where a lot of people commute to work may have a great idea, too.

(B) The young couple that decides to open a doggy day care in a town where a lot of people commute to work may have a great idea, to.

(C) The young couple who decides to open a doggy day care in a town where a lot of people commute to work may have a great idea, to.

(D) The young couple which decides to open a doggy day care in a town where a lot of people commute to work may have a great idea, too.

798. Select the best sentence from among the given choices.

(A) Putting your business idea into words is a no-brainer if your starting a new company.

(B) Putting you're business idea into words is a no-brainer if you're starting a new company.

(C) Put your business idea into words is a no-brainer if you're starting a new company.

(D) Putting your business idea into words is a no-brainer if you're starting a new company.

799. Select the best sentence from among the given choices.

(A) The emphasis of your plan will differing depending on your goal, of course.

(B) The emphasis of your plan will differ depending on your goal, of coarse.

(C) The emphasis of your plan will differ depending on your goal, of course.

(D) The emphasis of your plan will differ depend on your goal, of course.

800. Select the best sentence from among the given choices.

(A) As you develop the essential idea behind the new direction, compare them to the idea that launched your business in the first place.

(B) Developing the essential idea behind the new direction, compare it to the idea that launched your business in the first place.

(C) Having developed the essential idea behind the new direction compare it to the idea that launched your business in the first place.

(D) As you develop the essential idea behind the new direction, compare it to the idea that launched your business in the first place.

801. Select the best sentence from among the given choices.

(A) Been excited about what you want to do is no guarantee of success.

(B) Being excited about what you want to do is no guarentee of success.

(C) Being excited about what you want to do is no guarantee of success.

(D) Being excited about what you want to do is not guaranteed of success.

802. Select the best sentence from among the given choices.

(A) If you're hoping to turn a personnel passion into a successful business, you need to ask yourself a simple question: Can it make a profit?

(B) If you're hoping to turn a personnel passion into a successful business you need to ask yourself a simple question: Can it make a profit?

(C) If you're hoping to turn a personal passion into a successful business, you need to ask yourself a simple question: Can it make a profit?

(D) If you're hoping to turn a personal passion into a successful business you need to ask yourself a simple question: Can it make a profit?

Questions 803 through 808 are based on the following passage. The passage is not complete. You have to select the best sentence or completion of a sentence from among the given choices.

The following excerpt is from Chess For Dummies *by James Eade (Wiley).*

If you're new to chess, don't despair. *SEE QUESTION 803* Everyone can learn to play a passable game of chess, and after you come on-board (no pun intended!), it's just a matter of time until you find someone you can play well against.

SEE QUESTION 804 — one player uses white pieces, and the other uses black. Each player gets 16 pieces to maneuver (although, technically, pawns aren't pieces, but I'll get to that). Players take turns moving one piece at a time, with the ultimate objective of checkmating their opponent's king.

Because chess has so many great rules and because the pieces all exercise their individuality with different moves and abilities, the game has lots of interesting nuances that you'll want to keep in mind as you play. I cover each aspect of the game in this book, so if you're a novice, you'll find sufficient information to get acquainted with chess; *SEE QUESTION 805*

Components of a chess game can be broken down into categories that are so fundamental that they're referred to as *elements*. The element of time, known as *development*, is one example. The element of force, known as *material*, is another. *SEE QUESTION 806*

The elements are all a part of what drives a game to the desired end result: *checkmate*. If the king is attacked and can't escape the attack, the aggressor has secured checkmate, and the game is over. However, checkmate doesn't always come to fruition — sometimes a game ends in *stalemate*, which is one way to draw. You can also have a situation called *check*, which is an attack on the king.

SEE QUESTION 807 — check can actually happen several times in a game, and if your opponent can effectively escape from check, you may just be wasting your time.

The militaristic character of chess is undeniable, but it also holds appeal for the confirmed peacenik. Although many of the strategies of war apply equally well to chess (divide and conquer, for example), many people gain ascetic pleasure from playing or watching a well-played game. Well-known patterns can appear with an unexpected twist and delight the observer. At an advanced level, you'll discover harmonies that lie just below the surface of the moves, and a move that breaks that harmony will feel as discordant as an off-key note in music. So take heart, consider the information this book provides, and allow yourself to get comfortable with the pieces, their powers, and all the exciting aspects of this strategic, creative game. *SEE QUESTION 808*

803. Select the best completion of the sentence from among the given choices.

(A) No chess jeans decides who can and can't play; take my word for it.

(B) No chess gene decides whom can and can't play; take my word for it.

(C) No chess gene decides who can and can't play; take my word for it.

(D) No chess gene decides whom can and can't play; take my word for it.

804. Select the best completion of the sentence from among the given choices.

(A) Chess, simply stated, is a board game for too

(B) Chess, simply stated, is a bored game for too

(C) Chess, simply stated, is a bored game for two

(D) Chess, simply stated, is a board game for two

805. Select the best completion of the sentence from among the given choices.

(A) if you already know how to play but want to hone your prowess, one can find plenty of information to help you do just that.

(B) if you already know how to play but want to hone your prowess, you'll find plenty of information to help you do just that.

(C) if you already know how to play but want to hone your prowess, you find plenty of information to help you do just that.

(D) if you already know how to play but want to hone your prowess, one finding plenty of information to help you do just that.

806. Select the best sentence from among the given choices.

(A) If one player deploys more force more quickly than the other player, it may be impossible for the latter player to defend against a subsequent invasion.

(B) If one player deploys more force more quick than the other player, it may be impossible for the later player to defend against a subsequent invasion.

(C) If one player deploys more force more quick than the other player, it may be impossible for the latter player to defend against a subsequent invasion.

(D) If one player deploys more force more quickly than the other player, it may be impossible for the later player to defend against a subsequent invasion.

807. Select the best completion of the sentence from among the given choices.

(A) One thing to note however is that placing your opponent in check doesn't necessarily mean you'll win

(B) One thing to note however is that placing your proponent in check doesn't necessarily mean you'll win

(C) One thing to note, however, is that placing your opponent in check doesn't not necessarily mean you'll win

(D) One thing to note, however, is that placing your opponent in check doesn't necessarily mean you'll win

808. Select the best sentence from among the given choices.

(A) Beside, unlike real warfare, the worst you'll suffer in your chess career is a bruised ego.

(B) Besides, unlike real warfare, the worst you'll suffer in your chess career is a bruised ego.

(C) Beside, unlike real warfare, the worst your suffer in your chess career is a bruised ego.

(D) Besides, unlike real warfare the worst you're suffer in your chess career is a bruised ego.

Questions 809 through 816 are based on the following passage.

This excerpt is from Dracula *by Bram Stoker.*

8 May.—I began to fear as I wrote in this book that I was getting too diffuse; but now I am glad that I went into detail from the first, for there is something so strange about this place and all in it that I cannot but feel uneasy. I wish I were safe out of it, or that I had never come. It may be that this strange night-existence is telling on me; but would that that were all! If there were any one to talk to I could bear it, but there is no one. I have only the Count to speak with, and he!—I fear I am myself the only living soul within the place. Let me be **prosaic** so far as facts can be; it will help me to bear up, and imagination must not run riot with me. If it does I am lost. Let me say at once how I stand—or seem to.

I only slept a few hours when I went to bed, and feeling that I could not sleep any more, got up. I had hung my shaving glass by the window, and was just beginning to shave. Suddenly I felt a hand on my shoulder, and heard the Count's voice saying to me, "Good-morning." I started, for it amazed me that I had not seen him, because the reflection of the glass covered the whole room behind me. In starting I had cut myself slightly, but did not notice it at the moment. Having answered the Count's salutation, I turned to the glass again to see how I had been mistaken. This time there could be no error, for the man was close to me, and I could see him over my shoulder. But there was no reflection of him in the mirror! The whole room behind me was displayed; but there was no sign of a man in it, except myself. This was startling, and, coming on the top of so many strange things, was beginning to increase that vague feeling of uneasiness which I always have when the Count is near; but at the instant I saw that the cut had bled a little, and the blood was trickling over my chin. I laid down the razor, turning as I did so half round to look for some sticking plaster. When the Count saw my face, his eyes blazed with a sort of demoniac fury, and he suddenly made a grab at my throat. I drew away, and his hand touched the string of beads which held the crucifix. It made an instant change in him, for the fury passed so quickly that I could hardly believe that it was ever there.

"Take care," he said, "take care how you cut yourself. It is more dangerous than you think in this country." Then seizing the shaving glass, he went on: "And this is the wretched thing that has done the mischief. It is a foul bauble of man's vanity. Away with it!" and opening the heavy window with one wrench of his terrible hand, he flung out the glass, which was shattered into a thousand pieces on the stones of the courtyard far below. Then he withdrew without a word. It is very annoying, for I do not see how I am to shave, unless in my watch-case or the bottom of the shaving-pot, which is fortunately of metal.

When I went into the dining-room, breakfast was prepared; but I could not find the Count anywhere. So I breakfasted alone. It is strange that as yet I have not seen the Count eat or drink. He must be a very peculiar man! After breakfast I did a little exploring in the castle. I went out on the stairs, and found a room looking towards the South. The view was magnificent, and from where I stood there was every opportunity of seeing it. The castle is on the very edge of a terrible precipice. A stone falling from the window would fall a thousand feet without touching anything! As far as the eye can reach is a sea of green tree tops, with occasionally a deep rift where there is a chasm. Here and there are silver threads where the rivers wind in deep gorges through the forests.

But I am not in heart to describe beauty, for when I had seen the view I explored further; doors, doors, doors everywhere, and all locked and bolted. In no place save from the windows in the castle walls is there an available exit.

The castle is a veritable prison, and I am a prisoner!"

809. What is the narrator's tone in the opening paragraph?

(A) relaxed and content

(B) uneasy and lonely

(C) excited and hopeful

(D) disappointed

810. Based on its usage in the excerpt, what is the best definition of the word *prosaic*?

(A) clear and direct

(B) imaginative

(C) capricious

(D) vague

811. When the narrator is in his room shaving, why is he so surprised when the Count puts his hand on the narrator's shoulder?

(A) The narrator was still half asleep and didn't expect to see the Count.

(B) The narrator expected to see someone else other than the Count.

(C) The narrator thought that the Count had already left the castle before breakfast.

(D) The Count's reflection did not appear in the mirror that the narrator was looking at.

812. What is the best definition of the word *salutation* as used in this sentence: "Having answered the Count's salutation, I turned to the glass again to see how I had been mistaken"?

(A) question

(B) greeting

(C) inquiry

(D) challenge

813. What is the Count's initial reaction when the narrator cuts himself while shaving?

(A) He offers to help the narrator tend to the wound.

(B) He becomes furious and tries to grab the narrator by the throat.

(C) He is calm and offers practical advice.

(D) He is stoic and shows no reaction at all.

814. What is the Count's reaction when he sees the narrator's crucifix?

(A) He becomes furious and throws the crucifix out the window.

(B) The crucifix has no effect on the Count because he isn't religious.

(C) He laughs and jokes about the narrator's vanity.

(D) The crucifix makes him withdraw immediately and become calm again.

815. Where is the castle located?

(A) on a hill overlooking a bleak landscape

(B) at the bottom of a gorge near a river

(C) on a cliff overlooking a beautiful forest

(D) deep in a dark forest

816. When the narrator becomes afraid that he is locked inside the castle, why doesn't he simply jump out the window?

(A) The windows are all locked.

(B) There are no windows in the castle.

(C) It would be impolite to leave via the windows.

(D) He would not survive the fall.

817. What is the best meaning of the word *veritable* in this sentence: "The castle is a veritable prison, and I am a prisoner"?

(A) actual

(B) fake

(C) spurious

(D) artificial

Questions 818 through 826 are based on the following passage.

This excerpt is from Chemistry For Dummies *by John T. Moore (Wiley).*

I really enjoy chemistry. It's far more than a simple collection of facts and a body of knowledge. I was a physics major when I entered college, but I was hooked when I took my first chemistry course. It seemed so interesting, so logical. I think it's fascinating to watch chemical changes take place, to figure out unknowns, to use instruments, to extend my senses, and to make predictions and figure out why they were right or wrong. The whole field of chemistry starts here — with the basics — so consider this chapter your jumping-off point. Welcome to the interesting world of chemistry.

This whole branch of science is all about *matter,* which is anything that has mass and occupies space. *Chemistry* is the study of the composition and properties of matter and the changes it undergoes, including energy changes.

Science used to be divided into very clearly defined areas: If it was alive, it was biology. If it was a rock, it was geology. If it smelled, it was chemistry. If it didn't work, it was physics. In today's world, however, those clear divisions are no longer present. You can find biochemists, chemical physicists, geochemists, and so on. But chemistry still focuses on matter and energy and their changes.

A lot of chemistry comes into play with that last part — the changes matter undergoes. Matter is made up of either pure substances or mixtures of pure substances. The change from one substance into another is what chemists call a *chemical change,* or *chemical reaction,* and it's a big deal because when it occurs, a brand-new substance is created.

So what are compounds and elements? Just more of the anatomy of matter. Matter is pure substances or mixtures of pure substances, and substances themselves are made up of either elements or compounds. (Chapter 3 dissects the anatomy of matter. And, as with all matters of dissection, it's best to be prepared — with a nose plug and an empty stomach.)

Science is far more than a collection of facts, figures, graphs, and tables. Science is a method for examining the physical universe. It's a way of asking and answering questions. However, in order for it to be called science, it must be testable. Being testable is what makes science different from faith.

For example, you may believe in UFOs, but can you test for their existence? How about matters of love? Does she love me? How much does she love me? Can I design a test to test and quantify that love? I think not. I have to accept that love on faith. It's not based in science, which is okay. Mankind has struggled with many great questions that science can't answer. Science is a tool that is useful in examining certain questions, but not all. You wouldn't use a front-end loader to eat a piece of pie, nor would you dig a ditch with a fork. Those are inappropriate tools for the task, just as science is an inappropriate tool for areas of faith.

Science is best described by the attitudes of scientists themselves: They're **skeptical**. They simply won't take another person's word for a phenomenon — it must be testable. And they hold onto the results of their experiments tentatively, waiting for another scientist to disprove them. Scientists wonder, they question, they strive to find out *why,* and they experiment — they have exactly the same attitudes that most small children have before they grow up. Maybe this is a good definition of scientists — they are adults who've never lost that wonder of nature and the desire to know.

Technology, the use of knowledge toward a very specific goal, actually developed before science. Ancient peoples cooked food, smelted ores, made beer and wine by fermentation, and made drugs and dyes from plant material. Technology initially existed without much science. There were few theories and few true experiments. Reasoning was left to the philosophers. Eventually alchemy arose and gave chemistry its experimental basis. Alchemists searched for ways to turn other metals into gold and, in doing so, discovered many new chemical substances and processes, such as distillation. However, it wasn't until the 17th century that experimentation replaced **serendipity**."

818. The author's tone in the passage can best be described as

(A) grim and sardonic

(B) amused and sarcastic

(C) disingenuous

(D) enthusiastic and informative

819. All of the following facts about chemistry first helped the author become hooked on the subject EXCEPT

(A) chemistry is logical.

(B) chemistry is interesting.

(C) chemistry is a branch of physics.

(D) chemistry allows you to test your predictions about how substances interact.

820. According to the passage, what is chemistry the study of?

(A) rocks

(B) living things

(C) things that don't work

(D) changes in matter and energy

821. According to the passage, how have the definitions of the different sciences changed recently?

(A) There is more of an overlap among the sciences now.

(B) The sciences have become more distinct from each other.

(C) The old definitions have been completely discarded.

(D) The have been no recent changes in the definitions of the different sciences.

822. Why does the author suggest that "a nose plug and an empty stomach" is the best way to prepare for an experiment involving dissection?

(A) Dissection involves eating, so it is best to have an empty stomach before you begin.

(B) The foul smell of the cadaver may make you want to vomit.

(C) Nose plugs are fashionable in the scientific community nowadays.

(D) The nose plug prevents you from smelling your fellow scientists.

823. According to the information given in the passage, which of the following could be properly tested by science?

(A) the existence of God

(B) the existence of the devil

(C) the existence of gravity

(D) the existence of angels

824. As it is used in the passage, what does the word *skeptical* mean?

(A) doubtful

(B) naive

(C) intelligent

(D) trusting

825. In what way does the passage imply that scientists are like children?

(A) They accept the world around them for what it is.

(B) They believe every word of the Bible without questioning it.

(C) They like to test adults' patience.

(D) They keep asking *why*.

826. As it is used in the passage, what does the word *serendipity* mean?

(A) investigation

(B) chance

(C) misfortune

(D) experimentation

Questions 827 through 835 are based on the following passage.

This excerpt is from Forensics For Dummies *by D. P. Lyle, MD (Wiley).*

Turn on the TV any night of the week, and you'll find crime scene investigators, or *criminalists,* tracking down criminals, crime lab technicians evaluating evidence, and even forensic pathologists conducting autopsies on shows detailing cases real or imagined. I don't think this newfound interest in all things forensic stems from some macabre fascination with death or a guilty **enchantment** with the criminal world. If you ask me, people simply are curious by nature and have a strong appetite for scientific knowledge. Remember everyone's fascination with the space program not too many years ago? The cool tools and magical feats of forensic science, such as making fingerprints appear from nowhere, identifying suspects by their shoe-prints, sniffing out a forger by the unique signature of a laser printer, and finding even the most obscure poisons, are proving equally fascinating.

If you lived in ancient Rome, you'd head to the forum when you wanted to discuss the news of the day. The town *forum* was a community meeting place for merchants, politicians, scholars, and citizens that doubled as a center for public justice. Steal your neighbor's toga, and the case would be tried at the forum.

The term *forensic* stems from the Latin word *forum* and applies to anything that relates to law. *Forensic science,* or criminalistics, is the application of scientific disciplines to the law.

The same tools and principles that drive scientific research in universities and identify cures in hospitals are used by forensic scientists to reveal how a victim died and, ideally, who was responsible. In the same way modern hospital laboratories employ professionals to deal with pathology (the study of diseases of the human body), toxicology (the study of drugs and poisons), and serology (the study of blood), modern forensic laboratories employ experts in forensic pathology, forensic toxicology, and forensic serology, all of whom use the principles and testing procedures of their medical specialties to help resolve legal issues and answer questions like: When and how did the victim die? Does the suspect's blood match the blood found at the crime scene? Was a suspect's unusual behavior caused by drug use?

Not long ago identifying, capturing, and convicting criminals depended primarily upon eyewitnesses and confessions. The world was smaller, communities more closely knit, and the extent of travel basically only as far as you could walk. Whenever anyone witnessed a crime, he likely knew the perpetrator. Case closed.

Trains, planes, and automobiles changed all that. Criminals can now rapidly travel far and wide, and with this newfound mobility they are less and less likely to be recognized by an eyewitness. Besides, eyewitness evidence these days frequently is proven to be unreliable.

For law enforcement to keep pace with these changes, other techniques for identifying criminals had to be developed. Science came to the rescue with methods that depend less on eyewitnesses to identify perpetrators or at least link them to their victims or crime scenes. Fingerprinting, firearms identification and gunshot residue analysis, hair and fiber studies, blood typing, DNA analysis, and many other scientific techniques now help solve crimes that would've remained unsolved in the past.

The marriage of science and law hasn't been without its setbacks. Many scientific breakthroughs are viewed with suspicion, if not downright hostility, until they become widely accepted. And before a science can ever enter the courtroom, it must be widely accepted. It should come as no surprise that before forensic science could develop, science in general had to reach a certain level of maturity.

827. According to the passage, why are TV shows about forensic science so popular?

(A) People have a macabre fascination with death.

(B) People take guilty pleasure in watching criminals in action.

(C) People are curious about nature and seek scientific knowledge.

(D) The passage does not specify.

828. According to the passage, forensic science can catch criminals by all of the following methods EXCEPT

(A) identifying a suspect's fingerprints.

(B) identifying the motive behind the criminal act.

(C) identifying the method used to print materials.

(D) identifying the presence of obscure poisons.

829. As used in the passage, what is the best meaning of the word *enchantment*?

(A) hostility

(B) distaste

(C) fascination

(D) guilt

830. Why does the author bring up the topic of ancient Rome in the passage?

(A) He is an amateur historian and likes showing off his knowledge of history.

(B) He wants to compare our knowledge of forensics during Roman times to our knowledge of forensics today.

(C) He wants to show how forensics has improved our knowledge of Ancient Rome.

(D) He wants to explain the origin of the word *forensic.*

831. Based on the information in the passage, which of the following is a true statement?

(A) Serology is the study of drugs and poisons, pathology is the study of human diseases, and toxicology is the study of the blood.

(B) Serology is the study of human diseases, pathology is the study of the blood, and toxicology is the study of drugs and poisons.

(C) Serology is the study of the blood, pathology is the study of human diseases, and toxicology is the study of drugs and poisons.

(D) Serology is the study of the blood, pathology is the study of drugs and poisons, and toxicology is the study of human diseases.

832. Which of the following questions does forensic science NOT help to resolve?

(A) Was drug use a factor in the crime?

(B) Does the suspect's blood match the blood found at the crime scene?

(C) What did the suspect have to gain by killing the victim?

(D) When and how did the victim die?

833. Before the advent of forensic science, what did investigators primarily rely on in order to identify, capture, and convict criminals?

(A) eyewitnesses and confessions

(B) fingerprint analysis

(C) gunshot residue analysis

(D) blood typing DNA analysis

834. How did increased access to modern transportation reduce the effectiveness of the old crime-solving methods?

(A) It meant that criminals could escape from the crime scene faster than before.

(B) It had no effect.

(C) It made eyewitness accounts less reliable.

(D) It made confessions less reliable.

835. Why did it take time for forensic science to become widely accepted in the courtroom?

(A) Eyewitness accounts are more reliable.

(B) Fingerprint analysis is more reliable.

(C) Most people have a solid understanding of science.

(D) People are often suspicious of scientific breakthroughs.

Questions 836 through 843 are based on the following passage.

This excerpt is from "2 B o N 2 B" by Kurt Vonnegut.

Everything was perfectly swell.

There were no prisons, no slums, no insane asylums, no cripples, no poverty, no wars.

All diseases were conquered. So was old age.

Death, barring accidents, was an adventure for volunteers.

The population of the United States was stabilized at forty-million souls.

One bright morning in the Chicago Lying-in Hospital, a man named Edward K. Wehling, Jr., waited for his wife to give birth. He was the only man waiting. Not many people were born a day any more.

Wehling was fifty-six, a mere stripling in a population whose average age was one hundred and twenty-nine.

X-rays had revealed that his wife was going to have triplets. The children would be his first.

Young Wehling was hunched in his chair, his head in his hand. He was so rumpled, so still and colorless as to be virtually invisible. His camouflage was perfect, because the waiting room had a disorderly and demoralized air, too. Chairs and ashtrays had been moved away from the walls. The floor was paved with spattered dropcloths.

The room was being redecorated. It was being redecorated as a memorial to a man who had volunteered to die.

A **sardonic** old man, about two hundred years old, sat on a stepladder, painting a mural he did not like. Back in the days when people aged visibly, his age would have been guessed at thirty-five or so. Aging had touched him that much before the cure for aging was found.

The mural he was working on depicted a very neat garden. Men and women in white, doctors and nurses, turned the soil, planted seedlings, sprayed bugs, spread fertilizer.

Men and women in purple uniforms pulled up weeds, cut down plants that were old and sickly, raked leaves, carried refuse to trash-burners.

Never, never, never—not even in medieval Holland nor old Japan—had a garden been more formal, been better tended. Every plant had all the loam, light, water, air and nourishment it could use.

A hospital orderly came down the corridor, singing under his breath a popular song:

If you don't like my kisses, honey,
Here's what I will do:
I'll go see a girl in purple,
Kiss this sad world toodle-oo.
If you don't want my lovin',
Why should I take up all this space?
I'll get off this old planet,
Let some sweet baby have my place.

The orderly looked in at the mural and the muralist. "Looks so real," he said, "I can practically imagine I'm standing in the middle of it."

"What makes you think you're not in it?" said the painter. He gave a satiric smile. "It's called 'The Happy Garden of Life,' you know."

"That's good of Dr. Hitz," said the orderly.

He was referring to one of the male figures in white, whose head was a portrait of Dr. Benjamin Hitz, the hospital's Chief Obstetrician. Hitz was a blindingly handsome man.

"Lot of faces still to fill in," said the orderly. He meant that the faces of many of the figures in the mural were still blank. All blanks were to be filled with portraits of important people on either the hospital staff or from the Chicago Office of the Federal Bureau of Termination.

"Must be nice to be able to make pictures that look like something," said the orderly.

The painter's face curdled with scorn. "You think I'm proud of this daub?" he said. "You think this is my idea of what life really looks like?"

"What's your idea of what life looks like?" said the orderly.

The painter gestured at a foul dropcloth. "There's a good picture of it," he said. "Frame that, and you'll have a picture a damn sight more honest than this one."

"You're a gloomy old duck, aren't you?" said the orderly.

"Is that a crime?" said the painter.

The orderly shrugged. "If you don't like it here, Grandpa—" he said, and he finished the thought with the trick telephone number that people who didn't want to live any more were supposed to call. The zero in the telephone number he pronounced "naught."

The number was: "2 B R 0 2 B."

It was the telephone number of an institution whose fanciful sobriquets included: "Automat," "Birdland," "Cannery," "Catbox," "De-louser," "Easy-go," "Good-by, Mother," "Happy Hooligan," "Kiss-me-quick," "Lucky Pierre," "Sheepdip," "Waring Blendor," "Weep-no-more" and "Why Worry?"

"To be or not to be" was the telephone number of the municipal gas chambers of the Federal Bureau of Termination.

836. According to the passage, what is the population of the United States in the time period in which the story is set?

(A) 1 million
(B) 40 million
(C) 400 million
(D) 40 billion

837. According to the passage, why is Mr. Wehling the only person in the waiting room at the maternity ward of the hospital?

(A) There are no diseases anymore.
(B) Everything is perfectly swell.
(C) Old age has been conquered.
(D) Not many people are born each day anymore.

838. Why does the passage refer to Edward K. Wehling, Jr. as "Young Wehling" and describe him as "a mere stripling," even though he is 56 years old?

(A) You are only as young as you feel.
(B) The average age of the population is 129.
(C) He is in exceptionally good health.
(D) He is actually only 26 years old.

839. According to the passage, the wall of the hospital ward is being decorated with a mural in honor of whom?

(A) Dr. Benjamin Hitz
(B) the writer of a popular song
(C) a man who had volunteered to die
(D) the hospital's chief obstetrician

840. What is the best meaning of the word *sardonic* as used in the passage?

(A) ignorant
(B) happy
(C) shameful
(D) cynical

841. Why are the municipal gas chambers of the Federal Bureau of Termination known by so many other nicknames, such as "Kiss-me-quick" and "Why Worry?"

(A) Because the government wanted a harmless way of cheering people up

(B) to disguise the true purpose of the Bureau

(C) Making up nicknames is a fun way to pass the time

(D) the nicknames accurately describe the purpose of the Bureau

842. In the description of the mural titled "The Happy Garden of Life," the weeds and the refuge are used as metaphors for

(A) humans who have outgrown their useful purpose in life.

(B) disease.

(C) old age.

(D) criminals.

843. Why does the artist of the mural reply with scorn when the orderly comments on his work?

(A) He is very modest and finds praise hard to accept.

(B) He thinks the orderly is making fun of the artist's hard work.

(C) He is proud of the mural and believes that it represents real life.

(D) He believes that the mural is dishonest and does not represent real life.

Questions 844–851 are based on the following passage.

This excerpt is from "The Tell-Tale Heart" by Edgar Allan Poe.

"TRUE! — nervous — very, very dreadfully nervous I had been and am; but why will you say that I am mad? The disease had sharpened my senses — not destroyed — not dulled them. Above all was the sense of hearing acute. I heard all things in the heaven and in the earth. I heard many things in hell. How, then, am I mad? Hearken! and observe how healthily — how calmly I can tell you the whole story.

It is impossible to say how first the idea entered my brain; but once conceived, it haunted me day and night. Object there was none. Passion there was none. I loved the old man. He had never wronged me. He had never given me insult. For his gold I had no desire. I think it was his eye! yes, it was this! He had the eye of a vulture — a pale blue eye, with a film over it. Whenever it fell upon me, my blood ran cold; and so by degrees — very gradually — I made up my mind to take the life of the old man, and thus rid myself of the eye forever.

Now this is the point. You fancy me mad. Madmen know nothing. But you should have seen me. You should have seen how wisely I proceeded — with what caution — with what foresight — with what dissimulation I went to work! I was never kinder to the old man than during the whole week before I killed him. And every night, about midnight, I turned the latch of his door and opened it — oh so gently! And then, when I had made an opening sufficient for my head, I put in a dark lantern, all closed, closed, that no light shone out, and then I thrust in my head. Oh, you would have laughed to see how cunningly I thrust it in! I moved it slowly — very, very slowly, so that I might not disturb the old man's sleep. It took me an hour to place my whole head within the opening so far that I could see him as he lay upon his bed. Ha! would a madman have been so wise as this? And then, when my head was well in the room, I undid the lantern cautiously — oh, so cautiously — cautiously (for the hinges creaked) — I undid it just so much that a single thin ray fell upon the vulture eye. And this I did for seven long nights — every night just at midnight—but I found the eye always closed; and so it was impossible to do the work; for it was not the old man who vexed me, but his Evil Eye. And every morning, when the day broke, I went boldly into the chamber, and spoke courageously to him, calling him by name in a hearty tone, and inquiring how he had passed the night. So you see he would have been a very profound old man, indeed, to suspect that every night, just at twelve, I looked in upon him while he slept.

Upon the eighth night I was more than usually cautious in opening the door. A watch's minute hand moves more quickly than did mine. Never before that night had I felt the extent of my own powers — of my sagacity. I could scarcely contain my feelings of triumph. To think that there I was, opening the door, little by little, and he not even to dream of my secret deeds or thoughts. I fairly chuckled at the idea; and perhaps he heard me; for he moved on the bed suddenly, as if startled. Now you may think that I drew back — but no. His room was as black as pitch with the thick darkness, (for the shutters were close fastened, through fear of robbers,) and so I knew that he could not see the opening of the door, and I kept pushing it on steadily, steadily.

I had my head in, and was about to open the lantern, when my thumb slipped upon the tin fastening, and the old man sprang up in bed, crying out — "Who's there?"

I kept quite still and said nothing. For a whole hour I did not move a muscle, and in the meantime I did not hear him lie down. He was still sitting up in the bed listening;—just as I have done, night after night, hearkening to the death watches in the wall."

844. What disease is the narrator referring to in the opening paragraph?

(A) madness

(B) anxiety

(C) eye cataracts

(D) acute hearing

845. The narrator's personality can best be described as

(A) kind, unbalanced, and passionate.

(B) timid, kind, and passionate.

(C) kind, passionate and compulsive.

(D) cunning, unbalanced, and compulsive.

846. How does the narrator attempt to convince the reader that he is not actually insane?

(A) by pointing out his ability to tell the story calmly and clearly

(B) by offering a valid reason he wanted to kill the old man

(C) by suggesting that it was the old man who was really insane

(D) by pleading insanity

847. According to the passage, why does the narrator want to kill the old man?

(A) because the old man insulted him

(B) so he would never have to look at the old man's diseased eye ever again

(C) to steal the old man's gold

(D) because he hated the old man's pet vulture

848. Why was the narrator unable to carry out his decision to kill the old man during the first week every time he opened the old man's bedroom door?

(A) The narrator was having second thoughts about murdering the old man.

(B) The old man was asleep, so the narrator could not see the "Evil Eye" that he wanted to get rid of.

(C) He couldn't open the bedroom door without waking the old man.

(D) He still needed to know where the old man kept his gold.

849. According to the passage, each morning the narrator tried to hide his intentions toward the old man by doing all of the following EXCEPT

(A) calling him by name.

(B) speaking to him in a cheerful way.

(C) casually asking him where he kept his gold.

(D) asking him how well he had slept.

850. What does the word *sagacity* mean as used in the sentence: "Never before that night had I felt the extent of my own powers—of my sagacity"?

(A) perception

(B) strength

(C) impulsiveness

(D) passion

851. What does the narrator do when the old man springs up in bed and cries out, "Who's there?"

(A) He quickly retreats and quietly closes the door.

(B) He stands perfectly still for over an hour.

(C) He apologizes to the old man for disturbing him.

(D) He springs at the old man and strangles him to death.

Questions 852 through 858 are based on the following passage. The passage is not complete. You have to select the best sentence or completion of a sentence from among the given choices.

This excerpt is from Staying Sharp For Dummies *by the American Geriatrics Society and the Health in Aging Foundation (Wiley).*

SEE QUESTION 852 The exciting thing is that science now provides evidence for what works and what doesn't. Training your brain no longer has to be a case of trial and error.

SEE QUESTION 853 With 100 billion cells, your brain is like the CEO of a giant corporation. How can something so small have so much responsibility? *SEE QUESTION 854*

Brain training is a growing area of interest, both in research and in the public mind. Exciting emerging evidence indicates that you *can* train your brain and, as a result, change your circumstances. But what works and what doesn't? Can everyone benefit from brain training?

SEE QUESTION 855 Although you may have heard that you're stuck with the brain you have, scientific research has now found that this isn't true!

You're probably familiar with the left brain and the right brain. Well, it's true that the brain is made up of left and right hemispheres, which do have different functions. However, the idea that some people are only left-brainers and others are only right-brainers isn't entirely true. For example, language skills are located in the left hemisphere and everyone uses this part of the brain! You don't need to hide behind the excuse that you're a right-brainer so you can't do math calculations. With the activities included in this book, you can get both halves of your brain working at their optimum levels.

SEE QUESTION 856 When you train one part of the brain, the whole brain benefits. You can think of the brain like an orchestra or a sports team. The message is the same — one star player can't carry the rest of the team.

Mental health refers to your state of being. Are you happy? When do you find yourself frustrated? Do you feel stressed out? What makes you feel anxious? These questions are important in determining how well your brain functions, so make sure you pay attention to your mental health. *SEE QUESTION 857*

Don't take your passions and hobbies for granted. Discover how they can make your brain more creative. A more creative brain is a smarter brain. *SEE QUESTION 858*

Getting swept into myriad things that demand your attention on a daily basis is easy. Yet, in this ever-demanding environment, finding time to quiet your brain and create a space for contemplation is increasingly important"

852. Select the best sentence from among the given choices.

(A) You want your brain to work at its best, whether you want to stay sharp to keep up with your children or to excel at you're work.

(B) You want your brain to work at its best, whether you want to stay sharp to keep up with your children or to Excel at you're work.

(C) You want your brains to work at its best, whether you want to stay sharp to keep up with your children or to Excel at your work.

(D) You want your brain to work at its best, whether you want to stay sharp to keep up with your children or to excel at your work.

853. Select the best sentence from among the given choices.

(A) The brain weighs a mere three pounds, yet it's responsible for the smooth running of your whole body.

(B) The brain weighs a mere three pounds, yet its responsible for the smooth running of your whole body.

(C) The brain weighs a mere three pounds, yet its responsible for the smooth running of your hole body.

(D) The brain weighs a mere three pounds, yet it's responsible for the smooth running of your hole body.

854. Select the best sentence from among the given choices.

(A) This understanding gives you the foundation for know how to best train your brain.

(B) This understanding gives you the foundation for knowing how to best training your brain.

(C) This understanding gives you the foundation for knowing how to best train your brain.

(D) This understanding gives you the foundation for know how to best training your brain.

855. Select the best sentence from among the given choices.

(A) People whom use their brains more efficiently tend to have better jobs, better relationships, and more happy and fulfilling lives.

(B) People who use their brains more efficiently tend to have better jobs, better relationships, and more happy and fulfilling lives.

(C) People whom use their brain more efficiently tend to have better jobs, better relationships, and more happy and fulfilling lives.

(D) People who use their brain more efficiently tend to have better jobs, better relationships, and more happy and fulfilling lives.

856. Select the best sentence from among the given choices.

(A) The different parts of the brain don't work in isolation, they work together as a team.

(B) The different parts of the brain don't work in isolation they work together as a team.

(C) The different part of the brain don't work in isolation; they work together as a team.

(D) The different parts of the brain don't work in isolation; they work together as a team.

857. Select the best sentence from among the given choices.

(A) Do so can make the difference between living a fulfilled life and living a frustrated one.

(B) Doing so can make the difference among living a fulfilled life and living a frustrated one.

(C) Doing so can make the difference between living a fulfilled life and living a frustrated one.

(D) Doing so can make the difference amongst living a fulfilled life and living a frustrated one.

858. Select the best sentence from among the given choices.

(A) Whether you're a music lover, a budding writer, or a person with dozens of other interests, you can choose from a range of activities to help your brain.

(B) Weather you're a music lover, a budding writer, or a person with dozens of other interests, you can chose from a range of activities to help your brain.

(C) Whether you're a music lover, a budding writer, or a person with dozens of other interests, you can chose from a range of activities to help your brain.

(D) Weather you're a music lover, a budding writer, or a person with dozens of other interests, you can choose from a range of activities to help your brain.

Questions 859 through 865 are based on the following passage.

This excerpt is from "The Monkey's Paw" by W. W. Jacobs.

Without, the night was cold and wet, but in the small parlour of Laburnam Villa the blinds were drawn and the fire burned brightly. Father and son were at chess, the former, who possessed ideas about the game involving radical changes, putting his king into such sharp and unnecessary perils that it even provoked comment from the white-haired old lady knitting placidly by the fire.

"Hark at the wind," said Mr. White, who, having seen a fatal mistake after it was too late, was amiably desirous of preventing his son from seeing it.

"I'm listening," said the latter, grimly surveying the board as he stretched out his hand. "Check."

"I should hardly think that he'd come to-night," said his father, with his hand poised over the board.

"Mate," replied the son.

"That's the worst of living so far out," bawled Mr. White, with sudden and unlooked-for violence; "of all the beastly, slushy, out-of-the-way places to live in, this is the worst. Pathway's a bog, and the road's a torrent. I don't know what people are thinking about. I suppose because only two houses in the road are let, they think it doesn't matter."

"Never mind, dear," said his wife, soothingly; "perhaps you'll win the next one."

Mr. White looked up sharply, just in time to intercept a knowing glance between mother and son. The words died away on his lips, and he hid a guilty grin in his thin grey beard.

"There he is," said Herbert White, as the gate banged to loudly and heavy footsteps came toward the door.

The old man rose with hospitable haste, and opening the door, was heard condoling with the new arrival. The new arrival also condoled with himself, so that Mrs. White said, "Tut, tut!" and coughed gently as her husband entered the room, followed by a tall, burly man, beady of eye and rubicund of visage.

"Sergeant-Major Morris," he said, introducing him.

The sergeant-major shook hands, and taking the proffered seat by the fire, watched contentedly while his host got out whiskey and tumblers and stood a small copper kettle on the fire.

At the third glass his eyes got brighter, and he began to talk, the little family circle regarding with eager interest this visitor from distant parts, as he squared his broad shoulders in the chair and spoke of wild scenes and doughty deeds; of wars and plagues and strange peoples.

"Twenty-one years of it," said Mr. White, nodding at his wife and son. "When he went away he was a slip of a youth in the warehouse. Now look at him."

"He don't look to have taken much harm," said Mrs. White, politely.

"I'd like to go to India myself," said the old man, "just to look round a bit, you know."

"Better where you are," said the sergeant-major, shaking his head. He put down the empty glass, and sighing softly, shook it again.

"I should like to see those old temples and fakirs and jugglers," said the old man. "What was that you started telling me the other day about a monkey's paw or something, Morris?"

"Nothing," said the soldier, hastily. "Leastways nothing worth hearing."

"Monkey's paw?" said Mrs. White, curiously.

"Well, it's just a bit of what you might call magic, perhaps," said the sergeant-major, offhandedly.

His three listeners leaned forward eagerly. The visitor absent-mindedly put his empty glass to his lips and then set it down again. His host filled it for him.

"To look at," said the sergeant-major, fumbling in his pocket, "it's just an ordinary little paw, dried to a mummy."

He took something out of his pocket and proffered it. Mrs. White drew back with a grimace, but her son, taking it, examined it curiously.

"And what is there special about it?" inquired Mr. White as he took it from his son, and having examined it, placed it upon the table.

"It had a spell put on it by an old fakir," said the sergeant-major, "a very holy man. He wanted to show that fate ruled people's lives, and that those who interfered with it did so to their sorrow. He put a spell on it so that three separate men could each have three wishes from it."

859. The passage describes Sergeant-Major Morris as

(A) short, burly, beady-eyed, and red-cheeked.

(B) short, skinny, beady-eyed, and red-cheeked.

(C) tall, burly, beady-eyed, and red-cheeked.

(D) tall, skinny, sharp-eyed, and red-cheeked.

860. Why does the son say "mate" to his father?

(A) They are the very best of friends.

(B) The son is informing the father that their game is over.

(C) His father is called Mate.

(D) He is asking about a mutual friend.

861. Why does Mr. White's wife ignore her husband's sudden complaint about living so far out of the way and instead say, "Never mind, dear, . . . perhaps you'll win the next one"?

(A) She misunderstood what he was complaining about.

(B) She wants to change the subject because they have no choice but to live there.

(C) She has realized that the real reason he is upset is that he has just lost the game.

(D) She is going senile.

862. Where has Sergeant-Major Morris been living for the past twenty years?

(A) Africa

(B) India

(C) Laburnam Villa

(D) The passage does not say.

863. Mr. White expresses interest in seeing all of the following exotic attractions EXCEPT

(A) jugglers.

(B) old temples.

(C) wild monkeys.

(D) fakirs.

864. According to the passage, what is special about the monkey's paw?

(A) It is very old and dry.

(B) It is mummified.

(C) It has had a magic spell placed on it.

(D) It used to belong to a very important monkey.

865. According to the passage, what was the old fakir's purpose when he placed the enchantment on the monkey's paw?

(A) He wanted to show that people who interfere with fate do so to their sorrow.

(B) He wanted to help people by granting them three wishes.

(C) He wanted to help the monkey whose paw had been taken.

(D) He wanted to show people that their wishes really can come true.

Questions 866 through 873 are based on the following passage.

This excerpt is from The War of The Worlds *by H. G. Wells.*

"Keep back! Keep back!"

A boy came running towards me.

"It's a-movin'," he said to me as he passed; "a-screwin' and a-screwin' out. I don't like it. I'm a-goin' 'ome, I am."

I went on to the crowd. There were really, I should think, two or three hundred people elbowing and jostling one another, the one or two ladies there being by no means the least active.

"He's fallen in the pit!" cried some one.

"Keep back!" said several.

The crowd swayed a little, and I elbowed my way through. Every one seemed greatly excited. I heard a peculiar humming sound from the pit.

"I say!" said Ogilvy; "help keep these idiots back. We don't know what's in the confounded thing, you know!"

I saw a young man, a shop assistant in Woking I believe he was, standing on the cylinder and trying to scramble out of the hole again. The crowd had pushed him in.

The end of the cylinder was being screwed out from within. Nearly two feet of shining screw projected. Somebody blundered against me, and I narrowly missed being pitched onto the top of the screw. I turned, and as I did so the screw must have come out, for the lid of the cylinder fell upon the gravel with a ringing concussion. I stuck my elbow into the person behind me, and turned my head towards the Thing again. For a moment that circular cavity seemed perfectly black. I had the sunset in my eyes.

I think everyone expected to see a man emerge—possibly something a little unlike us terrestrial men, but in all essentials a man. I know I did. But, looking, I presently saw something stirring within the shadow: greyish billowy movements, one above another, and then two luminous disks—like eyes. Then something resembling a little grey snake, about the thickness of a walking stick, coiled up out of the writhing middle, and wriggled in the air towards me—and then another.

A sudden chill came over me. There was a loud shriek from a woman behind. I half turned, keeping my eyes fixed upon the cylinder still, from which other tentacles were now projecting, and began pushing my way back from the edge of the pit. I saw astonishment giving place to horror on the faces of the people about me. I heard inarticulate exclamations on all sides. There was a general movement backwards. I saw the shopman struggling still on the edge of the pit. I found myself alone, and saw the people on the other side of the pit running off, Stent among them. I looked again at the cylinder, and ungovernable terror gripped me. I stood petrified and staring.

A big greyish rounded bulk, the size, perhaps, of a bear, was rising slowly and painfully out of the cylinder. As it bulged up and caught the light, it glistened like wet leather.

Two large dark-coloured eyes were regarding me steadfastly. The mass that framed them, the head of the thing, was rounded, and had, one might say, a face. There was a mouth under the eyes, the lipless brim of which quivered and panted, and dropped saliva. The whole creature heaved and pulsated convulsively. A lank tentacular appendage gripped the edge of the cylinder, another swayed in the air.

Those who have never seen a living Martian can scarcely imagine the strange horror of its appearance. The peculiar V-shaped mouth with its pointed upper lip, the absence of brow ridges, the absence of a chin beneath the wedgelike lower lip, the incessant quivering of this mouth, the Gorgon groups of tentacles, the tumultuous breathing of the lungs in a strange atmosphere, the evident heaviness and painfulness of movement due to the greater gravitational energy of the earth—above all, the extraordinary intensity of the immense eyes—were at once vital, intense, inhuman, crippled and monstrous. There was something fungoid in the oily brown skin, something in the clumsy deliberation of the tedious movements unspeakably nasty. Even at this first encounter, this first glimpse, I was overcome with disgust and dread.

866. Why does the author appear to misspell the words spoken by the boy when he says phrases like "It's a-movin'" and "I'm a-goin' 'ome, I am"?

(A) The story was written before automated spell-checkers were invented.

(B) The author is a terrible writer and doesn't understand the rules of spelling or grammar.

(C) The author wanted to display the boy's character to the reader by spelling the words in the manner in which the boy says them.

(D) The rules of spelling and grammar were very different when the story was written.

867. In the scene, who appears to be in a position of authority?

(A) the shop assistant from Woking

(B) Ogilvy

(C) the Thing

(D) the narrator

868. As the occupants of the cylinder begin to emerge, the mood of the spectators changes swiftly from

(A) horror to panic.

(B) ambivalence to excitement.

(C) horror and panic to excitement and anticipation.

(D) excitement and anticipation to horror and panic.

869. How does the crowd know that the cylinder has someone or something alive inside of it?

(A) The cylinder is being unscrewed from within.

(B) They can hear the cries of help from within.

(C) Cylinders of this size always contain living things.

(D) It's a lucky guess.

870. What does the crowd expect to see emerging from the cylinder?

(A) an alien with large eyes and tentacles

(B) a snake-like creature

(C) a bear-like creature

(D) a creature that resembles a human

871. What feature of the alien's appearance does the narrator find most disturbing?

(A) the alien's tentacles

(B) the alien's mouth

(C) the alien's eyes

(D) the lack of chin

872. Where did the cylinder apparently come from?

(A) Russia

(B) Mars

(C) Neptune

(D) The passage does not say.

873. Which of the following scenarios is LEAST likely to happen in the next part of the story?

(A) The narrator becomes firm friends with the aliens.

(B) The aliens attack the crowd.

(C) The humans regroup and attack the aliens.

(D) The aliens and humans enter a war against each other.

Questions 874 through 880 are based on the following passage. The passage is not complete. You have to select the best sentence or completion of a sentence from among the given choices.

The following excerpt is from Business Writing For Dummies *by Natalie Canavor (Wiley).*

In both your personal and professional lives, you may occasionally find cause to write complaints. When that happens, you get much better results if you do it well. A written complaint offers a great demonstration of how to use the planning process.

SEE QUESTION 874 You may not have achieved what you wanted or may feel disappointed, but written complaints last a long time — forever, more or less. People take written complaints and criticism very seriously. So never draft and send such a message in the heat of the moment. Step-by-step planning helps you remove yourself from the emotional context and attendant risks.

SEE QUESTION 875 For example, you might say, 'Hi Jack, how's it going? We noticed there's a long delay till our calls for service get handled. What's up?' This is a good, neutral way to start the interaction.

If making a call or having a conversation doesn't seem to help, plan a letter. Suppose a supplier has disappointed you with the quality of goods or services delivered. Perhaps computer maintenance work has been poorly performed. Articulating your *goal* is critical.

SEE QUESTION 876 Writing from anger is a self-indulgent approach that frequently boomerangs. You may not know an important part of the story, so proceed very cautiously before burning bridges. In any case, the world is small, and a person you attack may have friends you could encounter in the future.

Your goal may better be stated as one or more of the following:

- Resolve a dispute
- Solve a problem
- Gain a concession
- Get a refund
- Get an apology or acknowledgment

SEE QUESTION 877 Putting your reader on the defensive is never to your advantage. Stick to the facts, not how you feel. Adopt a tone that conveys an assumption that the problem can be fixed. As the saying says, no point biting off your nose to spite your face. Is the disappointing supplier the only one who has what you need? Will finding a new source threaten your production deadlines or up the costs? Review the ramifications to help you feel more objective. Resolve to give the other party a chance to perform.

For example, you can complain about a computer maintenance issue:

Dear Bob,

SEE QUESTION 878 *During the first quarter of this year, we made 16 calls to your office and in 12 cases, response took two to three days. As you know, the network's critical to all our operations and such delays are expensive for us.*

SEE QUESTION 879.

Please look into this and get back to me at your earliest convenience. I'd like to know why the problem is happening and what steps you can take to deliver the service we need.

Thank you for your immediate attention. I hope these issues can be quickly resolved.

Best, Elaine

The tone and language are low-key and neutral, and Bob will notice that Elaine sees the problem as fixable. But he'll have no trouble recognizing that the contract is at risk. ***SEE QUESTION 880***

874. Select the best sentence from among the given choices.

(A) In any situation first thoroughly review the pros and cons of putting a complaint in writing at all.

(B) In any situation, first, thoroughly reviewing the pros and cons of putting a complaint in writing at all.

(C) In any situation, first thoroughly review the pros and cons of putting a complaint in writing at all.

(D) In any situation first thoroughly reviewing the pros and cons of putting a complaint in writing at all.

875. Select the best sentence from among the given choices.

(A) Bring up the problem in a telephone or in person conversation may be a smart way to deal with the complaint, depending on the situation and weather you can keep your cool.

(B) Bringing up the problem in a telephone or in-person conversation may be a smart way to deal with the complaint, depending on the situation and weather you can keep your cool.

(C) Bring up the problem in a telephone or in person conversation may be a smart way to deal with the complaint, depending on the situation and whether you can keep your cool.

(D) Bringing up the problem in a telephone or in-person conversation may be a smart way to deal with the complaint, depending on the situation and whether you can keep your cool.

876. Select the best sentence from among the given choices.

(A) Your goal in a complaint letter is never — no matter how you feel — to let off steam.

(B) Your goal in a complaint letter is never no matter how you feel to let off steam.

(C) Your goal in a complaint letter is never — no matter how you feeling — to let off steam.

(D) Your goal in a complaint letter is not never — no matter how you feel — to let off steam.

877. Select the best sentence from among the given choices.

(A) Control your tone also helps you achieve your purpose.

(B) Controlling your tone also helps you achieve your purpose.

(C) Control your tone also helps you achieving your purpose.

(D) Controlling your tone also helps you achieve your propose.

878. Select the best sentence from among the given choices.

(A) I looked into several complaints from three of my departments last week, and the records show that service on our network has been slow.

(B) I had looked into several complaints from three of my departments last week, and the records show that service on our network has been slow.

(C) I will look into several complaints from three of my departments last week, and the records show that service on our network has been slow.

(D) I will be looking into several complaints from three of my departments last week, and the records show that service on our network has been slow.

879. Select the best sentence from among the given choices.

(A) Of coarse, this is not the service level we signed on for or experienced in the prior year.

(B) Of course this is not the service level we signed on for or experienced in the prior year.

(C) Of coarse this is not the service level we signed on for or experienced in the prior year.

(D) Of course, this is not the service level we signed on for or experienced in the prior year.

880. Select the best sentence from among the given choices.

(A) Note how using specific facts support the goal and provide the best shot at remedying the situation.

(B) Note how using specific facts supports the goal and provides the best shoot at remedying the situation.

(C) Note how using specific facts supports the goal and provides the best shot at remedying the situation.

(D) Noting how using specific facts supports the goal and provides the best shot at remedying the situation.

Questions 881 through 888 are based on the following passage.

The following excerpt is from Fit and Healthy For Dummies *by Carol Ann Rinzler (Wiley).*

You are what you eat. You are also how you eat. And when you eat.

Choosing a varied diet of healthful foods supports any healthy mind and body, but which healthful foods you choose says much about your personal tastes as well as the culture from which you come.

How you eat may do the same: Do you use a knife and fork? A pair of sticks? Your hands and a round of bread? Each is a cultural statement. As for when you eat (and when you stop), that is a purely personal physiological response to signals from your digestive organs and your brain: "Get food now!" or "Thank you, that's enough."

If you read chapter by chapter through this book, you can follow what you eat and drink as it moves from your plate to your mouth to your digestive tract and into every tissue and cell. Along the way, you discover how your organs and systems work. You observe firsthand why some foods and beverages are essential to your health. And you find out how to manage your diet so that you can get the biggest bang (nutrients) for your buck (calories).

Technically speaking, nutrition is the science of how the body uses food. In fact, nutrition is life. All living things, including you, need food and water to live. Beyond that, you need good food, meaning food with the proper nutrients, to live well. If you don't eat and drink, you'll die. Period. If you don't eat and drink nutritious food and beverages:

Your bones may bend or break (not enough calcium).

Your gums may bleed (not enough vitamin C).

Your blood may not carry oxygen to every cell (not enough iron).

And on, and on, and on. Understanding how good nutrition protects you against these dire consequences requires a familiarity with the language and concepts of nutrition. Knowing some basic chemistry is helpful. (Don't panic: Chemistry can be a cinch when you read about it in plain English.) A smattering of sociology and psychology is also useful because although nutrition is mostly about how food revs up and sustains your body, it's also about the cultural traditions and individual differences that explain how you choose your favorite foods.

To sum it up: Nutrition is about why you eat what you eat and how the food you get affects your body and your health.

Nutrition's primary task is figuring out which foods and beverages (in what quantities) provide the energy and building material you need to construct and maintain every organ and system. To do this, nutrition concentrates on food's two basic attributes: energy and nutrients.

Energy is the ability to do work. Virtually every bite of food gives you energy, even when it doesn't give you nutrients. The amount of energy in food is measured in calories, the amount of heat produced when food is burned (metabolized) in your body cells. You can read all about calories in Chapter 3. But right now, all you need to know is that food is the fuel on which your body runs. Without enough food, you don't have enough energy.

Essential nutrients for human beings include many well-known vitamins and minerals, several amino acids (the so-called building blocks of proteins), and at least two fatty acids.

Identifying nutrients is one thing. Making sure you get them into your body is another. Here, the essential idea is to keep nutritious food nutritious by preserving and protecting its components.

Some people see the term food processing as a nutritional dirty word. Or words. They're wrong. Without food processing and preservatives, you and I would still be forced to gather (or kill) our food each morning and down it fast before it spoiled.

Considering how vital food preservation can be, you may want to think about when you last heard a rousing cheer for the anonymous cook who first noticed that salting or pickling food could extend food's shelf life. Or for the guys who invented the refrigeration and freezing techniques that slow food's natural tendency to degrade.

881. The passage says that all of the following factors affect your choice of healthful foods EXCEPT

(A) the country you come from.

(B) the culture you live in.

(C) your budget.

(D) your personal tastes.

882. According to the passage, nutrition is described as all of the following EXCEPT

(A) the science of how the body uses food.

(B) life.

(C) necessary to live well.

(D) necessary to live a happy life.

883. According to the passage, all of the following are nutrients EXCEPT

(A) calcium.

(B) vitamin C.

(C) iron.

(D) nickel.

884. Fill in the blanks to correctly complete the sentence:

_______________ is defined as the ability to do work. _______________ is the fuel on which your body runs.

885. According to the passage, what is produced when food is metabolized in the body?

(A) heat

(B) light

(C) calories

(D) cells

886. According to the passage, essential nutrients for the human body include

(A) vitamins and minerals only.
(B) vitamins and fatty acids only.
(C) amino acids and fatty acids only.
(D) vitamins and minerals, amino acids, and fatty acids.

887. According to the passage, what is the author's opinion regarding food processing?

(A) She considers it a nutritional dirty word.
(B) She is strongly against it.
(C) She is strongly in favor of it.
(D) She is ambivalent about it.

888. What is the best meaning of the word *degrade* as used in the sentence fragment: "Or for the guys who invented the refrigeration and freezing techniques that slow food's natural tendency to degrade"?

(A) become less important
(B) spoil
(C) to achieve less
(D) to be awarded a grade D

Questions 889 through 896 are based on the following passage.

The following excerpt is from 3D Printing For Dummies *by Kalani Kirk Hausman and Richard Horne (Wiley).*

An amazing transformation is currently underway in manufacturing, across nearly all types of products — a transformation that promises to remake the future into a sustainable and personally customized environment. In this fast-approaching future, everything we need — from products to food, and even our bodies themselves — can be replaced or reconstructed rapidly and with very minimal waste. This is not the slow change of progress from one generation of iPhone to the next but instead a true revolution, mirroring the changes that introduced the world to the Industrial Age and then brought light and electricity to our homes and businesses.

This will not be a "bloodless coup" by any means; any truly fundamental change that spans all aspects of the global economy will, by its nature, be disruptive. But traditional inefficient ways of producing the next year's model will surely give way to entirely new opportunities impossible to imagine before. The technology behind this transformation is referred to as *additive manufacturing, 3D printing,* or *direct digital manufacturing.*

By whatever name, in the coming decade this technology will be used to construct everything from houses to jet engines, airplanes, food, and even replacement tissues and organs made from your own cells! Every day new applications of 3D printing are being discovered and developed all over the world. And even in space: NASA is testing designs that will function in zero gravity, on the airless moon, and even to support human exploration of other planets like Mars. Hold on tight, because in the chapters ahead we cover a lot of incredibly new and fantastic technologies — and before the end, we show you how you can get involved in this amazing transformation yourself by building and using a 3D printer at home.

So, what is "additive manufacturing," you might ask? Additive manufacturing is a little like the "replicators" in the *Star Trek* universe, which allow the captain to order "Tea, Earl Grey, hot" and have a cup filled with liquid appear fully formed and ready for consumption. We are not quite to that level, but today's 3D printers perform additive manufacturing by taking a 3D model of an object stored in a computer, translating it into a series of very thin layers, and then building the object one layer at a time, stacking up material until the object is ready for use.

3D printers are much like the familiar desktop printer you already use at work or in your home to create copies of documents transmitted electronically or created on your computer, except that a 3D printer creates a solid three-dimensional object out of a variety of materials, not just a simple paper document.

Since the time of Johannes Gutenberg, creating multiple printed documents has brought literacy to the world. Today, when you click the Print button in a word processor application, you merge the functions of writers, stenographers, editors (spell-check), layout, illumination (coloring and adding in images), and press reproduction all into a single task, and with the click of a few more buttons, you can post the document you create onto the Internet and allow it to be shared, downloaded, and printed out by others all over the world.

3D printing does the exact same thing for objects: Designs and virtual 3D models for physical objects can be shared, downloaded, and then printed out into physical form. It's hard to imagine what Johannes Gutenberg would have made of that.

889. According to the initial paragraph of the passage, what two advantages will additive manufacturing have over traditional manufacturing methods?

(A) Although it produces more waste, it will be cheaper and faster than traditional methods.

(B) Although it is slower, it is cheaper and produces less waste than traditional methods.

(C) It is sustainable and personally customizable.

(D) It will be cheaper and personally customizable.

890. Why do the authors compare the advent of additive manufacturing to the changes that brought about the Industrial Age?

(A) They want to show how similar the advent of additive manufacturing is to the progress from one generation of the iPhone to the next.

(B) Additive manufacturing was invented during the Industrial Age.

(C) Additive manufacturing was a prerequisite for the Industrial Age to occur.

(D) They want to show how much additive manufacturing will revolutionize our lives.

891. Why do the authors warn that the revolution brought about by this new technology "will not be a 'bloodless coup'"?

(A) It will be disruptive as it brings swift changes to all aspects of the economy.

(B) It will bring gradual changes to only some parts of the economy.

(C) New technologies always cause injuries or deaths before all the kinks have been ironed out.

(D) It will cause the government to fall, and some leaders may be executed.

892. According to the passage, 3D printers are

(A) available only to NASA.

(B) too technical and expensive for the average person to own.

(C) so easy to use and make, you can build one yourself.

(D) not actually real but may become so in the future.

893. Why do the authors compare 3D printers to the "replicators" in *Star Trek*?

(A) because 3D printers can be used to manufacture replicators

(B) to provide a clear example of a similar device that the reader may be familiar with

(C) to show the differences between the devices

(D) because everyone loves *Star Trek*

894. Who was Johannes Gutenberg?

(A) the inventor of the first 3D printer

(B) the inventor of the replicator

(C) the inventor of the printing press

(D) the author of best-selling books on literacy

895. According to the passage, which of the following is a true statement?

(A) A 3D printer stores an object in a cupboard, translating it into a series of very thick slices, and then builds the object two layers a time.

(B) A 3D printer stores an object in a computer, translating it into a series of very thin slices, and then builds the object one layer at a time.

(C) A 3D printer stores an object in a computer, translating it into a series of very thick slices, and then builds the object several layers at a time.

(D) A 3D printer stores an object in a computer, translating it into a series of very thin slices, and then builds the object five layers at a time.

896. Why do the authors end the excerpt with the sentence "It's hard to imagine what Johannes Gutenberg would have made of that"?

(A) to show that Gutenberg was a secretive person whose thoughts were difficult to read

(B) to show that Gutenberg would have expected additive manufacturing to have happened sooner rather than later

(C) to show that Gutenberg would not have approved of 3D printing

(D) to show how amazed Gutenberg would be to see how far printing has progressed since his time

Questions 897 through 904 are based on the following passage.

The following excerpt is from Wine For Dummies *by Ed McCarthy and Mary Ewing-Mulligan (Wiley).*

We know plenty of people who enjoy drinking wine but don't know much about it. (Been there, done that ourselves.) Knowing a lot of information about wine definitely isn't a prerequisite to enjoying it. But familiarity with certain aspects of wine can make choosing wines a lot easier, enhance your enjoyment of wine, and increase your comfort level. You can master as much or as little as you like. The journey begins here.

In its most basic form, winemaking is that simple. After the grapes are crushed, *yeasts* (tiny one-celled organisms that exist naturally in the vineyard and, therefore, on the grapes) come into contact with the sugar in the grapes' juice and gradually convert that sugar into alcohol. Yeasts also produce carbon dioxide, which evaporates into the air. When the yeasts are done working, your grape juice is wine. The sugar that was in the juice is no longer there — alcohol is present instead. (The riper and sweeter the grapes, the more alcohol the wine will have.) This process is called *fermentation.*

Fermentation is a totally natural process that doesn't require man's participation at all, except to put the grapes into a container and release the juice from the grapes. Fermentation occurs in fresh apple cider left too long in your refrigerator, without any help from you. We read that even milk, which contains a different sort of sugar than grapes do, develops a small amount of alcohol if left on the kitchen table all day long.

Speaking of milk, Louis Pasteur is the man credited with discovering fermentation in the 19th century. That's discovering, not inventing. Some of those apples in the Garden of Eden probably fermented long before Pasteur came along. (Well, we don't think it could have been much of an Eden without wine!)

Now if every winemaker actually made wine in as crude a manner as we just described, we'd be drinking some pretty rough stuff that would hardly inspire us to write a book about wine. But today's winemakers have a bag of tricks as big as a sumo wrestler's appetite, which is one reason no two wines ever taste exactly the same.

The men and women who make wine can control the type of container they use for the fermentation process (stainless steel and oak are the two main materials) as well as the size of the container and the temperature of the juice during fermentation — and every one of these choices can make a real difference in the taste of the wine.

After fermentation, winemakers can choose how long to let the wine *mature* (a stage when the wine sort of gets its act together) and in what kind of container. Fermentation can last three days or three months, and the wine can then mature for a couple of weeks or a couple of years or anything in between. (If you have trouble making decisions, don't ever become a winemaker.)

Obviously, one of the biggest factors in making one wine different from the next is the nature of the raw material, the grape juice. Besides the fact that riper, sweeter grapes make a more alcoholic wine, different *varieties* of grapes (Chardonnay, Cabernet Sauvignon, or Merlot, for example) make different wines. Grapes are the main ingredient in wine, and everything the winemaker does, he does to the particular grape juice he has.

897. The authors suggest that learning more information about wine

(A) is a prerequisite to enjoying wine.

(B) can make choosing wines a lot easier.

(C) will make you drink more.

(D) will make you seem pretentious.

898. According to the passage, when yeasts are placed in grape juice, they produce all of the following EXCEPT

(A) sugar.

(B) alcohol.

(C) carbon dioxide.

(D) wine.

899. According to the passage, fermentation occurs naturally in

(A) newly refrigerated milk.

(B) milk left at room temperature.

(C) pure water.

(D) empty refrigerators.

900. Who was Louis Pasteur?

(A) He discovered fermentation.

(B) He discovered yeasts.

(C) He invented wine.

(D) He invented apple cider.

901. Why do the authors say, "Well, we don't think it could have been much of an Eden without wine!"?

(A) They know that wine was invented in Eden.

(B) Eden is famous for its wide variety of wine.

(C) The best gardens for growing grapes are found just east of Eden.

(D) They're attempting to be humorous.

902. According to the passage, *after* all the ingredients have been collected and prepared, winemakers can still control the taste of the wine produced during the fermentation process by selecting all of the following factors EXCEPT

(A) the material used for the brewing container.

(B) the temperature of the juice.

(C) the type of grapes used.

(D) the size of the brewing container.

903. According to the passage, how do winemakers affect the flavor of the wine *after* the fermentation process is complete?

(A) by letting the wine mature for a particular amount of time

(B) by bottling and selling the wine as soon as possible

(C) by adding more grape juice

(D) by selecting different grapes

904. What determines whether a particular wine is considered a Chardonnay, a Cabernet Sauvignon, or a Merlot?

(A) the label on the bottle

(B) the country that the grapes come from

(C) the type of yeasts used

(D) the variety of grapes used

Questions 905 through 912 are based on the following passage.

The following excerpt is from Signing For Dummies *by Adan R. Penilla and Angela Lee Taylor (Wiley).*

Signing isn't difficult, although moving your hands, body, and face to convey meaning instead of just using your voice may seem odd at first. But with time, practice, and interaction, you'll see that hand movements can be meaningful. Your goal and reward is being able to meet and communicate with a whole new group of people — people who share your opinions, hobbies, and more. That's definitely worth the initial awkwardness!

This chapter illustrates the manual alphabet in American Sign Language and talks about hand and body movements. Here, we show you the basics of making handshapes and using facial expressions and body language to get your ideas across. And we start off by reassuring you that you already know some signs. Trust us — you do.

For example, Sign is interwoven in your gestures when you use your index finger to motion to someone to "come here," when you shake your head "yes" and "no," and when you give someone the "evil eye." When you put these in signing context, you convey volumes of information.

Iconic or *natural* signs look like what they mean — the up and down motion of brushing your teeth that means **toothbrush,** for instance, or the right and left punches that mean **boxing.** Iconic signs always show action.

If you have trouble reading someone's signs, check the context and then ask yourself, "What could this person mean?" Remember that it's okay to ask someone to repeat something, just like you do when you don't understand someone speaking to you. You can show a signer you're "listening" by nodding your head. If at any time someone is signing something to you and you begin not to understand, stop the person and let her know what you did understand and where you stopped understanding. This is perfectly acceptable. Don't wait for the person to finish a long, drawn-out thought and then say, "I don't understand."

Remember not to watch the signer's hands primarily. You want to watch the signer's hands through your peripheral vision. Keep your eyes on the whole picture, from the signer's abdomen on up to her head. The eyes, face, hands, and body movements tell the whole story.

You already know that "speaking" ASL is mostly a matter of using your fingers, hands, and arms. What you may not understand yet is that facial expressions and body language are important and sometimes crucial for conveying and understanding signs and their meaning. If you're focused only on a signer's hands, you can easily miss the slightest rolling of the eyes, a raised eyebrow, or the signer "pointing" at something with his eyes. So expect to see hands on hips in frustration, eyes open wide in shock, and hands on mouths covering a hearty laugh. You know these gestures already and are off to a good start.

Signers use the manual alphabet all the time, especially beginners. Signers *fingerspell* — spell using the manual alphabet — certain words and, at first, people's names. So as a beginner, feel free to fingerspell any word you don't know the sign for. If you want to fingerspell two or more words in a row, such as a title or someone's first and last name, pause for just a second between each word.

905. Based on the information in the passage, which of the following is a true statement?

(A) Signing uses your hands, toes, and face to convey meaning.

(B) Signing uses your hands, body, and ears to convey meaning.

(C) Signing uses your hands, body, and face to convey meaning.

(D) Signing uses your hands, shoulders, knees, and toes to convey meaning.

906. According to the passage, what is an *iconic* or *natural* sign?

(A) a complex sign that only the most advanced users can understand

(B) a passive sign that requires only the use of your voice

(C) an action sign that looks like what it means

(D) a sign that is used to convey emotions

907. If you are having trouble understanding someone's signs, which of the following actions would be unacceptable?

(A) asking the person to repeat what he or she just said

(B) stopping the person and letting him or her know where you stopped understanding

(C) slapping your forehead and shouting, "Speak up, fool!"

(D) considering the context of the conversation and imagining what the other person could have meant

908. According to the passage, what is ASL?

(A) Australian Sign Language

(B) American Sign Language

(C) Alternative Sign Language

(D) American Signing Lessons

909. Based on the information in the passage, which of the following is a true statement?

(A) You should watch the signer's hands primarily in order to understand the message.

(B) You should watch the signer's face primarily in order to understand the message.

(C) One only needs to watch the signer's abdomen in order to understand the message.

(D) You should watch the signer's abdomen on up to the signer's head in order to understand the message.

910. Based on the information in the passage, what is *fingerspelling*?

(A) writing letters on a sheet of paper

(B) signing the individual letters with your fingers

(C) an alternative name for signing

(D) when a signer performs a magic trick

911. According to the passage, what should you do if you want to fingerspell more than one word?

(A) pause for just a second between each pair of words

(B) spell them as quickly as possible to avoid confusion

(C) use ASL signs for all the other words after the initial word

(D) you should never fingerspell more than one word at a time

912. According to the passage, why would a person with perfectly good hearing bother to learn how to sign?

(A) to feel superior to deaf people

(B) to understand how difficult it is for deaf people to communicate with each other

(C) to communicate with a whole new group of people

(D) they are bored and can't think of anything else to do with their time

Questions 913 through 920 are based on the following two poems by WWI veteran Siegfried Sassoon.

Survivors

No doubt they'll soon get well; the shock and strain
Have caused their stammering, disconnected talk.
Of course they're 'longing to go out again,' —
These boys with old, scared faces, learning to walk.
They'll soon forget their haunted nights; their cowed
Subjection to the ghosts of friends who died,—
Their dreams that drip with murder; and they'll
be proud Of glorious war that shatter'd all their
pride... Men who went out to battle, grim and glad;
Children, with eyes that hate you, broken and mad.

Craiglockart Hospital. October, 1917. Siegfried Sassoon

Suicide in the Trenches

I knew a simple soldier boy
Who grinned at life in empty joy,
Slept soundly through the lonesome dark,
And whistled early with the lark.

In winter trenches, cowed and glum,
With crumps and lice and lack of rum,
He put a bullet through his brain.
No one spoke of him again.

You smug-faced crowds with kindling eye
Who cheer when soldier lads march by,
Sneak home and pray you'll never know
The hell where youth and laughter go.

913. What is the author's tone in the first poem?

(A) ironic
(B) sincere
(C) jovial
(D) proud

914. Which of the following best summarizes the main theme that both poems share?

(A) the glory of war
(B) the horrors of war
(C) our brave war heroes
(D) fight the good fight

915. The phrase "These boys with old, scared faces, learning to walk" could mean all of the following EXCEPT

(A) the soldiers are slowly recovering from their physical injuries.
(B) the soldiers are slowly recovering from their psychological injuries.
(C) the soldiers are so old that they have forgotten how to walk properly.
(D) the soldiers are slowly readjusting to normal life.

916. What is the most likely reason that the author included the fact that he had written the first poem in a hospital?

(A) He was an injured war veteran and wrote the poem while recovering from his injuries in the hospital.
(B) He works at a hospital.
(C) He likes writing poems in the hospital.
(D) He was joking.

917. In the second poem, what is the author's attitude toward the supporters of the war?

(A) He respects their opinion but disagrees with them.
(B) He agrees with them fully.
(C) He has utter contempt for them.
(D) He is ambivalent toward them.

918. At the end of the first poem, what does the phrase "Men who went out to battle, grim and glad; Children, with eyes that hate you, broken and mad" mean?

(A) Soldiers make terrible parents.
(B) The soldiers went to war as men but came back broken and almost insane.
(C) Children should be sent to war rather than soldiers.
(D) The children of the soldiers will not forgive you.

919. What is the "hell" that is referred to in the phrase "The hell where youth and laughter go"?

(A) losing the war

(B) war

(C) coming home from the war

(D) the place where the devil lives

920. What would the author's opinion be about people who organize a parade titled "Our brave soldiers' return from the war"?

(A) He would be in favor of it because it would celebrate the soldiers' bravery.

(B) He would be ambivalent about it.

(C) He would be totally against it.

(D) He may publicly state that he is against it but would secretly want to attend.

Questions 921 through 928 are based on the following passage.

The following excerpt is from Writing Children's Books For Dummies *by Lisa Rojany Buccieri and Peter Economy (Wiley).*

For many, dreams of writing or illustrating a children's book remain just that — dreams — because they soon find out that writing a really good children's book is *hard.* Not only that, but actually getting a children's book published is even harder. If you don't know the conventions and styles, if you don't speak the lingo, if you don't have someone to advocate for your work, or if you or your manuscript doesn't come across as professional, you'll be hard pressed to get your manuscript read and considered, much less published.

Consider this chapter your sneak peek into the world of children's publishing. We fill you in on the basics of children's book formats, creating a productive writing zone, employing key storytelling techniques, revising your manuscript, and getting your story into the hands of publishers who sell to the exact children's audience you're targeting.

Every bestselling children's book author started with a story idea — just like yours. Also, many of today's most successful writers were rejected time after time until they finally found someone who liked what he or she read or saw and decided to take a chance. Follow your dreams. Feed your passion. Never give up. The day your children's book is published, we'll be cheering for you.

Before you do anything else, figure out what kind of children's book you're writing (or want to write). Manuscripts are published in several tried-and- true formats, with new ones developed every year. *Formats* involve the physical characteristics of a book: page count, *trim size* (width and height), whether it's color or black and white, has lots of pictures or lots of words, is hardcover or softcover, comes as an e-book or an app — or both. There are also lots of genres your book may (or may not) fall into. So figuring out your format and genre will help you determine exactly how to write and present your book.

You also need to ask yourself: Who is my audience? Believe it or not, *children* isn't the correct answer. Children of a particular age bracket, say *infant to age 2*, or *ages 3 to 8,* may come closer to defining the target age you're trying to reach, but are they really the ones who buy your book? Because books are ushered through the process by grown-ups — signed up by agents, acquired and edited by editors, categorized by publishers, pushed by sales reps, shelved and sold by booksellers, and most often purchased by parents and other adults — your audience is more complicated than you may think.

If you thought you could just grab a pen and paper and jump right in to writing, you're right! But you may also want to consider what will happen when your life starts to intrude on your writing time. How do you work around the children needing to be fed and your desk being buried under mounds of bills and old homework? How do you figure out when it's best to write? In Chapter 4, we talk about the importance of making a writing schedule and sticking to it. We also emphasize finding a space of your own for writing and making that space conducive to productivity and creativity.

After you figure out how to get to work, you have to decide what you're going to write about. Coming up with an interesting idea for a story isn't necessarily as easy as you may think, which is why we provide lots of ways to boot up your idea factory in Chapter 5. We also have ways to get you unstuck if you find yourself with a mysterious case of writer's block.

As soon as you have your good idea, it's time to get out there and research to make sure the idea fits your target audience. We cover the hows and whys of researching your audience, of figuring out what children like and what is important in their lives, and then researching the topic itself in Chapter 6.

By making sure your fiction story features these key elements, you'll be one step closer to publishing success.

921. According to the passage, all of the following are reasons many potential writers never achieve their dream of getting a children's book published EXCEPT

(A) writing a really good children's book is hard.

(B) they don't know the conventions or styles that publishers like.

(C) they demand too much money for their books.

(D) they don't know the jargon used by publishers and appear unprofessional.

922. According to the passage, what should you do if your idea for a children's story is rejected?

(A) give up

(B) change your story completely

(C) keep trying until you find a publisher who is willing to take a chance on you

(D) write a different book for adults instead

923. What is the first thing you should do after deciding to write a children's book?

(A) decide what type of children's book you want to write

(B) have at least one child

(C) find a good publisher

(D) decide who your target audience will be

924. Based on the information in the passage, fill in the blanks to correctly complete the sentence:

Formats involve the ______________ characteristics of a book, including page count, ______________ (width and height), and the cover type (______________).

925. What is the best way to prevent your other responsibilities from intruding upon your writing time?

(A) writing whenever you have a few minutes to spare

(B) ignoring all your other responsibilities and just writing

(C) making a writing schedule and stick to it

(D) splitting your time 50-50 between writing and your other responsibilities

926. What is writer's block?

(A) when a group of writers get together and hold a block party

(B) when a writer's other responsibilities block his or her attempts to write

(C) when a writer manages to write a large block of writing in one sitting

(D) when a writer cannot think of anything to write

927. Once you have a good idea for your children's story, what should you do next?

(A) celebrate

(B) do research to make sure your idea fits your target audience

(C) find a publisher

(D) think of a good ending to your story

928. What is the author's tone throughout the passage?

(A) sarcastic

(B) ambivalent

(C) pessimistic

(D) realistic but encouraging

Questions 929 through 937 are based on the following passage.

The following excerpt is from "The White Snake" by Jacob Grimm and Wilhelm Grimm.

A long time ago there lived a king who was famed for his wisdom through all the land. Nothing was hidden from him, and it seemed as if news of the most secret things was brought to him through the air. But he had a strange custom; every day after dinner, when the table was cleared, and no one else was present, a trusty servant had to bring him one more dish. It was covered, however, and even the servant did not know what was in it, neither did anyone know, for the king never took off the cover to eat of it until he was quite alone.

This had gone on for a long time, when one day the servant, who took away the dish, was overcome with such curiosity that he could not help carrying the dish into his room. When he had carefully locked the door, he lifted up the cover, and saw a white snake lying on the dish. But when he saw it he could not deny himself the pleasure of tasting it, so he cut of a little bit and put it into his mouth. No sooner had it touched his tongue than he heard a strange whispering of little voices outside his window. He went and listened, and then noticed that it was the sparrows who were chattering together, and telling one another of all kinds of things which they had seen in the fields and woods. Eating the snake had given him power of understanding the language of animals.

Now it so happened that on this very day the queen lost her most beautiful ring, and suspicion of having stolen it fell upon this trusty servant, who was allowed to go everywhere. The king ordered the man to be brought before him, and threatened with angry words that unless he could before the morrow point out the thief, he himself should be looked upon as guilty and executed. In vain he declared his innocence; he was dismissed with no better answer.

In his trouble and fear he went down into the courtyard and took thought how to help himself out of his trouble. Now some ducks were sitting together quietly by a brook and taking their rest; and, whilst they were making their feathers smooth with their bills, they were having a confidential conversation together. The servant stood by and listened. They were telling one another of all the places where they had been waddling about all the morning, and what good food they had found; and one said in a pitiful tone: 'Something lies heavy on my stomach; as I was eating in haste I swallowed a ring which lay under the queen's window.' The servant at once seized her by the neck, carried her to the kitchen, and said to the cook: 'Here is a fine duck; pray, kill her.' 'Yes,' said the cook, and weighed her in his hand; 'she has spared no trouble to fatten herself, and has been waiting to be roasted long enough.' So he cut off her head, and as she was being dressed for the spit, the queen's ring was found inside her.

The servant could now easily prove his innocence; and the king, to make amends for the wrong, allowed him to ask a favour, and promised him the best place in the court that he could wish for. The servant refused everything, and only asked for a horse and some money for travelling, as he had a mind to see the world and go about a little. When his request was granted he set out on his way, and one day came to a pond, where he saw three fishes caught in the reeds and gasping for water. Now, though it is said that fishes are dumb, he heard them lamenting that they must perish so miserably, and, as he had a kind heart, he got off his horse and put the three prisoners back into the water. They leapt with delight, put out their heads, and cried to him: 'We will remember you and repay you for saving us!'

He rode on, and after a while it seemed to him that he heard a voice in the sand at his feet. He listened, and heard an ant-king complain: 'Why cannot folks, with their clumsy beasts, keep off our bodies? That stupid horse, with his heavy hoofs, has been treading down my people without mercy!' So he turned on to a side path and the ant-king cried out to him: 'We will remember you—one good turn deserves another!'

929. According to the opening paragraph, what strange custom does the king have?

(A) He receives news from all over the kingdom via carrier pigeon.

(B) He eats dinner alone every night.

(C) He eats a secret dish each night.

(D) He clears the table instead of leaving it for his servants to do.

930. Why does the trusted servant take the dish to his own room instead of bringing it directly to the king?

(A) He wants to make sure it hasn't been poisoned.

(B) He wants to make sure it contains the correct meal.

(C) He is overcome by curiosity.

(D) He loves the taste of snake.

931. What happens as soon as the servant tries the snake?

(A) He spits out the food because he hates the taste of snake.

(B) He quickly brings the rest of the meal to the king.

(C) He begins talking to the birds.

(D) He hears a strange whispering of little voices outside his window.

932. When the queen's ring goes missing, why does suspicion of the theft fall on the trusted servant?

(A) He has already been caught stealing the king's meals.

(B) He has access to everywhere in the castle.

(C) He is a suspicious character whom nobody trusts.

(D) He has been seen wearing the ring.

933. How does the servant learn the whereabouts of the queen's ring?

(A) He overhears a conversation between some ducks.

(B) He overhears some other servants discussing the theft.

(C) He overhears some sparrows chattering by his window.

(D) The white snake tells him about it.

934. How does the servant manage to reveal the location of the ring inside the duck without revealing his secret ability?

(A) He kills the duck and removes the ring.

(B) He orders the cook to kill and prepare the duck for dinner.

(C) He asks the queen to search the duck herself.

(D) He brings the duck directly to the king.

935. What reward does the servant ask for from the king in return for finding the ring?

(A) the best place in the court

(B) another taste of the king's white snake meal

(C) a horse and some money for traveling

(D) the queen's ring

936. What does the servant do when he encounters some fish one day while on his travels?

(A) He releases them from prison.

(B) He kills and eats them.

(C) He saves their lives.

(D) He puts them back in the reeds.

937. What is likely to be the moral of the story?

(A) One good deed deserves another.

(B) No good deed goes unpunished.

(C) The early bird gets the worm.

(D) Honesty is the best policy.

Questions 938 through 945 are based on the following passage.

The following excerpt is from The Secret Life of Dust *by Hannah Holmes (Wiley).*

Flying diatoms don't add significantly to the airborne vegetable matter, in terms of simple tonnage. But when these glass-shelled algae do take a spin through the atmosphere, they raise interesting questions. They seem to defy the size limit for far-flying dust, for one thing. And they may sometimes fly with a purpose.

Michael Ram, a professor of physics at the University of Buffalo, has become an expert at teasing these tiny organisms out of ice cores from Antarctica and Greenland. Deep glaciers preserve thousands upon thousands of fine layers, each representing a year. And trapped in each layer is a sprinkling of fallen desert dust, Stardust, volcanic ash, pollen, insect parts — and diatoms. Ram melts a bit of ice, then puts the remaining sediment under a microscope.

The diatoms, he says, stand out due to their geometric perfection. Desert dust, under the microscope, resembles shattered rock. But diatoms often resemble delicately etched pill-boxes or broken shards of the same.

Most diatoms spend their brief lives adrift in rivers, ponds, lakes, and oceans. And when they die, their little shells sink. Ram says the ideal source of diatom dust is a shallow lake that shrinks in the dry season, exposing the sediment at its edges to the wind. Africa and the western United States are both pocked with excellent candidates.

Ram originally intended to use the diatoms he found to trace the source of the dust and diatoms in each sample: if the ice of one century was rich in North American diatoms, and the next century's ice held African diatoms, he could conclude that the prevailing wind had shifted. This might reveal something about the dynamics of climate change.

But Ram's diatoms proved coy about their place of origin. Many of them look alike. Scientists with more diatom expertise are pursuing this line of inquiry.

And Ram's diatoms have caused additional head scratching. Generally, scientists don't expect things much larger than a few hundredths of a hair's width to fly long distances. But Ram has seen disks as wide as a hundred, or even two hundred, microns — that's a whopping two hairs in diameter. "These diatoms are large, but they have a large surface area, and they're light," Ram speculates in the accent that remains from his European upbringing. "They're like Frisbees. They're very aerodynamic."

The size of the diatoms may also relate to the strength of the wind that lifted them. An uncommonly strong wind can lift uncommonly large dust, as a survey of hailstone cores has suggested. Carried up into a storm cloud and then coated in ice until they fell again have been such "dusts" as small insects, birds, and at least one gopher tortoise. Perhaps a large diatom is not such a challenge.

But a third source of puzzlement is what appears to be a complete colony of diatoms that evidently dwelled smack atop the Greenland glacier about four hundred years ago. It is common for living diatoms to blow into melt pools at the edges of glaciers and there start a family. But the founder of the little clan Ram discovered apparently flew all the way to the center of the immense island before dropping into a puddle. And that pioneer was still in good enough shape to launch a modest dynasty.

938. The best title for this passage is

(A) "A Scientific Study of Plants."

(B) "Diatoms: Flying Wonders of Nature."

(C) "A Year in the Life of Diatoms."

(D) "Professor Ram, Hero of Biology."

939. According to the passage, "flying diatoms" are

(A) living or dead algae transported through the air.

(B) dead algae transported through the air.

(C) small pieces of metal.

(D) winged ants.

940. According to the passage, why does professor Ram compare diatoms to Frisbees?

(A) Professor Ram invented the Frisbee.

(B) Frisbees are smaller than diatoms.

(C) Professor Ram is also an expert on Frisbees.

(D) He wants to give his audience a familiar example of a large object that can fly long distances.

941. Scientists who study diatoms are seeking the answers to all the following puzzles EXCEPT

(A) how diatoms sometimes appear to fly with a purpose.

(B) where diatoms spend most of their brief lives.

(C) how a single diatom could find a small puddle in the center of a large country like Greenland.

(D) how diatoms are able to defy the size limit for far-flying dust.

942. As it is used in the context of the passage, the word *teasing* means

(A) interesting.

(B) enclosing.

(C) extracting.

(D) making fun of.

943. According to the passage, what unusual feature of diatoms stands out when they are viewed under a microscope?

(A) their geometric perfection

(B) their Frisbee-like shape

(C) their bright colors

(D) their resemblance to shattered rock

944. Based on the information in the passage, fill in the blanks to correctly complete the sentence:

The ideal source of diatom dust is a ______________ that shrinks in the dry season, exposing the ______________ at its edges to the wind.

945. Why does the author, Hannah Holmes, mention the gopher tortoise?

(A) She is using the gopher tortoise as a metaphor.

(B) She wants to reinforce the idea that heavy objects can be lifted and transported by strong winds.

(C) Gopher tortoises feed on the diatoms.

(D) Gopher tortoises are often found covered in diatom dust.

Questions 946 through 955 are based on the following passage. The passage is not complete. You have to select the best sentence or completion of a sentence from among the given choices.

The following excerpt is from YouTube Channels For Dummies *by Rob Ciampa and Theresa Moore (Wiley).*

Anyone that wants to show off their video prowess or share their vision with the world can hang a virtual shingle on YouTube by starting their own channel. *SEE QUESTION 946* These days, you can multiply those stubby digits by 100 million to count the number of YouTube channels. *SEE QUESTION 947*

Having more than 500 million channels can make getting noticed on your channel feel like searching for a virtual needle in an online haystack. *SEE QUESTION 948* But it's not all bad news — you also have an advantage over your counterpart in the 1940s. *SEE QUESTION 949* Today? Not so much. In fact, if you just want a platform for presenting some of your video work, YouTube can make that possible without you having to fork over one thin dime.

Knowing that YouTube is free should reduce some of your worries — at least from a financial perspective. Couple that with the size and diversity of the YouTube audience — and the endless number of topics that interest them — it's easy to believe that you have a fair chance of success for your channel. That's true, up to a point — the point being that, if you want your channel to thrive, you need to provide your viewers with compelling content.

SEE QUESTION 950 But content merely makes up the first part of the equation; the rest depends on how you bring viewers to that content — YouTube is free, video production certainly is not. Unless you want to shell out money from your own pocket, you need to generate some funds to produce content for your channel. In the world of YouTube, one major way to generate such funds is through advertising revenue — *SEE QUESTION 951* How much depends on your needs and ambitions, but increased revenue can lead to better production values, which brings it all back to more revenue.

SEE QUESTION 952

Like snowflakes on a winter day, or episodes of *Law and Order*, there are more topics that viewers can appreciate on YouTube than any human can count. *SEE QUESTION 953*

On the downside, you're not the only one hoping to get noticed on YouTube. Many others with the very same intention are looking to build an audience for their YouTube channels, too. (*SEE QUESTION 954* The number exceeds the number of those pre-approved credit card applications that plague your mailbox, so we're talking lots.)

Your journey on YouTube begins with knowing your strengths. Some users relish documenting the quirks of their existence to the gentle amusement of others. Others have some type of expertise to share. *SEE QUESTION 955* — the list could go on and on. Even businesses realize it's a great place to inform consumers about their products or provide a great level of customer service. Regardless of your passion, a potential audience is waiting for you.

946. Select the best sentence from among the given choices.

(A) Of course, when television began, us humans had more toes than the TV had channels.

(B) Of course when television began we humans had more toes than the TV had channels.

(C) Of course when television began us humans had more toes than the TV had channels.

(D) Of course, when television began, we humans had more toes than the TV had channels.

947. Select the best sentence from among the given choices.

(A) That make running a successful YouTube channel seem a bit more daunting.

(B) That makes running a successful YouTube channel seem a bit more daunting.

(C) That make run a successful YouTube channel seemed a bit more daunting.

(D) That makes run a successful YouTube channel seemed a bit more daunting.

948. Select the best sentence from among the given choices.

(A) Yet, regardless of the steep increase in competition, the intention has always been the same — getting people to watch your channel.

(B) Yet, irregardless of the steep increase in competition, the intension has always been the same — getting people to watch your channel.

(C) Yet, irregardless of the steep increase in competition, the intention has always been the same — getting people to watch your channel.

(D) Yet, regardless of the steep increase in competition, the intension has always been the same — getting people to watch your channel.

949. Select the best sentence from among the given choices.

(A) Back then, it takes a great deal of capital to get started on television.

(B) Back then, it will take a great deal of capitol to get started on television.

(C) Back then, it took a great deal of capital to get started on television.

(D) Back then, it took a great deal of capitol to get started on television.

950. Select the best sentence from among the given choices.

(A) Say that your channel needs to host solid content that people actually want to see seems as glaringly obvious as saying a hamburger joint must make a good burger in order to surviving.

(B) Say that your channel needs to host solid content that people actually want to see seems as glaringly obvious as saying a hamburger joint must make a good burger in order to survive.

(C) Saying that your channel needs to host solid content that people actually want to see seems as glaringly obvious as saying a hamburger joint must make a good burger in order to surviving.

(D) Saying that your channel needs to host solid content that people actually want to see seems as glaringly obvious as saying a hamburger joint must make a good burger in order to survive.

951. Select the best completion of the sentence from among the given choices.

(A) — and it came as no surprise that the more viewers you can attract, the greater your potential to generate advertising revenue.

(B) — and it should come as no surprise that the more viewers you can attract, the greater your potentially to generate advertising revenue.

(C) — and it should come as no surprise that the more viewers you can attract, the greater your potential to generate advertising revenue.

(D) — and it came as no surprise that the more viewers you can attract, the greater your potentially to generate advertising revenue.

952. Select the best sentence from among the given choices.

(A) But before one starts worrying about all that money you're going to make, lets take a look at what it takes to get started on a YouTube channel for you or your business.

(B) But before you start worrying about all that money your going to make, lets take a look at what it takes to get started on a YouTube channel for you or your business.

(C) But before you start worrying about all that money you're going to make, let's take a look at what it takes to get started on a YouTube channel for you or your business.

(D) But before one starts worrying about all that money you're going to make, let's take a look at what it takes to get started on a YouTube channel for you or your business.

953. Select the best sentence from among the given choices.

(A) And since you all ready love making videos and most like exhibit some expertise or viewpoint to share with the world, YouTube may be your best creative outlet.

(B) And since you already love making videos and most likely exhibiting some expertise or viewpoint to share with the world, YouTube may be your best creative outlet.

(C) And since you all ready love making videos and most likely exhibit some expertise or viewpoint to share with the world, YouTube may be your best creative outlet.

(D) And since you already love making videos and most likely exhibit some expertise or viewpoint to share with the world, YouTube may be your best creative outlet.

954. Select the best sentence from among the given choices.

(A) "How many"? you ask.

(B) "How many?" you ask.

(C) "How many you ask"?

(D) "How many," you ask?

955. Select the best completion of the sentence from among the given choices.

(A) Then you have performers whom regard the video hosting site as his personal stage

(B) Then you have performers who regard the video hosting site as their personal stage

(C) Then you have performers whom regard the video hosting site as their personal stage

(D) Then you have performers who regard the video hosting site as his personal stage

Questions 956 through 964 are based on the following passage. The passage is not complete. You have to select the best sentence or completion of a sentence from among the given choices.

The following excerpt is from Twitter For Dummies *by Laura Fitton (Wiley).*

You may have heard of Twitter but have no idea what it actually is. *SEE QUESTION 956* — whether you know them personally or not. It also lets you share what you're doing with the world — everyone from your family and friends to complete strangers. (*SEE QUESTION 957*) MIT Professor Andrew McAfee (@amcafee) describes Twitter this way: "With Twitter, my friends are never far away."

McAfee was most certainly right, because Twitter's company data in July 2014 showed that 115 million active monthly users were sending more than 53 million Tweets daily. *SEE QUESTION 958* Additionally, of those 53 million Tweets, almost 40 percent were sent from mobile devices such as cellphones and tablets.

SEE QUESTION 959 It's a social network — a digital abstraction that interested in (whether you know them personally or not) — that you can access from your computer or your mobile device anywhere that has an Internet connection.

SEE QUESTION 960, through the Twitter website (https:// twitter.com), through the Twitter application on a mobile device, or by way of the numerous third-party applications that are available for both.

Think you can't say anything meaningful in 140 characters? Think again. *Twitterers* (people who use Twitter) are not only innovating clever forms of one-liners, haiku, quotes, stories, and humor, but also including images and links to things like websites and blog posts, which carry a lot more information and context. Writing 140-character messages seems trivial. *SEE QUESTION 961* Consider: "Man Lands on Moon."

SEE QUESTION 962 When you think about how millions of people around the world are posting Twitter messages, following other people's Twitter streams, and responding to one another, you can start to see the significance behind Twitter's appeal. In fact, Twitter has noticed that it acts like a "pulse of the planet," a record of what everyone is thinking about, talking about, doing, and feeling — right now. Now, that's pretty interesting!

True, Twitter can look like it's full of noise. But once you find interesting people and accounts to follow, your Twitter stream shifts from a cascade of disjointed chatter to one of the most versatile, useful online communications tools yet seen — that is, if you take the time to find out how to use that tool correctly.

Twitter is a great way for you or your company to connect with large numbers of people quickly and personally, just as though you were having a conversation. *SEE QUESTION 963* Or, if you prefer a work metaphor, Twitter is like the office water cooler, where any number of informal (or formal) conversations can take place.

SEE QUESTION 964 The web offers a lot of information. Twitter can turn those long articles, lengthy conversations, and far-reaching connections into easily digestible facts, thoughts, questions, ideas, concepts, and sound bites. In other words, when you have only 140 characters, you have to be succinct.

956. Select the best completion of the sentence from among the given choices.

(A) Twitter is basic a powerful social network that allows you to keep up with the people, businesses, and organizations you're interested in

(B) Twitter is basically a powerful social network that allows you to keep up with the people, businesses, and organizations you're interested in

(C) Twitter is basic a powerful social network that allows one to keep up with the people, businesses, and organizations you're interested in

(D) Twitter is basically a powerful social network that allows one to keep up with the people, businesses, and organizations you're interested in

957. Select the best sentence from among the given choices.

(A) You're have to bare with us to find out why you would want to do that.

(B) You'll have to bare with us to find out why you would want to do that.

(C) You have to bear with us to find out why you would want to do that.

(D) You'll have to bear with us to find out why you would want to do that.

958. Select the best sentence from among the given choices.

(A) That's a whole lot of tweeting?

(B) That's a whole lot of tweeting!

(C) That's a hole lot of tweeting!

(D) That's a hole lot of tweeting?

959. Select the best sentence from among the given choices.

(A) Twitter is a fast-evolving, surprisingly powerful new way to exchange ideas and information and to stay in touch with people, businesses, and organizations that you care about.

(B) Twitter is a fast evolving, surprising powerful new way to exchange ideas and information and to stay in touch with people, businesses, and organizations that you care about.

(C) Twitter is a fast-evolving, surprising powerful new way to exchange ideas and information and to stay in touch with people, businesses, and organizations that you care about.

(D) Twitter is a fast evolving, surprisingly powerful new way to exchange ideas and information and to stay in touch with people, businesses, and organizations that you care about.

960. Select the best completion of a sentence from among the given choices.

(A) Twitter has one central feature, it lets users instantly post entries of 140 characters or less, known as *Tweets*

(B) Twitter has one central feature: It lets users instantly post entries of 140 characters or less, known as *Tweets*

(C) Twitter has one central feature, it let users instantly post entries of 140 characters or less, known as *Tweets*

(D) Twitter has one central feature: It let's users instantly post entries of 140 characters or less, known as *Tweets*

961. Select the best sentence from among the given choices.

(A) But writing headlines and very short advertising copy is famously hard to do real good, and the right words can be quite powerful.

(B) But writing headlines and very short advertising copy is famously hard to do real well, and the right words can be quite powerful.

(C) But writing headlines and very short advertising copy is famously hard to do really good, and the right words can be quite powerful.

(D) But writing headlines and very short advertising copy is famously hard to do really well, and the right words can be quite powerful.

962. Select the best sentence from among the given choices.

(A) Twitter sound simple — deceptive simple.

(B) Twitter sounds simply — deceptively simply.

(C) Twitter sounds simple — deceptively simple.

(D) Twitter sound simply — deceptively simple.

963. Select the best sentence from among the given choices.

(A) In tech-speak, Twitter is a microblogging tool; however, you can more easily think of Twitter as a giant cocktail party with dozens of conversations you can join (or start) at any moment.

(B) In tech-speak, Twitter is a microblogging tool however you can more easily think of Twitter as a giant cocktail party with dozens of conversations you can join (or start) at any moment.

(C) In tech-speak, Twitter is a microblogging tool however, you can more easy think of Twitter as a giant cocktail party with dozens of conversations you can join (or start) at any moment.

(D) In tech-speak, Twitter is a microblogging tool; however, you can more easy think of Twitter as a giant cocktail party with dozens of conversations you can join (or start) at any moment.

964. Select the best sentence from among the given choices.

(A) If you're familiar with blogs, instant messaging, and web-based journals, you can start to understand what makes Twitter very unique.

(B) If you're familiar with blogs, instant messaging, and web-based journals, you can start to understand what makes Twitter most unique.

(C) If you're familiar with blogs, instant messaging, and web-based journals, you can start to understand what makes Twitter unique.

(D) If you're familiar with blogs, instant messaging, and web-based journals, you can start to understand what makes Twitter the uniquest.

Questions 965 through 972 are based on the following passage.

This excerpt is from "Rip Van Winkle" by Washington Irving.

Whoever has made a voyage up the Hudson must remember the Catskill Mountains. They are a branch of the great Appalachian family, and are seen away to the west of the river, swelling up to a noble height, and **lording it over** the surrounding country. Every change of season, every change of weather, indeed, every hour of the day, produces some change in the magical hues and shapes of these mountains, and they are regarded by all the goodwives, far and near, as perfect barometers.

At the foot of these fairy mountains the traveler may have seen the light smoke curling up from a village, whose shingle roofs gleam among the trees, just where the blue tints of the upland melt away into the fresh green of the nearer landscape. It is a little village of great age, having been founded by some of the Dutch colonists in the early times of the province, just about the beginning of the government of the good Peter Stuyvesant (may he rest in peace!), and there were some of the houses of the original settlers standing within a few years, built of small yellow bricks brought from Holland, having latticed windows and gable fronts, surmounted with weathercocks.

In that same village, and in one of these very houses, there lived, many years since, while the country was yet a province of Great Britain, a simple, good-natured fellow, of the name of Rip Van Winkle. He was a descendant of the Van Winkles who figured so gallantly in the chivalrous days of Peter Stuyvesant, and accompanied him to the siege of Fort Christina. He inherited, however, but little of the martial character of his ancestors. I have observed that he was a simple, good-natured man; he was, moreover, a kind neighbor and an obedient, henpecked husband.

Certain it is that he was a great favorite among all the goodwives of the village, who took his part in all family squabbles; and never failed, whenever they talked those matters over in their evening gossipings, to lay all the blame on Dame Van Winkle. The children of the village, too, would shout with joy whenever he approached. He assisted at their sports, made their playthings, taught them to fly kites and shoot marbles, and told them long stories of ghosts, witches, and Indians. Whenever he went dodging about the village, he was surrounded by a troop of them, hanging on his skirts, clambering on his back, and playing a thousand tricks on him; and not a dog would bark at him throughout the neighborhood.

The great error in Rip's composition was a strong dislike of all kinds of profitable labor. It could not be from the want of perseverance; for he would sit on a wet rock, with a rod as long and heavy as a lance, and fish all day without a murmur, even though he should not be encouraged by a single nibble. He would carry a fowling piece on his shoulder for hours together, trudging through woods and swamps, and up hill and down dale, to shoot a few squirrels or wild pigeons. He would never refuse to assist a neighbor even in the roughest toil, and was a foremost man at all country frolics for husking Indian corn, or building stone fences; the women of the village, too, used to employ him to run their errands, and to do such little odd jobs as their less obliging husbands would not do for them. In a word, Rip was ready to attend to anybody's business but his own; but as to doing family duty, and keeping his farm in order, he found it impossible.

His children, too, were as ragged and wild as if they belonged to nobody. His son Rip promised to inherit the habits, with the old clothes, of his father. He was generally seen trooping like a colt at his mother's heels, equipped in a pair of his father's cast-off breeches, which he had much ado to hold up with one hand, as a fine lady does her train in bad weather.

Rip Van Winkle, however, was one of those happy mortals, of foolish, well-oiled dispositions, who take the world easy, eat white bread or brown, whichever can be got with least thought or trouble, and would rather starve on a penny than work for a pound. If left to himself, he would have whistled life away in perfect contentment; but his wife kept continually dinning in his ear about his idleness, his carelessness, and the ruin he was bringing on his family. Morning, noon, and night, her tongue was incessantly going, and everything he said or did was sure to produce a torrent of household eloquence. Rip had but one way of replying to all lectures of the kind, and that, by frequent use, had grown into a habit. He shrugged his shoulders, shook his head, cast up his eyes, but said nothing. This, however, always provoked a fresh volley from his wife; so that he was fain to draw off his forces, and take to the outside of the house — the only side which, in truth, belongs to a **henpecked** husband.

965. What is the best meaning of the phrase *lording it over* as it is used in this sentence: "They are a branch of the great Appalachian family, and are seen away to the west of the river, swelling up to a noble height, and lording it over the surrounding country"?

(A) acting in an upper-class manner

(B) dominating

(C) wandering about

(D) hiding from

966. What is the name of the village in which Rip lives?

(A) Hudson

(B) Catskill

(C) Fort Christina

(D) The passage does not say.

967. What is the best meaning of the word *henpecked* as it is used in this sentence: "This, however, always provoked a fresh volley from his wife; so that he was fain to draw off his forces, and take to the outside of the house — the only side which, in truth, belongs to a henpecked husband"?

(A) lazy

(B) chicken farmer

(C) downtrodden

(D) resourceful

968. Whom do the housewives of the village usually blame when Rip and his family get into an argument with each other?

(A) Rip
(B) Rip's father
(C) Rip's wife
(D) Rip's son

969. Which of the following best describes the pants that Rip's son usually wears?

(A) They resemble the train of a lady's expensive dress.
(B) They're much too large for him.
(C) They fit snugly.
(D) They're fashionable and expensive.

970. What is Rip's main character flaw?

(A) He gives up easily.
(B) He has a strong dislike of all kinds of profitable labor.
(C) He is lazy and avoids helping his neighbors.
(D) He has an unpleasant personality that causes most people to dislike him.

971. Which of the following best describe Rip's character?

(A) complex, bad-tempered, and sarcastic
(B) complex, good-natured, kind, and obedient
(C) simple, good-natured, kind, and obedient
(D) simple, kind, and sarcastic

972. Which of the following phrases best sums up Rip's attitude toward life?

(A) Curiosity killed the cat.
(B) A rolling stone gathers no moss.
(C) Strike while the iron is hot.
(D) Don't worry; be happy.

Questions 973 through 980 are based on the following passage.

This excerpt is from The Strange Case of Dr. Jekyll and Mr. Hyde *by Robert Louis Stevenson.*

Nearly a year later, in the month of October, 18—, London was startled by a crime of singular ferocity and rendered all the more notable by the high position of the victim. The details were few and startling. A maid servant living alone in a house not far from the river, had gone up-stairs to bed about eleven. Although a fog rolled over the city in the small hours, the early part of the night was cloudless, and the lane, which the maid's window overlooked, was brilliantly lit by the full moon. It seems she was romantically given, for she sat down upon her box, which stood immediately under the window, and fell into a dream of musing. Never (she used to say, with streaming tears, when she narrated that experience), never had she felt more at peace with all men or thought more kindly of the world. And as she so sat she became aware of an aged and beautiful gentleman with white hair, drawing near along the lane; and advancing to meet him, another and very small gentleman, to whom at first she paid less attention. When they had come within speech (which was just under the maid's eyes) the older man bowed and accosted the other with a very pretty manner of politeness.

It did not seem as if the subject of his address were of great importance; indeed, from his pointing, it sometimes appeared as if he were only inquiring his way; but the moon shone on his face as he spoke, and the girl was pleased to watch it, it seemed to breathe such an innocent and old-world kindness of disposition, yet with something high too, as of a well-founded self-content. Presently her eye wandered to the other, and she was surprised to recognise in him a certain Mr. Hyde, who had once visited her master and for whom she had conceived a dislike. He had in his hand a heavy cane, with which he was trifling; but he answered never a word, and seemed to listen with an ill-contained impatience. And then all of a sudden he broke out in a great flame of anger, stamping with his foot, brandishing the cane, and carrying on (as the maid described it) like a madman. The old gentleman took a step back, with the air of one very much surprised and a trifle hurt; and at that Mr. Hyde broke out of all bounds and clubbed him to the earth. And next moment, with ape-like fury, he was trampling his victim under foot and hailing down a storm of blows, under which the bones were audibly shattered and the body jumped upon the roadway. At the horror of these sights and sounds, the maid fainted.

It was two o'clock when she came to herself and called for the police. The murderer was gone long ago; but there lay his victim in the middle of the lane, incredibly mangled. The stick with which the deed had been done, although it was of some rare and very tough and heavy wood, had broken in the middle under the stress of this insensate cruelty; and one splintered half had rolled in the neighbouring gutter — the other, without doubt, had been carried away by the murderer. A purse and a gold watch were found upon the victim: but no cards or papers, except a sealed and stamped envelope, which he had been probably carrying to the post, and which bore the name and address of Mr. Utterson.

This was brought to the lawyer the next morning, before he was out of bed; and he had no sooner seen it, and been told the circumstances, than he shot out a solemn lip. "I shall say nothing till I have seen the body," said he; "this may be very serious. Have the kindness to wait while I dress." And with the same grave countenance he hurried through his breakfast and drove to the police station, whither the body had been carried. As soon as he came into the cell, he nodded.

"Yes," said he, "I recognise him. I am sorry to say that this is Sir Danvers Carew."

"Good God, sir," exclaimed the officer, "is it possible?" And the next moment his eye lighted up with professional ambition. "This will make a deal of noise," he said. "And perhaps you can help us to the man." And he briefly narrated what the maid had seen, and showed the broken stick.

Mr. Utterson had already quailed at the name of Hyde; but when the stick was laid before him, he could doubt no longer; broken and battered as it was, he recognised it for one that he had himself presented many years before to Henry Jekyll.

"Is this Mr. Hyde a person of small stature?" he inquired.

"Particularly small and particularly wicked-looking, is what the maid calls him," said the officer.

Mr. Utterson reflected; and then, raising his head, "If you will come with me in my cab," he said, "I think I can take you to his house."

973. What is the meaning of the phrase "high position of the victim" as it's used in the passage?

(A) The victim was one of the highest paid maids in London.

(B) The victim had been taking illegal drugs.

(C) The victim was an important person.

(D) The victim was standing on a ledge high above the ground.

974. At approximately what time did the murder take place?

(A) just after 2:00 a.m.

(B) around noon

(C) shortly after 11 p.m.

(D) shortly before 11 p.m.

975. What was the murder victim's name?

(A) Sir Danvers Carew

(B) Mr. Utterson

(C) Dr. Jekyll

(D) Mr. Hyde

976. What can you infer based on the fact that the victim's purse and gold watch were found on the body?

(A) The attacker planted them on the victim.

(B) The victim sold gold watches for a living.

(C) The motive for the murder was probably not robbery.

(D) The attacker dropped them during his escape.

977. What connection does Mr. Utterson have to the murder weapon?

(A) He used it to kill the victim.

(B) He gave it to Mr. Hyde many years ago.

(C) He gave it to Dr. Jekyll many years ago.

(D) He has never seen it before in his life.

978. Mr. Hyde is described as all the following EXCEPT

(A) white-haired.

(B) ill-tempered.

(C) wicked-looking.

(D) a person of small stature.

979. Why does the officer's eye light up "with professional ambition" when he discovers the identity of the murder victim?

(A) The victim was also a policeman and a personal rival of the officer.

(B) The victim was the son of the chief of police.

(C) The officer realized that solving such a high-profile crime would help his career.

(D) The officer realized that he can now arrest the lawyer.

980. Why does the maid initially pay more attention to the older gentleman in the alley?

(A) He's a very short man.

(B) He speaks in a very loud voice.

(C) He is carrying a heavy cane.

(D) She thinks he's handsome.

Questions 981 through 988 are based on the following passage.

This excerpt is from Fermenting For Dummies *by Marni Wasserman and Amelia Jeanroy (Wiley).*

Before the days of refrigerators, people had to do something to keep their foods from going bad. Fermentation is one of those incredible preservation methods still used today. You can preserve foods in so many different ways: You can freeze them, can them, dry them for storage, or ferment them. These days, few people know and love the art of fermentation, but it's an art that has existed for many years past and, when you discover it, a world of splendor opens up!

Fermented foods are returning to the modern kitchen. The art of fermentation precedes history and happens by capturing and controlling the growth of bacteria, molds, and yeasts, and falling in love with the presence of lactobacilli found on the surface of all things. You'll discover more about the importance of these healthy living microbes in fermentation as you read on.

Fermentation is a unique, natural, and fun way to preserve your food, discover new flavors and recipes, and go on a mind-bending adventure through various cultures and through an ancient history of food that has existed for centuries around the world. If you're lucky, fermentation can even act as a tool for self-discovery and a vehicle for self-exploration in health and healing.

Fermented foods are all around you. You may not realize it, but you're likely already a consumer of one or more fermented food products. Have you had any sourdough bread, soy sauce, tofu, yogurt, cheese, or a glass of cider or wine lately? Does your sandwich come with a salty pickle or some sauerkraut on the side? You can thank the process of fermentation for these items.

Fermentation turns sugars to alcohol or other acids using yeast and bacteria. The chemical change often involves increasing the acidic environment and develops in places without oxygen (*anaerobic* conditions). It's a low-cost, highly efficient way of preserving foods.

Fermented foods have existed for centuries as populations around the globe learned how to capture the slow decomposition process of organic materials and preserve them by adding salts, sugars, or yeasts. They controlled mold and promoted good bacteria with the intention of maximizing the shelf life of their foods, enhancing flavors, or gaining health benefits.

Getting to know the art of fermentation also gets you familiar with the beauty of bacteria and its desirable presence in your food products. The changes caused by fermentation can be both good and bad. When fermentation occurs naturally, the food can smell or taste "off" (think of sour milk), but when you control the fermentation process, you can actually have some incredible results! When you execute fermentation processes properly, something that could have turned rotten instead turns into a consumable product. That's right — bacteria, yeasts, and molds will soon become your new best friends.

When fermenting foods, the key to developing the perfect environment and flavor and gaining all the great health benefits is to be confident, experiment, and do your best to create the utmost environment for fermentation, with proportional ingredients to support its growth. Some recipes are more challenging than others or require longer fermentation time, but plenty of fun and simple recipes are out there for beginners."

981. Before the days of refrigerators, people preserved foods by each of the following methods EXCEPT

(A) freezing.

(B) canning.

(C) drying.

(D) fermenting.

982. What is the authors' opinion regarding bacteria, molds, and yeasts?

(A) They have no place in a clean kitchen.

(B) They destroy foods and make them go stale.

(C) They are a necessary evil whose presence should be minimized wherever possible.

(D) The authors love them.

983. Fermentation is a ____________ way to preserve your food.

(A) modern and ancient

(B) natural and ancient

(C) modern and natural

(D) natural and artificial

984. According to the passage, fermented foods include all of the following EXCEPT

(A) cider and wine.

(B) freshly squeezed apple juice.

(C) pickles.

(D) sourdough bread.

985. According to the passage, what is *anaerobic fermentation?*

(A) a process involving yeast and bacteria that requires oxygen

(B) a process involving yeast and bacteria that does not require oxygen

(C) a process involving oxygen and bacteria that does not require yeast

(D) a process involving oxygen and yeast that does not require bacteria

986. According to the passage, why is it important to control the conditions of fermentation?

(A) Fermentation always produces tasty consumable products.

(B) Fermentation always produces rotten, inedible products.

(C) The changes caused by fermentation can be either good or bad, or they can be both good and bad, depending on the conditions.

(D) If conditions aren't controlled, too much alcohol may be produced.

987. According to the passage, controlling mold and promoting good bacteria produces all of the following advantages to the finished product EXCEPT

(A) longer shelf life.

(B) added health benefits.

(C) increased alcohol content.

(D) better taste.

988. According to the passage, fermentation has each of the following benefits EXCEPT

(A) it takes only one day to complete.

(B) it's fun.

(C) it's efficient.

(D) it's cheap.

Questions 989 through 998 are based on the following passage.

This excerpt is from The Metamorphosis *by Franz Kafka.*

One morning, when Gregor Samsa woke from troubled dreams, he found himself transformed in his bed into a horrible vermin. He lay on his armour-like back, and if he lifted his head a little he could see his brown belly, slightly domed and divided by arches into stiff sections. The bedding was hardly able to cover it and seemed ready to slide off any moment. His many legs, pitifully thin compared with the size of the rest of him, waved about helplessly as he looked.

"What's happened to me?" he thought. It wasn't a dream. His room, a proper human room although a little too small, lay peacefully between its four familiar walls. A collection of textile samples lay spread out on the table — Samsa was a travelling salesman — and above it there hung a picture that he had recently cut out of an illustrated magazine and housed in a nice, gilded frame. It showed a lady fitted out with a fur hat and fur boa who sat upright, raising a heavy fur muff that covered the whole of her lower arm towards the viewer.

Gregor then turned to look out the window at the dull weather. Drops of rain could be heard hitting the pane, which made him feel quite sad. "How about if I sleep a little bit longer and forget all this nonsense," he thought, but that was something he was unable to do because he was used to sleeping on his right, and in his present state couldn't get into that position. However hard he threw himself onto his right, he always rolled back to where he was. He must have tried it a hundred times, shut his eyes so that he wouldn't have to look at the floundering legs, and only stopped when he began to feel a mild, dull pain there that he had never felt before.

"Oh, God," he thought, "what a strenuous career it is that I've chosen! Travelling day in and day out. Doing business like this takes much more effort than doing your own business at home, and on top of that there's the curse of travelling, worries about making train connections, bad and irregular food, contact with different people all the time so that you can never get to know anyone or become friendly with them. It can all go to Hell!" He felt a slight itch up on his belly; pushed himself slowly up on his back towards the headboard so that he could lift his head better; found where the itch was, and saw that it was covered with lots of little white spots which he didn't know what to make of; and when he tried to feel the place with one of his legs he drew it quickly back because as soon as he touched it he was overcome by a cold shudder.

He slid back into his former position. "Getting up early all the time," he thought, "it makes you stupid. You've got to get enough sleep. Other travelling salesmen live a life of luxury. For instance, whenever I go back to the guest house during the morning to copy out the contract, these gentlemen are always still sitting there eating their breakfasts. I ought to just try that with my boss; I'd get kicked out on the spot. But who knows, maybe that would be the best thing for me. If I didn't have my parents to think about I'd have given in my notice a long time ago, I'd have gone up to the boss and told him just what I think, tell him everything I would, let him know just what I feel. He'd fall right off his desk! And it's a funny sort of business to be sitting up there at your desk, talking down at your **subordinates** from up there, especially when you have to go right up close because the boss is hard of hearing. Well, there's still some hope; once I've got the money together to pay off my parents' debt to him — another five or six years I suppose — that's definitely what I'll do. That's when I'll make the big change. First of all though, I've got to get up, my train leaves at five."

He was still hurriedly thinking all this through, unable to decide to get out of the bed, when the clock struck quarter to seven. There was a cautious knock at the door near his head. "Gregor," somebody called — it was his mother — "it's quarter to seven. Didn't you want to go somewhere?" That gentle voice! Gregor was shocked when he heard his own voice answering, it could hardly be recognized as the voice he had had before. As if from deep inside him, there was a painful and uncontrollable squeaking mixed in with it, the words could be made out at first but then there was a sort of echo which made them unclear, leaving the hearer unsure whether he had heard properly or not. Gregor had wanted to give a full answer and explain everything, but in the circumstances contented himself with saying: "Yes, mother, yes, thank-you, I'm getting up now."

989. What appears to have happened to Gregor Samsa during the previous night?

(A) He was out drinking late and is now feeling hung-over.

(B) He was sleepwalking and has now woken up in the wrong room.

(C) He was transformed into a rat.

(D) He was transformed into a giant cockroach.

990. Based on the information in the passage, which of the following is a true statement?

(A) Gregor Samsa is a hotel inspector who hates his job.

(B) Gregor Samsa is a traveling salesman who loves his job.

(C) Gregor Samsa is a factory owner who loves his job.

(D) Gregor Samsa is a traveling salesman who hates his job.

991. What is the most likely reason that Gregor Samsa has the picture of the lady in his room?

(A) The lady is his wife.

(B) The lady is his mother.

(C) He sells picture frames.

(D) He is lonely and wishes he were in a relationship.

992. Why does Gregor Samsa close his eyes while trying to get off the bed?

(A) Bright sunshine is flooding into the room.

(B) He realizes he is dreaming and wants to wake up.

(C) He doesn't want to have to look at his floundering legs.

(D) He's tired and needs to sleep.

993. According to the passage, all of the following are part of the curse of traveling EXCEPT

(A) bad and irregular food.

(B) carrying heavy luggage.

(C) superficial relationships.

(D) worries about making train connections.

994. What is the most likely reason that Gregor's boss likes sitting on top of his desk rather than using a chair?

(A) His office chair is broken.

(B) His desk is extremely comfortable.

(C) He likes to appear superior.

(D) He is partially deaf, and sitting on his desk helps him hear his employees' concerns.

995. Why does Gregor not give a full explanation of his situation to his mother when she comes to his door to wake him up?

(A) He wants to end the conversation quickly before his mother realizes how strange his voice sounds.

(B) He hates his mother and doesn't want to talk to her.

(C) His throat is sore and it hurts him to talk.

(D) She's being too nosy.

996. All of the following factors add to the overall feeling of despair that Gregor is experiencing EXCEPT

(A) his relationship with his wife.

(B) financial pressure from his parents' debt.

(C) the weather outside.

(D) the strenuous demands of his job.

997. Why doesn't Gregor quit his job?

(A) He respects his boss too much to quit.

(B) He loves his job.

(C) He needs to pay off his parents' debt to his boss.

(D) He enjoys all the perks of the job.

998. As used in the passage, what is the best meaning of the word *subordinates?*

(A) superiors

(B) employees

(C) peers

(D) masters

Essays

For Questions 999 through 1,001, read and utilize the passages to write an extended response to each prompt. Each question should take approximately 45 minutes to complete.

999. The minimum age required to apply for a driver's license varies from state to state. Although most states require drivers to be 16 or 17, in some states like Alaska, 14-year-olds can apply for their learner's permit. Some safety experts and politicians have proposed raising the minimum driving age to 18. The following articles present arguments both in favor of and against raising the minimum driving age. In your response, analyze both positions presented in the two articles and explain which one is best supported. Incorporate relevant and specific evidence from both sources to support your response.

Passage 1

Watching your child get behind the wheel for the first time when you don't yet trust him to clean up his own room can be a scary moment for any parent. Scientific evidence shows that the brain of an average teen operates very differently from that of an average adult and that younger teens often make careless decisions that can put their own lives and the lives of others in danger. The typical teenager's mind is easily distracted; texting while driving, chatting with friends who are passengers, and speeding to impress their peers are all examples of dangerous behaviors that the typical teen is more likely to engage in while driving.

Smartphones and other similar technological distractions appear to be much more important to younger teenagers. A sudden phone call from a best friend (or a crush) seems much more important to them than paying attention to the road. By the age of 18, however, there has been an adjustment in the teenager's brain that makes this technology appear not so important.

Drinking and driving is a problem at all ages, but it is more so for younger teens. Younger teenagers have a particularly low tolerance for alcohol, which can lead to devastating results once they get behind the wheel. The average 16-year-old is simply not mature enough to make responsible decisions — so why take the risk?

Younger teens are also not experienced enough to be trusted to handle the multitude of potentially life-or-death decisions that driving requires. This problem is compounded by the average teenager's 'need for speed.' Whether they are speeding to impress their friends or simply for the cheap thrill it gives them, teenagers pose a significant risk to their own safety and the safety of others.

Keeping teenagers safe is the number one argument for raising the minimum driving age. Data provided by the Insurance Institute for Highway Safety show that twice as many fatal crashes involve 16- to 17-year-olds than 18- to 19-year-olds, so it simply makes sense to raise the minimum driving age.

Passage 2

Recently, some politicians have proposed raising the minimum driving age to 18 years old in order to reduce the number of fatalities each year due to teen-related driving accidents. They often cite the age of young teen drivers as the leading cause of road accidents and suggest that simply by raising the minimum driving age, the problem will be resolved. Although the motives of these politicians may be noble, they have actually misunderstood the root of the problem, and the solution they propose may actually make things worse.

It is not the age of the driver that matters — it is the driver's experience that counts.

No matter at what age a teenager first begins to drive, he or she begins with zero driving experience. An 18-year-old who is a new driver has just as little experience behind the wheel as a 16-year-old novice. Data from the Insurance Institute for Highway Safety backs this up by showing that raising the driving age does not actually prevent teen driver crashes — it just delays them. According to their statistics, the death rate due to driving accidents in Connecticut (where the driving age is 16) is the highest among 16-year-olds, but in New Jersey (where the minimum licensing age is 17), it is the highest among 17-year-olds. So it is not the age of the driver that matters — it is the inexperience of the driver that leads to some accidents.

Kate Willette of Seattle's SWERVE Driving School agrees. "It's careful and extensive training, more than age, that prepares teenagers to be safe drivers," she argues.

Also, raising the minimum driving age to 18 would prevent many teenagers from getting the proper driving training they need to become safe, reliable drivers. Many high schools offer driver's education classes, and many relatives who are experienced drivers are happy to give their son or daughter driving lessons on the weekends. But if a teenager cannot legally start learning to drive until the age when he or she may have already left home, there may not be anyone nearby to teach him or her to drive safely.

Because inexperience (rather than age) appears to be the main cause of many accidents, then raising the driving age to 18 or 30 or even 50 won't help. Teens have to get their driving experience somehow, and the only place they can do that is behind the wheel.

1,000. The following articles present arguments both in favor of and against enforcing school uniforms for all students. In your response, analyze both positions presented in the two articles and explain which one is best supported. Incorporate relevant and specific evidence from both sources to support your response.

Passage 1

There are many reasons why enforcing school uniforms for all students is the correct thing to do. First, students' behavior improves, and they tend to perform better academically when they wear a uniform. Second, not having to make clothing decisions makes mornings easier for both the child and the parent. Third, it enforces controls on acceptable school attire and reduces bullying for those children who cannot afford the latest expensive sneakers or other fashionable clothes.

Educators and experts who support school uniforms agree that uniforms contribute positively to the behavior of students and that they perform better when there is less of a focus on fashion in the classroom and more on learning. A recent study by Virginia Draa, an assistant professor at Youngstown State University, followed 64 schools in Ohio and concluded that those schools with uniform policies had improved records in attendance, graduation, and suspension rates. Uniforms make students feel more professional and give them a sense of school pride, which encourages them to behave accordingly.

When students know exactly what they have to wear each day for school, mornings become much easier because there is no debate on what clothes the students want to wear to school. Things like modesty issues are no longer a problem, and the problems of offensive t-shirts and gang colors are eliminated. In addition, teachers are spared the extra task of having to monitor their students' attire and send home offenders when a school uniform policy is in place.

Experts who support the school uniform policy also believe that wearing uniforms decreased bullying and teasing related to clothes. This opinion appears to be supported by experience — for example, a school district in North Jersey recently reported that implementing school uniforms has directly reduced bullying. After all, not everyone can afford the latest fashion accessories, and clothes can be used as a powerful weapon to tease and intimidate poor students. School uniforms even the playing field because everyone is dressed the same. This allows students to focus on developing their personality rather than their sense of fashion.

Today's students already have too many distractions, so doesn't it make sense to remove yet another one by enforcing a strict school uniform policy in all schools that helps students focus on their studies, reduces undesirable behavior, and fosters a sense of pride and belonging in their school?

Passage 2

Some people think that all students should be forced to wear school uniforms — but they are idiots who don't know what they are talking about. Forcing people to wear school uniforms is immoral, makes them oblivious to the latest fashion trends, and makes everyone look and act like little robots.

First of all, forcing students to wear school uniforms is immoral since it restricts the student's right to free expression and goes against the idea of a free society. I thought we lived in America — not communist Russia! What gives a school administrator (who probably earns less in one year than what I spend on clothes in a month) the right to force his stupid ideas of what clothing is appropriate on me and everyone else? If students should have to wear uniforms, then it only makes sense that the teachers should be forced to wear them too. Let's see how they like being told what to wear!

And have you seen the state of most school uniforms? To say that they are ugly would be a major understatement. I wouldn't be seen dead wearing a below-the-knee length pleated skirt and buckled shoes — yuck! Get a grip, people! Not only are school uniforms as ugly as sin, but they also make everyone look the same. How am I supposed to judge whether a new girl in my class is worthy of my company if I can't immediately dismiss her based on her lack of fashion sense (or her lack of ability to afford designer clothes)? What's the point of being able to afford the latest Mui Mui shoes and Gucci tops if I can't flaunt them in front of everyone at school each day?

In conclusion, imposing school uniforms on students is immoral, stupid, and should obviously be illegal!

1,001. In your response, analyze the relationship between Passage 2 and the enduring truth expressed in the quotation from Justice Harlan in Passage 1. How well does Passage 2 relate Justice Harlan's statement to the ideas of affirmative action? Incorporate relevant and specific evidence from the quotation and the passage, as well as your knowledge of affirmative action, to support your analysis.

Passage 1

Quotation: "Our Constitution is color-blind, and neither knows nor tolerates classes among citizens. In respect of civil rights, all citizens are equal before the law. The humblest is the peer of the most powerful." —John Marshall Harlan, Supreme Court Justice, 1896

Passage 2

Affirmative action in the United States arose from the effort to ameliorate the disparate access of historically disadvantaged groups to employment and educational opportunities.

With its inception in governmental executive orders, affirmative action meant only positive action designed to remedy the present effects of past discrimination.

The earliest use of the modern-day term affirmative action can be found in Executive Order 10925 initiated by President John F. Kennedy. It specifically refers to nondiscrimination in the employment processes of federal contractors: The contractor will take affirmative action to ensure that applicants are employed, and that employees are treated during employment, without regard to their race, creed, color, or national origin.

Similarly, the Civil Rights Act of 1964 contains the following reference to affirmative action: In administering a program regarding which the recipient [of federal funding] has previously discriminated against persons on the ground of race, color, or national origin, the recipient must take affirmative action to overcome the effects of prior discrimination.

Broadly conceived, affirmative action can be understood as positive action through programs initiated by governmental entities that benefit certain groups. Harvard legal scholar Randall Kennedy defines affirmative action as "policies that offer individuals deemed to be affiliated with a beneficiary group a preference over others in competitions for employment, education, or other valued resources."

The courts, bureaucracy, and the legislature have all been involved in interpreting affirmative action.

We examine the decisive turning point in judicial thought that moved from remedial, disparate-impact affirmative action designed to address a legal wrong to a singular, nonremedial rationale based on the educational benefits of diversity as a "compelling state interest."

We further highlight the Supreme Court's interpretive shift in relation to the Equal Protection Clause from protection of the rights of minorities to protection of the rights of all citizens, including White Americans. This interpretation has been the centerpiece of subsequent legal challenges to affirmative action.

Source: *Affirmative Action at a Crossroads* by Edna Chun and Alvin Evans (Wiley).

2 The Answers

IN THIS PART . . .

Review the answers to all 1,001 questions.

Study the answer explanations to better understand the concepts being covered.

Chapter **5**

The Answers

Chapter 1

1. **A. −13**

Substitute the value of *x* into the function by replacing the *x* with −5:

$$f(x) = 2x - 3$$
$$f(-5) = 2(-5) - 3$$

Then simplify the right-hand side of the equation:

$$f(-5) = -10 - 3$$
$$= -13$$

Choice (A) is the correct answer.

2. **C.** $-3 \le x < 5$

Deal with each part of the statement separately: "*x* is less than 5" can be written as $x < 5$, and "*x* is greater than or equal to −3" can be written as $x \ge -3$, or $-3 \le x$. Now combine both statements by placing *x* in the middle: $-3 \le x < 5$. Hence, Choice (C) is correct.

3. **D. −5**

There are at least two ways to solve this problem: 1) substitute in the answer choices to see which one works or 2) solve the quadratic equation.

Method 1: Substitute in each answer choice.

When you substitute $x = -2$ into the left-hand side of the equation, you get $(-2)^2 + 3(-2) = 4 - 6 = -2$. Because $-2 \ne 10$, Choice (A) is incorrect.

When you substitute $x = 5$ into the left-hand side of the equation, you get $(5)^2 + 3(5) = 25 + 15 = 40$. Because $40 \ne 10$, Choice (B) is incorrect.

When you substitute $x=7$ into the left-hand side of the equation, you get $(7)^2+3(7)=49+21=70$. Because $70\neq 10$, Choice (C) is incorrect.

When you substitute $x=-5$ into the left-hand side of the equation, you get $(-5)^2+3(-5)=25-15=10$. Because $10=10$, Choice (D) is the correct answer.

Method 2: Solve the quadratic. You can solve the quadratic equation by factoring. Subtract 10 from both sides to set the equation equal to zero:

$$x^2+3x-10=0$$

Factoring the equation gives you

$$(x-2)(x+5)=0$$

For the answer to be zero, either $(x-2)$ or $(x+5)$ has to equal zero (because any number times zero equals zero). Set each set of parentheses equal to zero and solve for x to find the solutions: $(x-2)=0$ gives you $x=2$, and $(x+5)=0$ gives you $x=-5$. Hence, Choice (D) is correct.

---

4. **B. $6.24**

First, you need to determine the number of hours that Jim rented the lawnmower for: There are 3 hours from 9:00 a.m. till noon (12:00 p.m.) and 5.5 hours from noon till 5:30 p.m., for a total of $3+5.5=8.5$ hours. Then you can find the hourly cost by dividing the total cost by the number of hours:

$$\frac{\$53.04}{8.5}=\$6.24$$

Hence, Choice (B) is correct.

---

5. **C. –3**

Substitute the given values of x and y into the expression:

$$6x-3y^2=6(12)-3(-5)^2$$

Then use the correct order of operations to simplify: Remember PEMDAS — (Parentheses, then Exponents, then Multiplication and Division, and then Addition and Subtraction). So first evaluate the exponent, then perform the multiplication, and finally perform the subtraction:

$$=72-3(25)$$
$$=72-75$$
$$=-3$$

Hence, Choice (C) is correct.

ANSWERS 1–100

6. B. \$2,585

Alex's total salary equals his base salary (\$650) plus commission. The 9% commission applies only to his sales in excess of \$10,000 (but not the initial \$10,000 worth of sales). He sold 7 cars worth an average of \$4,500 each, for a total of $7 \times \$4,500 = \$31,500$ in sales. Alex's commission is therefore $0.09(\$31,500 - \$10,000) = \$1,935$. Alex's total salary equals $\$650 + \$1,935 = \$2,585$, making Choice (C) correct.

7. D. $10\sqrt{2}$

Combine the two radicals by multiplying the contents of each radical together, giving you $\sqrt{(20)(10)} = \sqrt{200}$. The largest factor of 200 that has an integer square root is 100, so you can rewrite the expression as $\sqrt{(100)(2)}$. Split the radical back into two separate radicals, giving you $\sqrt{100} \cdot \sqrt{2}$. Then simplify to get the final answer, which is $10\sqrt{2}$. Hence, Choice (D) is correct.

8. A. 2.0×10^3

There are 1,000 millimeters in a meter, so convert the width of the microscope slide from millimeters into meters by dividing by 1,000 (or multiplying by 10^{-3}) to get 50×10^{-3} meters. Then, to find the number of hairs that can fit on the slide, you need to divide the width of the slide by the width of one hair.

$$= \frac{50 \times 10^{-3}}{2.5 \times 10^{-5}}$$

Many people make errors entering this on a calculator, so it's usually easier and quicker to perform this calculation by hand. Start by dividing 50 by 2.5 to get 20; then divide the powers of 10 by subtracting the bottom exponent from the top exponent:

$$= 20 \times 10^{-3-(-5)}$$
$$= 20 \times 10^{-3+5}$$
$$= 20 \times 10^{2}$$

Now convert into scientific notation by rewriting 20 as 2×10 (so the leading coefficient is between 1 and 9.9); then multiply the powers of 10 by adding the exponents:

$$= (2 \times 10) \times 10^2$$
$$= 2 \times 10^1 \times 10^2$$
$$= 2 \times 10^{1+2}$$
$$= 2 \times 10^3$$

Hence, Choice (A) is correct.

9. **D. $125 + 35x \leq 475$**

The total budget has to be less than or equal to \$475, so you can rule out Choices (A) and (C). The cost of renting the room is fixed at \$125, so this amount doesn't depend upon the number of people attending the party. Hence, Choice (B) is incorrect.

Because there are 35 people and each lunch cost *x* dollars, you need to multiply *x* by 35, making Choice (D) the correct answer.

10. **C. \$44,693**

Calculate how much Jenny's salary rose during the past four years as follows. First find the difference in salary:

$$\$32,433 - \$22,625 = \$9,808$$

Divide this by 4 to calculate the average rise per year:

$$\frac{\$9,808}{4} = \$2,452$$

Multiply this by 5 to calculate her salary increase over the next 5 years:

$$\$2,452 \times 5 = \$12,260$$

Add this to her current salary:

$$\$32,433 + \$12,260 = \$44,693$$

Choice (C) is the correct answer.

11. **D. $3n - 22$**

Mrs. Black's math class has 22 students less than $3n$. This can be written as $3n - 22$. Hence, Choice (D) is the correct answer.

12. **C. (3, 4.7) and (11, 11.5)**

By plotting the number of weeks along the *x*-axis and the height along the *y*-axis, Denise will place data points in the correct location on the coordinate grid.

13. **A. $y = 0.85x + 2.15$**

Find the slope, *m*, by substituting the coordinates of two data points listed in the table into the slope formula:

$$m = \frac{y_2 - y_1}{x_2 - x_1}$$

Using the points (3, 4.7) and (11, 11.5), for example, gives you

$$\begin{aligned} m &= \frac{11.5-4.7}{11-3} \\ &= \frac{6.8}{8} \\ &= 0.85 \end{aligned}$$

Because you now know the slope, you can calculate the y-intercept (b) by substituting any of the data points into the given equation. For example, using (1, 3.0) gives you

$$\begin{aligned} y &= mx+b \\ 3 &= 0.85(1)+b \\ b &= 2.15 \end{aligned}$$

Therefore, the equation is $y = 0.85x + 2.15$, making Choice (A) the correct answer.

---

14. **B. Week 17**

Because the slope of the linear equation is 0.85, the sunflower grows 0.85 cm per week. By Week 13, the sunflower was 13.2 cm tall. It therefore needs to grow an additional 3.4 cm to reach a height of 16.6 cm. This will take an additional four weeks, because

$$\frac{3.4}{0.85} = 4$$

Hence, the sunflower will reach a height of 16.6 cm at Week 17.

Another way to solve this problem is to use the equation from the preceding question, $y = 0.85x + 2.15$, and set y = 16.6 and solve for x:

$$\begin{aligned} 16.6 &= 0.85x+2.15 \\ 14.45 &= 0.85x \\ \frac{14.45}{0.85} &= x \\ 17 &= x \end{aligned}$$

Hence, Choice (B) is the correct answer.

---

15. **C. 40 minutes**

According to the graph, the patient's blood sugar began to increase immediately after she ate the candy bar and reached a peak after 2/3 of an hour (40 minutes) before falling again. Hence, Choice (C) is correct.

16. **B. 11.9**

The height of the cone is given as 6 inches, and the diameter of the cone is given as $2\frac{3}{4}$ (or 2.75) inches. The radius equals half the diameter and hence equals 1.375 cm.

You can find the volume of a cone by plugging these values into the following equation:

$$\begin{aligned} V &= \frac{1}{3}\pi r^2 h \\ &= \frac{1}{3}(3.14)(1.375)^2(6) \\ &= 11.879 \end{aligned}$$

Rounding to one decimal place gives you 11.9 cubic inches, so the correct answer is Choice (B).

17. **9**

The inequality $15 + 5x \leq 60$ represents the number of pairs of socks Anne can order from the company. Subtracting 15 from each side of the inequality gives you $5x \leq 45$. This can be reduced further by dividing both sides by 5, giving you $x \leq 9$:

$$\begin{aligned} 15 + 5x &\leq 60 \\ 5x &\leq 45 \\ x &\leq 9 \end{aligned}$$

18. **B. 5.4**

The sum of the nine scores that were plotted on the line graph is 49: $2+3+4+4+5+6+6+9+10=49$. Dividing the sum by 9 gives you $5.\overline{44}$. Rounding to one decimal place gives you 5.4, so Choice (B) is the correct answer.

19. **C. 6**

Because the modal score (the mode) is 6, more students must have scored a 6 than any other score. Hence, the tenth student must have also scored 6.

You can also check that this score gives the correct median by placing all the scores in ascending order and picking the average of the middle two numbers.

2, 3, 4, 4, 5, 6, 6, 6, 9, 10

The middle two numbers are 5 and 6, so the median is

$$\frac{5+6}{2} = 5.5$$

20. **D. 80%**

The probability of snow on Tuesday is 20%. Therefore, the probability that it will not snow on Tuesday is $100\% - 20\% = 80\%$.

21. **5.6%**

Calculate the probability that it will snow on all three days by multiplying all three probabilities together. When plugging these percentages into your calculator you can press the % button on the calculator after typing in each number.

$$(70\%)(20\%)(40\%) = 0.056$$

To convert this decimal answer into a percentage, simply multiply it by 100 to get

$$0.056 \times 100 = 5.6\%$$

22. **A. 33%**

There are three cases you need to consider:

Case 1: Snow on Monday (70%) and Tuesday (20%) but not Wednesday. (*Note:* The probability it won't snow on a day is 100% minus the probability that it will, so the probability it won't snow on Wednesday is $100\% - 40\% = 60\%$.) When plugging these percentages into your calculator you can press the % button on the calculator after typing in each number.

$$(70\%)(20\%)(60\%) = 0.084$$

To convert this decimal answer into a percentage simply multiply it by 100 to get 8.4%.

Case 2: Snow on Monday (70%) and Wednesday (40%) but not Tuesday $(100\% - 20\% = 80\%)$.

$$(70\%)(80\%)(40\%) = 0.224 = 22.4\%$$

Case 3: Snow on Tuesday (20%) and Wednesday (40%) but not Monday $(100\% - 70\% = 30\%)$.

$$(30\%)(20\%)(40\%) = 0.024 = 2.4\%$$

Now add the probabilities from each case to find the total probability of snowing two out of the three days:

$$8.4\% + 22.4\% + 2.4\% = 33.2\%$$

This equals 33% when rounded to the nearest whole number. Hence, Choice (A) is correct.

23. **C. 31,000**

Round each number to the nearest thousand and then add.

$$5{,}000 + 5{,}000 + 9{,}000 + 0 + 12{,}000 = 31{,}000$$

Hence, Choice (C) is the correct answer.

24. **C. 2,500,000**

You can find the volume of the pyramid by plugging the given dimensions into the volume equation, where B is the area of the base and h is the height of the pyramid. The base is a square, so the area of the base is the length of a side squared (s^2):

$$\begin{aligned} V &= \frac{1}{3}Bh \\ &= \frac{1}{3}(225^2)150 \\ &= 2{,}531{,}250 \end{aligned}$$

Rounding gives you 2,500,000 cubic meters, so the correct answer is Choice (C).

25. **B. 60**

The *range* of the set is simply the difference between the largest number and the smallest:

$$101 - 41 = 60$$

Hence, the correct answer is Choice (B).

26. **C. 71**

Because the members of Set A are already ordered from smallest to biggest, the median of the set is simply the middle value. Hence, the correct answer is 71, Choice (C).

27. **C. 71**

Because the members of Set A are equally spaced (a gap of 10 between neighbors), the mean is equal to the median.

Alternatively, you can find the mean by adding all the values together and dividing this sum by the number of values. There are seven numbers, so

$$\frac{41+51+61+71+81+91+101}{7}=\frac{497}{7}=71$$

Hence, the correct answer is Choice (C).

28. **D. $\frac{3}{11}$**

Divide the given number of yards by the number of yards in 1 mile:

$$\frac{480}{1{,}760}$$

Reduce the fraction to its lowest terms. Dividing both the numerator and the denominator by 10 gives you

$$\frac{48}{176}$$

Now, dividing both the numerator and the denominator by 8 followed by 2 gives you

$$\frac{6}{22}=\frac{3}{11}$$

Another option is to find $480 \div 1{,}760$, get a decimal answer, and use the calculator's decimal-to-fraction key.

Hence, the correct answer is Choice (D).

29. **D. Catty McCatface**

Because the whole-number part of each cat's tail length equals 7, you can ignore this and focus solely on the fractional part of each length. Hence, you only need to determine which of the following fractions (corresponding to each cat) is the greatest:

$$\frac{3}{4}, \frac{3}{8}, \frac{11}{16}, \frac{25}{32}$$

The lowest common denominator for all the fractions is 32, so you can rewrite each fraction in terms of this common denominator to get

$$\frac{24}{32}, \frac{12}{32}, \frac{22}{32}, \frac{25}{32}$$

Hence, Choice (D) is the correct answer.

30. **B. 1:4**

There are a total of 100 senators, 20 of whom are female. Therefore, there must be 80 male senators. To find the ratio of female senators to male senators, divide the number of female senators by the number of male senators:

$$\frac{20}{80}$$

Reduce this fraction to its lowest terms by dividing both the numerator and the denominator by 20:

$$\frac{1}{4}$$

Hence, Choice (B) is the correct answer.

31. **B. Car B**

To find the best gas mileage, divide the distance traveled by the number of gallons of gas used for each car:

$$\text{Car A: } \frac{102.3}{11.5} = 8.896$$

$$\text{Car B: } \frac{78.1}{7.9} = 9.886$$

$$\text{Car C: } \frac{57.8}{6.2} = 9.323$$

$$\text{Car D: } \frac{142.9}{15.9} = 8.987$$

Hence, Choice (B) is the correct answer.

32. **B. 11**

Each roll of the die has a one in six chance of landing on any of the six numbers. Therefore, multiplying the number of rolls by $\frac{1}{6}$ will give you an estimate of how many times a 6 is likely to appear.

$$\frac{1}{6} \cdot 66 = 11$$

33. $\frac{125}{216}$

Consider each roll of the die separately. The probability of not rolling a 1 on each roll equals $\frac{5}{6}$ because there are five other numbers that can appear (2, 3, 4, 5, and 6).

Now multiply all three probabilities together to find the overall probability of rolling no 1s.

$$\frac{5}{6} \cdot \frac{5}{6} \cdot \frac{5}{6} = \frac{125}{216}$$

34. **B. 8 million**

Let p equal the number of phones sold and b equal the number of exploding batteries. You are told that p is inversely proportional to b, which means that as b increases, p decreases. You can express this relationship as follows, where k equals a constant:

$$p = \frac{k}{b}$$

Substitute the given values for p and b into the equation to find k:

$$88 = \frac{k}{2}$$
$$k = 176$$

The equation now becomes $p = \frac{176}{b}$.

Now substitute $b = 22$ into the equation to find the corresponding value of p:

$$p = \frac{176}{22} = 8$$

Hence, Choice (B) is the correct answer.

35. **C. 18.75 m**

Set up a proportion with the unknown variable (actual length) as the numerator of the fraction and the scaled length as the denominator:

$$\frac{\text{actual length}}{\text{scaled length}} = \frac{5}{2}$$

Substitute the given values into the proportion and let x equal the unknown length:

$$\frac{x}{7.5} = \frac{5}{2}$$

Multiply both sides by 7.5 to solve for x:

$$x = 7.5\left(\frac{5}{2}\right)$$
$$= 18.75$$

Alternatively, cross-multiply to get $2x = 37.5$ and then divide both sides by 2 to get 18.75.

Hence, Choice (C) is the correct answer.

36. **A. 4.8 miles**

The total fare (not including tip) consists of a set initial fee of $2.50 plus a variable cost depending on the number of miles traveled, *x*:

$$\$14.50 = \$2.50 + \text{variable cost}$$

Hence, the variable cost equals $12.00.

Because every $\frac{1}{5}$ of a mile traveled costs an additional $0.50, multiplying by 5 shows that 1 mile costs $2.50. Divide the variable cost ($12) by the cost per mile ($2.50) to find the number of miles traveled:

$$\frac{12}{2.5} = 4.8$$

Hence, Choice (A) is the correct answer.

37. **3.75%**

You can use the following formula to calculate the annual interest rate:

$$\text{interest rate} = \frac{(\text{new balance} - \text{old balance})}{\text{old balance}} \cdot \frac{100}{1}$$

Plug in the given values to find the annual interest rate:

$$\text{interest rate} = \frac{(726.25 - 700)}{700} \cdot \frac{100}{1}$$

Hence, the interest rate as 3.75%.

Alternatively, the interest formula is

$$I = Prt$$

where *I* is the interest earned, *P* is the principal, *r* is the interest rate, and *t* is the time. Substituting in the values gives you

$$26.25 = (700)(r)(1)$$

$$\frac{26.25}{700} = 0.0375$$

To convert this decimal answer into a percentage, simply multiply it by 100 to get 3.75%.

38. **C. $P = 950x + 725y$**

The total payroll equals the cost of *x* cooks plus *y* waiters. Each cook earns an average of $950, so the payroll for *x* cooks equals 950*x*. Similarly, there are *y* waiters who earn an average of $725 each, so the payroll for *y* waiters equals 725*y*. Hence, the total payroll for the cooks and the waiters is given by

$$P = 950x + 725y$$

39. C. 7 waiters

Becky's total payroll cannot exceed \$9,825. The amounts she spends on the five cooks equals $5(\$950) = \$4,750$. The maximum amount that she has left to spend on the waiters is $\$9,825 - \$4,750 = \$5,075$.

Each waiter receives an average of \$725 per week, so the maximum number of waiters that she can employ is

$$\frac{\$5,075}{\$725} = 7$$

Hence, Choice (C) is the correct answer.

40. B. 62

Notice that $\frac{4}{7}x$ is exactly twice $\frac{2}{7}x$. Because $\frac{2}{7}x = 31$, you can simply double both sides of the equation to get

$$\frac{4}{7}x = 62$$

Therefore, Choice (B) is the correct answer.

41. \$552.50

The total fee includes the cost of a large van (\$125), plus the cost of 3 professional movers for 5 hours, plus the cost of the miles driven.

The cost of 3 professional movers for 5 hours is

$$3(18)(5) = \$270$$

The cost of the miles driven is

$$42(\$3.75) = \$157.50$$

Hence, the total cost equals

$$\$125 + \$270 + \$157.50 = \$552.50$$

42. C. \$537

Calculate Jenny's bill when 6% tax is added as follows:

$$(1.06)(\$450) = \$477$$

Now calculate the tip for the 3 professional movers:

$$3(\$20) = \$60$$

Now add the tip amount to the rest of the bill to get

$$\$477 + \$60 = \$537$$

Hence, Choice (C) is the correct answer.

43. **A. (4,1)**

Point A is located 4 along the x-axis and 1 along the y-axis. The x-coordinate always comes first, followed by the y-coordinate, making Choice (A) the correct answer.

44. **B. $\frac{3}{4}$**

Find the slope by substituting the coordinates of A and B from the graph into the slope formula, which is

$$m = \frac{y_2 - y_1}{x_2 - x_1}$$

Using the x and y coordinates of point B, located at $(-4, -5)$, and point A, located at $(4, 1)$, gives you

$$m = \frac{1-(-5)}{4-(-4)}$$
$$= \frac{3}{4}$$

45. **B. $y = \frac{3}{4}x - 2$**

Find the slope by substituting the coordinates of A and B from the graph into the slope formula, which is

$$m = \frac{y_2 - y_1}{x_2 - x_1}$$

Using the x and y coordinates of point B, located at $(-4, -5)$, and point A, located at $(4, 1)$, gives you

$$m = \frac{1-(-5)}{4-(-4)}$$
$$= \frac{3}{4}$$

The y intercept (b) of the graph equals -2 (where the graph crosses the y axis). Hence, the equation of the line in the form $y = mx + b$ equals

$$y = \frac{3}{4}x - 2$$

Hence, Choice (B) is correct.

46. **C. $13,000**

Let the original price of the car equal x. Jessica gets a discount of 45%, which means that she has to pay only 55% of the original price. She paid $7,150. Therefore,

$$\$7{,}150 = (0.55)x$$

Solve for x by dividing both sides of the equation by 0.55:

$$x = \$13{,}000$$

Choice (C) is the correct answer.

---

47. **A. 24 feet**

Set up a proportion for the mailbox with the height as the numerator of the fraction and the shadow length as the denominator:

$$\frac{\text{height}}{\text{shadow}} = \frac{4}{5.5}$$

Substitute the given shadow length of the tree into the proportion and let x equal the unknown height of the tree:

$$\frac{x}{33} = \frac{4}{5.5}$$

Multiply both sides by 33 to solve for x:

$$\begin{aligned} x &= 33\left(\frac{4}{5.5}\right) \\ &= 24 \end{aligned}$$

Alternatively, you can solve the proportion by cross-multiplying and then dividing both sides by 5:

$$5x = 4(33)$$
$$x = 24$$

Choice (A) is the correct answer.

---

48. **C. 15 inches**

Because the triangle is a right triangle, you can use the Pythagorean theorem, which states that $a^2 + b^2 = c^2$, where side c equals the length of the hypotenuse and a and b are the legs. Let the missing side equal a. Substitute the given values into the equation and solve for a:

$$\begin{aligned} a^2 + 8^2 &= 17^2 \\ a^2 + 64 &= 289 \\ a^2 &= 225 \\ a &= 15 \end{aligned}$$

Hence, Choice (C) is the correct answer.

49. **C. –7**

From the line graph, you can see that $A=-9$ and $E=-2$. Therefore, A minus E equals

$$(-9)-(-2)$$

Subtracting a negative number is the same as adding, so

$$-9+2=-7$$

Hence, Choice (C) is the correct answer.

50. **B. 0**

From the line graph, you can see that $A=-9$, $C=7$, $D=0$, and $E=-2$. Therefore, A times C times D times E equals

$$(-9)(7)(0)(-2)=0$$

Multiplying any number by zero equals zero, so Choice (B) is the correct answer.

51. **D. $-A>|E|+|B|$**

From the line graph, you can see that

$$|A|=9,\ |B|=4,\ |C|=7,\ |D|=0,\ |E|=2$$

Plugging these values into each answer choice gives you

(A) $9<7$, which is false

(B) $0>2$, which is false

(C) $-2<-9$, which is false

(D) $9>2+4$, which is true

Hence, Choice (D) is the correct answer.

52. **C. 8**

There are at least two ways to solve this problem: substitution or solving the quadratic.

Method 1: Substitute in each answer choice. Substitute each choice into the equation and check whether the resulting value on the left-hand side equals the value on the right-hand side of the equation. Only Choice (C) works:

$$(8)^2-5(8)=24$$
$$64-40=24$$

Method 2: Solve the quadratic. Solve the quadratic equation by subtracting 24 from both sides to set the equation equal to zero:

$$x^2 - 5x - 24 = 0$$

Then factor:

$$(x+3)(x-8) = 0$$

To get an answer of zero, one of the values in parentheses must equal zero. This gives you two possible solutions: $x = -3$ and $x = 8$. Hence, Choice (C) is the correct answer.

---

53. **C.** $x^2 + y^2 + 2xy$

Rewrite the equation as follows:

$$(x+y)^2 = (x+y)(x+y)$$

Then use FOIL to multiply each term in the first set of parentheses by each term in the second set of parentheses. The word *FOIL* is an acronym for the four terms of the product:

First (the first terms of each binomial are multiplied together)

Outer (the first term of the first binomial and the second term of the second are multiplied)

Inner (the second term of the first binomial and first term of the second are multiplied)

Last (the last terms of each binomial are multiplied)

This gives you

$$\begin{aligned}(x+y)(x+y) &= x^2 + xy + xy + y^2 \\ &= x^2 + 2xy + y^2\end{aligned}$$

Hence, Choice (C) is the correct answer.

---

54. **D. 216**

You can determine the surface area (*SA*) of a cube with the following equation, in which *s* is the length of a side:

$$SA = 6s^2$$

You know the surface area equals 216 cubic inches, so you can substitute this into the equation for *SA* and solve for *s*:

$$216 = 6s^2$$

Dividing both sides by 6 gives you

$$36 = s^2$$

Hence, $s = 6$.

A cube is a special type of rectangular prism in which the length (*l*), the width (*w*), and the height (*h*) are all equal. The volume of a rectangular prism is given by

$$V = lwh$$

Substituting $l = 6$, $w = 6$, and $h = 6$ into the equation shows the volume equals 216 cubic inches. Hence, Choice (D) is the correct answer.

55. **B. $9\sqrt{2}$**

Split 162 into two factors (making sure that the square root of one of the factors has an integer value) as follows:

$$\sqrt{162} = \sqrt{81 \cdot 2}$$

Now separate the factors, giving each its own square root sign:

$$\sqrt{81 \cdot 2} = \sqrt{81} \cdot \sqrt{2}$$

Simplify the factor that has an integer value as its square root:

$$\sqrt{81} \cdot \sqrt{2} = 9\sqrt{2}$$

Hence, Choice (B) is the correct answer.

56. **B. 11 and 12**

129 lies between the square numbers 121 and 144. Therefore, $\sqrt{121} < \sqrt{129} < \sqrt{144}$, which reduces to

$$11 < \sqrt{129} < 12$$

Hence, Choice (B) is the correct answer.

57. **C. $\frac{3}{10}$**

Adding all the nuts together gives you a total of 40 nuts. Twelve of these are cashews, so the fraction of cashews present in the bag is

$$\frac{12}{40}$$

Reduce to lowest terms by dividing both the numerator and the denominator by 4:

$$\frac{3}{10}$$

58. **D.** $\frac{1}{260}$

There are 3 peanuts out of a total of 40 nuts. The probability of selecting a peanut on the first pick is therefore

$$\frac{3}{40}$$

There are now 2 peanuts left out of a total of 39 nuts. The probability of selecting a peanut on the second pick is therefore

$$\frac{2}{39}$$

To find the probability of both events happening, you multiply the probabilities together:

$$\frac{3}{40}\cdot\frac{2}{39}$$

Cross-cancel the fractions by diving both the numerator of the second fraction and the denominator of the first fraction by 2 to get

$$\frac{3}{20}\cdot\frac{1}{39}$$

Continue cross-canceling the fractions by dividing both the numerator of the first fraction and the denominator of the second fraction by 3 to get

$$\frac{1}{20}\cdot\frac{1}{13}$$

Now multiply the fractions together to get

$$\frac{1}{260}$$

59. **C. $0.13**

To find the average cost per nut, simply divide the total cost by the number of nuts:

$$\frac{\$5.20}{40}=\$0.13$$

Hence, Choice (C) is the correct answer.

60. **10.**

Add $2x$ to both sides of the equation:

$$19 = 2x - 1$$

Now add 1 to both sides of the equation:

$$20 = 2x$$

Divide both sides by 2:

$$x = 10$$

61. **B. −2**

Substitute $y = 5$ into the equation of the line to get

$$5 - 4x = 13$$

Add $4x$ to both sides:

$$5 = 13 + 4x$$

Now subtract 13 from both sides:

$$-8 = 4x$$

Divide both sides by 4 to find x:

$$-2 = x$$

Hence, Choice (B) is the correct answer.

62. **4, 13**

The equation of the line is given as

$$y - 4x = 13$$

The slope-intercept form of a line is given by $y = mx + b$, where m represents the slope and b equals the y-intercept. Add $4x$ to both sides of the equation to put it in slope-intercept form:

$$y = 4x + 13$$

Hence, the slope is 4, and the y-intercept equals 13.

63. **B. 123**

Set up a proportion with the number of defective bulbs as the numerator of the fraction and the total number of bulbs as the denominator:

$$\frac{\text{defective bulbs}}{\text{total bulbs}} = \frac{1}{25}$$

Substitute the given value for the total number of bulbs into the proportion, and let x equal the unknown number of defective bulbs:

$$\frac{x}{3{,}075} = \frac{1}{25}$$

Multiply both sides by 3,075 to solve for x:

$$x = 3{,}075\left(\frac{1}{25}\right)$$
$$= 123$$

Alternatively, you can solve the proportion by cross-multiplying and then dividing both sides by 25:

$$25x = 3{,}075(1)$$
$$x = 123$$

Hence, Choice (B) is the correct answer.

---

64. **D. 210**

The width of the rectangle is given as 7 inches. Note that the length of the rectangle is 2.5 feet, which needs to be multiplied by 12 to convert into inches:

$$l = 2.5(12) = 30$$

Multiply the length by the width to calculate the area of the rectangle:

$$A = lw = (30)(7) = 210$$

Hence, Choice (D) is the correct answer.

---

65. **C. 3:1**

The perimeter P of a rectangle of length l and width w is given by the following formula:

$$P = 2l + 2w$$

The new length of the rectangle is $3l$ and the new width is $3w$, so the new perimeter will simply be 3 times longer than the old perimeter:

$$P_{new} = 2(3l) + 2(3w)$$
$$P_{new} = 3(2l + 2w)$$
$$P_{new} = 3P_{old}$$

Hence, the ratio of the new perimeter to old perimeter is 3:1, making Choice (C) correct.

66. **D. 9:1**

The area A of a rectangle of length l and width w is

$$A = lw$$

Because the new length of the rectangle is $3l$ and the new width is $3w$, the new area will be 9 times larger than the old area:

$$A_{new} = (3l)(3w)$$
$$A_{new} = 9(lw)$$
$$A_{new} = 9A_{old}$$

Hence, the ratio of the new area to old area equals 9:1, making Choice (D) correct.

67. **0.375**

Use long division to divide the numerator (3) by the denominator (8) to get 0.375.

68. **D. 2.97×10^5**

Rewrite the number with the smaller power of ten (1.7×10^4) so that it has the same power of ten as the larger number:

$$1.7 \times 10^4 = 0.17 \times 10^5$$

Now rewrite the sum using the newly converted number:

$$2.8 \times 10^5 + 0.17 \times 10^5$$

Because the powers of ten for the two numbers are now the same, you can simply add the coefficients (the decimal parts) and keep the 10^5 as it is:

$$2.8 \times 10^5 + 0.17 \times 10^5 = (2.8 + 0.17) \times 10^5$$
$$= 2.97 \times 10^5$$

Hence, Choice (D) is the correct answer.

69. **D. 3.2×10^4**

When multiplying numbers in scientific notation, multiply the coefficients as follows:

$$8 \times 4 = 32$$

Because the powers both have a base equal to 10, you can multiply them simply by adding the exponents together:

$$(10^6)(10^{-3}) = 10^{6-3} = 10^3$$

Combine both parts of your answer and write it in scientific notation:

$$32\times10^3 = 3.2\times10^4$$

Hence, Choice (D) is the correct answer.

70. **parallel, equal, perpendicular, negative reciprocals**

Two lines that never meet are called parallel lines, and their slopes are equal. Two lines that meet at right angles are called perpendicular lines, and their slopes are negative reciprocals.

71. **$0.27**

Calculate the range by subtracting the smallest value from the largest value:

$$\$3.56 - \$3.29 = \$0.27$$

72. **B. $3.43**

Add the four values together to find the sum of the prices as follows:

$$\$3.29 + \$3.38 + \$3.47 + \$3.56 = \$13.70$$

Divide the sum by 4 to get the average price:

$$\frac{\$13.70}{4} = \$3.425$$

Rounding up to the nearest cent gives you $3.43 per gallon; therefore, Choice (B) is the correct answer.

Alternatively, because the numbers are equally spaced, the mean will be the same as the median. You could find the mean simply by averaging the middle two numbers to get the same answer. (Also, when numbers are evenly spaced, averaging only the first and last numbers works, too.)

73. **D. $11.76**

Each week, the average price of gasoline rises by $0.09 per gallon. The price in Week 4 equals $3.56, so four weeks later (in Week 8), the price will have risen by

$$4\times(\$0.09) = \$0.36$$

Therefore, the average price per gallon in Week 8 equals

$$\$3.56 + \$0.36 = \$3.92$$

Note that the question stem asks how much 3 gallons of gasoline would cost, so you need to multiply by 3 to get the final answer.

$$3(\$3.92) = \$11.76$$

Hence, Choice (D) is the correct answer.

74. **C. p^{20}**

Substitute the values for x and y into the expression. Then divide the values in the parentheses (using the quotient rule) by subtracting their powers $(7-(-3)=10)$:

$$\left(\frac{p^7}{p^{-3}}\right)^2=\left(p^{10}\right)^2$$

Simplify further (by using the power rule) by multiplying the exponents together: p^{20}. Hence, the correct answer is Choice (C).

75. **B. 1**

Any expression to the power zero equals 1. Hence, the correct answer is Choice (B).

76. **A. 1**

Substitute the values for x, y, and z into the expression:

$$\left(p^7\right)\left(p^{-3}\right)^2\left(\frac{1}{p}\right)$$

Use the power rule on the middle term (multiply the exponents) to simplify the expression:

$$\left(p^7\right)\left(p^{-6}\right)\left(\frac{1}{p}\right)$$

Use the product rule on the first two terms by adding their exponents:

$$\left(p^1\right)\left(\frac{1}{p}\right)$$

Simplifying further gives you

$$\frac{p}{p}=1$$

Hence, the correct answer is Choice (A).

77. **C. $\frac{1}{9}$**

Substitute the value of x into the function by replacing the x with -3:

$$f(-3)=\frac{10-(-3)^2}{(-3)^2}$$

Then simplify the right-hand side of the equation:

$$f(-3) = \frac{10-(9)}{9}$$
$$= \frac{1}{9}$$

Choice (C) is the correct answer.

78. **acute, supplementary, obtuse, congruent**

Angle 2 is an <u>acute</u> angle and is <u>supplementary</u> to angle 1. Angle 5 is an <u>obtuse</u> angle and is <u>congruent</u> to angle 8.

79. **C. 135°**

Angle 3 is congruent to the 45° angle because it's formed by a pair of parallel lines cut by a transversal, and these angles are corresponding angles. Angle 1 is supplementary to angle 3, so you can calculate the measure of angle 1 as follows:

$$180-45=135$$

Hence, Choice (C) is correct.

80. **20**

Angle 1 equals 135° because it's supplementary to angle 3, which corresponds to the 45° angle. The angle represented by the expression $5x+35$ is congruent to angle 1 (because vertical angles are congruent) and therefore also equals 135°.

$$5x+35=135$$

Solve for x by subtracting 35 from both sides of the equation and then dividing by 5:

$$5x=100$$
$$x=20$$

81. **45**

The sail is shaped like a right isosceles triangle, meaning that the largest angle is 90° and the remaining two angles are equal to each other. Let x equal one of the unknown angles. The angles in a triangle add up to 180°, so

$$90+2x=180$$

Subtracting 90 from both sides and solving for x gives you

$$2x=90$$
$$x=45$$

82. **C. 90°**

The sum of the angles of any triangle equals 180°; hence,

$$\begin{aligned} 5x + 9x + 14x &= 180 \\ 28x &= 180 \end{aligned}$$

Solving for x gives you $x = \frac{180}{28}$, which reduces to $x = \frac{45}{7}$.
To find the largest angle, substitute $x = \frac{45}{7}$ into $14x$:

$$14\left(\frac{45}{7}\right)$$

This reduces to $2\left(\frac{45}{1}\right) = 90$.

A quicker method to solve the question is to realize that the largest angle ($14x$) is equal to the sum of the other two angles $(5x + 9x)$; therefore, the largest angle must equal half of the sum of the three angles (half of 180°).

83. **D. 24 dozen**

Set up a proportion with the unknown variable (the number of cookies in dozens) as the numerator of the fraction and the number of cups of brown sugar as the denominator:

$$\frac{\text{dozens of cookies}}{\text{cups of sugar}} = \frac{2}{\left(\frac{3}{8}\right)}$$

Remember that when you divide by a fraction, you can simply invert the fraction and multiply instead. Hence, you can simplify the nasty-looking proportion as follows:

$$\frac{\text{dozens of cookies}}{\text{cups of sugar}} = 2\left(\frac{8}{3}\right)$$

This simplifies further to

$$\frac{\text{dozens of cookies}}{\text{cups of sugar}} = \frac{16}{3}$$

Substitute the given values into the proportion, letting x equal the unknown number of cookies (in dozens):

$$\frac{16}{3} = \frac{x}{4.5}$$

Multiply both sides by 4.5 to get

$$4.5\left(\frac{16}{3}\right) = x$$

Simplifying further gives you $x = 24$, so Choice (D) is the correct answer.

84. **A.** $15x^2 - 17x - 4$

When multiplying polynomials, look at what type of polynomials you're multiplying. In this case, because it's a binomial times a binomial, you can use the FOIL method (First terms, Outer terms, Inner terms, Last terms). This results in $15x^2 - 20x + 3x - 4$, which simplifies to Choice (A), $15x^2 - 17x - 4$.

85. **C. 0.007**

The first digit to the right of the decimal point is called the *tenths digit.* The second digit to the right of the decimal point is called the *hundredths digit.* The third digit to the right of the decimal point is called the *thousandths digit*, making Choice (C) the correct answer.

86. **B. $17.40**

For a 27-word advertisement, the total cost consists of two parts: a fixed cost of $5.50 for the first 10 words plus the cost of the additional 17 words at $0.70 each:

$$\$5.50 + 17(0.70) = \$17.40$$

Hence, Choice (B) is correct.

87. **9.25**

To find the average, add all the values together and divide this sum by 4, the number of values:

$$\frac{8.8 + 12.7 + 9.4 + 6.1}{4} = \frac{37}{4} = 9.25$$

88. **A.** $\frac{170 \times 8.8}{3}$

The table lists the average number of calories used per hour per pound of weight for cycling as 8.8. Therefore, if the 170-pound man cycled for one hour, he would use 170×8.8 calories. However, the man cycled for only 20 minutes (one-third of an hour), so you need to divide this by 3 to get the correct answer:

$$\frac{170 \times 8.8}{3}$$

Hence, Choice (A) is correct.

89. **45°**

The entire circular pizza equals 360°. Because there are 8 equally sized pieces, the innermost angle of each slice is

$$\frac{360}{8}=45$$

90. **C. $2.25\pi+18$**

The equation for the circumference of a circle is $C=\pi d$. Substituting the value of the diameter into the equation gives you

$$C=18\pi$$

The perimeter of the slice is the distance around the edge of the slice, which equals two radii (2 times 9 inches) plus the length of the curved edge. There are eight pieces of pizza, so the length of the curved edge of the slice represents one-eighth of the entire circumference:

$$\text{curved edge}=\frac{18\pi}{8}=2.25\pi$$

The perimeter of the slice equals $2.25\pi+18$ inches, so the correct answer is Choice (C).

91. **A. 20.25π**

The equation for the area of a circle is $A=\pi r^2$. Substituting the value of the radius into the equation gives you

$$A_{\text{pizza}}=\pi\left(9^2\right)=81\pi$$

The area of two slices equals one-quarter of the entire area:

$$A_{\text{slices}}=\frac{81\pi}{4}$$

Hence, the area of two slices equals 20.25π square inches, so Choice (A) is correct.

92. **B. $x=4$, $y=7$**

From the diagram, you can see that the width of the lawn is 9 m and the length of the lawn is 22 m. Therefore, the value of x is 4 $(\text{or } 9-5)$ meters, and the value of y is 7 $(\text{or } 22-15)$ meters.

93. **A. $24**

The area of the lawn can be split into two rectangles whose dimensions are as follows: rectangle 1 (9 by 15) and rectangle 2 (x by y). From the figure, you can see that the value of x is 4 $(9-5)$ meters and the value of y is 7 $(22-15)$ meters. Now calculate the total as follows:

$$A_{\text{total}} = (9\times 15)+(4\times 7) = 163 \text{ square meters}$$

The cost of the lawn fertilizer is $0.15 per square meter, so to find the total cost, multiply $0.15 by the number of square meters:

$$163\times(\$0.15) = \$24.45$$

Rounding to the nearest dollar gives you $24, so Choice (A) is correct.

94. **A. 2 cm**

The equation for the area of a circle is $A=\pi r^2$, and the equation for the circumference of a circle is $C=2\pi r$. Because the circumference of this particular circle happens to equal its area, you can set the equations equal to each other and solve for r. Dividing both sides of the equation by πr gives you

$$2\pi r = \pi r^2$$

$$\frac{2\pi r}{\pi r} = \frac{\pi r^2}{\pi r}$$

$$2 = r$$

Therefore, Choice (A) is the correct answer.

95. **C. $\frac{1}{32}$**

The probability of tossing one head during a single toss of a fair coin is $\frac{1}{2}$. Therefore, the probability of tossing 5 heads in a row equals

$$\frac{1}{2}\times\frac{1}{2}\times\frac{1}{2}\times\frac{1}{2}\times\frac{1}{2}=\frac{1}{32}$$

Hence, Choice (C) is the correct answer.

96. **B. 16 degrees**

The temperature rose 9 degrees in the 3-hour period between 5:00 a.m. and 8:00 a.m. This is an increase of 3 degrees per hour. There are 9 hours between 5:00 a.m. and 2:00 p.m. (7 hours from 5:00 a.m. to noon plus 2 hours from noon to 2:00 p.m.), so the total increase in temperature equals

$$9\times 3 = 27 \text{ degrees}$$

At 5:00 a.m., the temperature was −11 degrees, so an increase of 27 degrees will make the temperature at 2:00 p.m. equal to

$$27 - 11 = 16 \text{ degrees}$$

Hence, Choice (B) is correct.

97. **B. $4.10**

Convert 6% to its decimal form by dividing by 100 to get 0.06. Multiply the price of the shirt by the sales tax percentage:

$$(0.06) \times (\$68.30) = \$4.098$$

Rounding to the nearest cent gives you $4.10, so Choice (B) is the correct answer.

98. **A. 2.25**

To find the volume in cubic feet, first convert the width and the length of the prism from inches to feet by dividing each value by 12:

$$l = \frac{18}{12} = 1.5$$

$$w = \frac{9}{12} = 0.75$$

Then substitute the values of each dimension in feet into the volume formula for a rectangular prism:

$$\begin{aligned} V &= lwh \\ &= 1.5 \times 0.75 \times 2 \\ &= 2.25 \text{ cubic feet} \end{aligned}$$

Hence, Choice (A) is the correct answer.

99. **5**

For a right triangle, you can calculate the length of the hypotenuse with the Pythagorean theorem, $a^2 + b^2 = c^2$, where a and b are the legs and c is the hypotenuse. Substitute the given sides into the formula and solve for c:

$$\begin{aligned} 3^2 + 4^2 &= c^2 \\ 9 + 16 &= c^2 \\ 25 &= c^2 \\ 5 &= c \end{aligned}$$

100. **A. 6**

The area of a triangle is $A = \frac{1}{2}bh$, where b is the base of the triangle and h is the triangle's height. This is a right triangle, so the base and the height are equal to the lengths of the legs. Substituting in the values of the triangle's base and height gives you

$$A = \frac{1}{2}(4)(3) = 6$$

Hence, the correct answer is Choice (A).

101. **A. 36**

The volume of a right prism is given by the base area times the prism's height:

$$V = Bh$$

The area of the triangular base is 6 $\left(B = \frac{1}{2}(4)(3) = 6\right)$. The prism is on its side, so its height is the edge labeled 6 in the figure. Substituting these values into the volume formula gives you

$$V = 6 \times 6 = 36$$

Hence, the correct answer is Choice (A).

102. **A. 3**

Substitute in the values of $a = -3$ and $b = 2$ into the equation:

$$\frac{(-3)^2 - 3(2)}{(-3)} + 4$$

Then simplify the expression:

$$\begin{aligned}\frac{9-6}{(-3)} + 4 &= \frac{3}{-3} + 4 \\ &= -1 + 4 \\ &= 3\end{aligned}$$

Hence, the correct answer is Choice (A).

103. **C. 10**

Each term of a geometric sequence is found by multiplying the preceding term by the same number (*r*). To find the value of *r*, divide the second term by the first:

$$\frac{-270}{810} = -\frac{1}{3}$$

You can check that this works by multiplying the second term (–270) by *r* and confirming that you get the third term (90):

$$-270 \times \left(-\frac{1}{3}\right) = 90$$

The fourth term in the sequence is −30, so the next term in the sequence is 10:

$$-30\times\left(-\frac{1}{3}\right)=10$$

Hence, the correct answer is Choice (C).

104. D. 89

Multiply the score by the number of students for each row of the frequency table:

Score	Number of Students	Total Score
72	1	$72\times1=72$
85	3	$85\times3=255$
90	4	$90\times4=360$
100	2	$100\times2=200$

Find the sum of the total scores:

$$72+255+360+200=887$$

Now divide by 10 to find the average score of the 10 students:

$$\frac{887}{10}=88.7$$

An alternative approach is to plug in the values from the table into the weighted average formula:

$$\frac{72(1)+85(3)+90(4)+100(2)}{10}=88.7$$

This rounds up to 89. Hence, Choice (D) is the correct answer.

105. C. 91

Remove the two lowest scores from the table (72 and 85). Multiply the remaining score by the remaining number of students for each row of the frequency table:

Score	Number of Students	Total Score
72	0	$72\times0=0$
85	2	$85\times2=170$
90	4	$90\times4=360$
100	2	$100\times2=200$

Find the sum of the total scores:

$$170 + 360 + 200 = 730$$

Now divide by 8 to find the average score of the 8 remaining students:

$$\frac{730}{8} = 91.25$$

An alternative approach is to plug the values from the table into the weighted average formula:

$$\frac{85(2) + 90(4) + 100(2)}{8} = 91.25$$

This rounds to 91, so Choice (C) is the correct answer.

---

106. **C.** $5x - 4y - z$

Remove the second set of parentheses by subtracting each term in the second set of parentheses from the terms within the first set of parentheses:

$$7x - 5y + 2z - 2x + y - 3z$$

Simplify by adding like terms:

$$5x - 4y - z$$

Hence, Choice (C) is the correct answer.

---

107. **C. 7 hours, 55 minutes**

Multiply 95 minutes by 5 to get the total number of minutes spent commuting each week:

$$95 \times 5 = 475 \text{ minutes}$$

To convert to hours, divide 475 by 60 and find the quotient and the remainder:

$$\frac{475}{60} = 7 \text{ remainder } 55$$

Therefore, the answer is 7 hours, 55 minutes, so the correct answer is Choice (C).

108. C. 20 inches

The area of the triangle is $A = \frac{1}{2}bh$, where b is the base and h is the height. Substituting in the base and area gives you

$$60 = \frac{1}{2}(6)h$$
$$60 = 3h$$
$$20 = h$$

The height is 20 inches, so the correct answer is Choice (C).

109. A. 2.56 km

The formula relating rate *(r)* to distance *(d)* and time *(t)* is

$$d = rt$$

Substitute the given values for speed (rate) and time into the equation to find the distance:

$$d = 320 \times 8$$
$$d = 2{,}560$$

Notice that this distance (2560) is in meters, but the question stem asks you to find the distance in kilometers. Divide by 1,000 to convert meters into kilometers. To divide 2,560.0 meters by 1,000, simply move the decimal point three places to the left to get 2.56 kilometers. Hence, Choice (A) is the correct answer.

110. C. $\frac{12}{7}$

Find the slope by substituting the coordinates of the two data points into the slope formula:

$$m = \frac{y_2 - y_1}{x_2 - x_1}$$
$$= \frac{5-(-7)}{8-1}$$
$$= \frac{12}{7}$$

Hence, Choice (C) is the correct answer.

111. C. $\frac{3}{8}$

On Monday, Andrea finished $\frac{1}{4}$ of her homework assignment, which means that she still had $\frac{3}{4}$ to complete. On Tuesday, she completed $\frac{1}{2}$ of the *remaining work*, which means that she completed an additional $\left(\frac{1}{2}\right)\times\left(\frac{3}{4}\right)=\frac{3}{8}$ of her homework. Find the total completed on Monday and Tuesday by adding the two fractions:

$$\frac{1}{4}+\frac{3}{8}$$

The lowest common denominator is 8, so the fraction of the homework completed so far is

$$\frac{2}{8}+\frac{3}{8}=\frac{5}{8}$$

Because Andrea has completed $\frac{5}{8}$ of her homework, she still has $\frac{3}{8}$ to complete. Hence, Choice (C) is the correct answer.

112. $236.70

Multiply Norman's hourly rate by the number of hours he worked to find his total gross pay for the week:

$$18\times\$13.15=\$236.70$$

113. 11, 9

The *mode* is simply the value that appears most often; hence, 11 is the mode of set *A* (because it appears more than any other value).

To find the median of set *A*, arrange the values in ascending order (from smallest to biggest) and select the middle value:

$$\{0, 2, 2, 3, 7, 11, 11, 11, 16, 37\}$$

Because there's an even number of values (10 values), the average of the middle two equals the median:

$$\frac{7+11}{2}=9$$

114. C. 10

To find the mean of set *A*, find the sum of the values and divide by the number of values in the set:

$$\frac{11+7+2+16+3+11+2+37+0+11}{10}=10$$

Hence, Choice (C) is the correct answer.

ANSWERS 101–200

115. C. 50

Note that anything to the zero power equals 1, so you can simplify the expression as follows:

$$5\times\left(1+3^2\right)$$

Then use the correct order of operations to simplify further: Remember PEMDAS (Parentheses, then Exponents, then Multiplication and Division, and then Addition and Subtraction). First, find the value of the terms within the parentheses by evaluating the exponent before adding the 1:

$$5\times(1+9)$$
$$5\times(10)$$

Then perform the multiplication to get 50. Hence, Choice (C) is the correct answer.

116. A. 2

Remove the parentheses by multiplying each term within the parentheses by the term outside the parentheses:

$$5(x-2)+x=2(3-x)$$
$$5x-10+x=6-2x$$

Group the x's together on the same side of the equation by adding $2x$ to both sides; then simplify:

$$5x-10+x+2x=6$$
$$8x-10=6$$

Now add 10 to both sides and divide by 8:

$$8x=16$$
$$x=2$$

Hence, Choice (A) is correct.

117. C. $a+c=95$, $9c+16a=1,380$

The number of adult tickets sold is a, and the number of child tickets sold is c. Because 95 tickets were sold in total, the equation for the number of tickets sold is

$$a+c=95$$

Create another equation for the money in terms of a and c. The price of each child's ticket is \$9, and the price of each adult's ticket is \$16. Therefore, the equation that represents the total revenue from ticket sales is

$$9c+16a=1,380$$

Hence, Choice (C) is correct.

118. C. 6

Because you know Fred has exactly 7 nickels, you can subtract 35 cents from the total: $1.45-0.35=1.10$. This remaining amount of money is the sum of value of q quarters and d dimes:

$$0.25q+0.1d=1.10$$

You also know that there are three times as many dimes as quarters, so $d=3q$. Combining the two equations (by substituting $3q$ for d), you get

$$\begin{aligned}0.25q+0.1(3q)&=1.10\\0.25q+0.3q&=1.10\\0.55q&=1.10\\q&=2\end{aligned}$$

Now that you know how many quarters there are, just triple it to find how many dimes: 6. Hence, Choice (C) is the correct answer.

119. C. 12

Rewrite the function by substituting in $x=-1$:

$$\begin{aligned}f(-1)&=8-4(-1)\\&=8-(-4)\\&=12\end{aligned}$$

Hence, Choice (C) is the correct answer.

120. C. 3

Rewrite the function by replacing $f(x)$ with -4:

$$\begin{aligned}f(x)&=8-4x\\-4&=8-4x\end{aligned}$$

Subtract 8 from both sides and then divide by -4 to find x:

$$\begin{aligned}-12&=-4x\\\frac{-12}{-4}&=\frac{-4x}{-4}\\3&=x\end{aligned}$$

Hence, Choice (C) is the correct answer.

121. **C.** $h = \frac{V}{\pi r^2}$

To isolate a particular variable, you undo the operations surrounding it. To isolate *h*, divide both sides of the formula by πr^2:

$$V = \pi r^2 h$$
$$\frac{V}{\pi r^2} = \frac{\pi r^2 h}{\pi r^2}$$
$$\frac{V}{\pi r^2} = h$$

This results in Choice (C) as the correct formula.

122. **6**

The number of different ways to place three different items in order is simply $3! = (3)(2)(1) = 6$.

Another way is to consider how many friends are left to sit in each chair. Any of the three friends can sit on the first seat; any of the remaining two friends can sit on the second seat; and there is only one friend left for the remaining seat. Multiply these results together to get six seating arrangements.

123. **D. 60 feet**

Set up a proportion for the stick with the height as the numerator of the fraction and the shadow length as the denominator:

$$\frac{\text{height}}{\text{shadow}} = \frac{3}{2.5}$$

Substitute the given shadow length of the clock tower into the proportion, letting *x* equal the unknown height of the tower:

$$\frac{x}{50} = \frac{3}{2.5}$$

Multiply both sides by 50 to solve for *x*:

$$x = 50\left(\frac{3}{2.5}\right)$$
$$x = 60$$

Alternatively, you can solve the proportion by cross-multiplying and then dividing by 2.5 to get

$$2.5x = 3(50)$$
$$2.5x = 150$$
$$x = 60$$

Hence, Choice (D) is the correct answer.

124. **B. 6 inches**

The Pythagorean theorem states that $a^2 + b^2 = c^2$, where side c equals the length of the hypotenuse. Let the missing side equal a. Substitute the given values into the equation and solve for a:

$$a^2 + 8^2 = 10^2$$
$$a^2 + 64 = 100$$
$$a^2 = 36$$
$$a = 6$$

Hence, Choice (B) is the correct answer.

125. **B.** $y = -\frac{3}{7}x + \frac{1}{9}$

Because you're looking for a line parallel to the given line, the new equation must have the same slope: $m = -\frac{3}{7}$. Because Choice (B) is the only equation with that slope, it's the correct answer.

126. **D.** $y = \frac{7}{3}x - 9$

Because you're looking for a line perpendicular to the given line, the new equation must have a slope that is the negative reciprocal of the slope of the given line: $m = \frac{7}{3}$. Because Choice (D) is the only equation with that slope, it's the correct answer.

127. **C. (7, −12)**

Substitute the x- and y-coordinates for each point into the equation to see which set of coordinates works. For (0, 9), you get $9 = -\frac{3}{7}(0) - 9$; this reduces to $9 = -9$, which is wrong, so Choice (A) is incorrect. For (7, 6), you get $6 = -\frac{3}{7}(7) - 9$, which reduces to $6 = -12$; this is wrong, so Choice (B) is incorrect. For (7, −12), you get $-12 = -\frac{3}{7}(7) - 9$, which reduces to $-12 = -12$; this is correct, so Choice (C) is the right answer. For (14, −9), you get $-9 = -\frac{3}{7}(14) - 9$, which reduces to $-9 = -15$; this is wrong, so Choice (D) is incorrect.

128. **A. Erica is 47, and Lisa is 26.**

Create a system of equations by defining Erica's age as e and Lisa's age as l. Using the information in the problem, you see that $e = 2l - 5$ and $e + l = 73$. To solve the system, substitute in the expression for e and solve:

$$\begin{aligned} e + l &= 73 \\ (2l - 5) + l &= 73 \\ 3l - 5 &= 73 \\ 3l &= 78 \\ l &= 26 \end{aligned}$$

Now that you know Lisa's age is 26, you can subtract this from 73 to get Erica's age, which is 47.

129. **A.** $\frac{3}{8}$

There are 6 blue marbles out of a total of 16, so the fraction of the marbles that are blue is

$$\frac{6}{16} = \frac{3}{8}$$

Hence, Choice (A) is the correct answer.

130. **C.** $\frac{1}{12}$

There are 5 red marbles out of 16 total, so the probability of selecting the first red marble is $\frac{5}{16}$. There are now 4 red marbles out of 15 total, so the probability of selecting the second red marble is $\frac{4}{15}$. You need both events to occur, so multiply the probabilities together:

$$\frac{5}{16} \times \frac{4}{15}$$

Cross-cancel before multiplying, and your answer will be in lowest terms:

$$\frac{1}{4} \times \frac{1}{3} = \frac{1}{12}$$

Hence, Choice (C) is the correct answer.

131. **B. The carton is a better value.**

To calculate the value of each container, divide the price of each container by the volume.

The volume of the carton is $V = lwh$, so the value is

$$\frac{\text{price}}{\text{volume}} = \frac{\$}{lwh} = \frac{\$4.20}{(3)(4)(7)} = \$0.05 \text{ per cubic inch}$$

The volume of the can is $V = \pi r^2 h$, so the value is

$$\frac{\text{price}}{\text{volume}} = \frac{\$}{\pi r^2 h} = \frac{\$6.79}{\pi\left(3^2\right)4} = \$0.06 \text{ per cubic inch}$$

This means the carton is cheaper per cubic inch, so Choice (B) is correct.

132. 24 months

The least common multiple of 6 and 8 is 24, so it will take 24 months before Tamara visits her dentist and her optician in the same week again.

133. D. 27.5 minutes

Set up a proportion with minutes as the numerator of the fraction and the number of laps as the denominator:

$$\frac{\text{minutes}}{\text{laps}} = \frac{11}{4}$$

Substitute the given number of laps into the proportion, letting x equal the unknown number of minutes:

$$\frac{x}{10} = \frac{11}{4}$$

Multiply both sides by 10 to solve for x, giving you $x = 27.5$.

Alternatively, you can solve the proportion by cross-multiplying and then dividing both sides of the equation by 4:

$$\begin{aligned} 4x &= 10(11) \\ 4x &= 110 \\ x &= 27.5 \end{aligned}$$

Hence, Choice (D) is the correct answer.

134. (4, 38) and (16, 62)

Each data point should be placed in the correct location on the coordinate grid by plotting the number of weeks along the x-axis and the height along the y-axis.

135. D. $y = 2x + 30$

Find the slope by substituting the coordinates of two data points listed in the table into the following formula:

$$m = \frac{y_2 - y_1}{x_2 - x_1}$$

Using the data from Week 0, point (0, 30), and Week 4, point (4, 38), for example, gives you a slope of 2:

$$m = \frac{38 - 30}{4 - 0} = \frac{8}{4} = 2$$

You can find the y-intercept (b) by looking at the table and selecting the y-value when $x = 0$:

$$b = 30$$

Therefore, the equation is $y = 2x + 30$. Choice (D) is the correct answer.

136. **C. Week 35**

You can see from the table that Barney can lift an additional 8 pounds every 4 weeks, which is equivalent to 2 additional pounds per week. Because Barney can already lift 30 pounds in Week 0, he needs to gain the strength to be able to lift an additional 70 pounds in order to reach his 100-pound target.

Dividing 70 by 2 additional pounds per week gives you 35 weeks. Hence, Barney will be able to lift 100 pounds at Week 35. Choice (C) is the correct answer.

137. **B. 9.5**

First, convert the length of the box from feet to inches by multiplying by 12 to get $l = 18$ inches. Then plug the values for l, w, and V into the equation for the volume of a box (or rectangular prism):

$$\begin{aligned} V &= lwh \\ 1{,}368 &= (18)(8)h \\ \frac{1{,}368}{(18)(8)} &= h \\ 9.5 &= h \end{aligned}$$

Hence, the correct answer is Choice (B).

138. **A.**

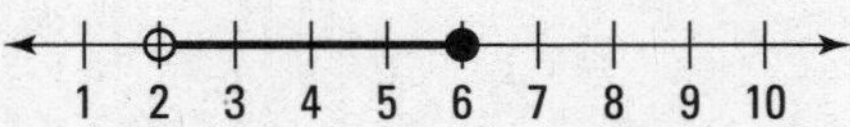

Divide each term of the inequality by 15 to get x on its own:

$$2 < x \le 6$$

Plot these endpoints on the graph with an open circle to represent < and a closed circle to represent ≤. Because x is trapped between the two endpoint values, Choice (A) is correct.

139. **C. 5.5**

The sum of the fish caught by the first 10 fishermen plotted on the line graph equals 55:

$$\begin{aligned}&1(1)+1(2)+2(3)+1(4)+2(7)+1(8)+2(10)\\&=1+2+6+4+14+8+20\\&=55\end{aligned}$$

Dividing the sum by 10 gives you an average of 5.5; hence, Choice (C) is the correct answer.

140. **B. 3**

Because the modal number of fish caught is 3, more fishermen must have caught 3 fish than any other number. Hence, the 11th fisherman must have caught 3 fish.

You can also check that the median actually does equal 4 if the 11th fisherman caught 3 fish by placing the number of fish caught in ascending order and then selecting the middle value:

1, 2, 3, 3, 3, 4, 7, 7, 8, 10, 10

Hence, Choice (B) is correct.

141. **9**

Subtract the smallest number of fish caught (1) from the largest number of fish caught (10) to find the range, which equals 9.

142. **A. 20%**

The probability of Daryl passing chemistry is 80%. Therefore, the probability that he will not pass chemistry is $100\% - 80\% = 20\%$.

143. **24%**

You can calculate Daryl's probability of passing all three tests by multiplying all three probabilities together. When plugging these percentages into your calculator you can press the % button on the calculator after typing in each number:

$$(50\%)(60\%)(80\%)=0.24$$

To convert this answer into a percentage, multiply it by 100 by moving the decimal point two places to the right: 100(0.24)= 24%.

ANSWERS 101–200

144. B. 46%

There are three cases you need to consider:

Case 1: Passing math (50%) and English (60%) but failing chemistry $(100\% - 80\% = 20\%)$. When plugging these percentages into your calculator, you can press the % button on the calculator after typing in each number.

$$(50\%)(60\%)(20\%) = 0.06$$

To convert this decimal answer into a percentage, multiply it by 100 by moving the decimal point two places to the right:

$$100(0.06) = 6\%$$

Case 2: Passing math (50%) and chemistry (80%) but failing English $(100\% - 60\% = 40\%)$.

$$(50\%)(40\%)(80\%) = 0.16 = 16\%$$

Case 3: Passing English (60%) and chemistry (80%) but failing math $(100\% - 50\% = 50\%)$.

$$(50\%)(60\%)(80\%) = 0.24 = 24\%$$

Now add the probabilities from each case to find the total probability of passing two out of the three tests:

$$6\% + 16\% + 24\% = 46\%$$

Hence, Choice (B) is correct.

145. B. 2,800

Round each number to the nearest hundred and then add:

$$700 + 400 + 800 + 300 + 600 = 2{,}800$$

Hence, Choice (B) is the correct answer.

146. $2.13

Calculate the range by subtracting the smallest value from the largest value:

$$\$5.29 - \$3.16 = \$2.13$$

147. D. $4.23

Add the four values together to find the sum of the prices; then divide by 4 to get the average:

$$\frac{\$5.29 + \$4.58 + \$3.87 + \$3.16}{4} = \$4.225$$

Rounding up to the nearest cent gives you $4.23 per pound; hence, Choice (D) is the correct answer.

148. D. $6.96

Each week, the average price of candy falls by $0.71 per pound. The price in Week 4 equals $3.16, so two weeks later (in Week 6), the price will have fallen by

$$2(\$0.71) = \$1.42$$

Therefore, the average price in Week 6 equals

$$\$3.16 - \$1.42 = \$1.74 \text{ per pound}$$

Note that the question asks how much 4 pounds of candy will cost, so you need to multiply by 4 to get the final answer:

$$4(\$1.74) = \$6.96$$

Hence, Choice (D) is the correct answer.

149. D. 1

Substitute the values for x, y, and z into the expression:

$$\left(p^{-2} \cdot p^{2}\right)^{p^3}$$

Then multiply the values in the parentheses using the product rule by adding their powers $(-2 + 2 = 0)$:

$$\left(p^{0}\right)^{p^3}$$

Anything to the power zero equals 1, and 1 to any power also equals 1. Hence, the correct answer is Choice (D).

150. **C. p^7**

Substitute the values for *x*, *y*, and *z* into the expression:

$$(p^3)(p^{-2})(p^2)^3$$

Use the power rule on the last term to simplify the expression (multiply the exponents):

$$(p^3)(p^{-2})(p^6)$$

Use the product rule by adding the exponents to get p^7. Hence, the correct answer is Choice (C).

151. **54 inches**

The perimeter *P* of a rectangle of length *l* and width *w* is given by

$$P = 2l + 2w$$

Substituting the values of *l* and *w* from the figure into the formula gives you

$$\begin{aligned} P &= 2(15) + 2(12) \\ &= 54 \text{ inches} \end{aligned}$$

152. **C. 15 inches**

You can find the length of the diagonal of the rectangular photo using the Pythagorean theorem, $a^2 + b^2 = c^2$, where *a* and *b* are the legs (sides) and *c* is the hypotenuse (diagonal). Substituting the given dimensions of the photo into the equations gives you

$$\begin{aligned} 9^2 + 12^2 &= c^2 \\ 81 + 144 &= c^2 \\ 225 &= c^2 \\ 15 &= c \end{aligned}$$

The diagonal is 15 inches, so Choice (C) is correct.

153. **B. $A = (15 - 2x)(12 - 2x)$**

The length of the frame is 15 inches, which includes a wooden border *x* inches wide on the left side and *x* inches wide on the right side. Hence, the length of the photo (not including the wooden border) is $15 - 2x$. Similarly, the width of the photo is $12 - 2x$, so the area of the photo is given by

$$A = (15 - 2x)(12 - 2x)$$

Choice (B) is correct.

154. **C. 100°**

The sum of the three angles in the figure equals 180° because they form a straight line:

$$x+3x+5x=180$$

Solving for *x* gives you

$$9x=180$$
$$x=20$$

Note that the question asks for the obtuse angle (between 90° and 180°), so substitute $x=20$ into the expression for the largest angle: $5x=5(20)=100$. Hence, the obtuse angle is 100°, making Choice (C) correct.

155. **B. 37.5%**

You can express the 3 out of 8 drivers who are speeding with the fraction $\frac{3}{8}$. To convert a fraction into a percentage, simply divide the numerator by the denominator and move the decimal point two places to the right:

$$\frac{3}{8}=0.375=37.5\%$$

Hence, Choice (B) is correct.

156. **D. 12 inches**

The area of the triangle is $A=\frac{1}{2}bh$, where *b* is the base and *h* is the height. Substituting in the values of the triangle's base and area gives you

$$48=\frac{1}{2}(8)h$$
$$48=4h$$
$$12=h$$

Hence, the correct answer is Choice (D).

157. **B. 0.02**

The first digit to the right of the decimal point is called the *tenths digit.* The second digit to the right of the decimal point is called the *hundredths digit,* making Choice (B) the correct answer.

158. B. $43.00

For a 13-mile trip, the total cost consists of two parts: a fixed cost of $25.50 for the first 8 miles plus the cost of the additional 5 miles at $3.50 per mile:

$$\$25.50 + 5(\$3.50) = \$43.00$$

Hence, Choice (B) is correct.

159. C. 3.5–4.0 hours

The table shows that a turkey weighing between 20 and 24 pounds takes from 3.5 to 4.0 hours to cook at a temperature of 375°F.

160. A. 10:30 a.m.

The table shows that a 16-pound turkey takes 3.0 hours to cook at a temperature of 375°F. Because Venus wants to serve a juicy turkey (which requires an additional 30 minutes to rest after it's removed from the oven) at 2:00 p.m., she must start cooking the turkey no later than 10:30 a.m. Hence, Choice (A) is correct.

161. 45

Notice that $\frac{6}{17}x$ is exactly three times as big as $\frac{2}{17}x$. Multiplying both sides of $\frac{2}{17}x = 15$ by 3 gives you

$$3\left(\frac{2}{17}x\right) = 3(15)$$

$$\frac{6}{17}x = 45$$

162. $40,000, $10,000

To save time, when you list Jack's annual salary during the five-year period, simply write the number of thousands:

{30, 30, 40, 40, 40}

The mode is the value that appears most often (40); hence, $40,000 is the mode. To find the range, subtract the smallest number from the largest: $40 - 30 = 10$. Hence, $10,000 is the range.

163. D. $40,000

To find the median, arrange the values in ascending order (from smallest to biggest) and select the middle value. To save time, you can simply write the number of thousands:

$$\{30, 30, 40, 40, 40\}$$

The middle number is 40, which stands for $40,000, so the correct answer is Choice (D).

164. $36,000

To find the mean, find the sum of five values and divide by 5. To save time, you can simply write the number of thousands:

$$\begin{aligned}&\frac{30+30+40+40+40}{5}\\&=\frac{180}{5}\\&=36\end{aligned}$$

This stands for $36,000.

165. A. $-\frac{6}{5}$

Find the slope by substituting the coordinates of two data points into the slope formula, where m is the slope and (x_1, y_1) and (x_2, y_2) are the coordinates of the points:

$$\begin{aligned}m&=\frac{y_2-y_1}{x_2-x_1}\\&=\frac{4-(-2)}{-2-3}\\&=-\frac{6}{5}\end{aligned}$$

Hence, Choice (A) is the correct answer.

166. A. $\sqrt{61}$

You can find the distance between two points via the following formula:

$$d=\sqrt{(x_2-x_1)^2+(y_2-y_1)^2}$$

Note that this formula is actually just the Pythagorean theorem solved for the hypotenuse, where one leg is the change in x values (x_2-x_1) and the other is the change in y values (y_2-y_1):

$$\begin{aligned}a^2+b^2&=c^2\\(x_2-x_1)^2+(y_2-y_1)^2&=d^2\end{aligned}$$

Substituting the given values for the two points in the figure into the equation gives you

$$\begin{aligned} d &= \sqrt{(3-(-2))^2 + ((-2)-4)^2} \\ &= \sqrt{5^2 + (-6)^2} \\ &= \sqrt{25+36} \\ &= \sqrt{61} \end{aligned}$$

Hence, Choice (A) is correct.

167. D. (0.5, 1)

To find the midpoint, you average the *x* and the *y* values. The coordinates of the midpoint of the two points on the line can be found via

$$\left(\frac{x_1+x_2}{2}, \frac{y_1+y_2}{2}\right)$$

Substituting the given values for the two points in the figure into the equations gives you

$$\left(\frac{3+(-2)}{2}, \frac{-2+4}{2}\right) = \left(\frac{1}{2}, \frac{2}{2}\right) = (0.5, 1)$$

Hence, Choice (D) is the correct answer.

168. B. 0.20 pounds

Because all the answer choices are in decimal format, convert the fraction into a decimal:

$$1\frac{3}{4} = 1.75$$

Subtract this answer from 1.95 to get 0.2 pounds. Hence, Choice (B) is the correct answer.

169. C. $697.20

Convert the tax percentage (17.0%) into a decimal by dividing by 100 (move the decimal point two places to the left), and then multiply by Tom's gross weekly salary:

$$(0.17)(\$840) = \$142.80$$

Subtract the tax amount from the gross salary to get the net salary:

$$\$840 - \$142.80 = \$697.20$$

Hence, Choice (C) is the correct answer.

170. **A. 10.0**

To find the volume in cubic feet, first convert the width and the height of the tank from inches to feet:

$$w = 1.5$$
$$h = 1\frac{2}{3} = \frac{5}{3}$$

Then substitute the values of each dimension (in feet) into the volume formula:

$$\begin{aligned} V &= lwh \\ &= 1.5 \times \frac{5}{3} \times 4 \\ &= 10 \end{aligned}$$

Hence, Choice (A) is the correct answer.

171. **D. 4.56×10^9**

In scientific notation, the coefficient (the leading part of the number) needs to be greater or equal to 1 but less than 10. Move the decimal point nine places to the left until the coefficient becomes 4.56. The power of ten is the number of places that the decimal point was moved. Hence, Choice (D) is the correct answer.

172. **20**

Because the hiker's path has formed two sides of a right triangle, the distance from home is the length of the hypotenuse, so use the Pythagorean theorem, $a^2 + b^2 = c^2$ (where a and b are the legs of the triangle and c is the hypotenuse). Substituting the given sides into the equation gives you

$$\begin{aligned} 12^2 + 16^2 &= c^2 \\ 144 + 256 &= c^2 \\ 400 &= c^2 \\ 20 &= c \end{aligned}$$

Therefore, $c = 20$ miles.

173. **B. 191.5**

After 5 months, Jeff should have lost $5(4.5) = 22.5$ pounds; therefore, he should weigh

$$\begin{aligned} 214 - 5(4.5) &= 214 - 22.5 \\ &= 191.5 \end{aligned}$$

Hence, the correct answer is Choice (B).

174. D. –4 and 5

Factoring the quadratic equation gives you

$$(x+4)(x-5)=0$$

Setting each set of parentheses equal to zero gives you two solutions: $x=-4$ and $x=5$. Hence, the correct answer is Choice (D).

Alternatively, you could simply plug in the values of each answer choice to see which one works.

175. D. 25

Subtracting the 8 games that ended in a draw leaves 30 games. If you let *x* equal the number of games the team lost, then 5*x* equals the number of games won. Set up an equation for the remaining games and solve for *x*:

$$\begin{aligned} 5x+x&=30\\ 6x&=30\\ x&=5 \end{aligned}$$

Therefore, the team lost 5 games and won five times as many, or 25 games, so the correct answer is Choice (D).

176. 34

After the first number, each subsequent number is found by adding the preceding two numbers together. For example, the third number (2) is the sum of the first two numbers $(1+1)$. Hence, the next number in the sequence will be $13+21=34$.

177. C. 49

Multiply the speed by the number of cars for each row of the frequency table.

Speed	Number of Cars	Total
30	2	$30\times2=60$
40	3	$40\times3=120$
50	1	$50\times1=50$
60	6	$60\times6=360$

To find the average, first find the sum of the totals:

$$60+120+50+360=590$$

Now divide by 12 to find the average of the 12 cars' speeds:

$$\frac{590}{12} = 49.17$$

Alternatively, you can simply substitute the values into the weighted average formula:

$$\frac{2(30)+3(40)+1(50)+6(60)}{12}$$
$$= \frac{590}{12} = 49.17$$

Rounding to the nearest whole number gives you 49 miles per hour. Hence, Choice (C) is the correct answer.

---

178. **D. 100%**

The difference between the lowest speed in the table (30 mph) and the fastest speed in the table (60 mph) is 30 mph. You find the percent increase by dividing this difference by the slowest speed and then multiplying by 100 (to change the decimal answer to a percent):

$$\frac{60-30}{30} \times \frac{100}{1}$$
$$= \frac{30}{30} \times \frac{100}{1}$$
$$= 100\%$$

Alternatively, the fastest speed (60) is double the slowest speed (30), which means it is 100% greater.

Hence, the correct answer is Choice (D).

---

179. **A. $8x - 7y$**

Multiply each term in the set of parentheses by the number in front of the parentheses:

$$2(7x-5y)-3(2x-y)$$
$$= 14x - 10y - 6x + 3y$$

Simplify by adding like terms:

$$8x - 7y$$

Hence, Choice (A) is the correct answer.

---

180. **B. $\frac{xy}{2}$**

Because 2 cookies cost y dollars, one cookie must cost half as much, $\frac{y}{2}$ dollars. Multiplying by x shows that x cookies will cost

$$x\left(\frac{y}{2}\right) = \frac{xy}{2}$$

Therefore, the correct answer is Choice (B).

ANSWERS 101–200

181. C. 8 and 9

Seventy-three lies between the square numbers 64 and 81:

$$\sqrt{64} < \sqrt{73} < \sqrt{81}$$

Taking the square root of each term gives you

$$8 < \sqrt{73} < 9$$

Hence, the correct answer is Choice (C).

182. A. 4.3 inches

The length of the third side of any triangle must be greater than the difference between the lengths of the other two sides. Similarly, the length of the third side of any triangle must be less than the sum of the lengths of the other two sides. Otherwise, all the sides of the triangle won't connect. If x equals the length of the missing side, then the allowed values of x are determined by

$$\begin{aligned} |10.2 - 5.8| < x < |10.2 + 5.8| \\ 4.4 < x < 16 \end{aligned}$$

Hence, Choice (A) is the correct answer.

183. C. 0

Evaluate the expression within each absolute value:

$$|-5| - |5| = 5 - 5 = 0$$

Hence, Choice (C) is the correct answer.

184. A. 9 inches x 15 inches x 11 inches

Because dice are rigid, you must round down the side lengths of each box to the nearest integer before calculating the box's volume (you can't have half a die). The rounded-down dimensions of each box and the associated volumes available for packing the dice are as follows:

$$\begin{aligned} 9 \times 15 \times 11 = 1{,}485 \\ 20 \times 7 \times 10 = 1{,}400 \\ 12 \times 7 \times 16 = 1{,}344 \\ 20 \times 7 \times 10 = 1{,}400 \end{aligned}$$

Hence, Choice (A) is the correct answer.

185. **8.6**

There are nine gaps between the vertical mark at 7.4 and the vertical mark at 10.1. Subtracting the endpoints gives you $10.1 - 7.4 = 2.7$, so each gap must represent $\frac{2.7}{9} = 0.3$. Point *A* is located four gaps beyond the 7.4 mark and therefore must be at

$$7.4 + 4(0.3) = 7.4 + 1.2 = 8.6$$

186. **C. $11:6:1$**

The figure shows that 55% of the students prefer dogs, 30% prefer cats, and 5% prefer rabbits, so the ratio of dogs to cats to rabbits is $55:30:5$. With 5 as the greatest common factor, this reduces to $11:6:1$; hence, Choice (C) is the correct answer.

187. **8**

The figure shows that 6% of the students preferred fish, compared to 4% who preferred rodents. Subtracting gives you a difference of 2%. Divide 2% by 100 to convert it into a decimal: 0.02. There are 400 students in total, so 2% of the students equals $0.02 \times (400) = 8$ students.

188. **C. $\frac{w}{x}$**

Multiplying the fractions together gives you

$$\frac{xyzp}{yzw} = 1$$

Simplifying gives you

$$\frac{xp}{w} = 1$$

Now solve for *p*. Multiplying both sides by *w* gives you $xp = w$, and dividing both sides by *x* gives you $p = \frac{w}{x}$. Hence, Choice (C) is the correct answer.

189. **C. $w - y > x - z$**

Look at each possible answer separately:

Because $w = x$, Choice (A) reduces to $y > z$; this is untrue, so Choice (A) is incorrect.

Although Choice (B) may appear correct because $y < z$, it's actually false when *w* and *x* are both negative, so Choice (B) is incorrect.

Because $w = x$, Choice (C) reduces to $-y > -z \rightarrow y < z$; this is true, making Choice (C) the correct answer.

Because $w = x$, Choice (D) reduces to $0 < y - z$. Adding z to both sides shows that $z < y$; this is untrue, so Choice (D) is incorrect.

190. **45, 225**

The price of each VIP ticket is \$45, and the price of each regular ticket is \$25. Let v equal the number of VIP tickets sold, and let r equal the number of regular tickets sold. The equation that represents the total tickets sold is

$$r + v = 270$$
$$r = 270 - v$$

And the equation that represents the total revenue is

$$25r + 45v = \$7{,}650$$

Substituting the value of r into the second equation gives you

$$25(270 - v) + 45v = 7{,}650$$
$$6{,}750 - 25v + 45v = 7{,}650$$
$$20v = 900$$
$$v = 45$$

Subtracting the number of VIP tickets, 45, from 270 gives you 225 regular tickets.

191. **C. 22**

You can write the product of the first six prime numbers as

$$2 \cdot 3 \cdot 5 \cdot 7 \cdot 11 \cdot 13$$

In this list, look for pairs of factors that, when multiplied, will give you one of the answer choices. You can rewrite this expression as

$$(2 \cdot 11) \cdot 3 \cdot 5 \cdot 7 \cdot 13 = (22) \cdot 3 \cdot 5 \cdot 7 \cdot 13$$

This shows that 22 is a factor. Hence, Choice (C) is the correct answer.

192. **D. 32**

Rewrite the function by substituting in $x = -4$:

$$f(-4) = (-4)^2 - 4(-4)$$
$$= 16 + 16$$
$$= 32$$

Hence, Choice (D) is the correct answer.

193. **C. 6 and −2**

Substitute $f(x)=12$ into the equation:

$$12=x^2-4x$$

Subtract 12 from both sides to set the equation equal to zero:

$$0=x^2-4x-12$$

Then factor:

$$(x-6)(x+2)=0$$

Set each set of parentheses equal to zero and solve for *x*. You get $x=6$ and $x=-2$. Hence, Choice (C) is the correct answer.

194. **A. 3^5**

Because there are three 3^4s, you can rewrite the expression $3^4+3^4+3^4$ as $3(3^4)=3^1\times 3^4$. Simplify using the product rule by adding the exponents: You get 3^5, so Choice (A) is correct.

195. **122°, 62°**

A straight line has an angle equal to 180°; therefore, *x* must equal 122, because

$$\begin{aligned} x+58&=180\\ x&=122 \end{aligned}$$

Because the sum of the angles of any triangle equals 180°, *y* must equal 62°, because $y+60+58=180$.

196. **12**

The central cube on each edge of the larger cube will have two sides painted. Because there are 12 edges, 12 cubes will have two sides painted.

197. **C. $\sqrt{41}$ inches**

The Pythagorean theorem states that $a^2+b^2=c^2$, where *c* equals the length of the hypotenuse and *a* and *b* are the legs. Substitute the given values into the equation and solve for *c*:

$$\begin{aligned} 4^2+5^2&=c^2\\ 16+25&=c^2\\ 41&=c^2\\ \sqrt{41}&=c \end{aligned}$$

Hence, Choice (C) is the correct answer.

198. **C.** $y = -6x - 1$

Because you're looking for a line parallel to the given line, the new equation has to have the same slope: $m = -6$. Because Choice (C) is the only equation with that slope, it's the correct answer.

199. **B.** $y = \frac{1}{6}x + \frac{1}{9}$

Because you're looking for a line perpendicular to the given line, the new equation has to have a slope that is the negative reciprocal of the slope of the given line: $m = \frac{1}{6}$. Because Choice (B) is the only equation with that slope, it's the correct answer.

200. **C.** $(-9, 45)$

At the point of intersection, the y values (and the x values) of the two lines are equal to each other. Therefore, set the line $y = -6x - 9$ equal to the line $y = -3x + 18$ and solve for x:

$$-6x - 9 = -3x + 18$$

Adding $6x$ to both sides and simplifying gives you

$$\begin{aligned} -9 &= 3x + 18 \\ -27 &= 3x \\ -9 &= x \end{aligned}$$

Substitute $x = -9$ into $y = -6x - 9$ (or into the other given equation) to find y:

$$y = -6(-9) - 9 = 45$$

Hence, Choice (C) is the correct answer.

201. **C.** $M + 7$

Using the information in the problem, you see that two years ago, Sammy was $M - 5$ years old. That means that today (2 years later), Sammy will be M – 3 years old.

$$(M - 5) + 2 = M - 3$$

In 10 years' time, Sammy will be

$$(M - 3) + 10 = M + 7$$

Hence, Choice (C) is correct.

202. **C. 6.321**

Convert each fraction into a decimal:

$$3\frac{1}{10} = 3.1$$
$$1\frac{11}{100} = 1.11$$
$$2\frac{111}{1,000} = 2.111$$

Now add the decimals:

$$3.100 + 1.110 + 2.111 = 6.321$$

Hence, Choice (C) is the correct answer.

203. **C. 1:1**

Let x equal the number of boys in Mr. Burke's class. The number of girls in the class equals $2x$. The chess club contains a quarter of the girls, $\frac{1}{4}(2x) = \frac{x}{2}$, and half the boys, $\frac{x}{2}$. Therefore, the ratio of girls to boys in the chess club is $\frac{1}{2} : \frac{1}{2}$, or 1:1. Hence, Choice (C) is the correct answer.

204. **B. the large can**

To calculate the cost per cubic inch of each container, divide the price of the container by the volume. The volume of a cylinder is $V = \pi r^2 h$, where r is the radius and h is the height, so the cost per cubic inch of the small can is

$$\frac{\$3.50}{\pi 2^2(10)} = \$0.028$$

The cost per cubic inch of the large can is

$$\frac{\$6.50}{\pi 4^2(5)} = \$0.026$$

The larger can costs less per cubic inch, so Choice (B) is the correct answer.

205. **231 seconds**

The factors of 21 are 7 and 3, and the factors of 77 are 7 and 11. The least common multiple of 21 and 77 is therefore the product of all the distinct non-repeating factors:

$$3 \times 7 \times 11 = 231 \text{ seconds}$$

An alternative method is to list the first few multiples of 21 and 77 until you reach the same number:

$$1\times77=77$$
$$2\times77=154$$
$$3\times77=231$$

$$1\times21=21$$
$$2\times21=42$$
$$3\times21=63$$
$$4\times21=84$$
$$5\times21=105$$
$$6\times21=126$$
$$7\times21=147$$
$$8\times21=168$$
$$9\times21=189$$
$$10\times21=210$$
$$11\times21=231$$

206. D. 12

The area of a trapezoid of height h is given by $A=\frac{1}{2}(b_1+b_2)h$, where b_1 and b_2 represent the lengths of the bases (the pair of parallel sides). Substitute the given values into the equation and solve for b:

$$38=\frac{1}{2}(7+b)4$$
$$38=2(7+b)$$
$$19=7+b$$
$$12=b$$

Hence, Choice (D) is the correct answer.

207. C. 1984–1985

From the graph, you can see that the largest gap between the level of imports and exports occurred in 1984–1985, making Choice (C) the correct answer.

208. D. 88 billion

You can find the average value for exports by finding the sum of exports and dividing by 6, the number of years:

$$\frac{68+78+90+90+92+110}{6}=88$$

The values in the chart represent billions, so Choice (D) is the correct answer.

209. B. 8.4 billion

You can find the total increase in imports (in billion Rs.) by subtracting the final value in 1987–88 from the initial value in 1982–83. Look at the darker bars and estimate their values for these years:

$$78 - 36 = 42$$

Five increases are shown on the graph, so you can find the average annual increase for imports by dividing by 5 to get 8.4. The numbers are in billions, making Choice (B) the correct answer.

210. C. 8 meters

Let *A* be the area of the smaller rug. The large rug is four times as big, so you can express its area as 4*A*. Hence, you can write a formula for the total area and solve for *A*:

$$A + 4A = 20$$
$$5A = 20$$
$$A = 4$$

Because the small rug has an area of 4 square meters, the length of one of its sides is

$$A = s^2$$
$$4 = s^2$$
$$2 = s$$

The perimeter *P* is

$$P = 4s = 4(2) = 8$$

Hence, the correct answer is Choice (C).

211. D. 25 students

Let *x* represent the total number of students in the class. The 10 students who received an A represent 40% of *x*; therefore,

$$0.4x = 10$$

Divide both sides by 0.4 to solve for *x*; then simplify:

$$x = \frac{10}{0.4}$$
$$x = \frac{100}{4}$$
$$x = 25$$

Hence, the correct answer is Choice (D).

212. C. 60°

The clock face is a circle that has 12 sections. Because the whole circle equals 360°, each section must be

$$\frac{360°}{12} = 30°$$

At 10:00 p.m., the hour hand is pointing at the 10 and the minute hand is pointing at the 12. There are two sections between 10 and 12, so the correct answer is 60°, which is Choice (C).

213. 8

From the table, you can see that the x values increase by 2 while the value of the function increases by 6 in each row. When x equals 2, $f(x) = 2$; therefore, when x equals 4, $f(x) = 8$.

214. C. 6 tanks

Calculate the number of miles the car can do on one tank by multiplying 32 by 13, which is 416 miles. Then divide the miles of the trip by the miles for one tank: $2{,}220 \div 416 = 5.336$. This means the correct answer is Choice (C), because five tanks wouldn't be enough to make it.

215. D. $\frac{9}{20}$

You can express 45% as both a decimal and a fraction. To convert a percentage into a decimal, simply divide by 100 (move the decimal point two places to the left) to get 0.45, which rules out Choices (A) and (B). Remember that to write a percentage as a fraction, you write the percent over 100 and simplify: $\frac{45}{100} = \frac{9}{20}$, which is Choice (D).

216. A. 25

The measure of the exterior angle of a triangle is equal to the sum of the nonadjacent interior angles of the triangle; therefore,

$$3x - 10 = 25 + (x + 15)$$

Solving for x gives you

$$2x = 50$$
$$x = 25$$

Hence, Choice (A) is correct.

217. D. $9x^3\sqrt{5}$

When combining radicals, you first have to check that the radicands (the expressions under the radical symbols) are the same. Because they are in this problem, you add the two coefficients together and leave the radicands alone:

$$\begin{aligned}3\sqrt{5x^6}+6\sqrt{5x^6}&=(3+6)\sqrt{5x^6}\\&=9\sqrt{5x^6}\end{aligned}$$

Because $\sqrt{x^6}=x^3$, you can simplify the expression even further to give you $9x^3\sqrt{5}$. Hence, Choice (D) is correct.

218. C. 0.3, $\frac{1}{3}$, $1\frac{2}{5}$, 250%

Comparing numbers in different forms can be difficult, so you want to rewrite them all in the same form (decimals are usually the easiest): $\frac{1}{3}=0.\overline{3}$, 0.3 is already a decimal, $1\frac{2}{5}=1.4$, and $250\%=2.5$. Now that they're all in decimal form, you need to remember what *ascending* means: smallest to largest. This means the order should be

$$0.3,\ 0.\overline{3},\ 1.4,\ 2.5$$

Substituting back in the original values, you get

$$0.3,\ \frac{1}{3},\ 1\frac{2}{5},\ 250\%$$

This is Choice (C).

219. C. circle; radius = 2 ft

Calculate the area and perimeter of each of the options. Recall that the perimeter is found by adding up all the sides or by using a circumference formula, and the area of a rectangle/square is found by multiplying length times width.

For Choice (A), the area of the rectangle equals 16 square feet, and the perimeter equals 20 feet, so Choice (A) is not the correct answer.

For Choice (B), the area of the square equals 25 square feet, and the perimeter equals 20 feet; hence, Choice (B) is not the correct answer.

For Choice (C), the area of the circle equals $A=\pi r^2=4\pi$ square feet, and the perimeter (circumference) equals $C=2\pi r=4\pi$ feet; hence, Choice (C) is the correct answer.

For Choice (D), the 3-4-5 right triangle is a special Pythagorean triple (with integer sides) you should have memorized. Because the base equals 4 feet and the height equals 3 feet, the triangle's area equals $A=\frac{1}{2}bh=\frac{1}{2}(3)(4)=6$ square feet, and the perimeter equals $3+4+5=12$ feet; hence, Choice (D) is not the correct answer.

220. B. 97

Because there's an average of 107 cups of coffee and each pot produces 10 cups, you can divide 107 by 10 and get 10.7 pots of coffee per hour. The store is open for 9 hours each day (5 hours from 7:00 a.m. till noon and 4 hours from noon till 4:00 p.m.), so it uses $10.7 \times 9 = 96.3$ pots of coffee on an average day. This means that the shop will need to brew 97 pots, Choice (B), to make sure there's enough coffee.

Alternatively, the coffee shop sells 107 cups per hour, which would be 9(107) or 963 cups per day. Dividing 963 cups by 10 cups per pot gives you 96.3 pots (which rounds up to 97 pots).

221. 968

One mile equals 5,280 feet; therefore, 11 miles equals $11 \times 5{,}280 = 58{,}080$ feet. Cory travels this distance in one hour; therefore, dividing by 60 gives you the distance traveled per minute (or speed). This equals $\frac{58{,}080}{60} = 968$ feet per minute.

222. D. $2^4 3^5$

Work backward from the answer choices to see which set of factors equals 3,888:

For Choice (A), $5^2 2^5 = 25 \times 32 = 800$, so it isn't the correct answer.

For Choice (B), $2^3 3^5 = 8 \times 243 = 1{,}944$, so it isn't the correct answer

For Choice (C), $3^4 5^3 = 81 \times 125 = 10{,}125$, so it isn't the correct answer.

For Choice (D), $2^4 3^5 = 16 \times 243 = 3{,}888$, so it's the correct answer.

223. C. 125

You can find the length of a side s of the cube from the formula for surface area, $SA = 6s^2$:

$$\begin{aligned} 150 &= 6s^2 \\ 25 &= s^2 \\ 5 &= s \end{aligned}$$

This means the volume of the cube is $V = s^3 = 5^3 = 125$ in.^{3}; hence, Choice (C) is the correct answer.

224. D. 1

Substitute the values for x, y, and z into the expression:

$$\left(\frac{(p^5)(p^{-4})}{p}\right)^5$$

Using the product rule by adding the powers $(5 + (-4) = 1)$ on the numerator gives you

$$\left(\frac{p}{p}\right)^5 = 1^5 = 1$$

Hence, the correct answer is Choice (D).

225. D. 105 feet

You can express the ratio of the sides of the triangle as

$$3x : 7x : 10x$$

Because the perimeter of the triangle is 210 feet, the sum of the sides of the triangle is

$$3x + 7x + 10x = 210$$

Solving for x gives you

$$20x = 210$$
$$x = 10.5$$

The longest side, $10x$, therefore equals 105 feet; hence, the correct answer is Choice (D).

226. A. $f(x) \leq 5$

Substitute a few positive integer values for x into the function to see whether you can see a trend:

$$f(1) = \frac{14+1}{2+1} = \frac{15}{3} = 5$$
$$f(2) = \frac{14+2}{2+2} = \frac{16}{4} = 4$$
$$f(3) = \frac{14+3}{2+3} = \frac{17}{5}$$

You can see that the maximum value of $f(x) = 5$; hence, the correct answer is Choice (A).

ANSWERS 201–300

227. C. $80+10\pi$

The length of the curved part of the semicircle equals half the circumference of the circle (whose diameter equals 20 mm). The circumference of a full circle is $C=\pi d$, so the length is

$$\frac{1}{2}(\pi d)=\frac{1}{2}(20\pi)=10\pi$$

The perimeter of the shape consists of this curved length plus the other three sides of the rectangle:

$$P=20+30+30+10\pi=80+10\pi$$

The correct answer is Choice (C).

228. B. $50\pi+600$

The area of the semicircle is half the area of the full circle (whose diameter equals 20 mm and whose radius equals 10 mm). The area of a full circle is $A=\pi r^2$, so

$$\frac{1}{2}\left(\pi r^2\right)=\frac{1}{2}\left(\pi 10^2\right)=50\pi$$

The area of the shape consists of the area of the semicircle plus the area of the rectangle:

$$A=50\pi+(20\times 30)=50\pi+600$$

Hence, the correct answer is Choice (B).

229. B. $3.58

Harry rented the power drill for 7 hours (3.5 hours from 8:30 a.m. until noon plus 3.5 hours from noon until 3:30 p.m.). To find the hourly cost, divide the total cost by the number of hours:

$$\begin{array}{r} 3.58 \\ 7\overline{)25.06} \\ -21 \\ 40 \\ -35 \\ 56 \\ -56 \\ 0 \end{array}$$

Hence, Choice (B) is the correct answer.

230. **C.** $\frac{4}{3}$

Substitute the given values of x and y into the equation:

$$\frac{(-3)^2-6(-3)+9}{(-3)^2-6(-3)}=\frac{9+18+9}{9+18}$$

Simplifying further gives you $\frac{36}{27}=\frac{4}{3}$. Hence, Choice (C) is correct.

231. **C. \$960**

Sammy's total salary equals his base salary plus commission. The 6% commission applies only to his sales in excess of \$1,000 (not the initial \$1,000 worth of sales). His total sales equal \$4,500, so his commission is therefore $0.06(\$4{,}500-\$1{,}000)=\$210$. Sammy's total salary equals $\$750+\$210=\$960$, making Choice (C) the correct choice.

232. **14**

Evaluate each radical expression separately and then add:

$$\sqrt{64}+\sqrt{36}=8+6=14$$

233. **D.** 4.08×10^{-2}

Move the decimal point to the right until the leading number is greater than or equal to 1 but less than 10; you get 4.08. Because you're moving the decimal point two places to the right, the exponent becomes −2. Hence, Choice (D) is correct.

234. **\$6.80**

The total budget is \$2,825, which includes the cost of renting the room ($3\times\$375=\$1{,}125$) and the cost x of each of the 250 bags of party favors. Therefore,

$$250x+1{,}125=2{,}825$$

Solving for x gives you $x=\$6.80$.

235. **\$96,000**

Calculate how much revenue each class of ticket generates by multiplying the number of seats in each class by the cost of each ticket:

$$40(\$1{,}200)+120(\$400)=\$96{,}000$$

236. C. 2:1

Calculate how much revenue each class of ticket generates by multiplying the number of seats sold in each class by the cost of the ticket:

First class: $40(\$1,200) = \$48,000$

Economy class: $60(\$400) = \$24,000$

Hence, the ratio of revenue from first class to economy is $48,000:24,000$, which reduces to $2:1$. Choice (C) is the correct answer.

237. A. 20%

Calculate the percent decrease as follows:

$$\frac{|\text{new price} - \text{old price}|}{\text{old price}} \times \frac{100}{1}$$

Substituting in the new and old prices of the ticket gives you

$$\frac{|\$1,200 - \$1,500|}{\$1,500} \times \frac{100}{1} = 20\%$$

Hence, Choice (A) is the correct answer.

238. $623

Subtract each of the deductions from Janet's gross salary:

$$\$1,012 - \$234 - \$128 - \$27 = \$623$$

239. B. 2.7%

Divide the amount spent on Social Security by the gross salary and multiply by 100:

$$\frac{27}{1,012} \times \frac{100}{1} = 2.668$$

Rounding the nearest tenth of a percent gives you 2.7%, so Choice (B) is correct.

240. C. Rotation 90° clockwise

Triangle *ODC* has been rotated 90° clockwise about the origin to map onto triangle *OBA*. Therefore, Choice (C) is the correct answer.

241. D. $\overline{DC}$

Find the slope of each line segment by using

$$\text{slope} = \frac{\text{rise or fall}}{\text{run}}$$

$\overline{OA}$ has a slope equal to −3, so you can eliminate Choice (A). $\overline{OB}$ has a slope equal to $-\frac{1}{3}$, so Choice (B) is wrong. $\overline{AB}$ has a positive slope, so you know you can eliminate Choice (C). $\overline{DC}$ has a slope equal to −1, so Choice (D) is correct.

242. B. y^4

Take the cube root of both sides to get

$$\left(x^3\right)^{\frac{1}{3}} = \left(y^{12}\right)^{\frac{1}{3}}$$

Simplify via the power rule by multiplying the exponents:

$$x = y^4$$

Hence, Choice (B) is correct.

243. C. 8:7

Brooke read 16 books, compared to Rachel's 14:

$$16:14 = 8:7$$

Hence, Choice (C) is correct.

244. B. 75%

Steve has read 8 books, compared to the 14 books read by Rachel, so Steve needs to read an additional 6 books to catch up to her. The required percent increase is

$$\left(\frac{\text{new value} - \text{old value}}{\text{old value}}\right) \times \frac{100}{1} = \frac{6}{8} \times \frac{100}{1} = 75\%$$

Hence, Choice (B) is correct.

245. C. Rachel read 100% more books than Steve read.

You can eliminate Choice (A), because you have no idea how many words each book contained (maybe Brooke's books contained fewer pages than either Steve's or Rachel's books). Choice (B) is incorrect because Steve read 8 books, which is more than half of the 14 books Rachel read. Choice (D) is also incorrect because Steve read 8 books, Rachel read 14 books, and Brooke read 16 books, for a total of 38 books.

Choice (C) is correct because Brooke read 16 books (exactly double the 8 books read by Steve). Therefore, Rachel read an additional 8 books, which is 100% of the number of books Steve read.

246. **D.**

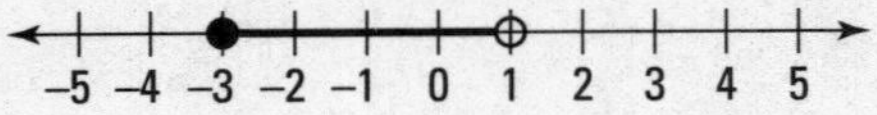

Subtract 5 from each term in the inequality to get $-3 \le x < 1$. The graph in Choice (D) correctly represents this range of possible values.

247. **B. 5**

The volume of a box (rectangular prism) is $V = lwh$, where l is the length, w is the width, and h is the height. Set the volumes of the two boxes equal to each other and solve for h:

$$(4)(2)(10) = (8)(2)h$$
$$80 = 16h$$
$$5 = h$$

Therefore, Choice (B) is the correct answer.

248. **A. 15**

Find the factors of each answer choice and then pick the one that contains the most unique prime factors.

Choice (A), 15, has the factors 1, 2, 3, 5, and 15, three of which are prime (2, 3, and 5).

Choice (B), 19, has the factors 1 and 19, only one of which is prime (19).

Choice (C), 27, has the factors 1, 3, 9, and 27, only one of which is prime (3).

Choice (D), 31, has the factors 1 and 31, only one of which is prime (31).

Hence, Choice (A) is correct.

249. **A. 2.5π**

The diameter of the circle is 5 inches (a third of 15 inches). Therefore, the circumference of the circle is

$$C = \pi d = 5\pi$$

But Peter cuts around only half of the circumference, because the paper is folded. Hence, Choice (A) is the correct answer.

250. A. Mrs. Croak

Because the whole-number part of the height of each frog's jump equals 5, you can focus solely on the fractional part of each jump. You only need to determine which of the following fractions (corresponding to each frog's hop) is the greatest:

$$\frac{4}{5}, \frac{3}{8}, \frac{11}{20}, \frac{7}{10}$$

The lowest common denominator for all the fractions is 40, so you can rewrite each fraction as follows:

$$\frac{32}{40}, \frac{15}{40}, \frac{22}{40}, \frac{28}{40}$$

Hence, Choice (A) is the correct answer.

Alternatively, to save time, if you recognize that $\frac{3}{8}$ is less than half, you can eliminate Choice (B) right away. You can also eliminate Choice (C) because $\frac{11}{20}$ is only slightly more than half. Then use 10 as the common denominator to determine that Choice (A) is greater than Choice (B), making Choice (A) the correct answer.

251. D. 13

You find the perimeter of the shape by adding the length of each side:

$$P=(x-7)+(x-2)+(x-1)+(x)+(x-3)$$

Set the perimeter equal to 52 and solve for *x*:

$$52=5x-13$$
$$65=5x$$
$$13=x$$

Hence, Choice (D) is the correct answer.

252. B. Kenneth was the slowest runner, and Usain was the fastest.

According to the table, Usain had the fastest time (the lowest number), and Kenneth had the slowest time.

253. C. $\frac{1}{12}$

Each roll of the die has a one-in-six chance of landing on any of the six numbers. Therefore, the chance of rolling a 6 is $\frac{1}{6}$.

The coin has an equal chance of landing on heads or tails, so the chance of landing on tails is $\frac{1}{2}$.

Multiplying both probabilities together gives you the overall probability of getting a 6 and tails:

$$\frac{1}{6}\cdot\frac{1}{2}=\frac{1}{12}$$

Hence, Choice (C) is correct.

254. **C.** $\frac{1}{6}$

Note that each roll of the die is independent of which numbers have been scored previously. Therefore, the chance of rolling a 6 is still $\frac{1}{6}$.

255. **B. 2 m/s²**

Let m equal the mass of the body and a equal its acceleration. Because you are told that a is inversely proportional to m, you know that $a=\frac{F}{m}$, where F equals the value of the constant force.

Substitute the given values for a and m into the equation to find F:

$$6=\frac{F}{5}$$
$$30=F$$

The equation now becomes $a=\frac{30}{m}$. Substitute $m=15$ into the equation to find the corresponding value of a:

$$a=\frac{30}{15}=2$$

Alternatively (and more easily), with an inverse proportion, you can use the following formula:

$$a_1m_1=a_2m_2$$

Substituting, you get:

$$6\times 5=a_2\times 15$$
$$a_2=2$$

Hence, Choice (B) is the correct answer.

256. **C. 97.5 feet**

Set up a proportion with the unknown variable (actual length) as the numerator of the fraction and the scaled length as the denominator:

$$\frac{\text{actual length}}{\text{scaled length}}=\frac{15}{2}$$

Substitute the given values into the proportion and let x equal the unknown length:

$$\frac{x}{13} = \frac{15}{2}$$

Multiply both sides by 13 to solve for x:

$$x = 13\left(\frac{15}{2}\right) = 97.5$$

Hence, Choice (C) is the correct answer.

257. B. 151 miles

The total fare (\$225.50) consists of three days of rental (at a rate of \$50 per day) plus \$0.50 multiplied by the number of miles traveled, x:

$$\$225.50 = 3(\$50) + x(\$0.50)$$

Solve for x to find the number of miles traveled:

$$\begin{aligned} 225.5 &= 150 + 0.5x \\ 75.5 &= 0.5x \\ 151 &= x \end{aligned}$$

Hence, Choice (B) is the correct answer.

258. A. 3.5%

You can use the following formula to calculate the annual interest rate:

$$\text{interest rate} = \frac{(\text{new balance} - \text{old balance})}{\text{old balance}} \cdot \frac{100}{1}$$

Plug in the given values to find the rate:

$$\text{interest rate} = \frac{(552.50 - 500)}{500} \cdot \frac{100}{1} = 10.5\%$$

This value is for three years of interest, so dividing by 3 gives you the annual simple interest rate, which equals 3.5%. Hence, Choice (A) is correct.

259. B. 150

Notice that $\frac{6}{11}x$ is exactly three times $\frac{2}{11}x$. Because $\frac{2}{11}x = 50$, you can multiply both sides of the equation by 3 to get

$$\frac{6}{11}x = 150$$

Hence, Choice (B) is the correct answer.

260. B. (2, 2)

Just by looking, you can see that the coordinates of the point that lies halfway between the two points on the graph are (2, 2). Alternatively, you can plug the coordinates of the two points into the midpoint formula:

$$M = \left(\frac{x_1 + x_2}{2}, \frac{y_1 + y_2}{2}\right)$$
$$= \left(\frac{0+4}{2}, \frac{1+3}{2}\right) = (2, 2)$$

Hence, Choice (B) is the correct answer.

261. C. $-\frac{1}{2}$

Find the slope by substituting the coordinates of the two points marked on the graph into the slope formula, where m is the slope and the points are (x_1, y_1) and (x_2, y_2):

$$m = \frac{y_2 - y_1}{x_2 - x_1}$$

Using the x- and y-coordinates of the points (0, 3) and (4, 1) gives you

$$m = \frac{1-3}{4-0} = -\frac{2}{4} = -\frac{1}{2}$$

Therefore, Choice (C) is correct.

262. C. $y = -\frac{1}{2}x + 3$

Find the slope by substituting the coordinates of the two points marked on the graph into the slope formula, where m is the slope and the points are (x_1, y_1) and (x_2, y_2):

$$m = \frac{y_2 - y_1}{x_2 - x_1}$$

Using the x- and y-coordinates of the points (0, 3) and (4, 1) gives you

$$m = \frac{1-3}{4-0} = -\frac{2}{4} = -\frac{1}{2}$$

The y-intercept of the graph, where the graph crosses the y-axis, equals 3. Hence, the equation of the line in the form $y = mx + b$ equals

$$y = -\frac{1}{2}x + 3$$

263. C. $80

Let the original price of the sweater equal x. Because the discount is 20%, that means that the sale price is 80% of the original price. Hence, $\$64 = (0.80)x$.

Solve for x by dividing both sides of the equation by 0.80. Therefore, $x = \$80$, making Choice (C) the correct answer.

264. A. 15 feet

Set up a proportion for the small triangle that includes the boy's height as the numerator and the base as the denominator:

$$\frac{\text{height}}{\text{base}} = \frac{5}{8}$$

Substitute the given base of the big triangle into the proportion, letting x equal the height of the tree:

$$\frac{x}{24} = \frac{5}{8}$$

Multiply both sides by 24 to solve for x:

$$x = 24\left(\frac{5}{8}\right) = 15$$

Hence, Choice (A) is the correct answer.

265. B. 35°

The sum of the angles of any triangle equals 180°. Because this is an obtuse isosceles triangle, the two remaining angles are equal to each other, so

$$\begin{aligned} x + x + 110 &= 180 \\ 2x &= 70 \end{aligned}$$

Solving for x gives you $x = 35$. Hence, Choice (B) is the correct answer.

266. D. 7.5

From the number line, you can see that $A = -5$ and $E = 2.5$. Therefore, E minus A equals

$$2.5 - (-5) = 2.5 + 5 = 7.5$$

Hence, Choice (D) is the correct answer.

267. A. −25

From the number line, you can see that $A = -5$, $B = -2.5$, and $C = -2$. Therefore, A times B times C equals

$$(-5)(-2.5)(-2) = -25$$

Hence, Choice (A) is the correct answer.

268. D. −7

From the number line, you can see that

$$|A| = 5,\ |B| = 2.5,\ |C| = 2,\ |D| = 1,\ |E| = 2.5,\ |F| = 3.5$$

Substituting these values into each answer choice gives you the following:

(A) $5 < 2$, which is false

(B) $1 > 2.5$, which is false

(C) $-2.5 < -5$, which is false

(D) $5 < 2.5 + 3.5$, which is true

269. B. $(x+4)(x-6) = 0$

First, write the left-hand side of the equation as the product of two pairs of parentheses with x as the leading term:

$$(x\quad)(x\quad) = 0$$

Then list all the possible pairs of factors of −24:

1, −24
2, −12
3, −8
4, −6
6, −4
8, −3
12, −2
24, −1

Now select the pair of factors that add up to the coefficient of the x-term in the equation, −2. You can save some time in this step if you apply some logic. The last term of the given equation is negative, so you know that one factor is positive and the other is negative. The factors need to have a difference of 2, so look at factors of 24 that are close together — 4 and 6 are only 2 units apart. Because the middle term is negative, the larger factor, 6, must be the negative one.

Substitute each value into the two pairs of parentheses:

$$(x+4)(x-6)=0$$

An alternative method involves using FOIL (first terms, outer terms, inner terms, last terms) on each answer choice to see which one is equal to the original quadratic equation. Only Choice (B) gives you the original equation, so Choice (B) is the correct answer.

270. **C. $x^2 + y^2 - 2xy$**

Rewrite the equation as follows:

$$(x-y)^2=(x-y)(x-y)$$

Then use FOIL (first terms, outer terms, inner terms, last terms) to multiply each term in the first set of parentheses by each term in the second set of parentheses:

$$\begin{aligned}(x-y)(x-y)&=x^2-xy-xy+y^2\\&=x^2-2xy+y^2\end{aligned}$$

Hence, Choice (C) is the correct answer.

271. **D. 64π**

The can has a circular base, so use the formula for the area of a circle to determine the radius of the can:

$$\begin{aligned}A&=\pi r^2\\16\pi&=\pi r^2\\4&=r\end{aligned}$$

If the label is removed and laid flat, it has the shape of a rectangle whose width is the height of the can (8 inches) and whose length is equal to the circumference of the can $(C=2\pi r)$. Hence,

$$\begin{aligned}A&=lw\\&=(2\pi r)h\\&=2\pi(4)8=64\pi\end{aligned}$$

Choice (D) is the correct answer.

272. **B. The median value is 58 inches, and the range is 12 inches.**

To find the median value, place the values in ascending order and select the middle value.

$$52,\ 55,\ 58,\ 61,\ 64\rightarrow 58$$

ANSWERS 201–300

Calculate the range by subtracting the smallest value from the largest value:

$$64-52=12$$

Hence, Choice (B) is correct.

273. **C. 58**

Add the five values together to find the sum of the heights. Then divide by 5 to find the average value:

$$\frac{52+55+58+61+64}{5}=\frac{290}{5}=58$$

Hence, Choice (C) is the correct answer.

274. **C. 6 feet, 1 inch**

Each year, Jacob's bush grows 3 inches. When Jacob was 14, the bush was 64 inches, so in 3 years' time, it will be 9 inches taller, which will make it 73 inches tall.

Divide by 12 to convert Jacob's height into feet and inches; 12 divides into 73 six whole times (6 feet) with a remainder of one (1 inch). Therefore, the correct answer is 6 feet, 1 inch, making Choice (C) the correct answer.

275. **C. 123**

Set up a proportion with the number of defective widgets as the numerator of the fraction and the number of widgets produced as the denominator:

$$\frac{\text{defective widgets}}{\text{total widgets}}=\frac{3}{50}$$

Substitute the given value for the total number of widgets into the proportion, letting x equal the unknown number of defective widgets:

$$\frac{x}{2{,}050}=\frac{3}{50}$$

Multiply both sides by 2,050 to solve for x:

$$x=2{,}050\left(\frac{3}{50}\right)=123$$

Hence, Choice (C) is the correct answer.

276. **C. 20π**

The outer radius of the donut is 10; therefore, the diameter is 20. The circumference is $C=\pi d=20\pi$. Hence, Choice (C) is the correct answer.

277. D. 3:1

The radius of the hole is 5, so you can find its area by substituting $r = 5$ into

$$\begin{aligned} A &= \pi r^2 \\ &= \pi(5^2) = 25\pi \end{aligned}$$

The outer radius of the donut is 10; therefore, you can find the total area (area of donut plus area of the hole) by substituting $r = 10$ into

$$\begin{aligned} A &= \pi r^2 \\ &= \pi(10^2) = 100\pi \end{aligned}$$

Subtracting the area of the hole from the area of the entire donut gives you the area of the shaded region:

$$100\pi - 25\pi = 75\pi$$

Therefore, the ratio of the area of the donut to the area of the hole equals

$$75\pi : 25\pi = 3:1$$

Hence, Choice (D) is correct.

278. A. 28

The question is asking about square yards, so convert the width and the length of the floor into yards (by dividing by 3) before you find its area. The length is 7 yards, and the width equals 4 yards.

The area A of a rectangle of length l and width w is

$$\begin{aligned} A &= lw \\ &= (4)(7) = 28 \end{aligned}$$

Hence, Choice (A) is the correct answer.

279. 218

The equation is given as

$$\frac{3{,}412 + w}{11} \leq 330$$

Rearrange the inequality to solve for w by multiplying both sides by 11 and then subtracting 3,412:

$$\begin{aligned} 3{,}412 + w &\leq 3{,}630 \\ w &\leq 218 \end{aligned}$$

280. B. 5.02×10^{-3}

The leading number needs to be greater than or equal to 1 but less that 10, so move the decimal point three places to the right to get 5.02. You now need to multiply this number by 10^{-3} to show that you moved the decimal point three places to the right. In scientific notation, the number is

$$5.02\times10^{-3}$$

Hence, Choice (B) is the correct answer.

281. blueberries, grapes

The longest bar on the graph corresponds to the blueberries; hence, they're the most popular fruit. The shortest bar belongs to the grapes, making them the least popular fruit.

282. C. 18

The bars on the graph show that approximately 30 people prefer oranges, compared to approximately 12 people who prefer bananas. The difference is about 18 people, making Choice (C) the correct answer.

283. D. 7:6

The bars on the graph show that approximately 30 people prefer oranges, compared to approximately 35 people who prefer apples. Hence, the ratio of the number of people who prefer apples to those who prefer oranges is 35:30, which you can reduce to 7:6, making Choice (D) the correct answer.

284. 0.3125

Use long division to divide the numerator (5) by the denominator (16) to get 0.3125:

$$\begin{array}{r} 0.3125 \\ 16\overline{)5.0000} \\ \underline{-48} \\ 20 \\ \underline{-16} \\ 40 \\ \underline{-32} \\ 80 \\ \underline{-80} \\ 0 \end{array}$$

285. **C. 5**

Because $f(x) = x$ and $f(x) = 15 - 2x$, you know that $x = 15 - 2x$. Adding $2x$ to both sides of the equation and then dividing by 3 gives you

$$3x = 15$$
$$x = 5$$

Hence, the correct answer is Choice (C).

Chapter 2

286. **B. She wanted to make sure women were given proper representation in the new government.**

Abigail expressed the desire of women to gain representation in the new government, making Choice (B) the correct answer. Choice (A) can be rejected because there was no mention of birthdays. You can also eliminate Choice (C), which is the opposite of what Abigail requested. Choice (D) is too extreme, because Abigail didn't want more power than her husband — she merely wanted women to have a voice in the new government.

287. **D. surprised and condescending**

From the excerpt, you can see that John Adams laughed at his wife's request — he was definitely being condescending (looking down on her). He also appeared surprised to hear that women might want to have a say in the laws that govern them. Therefore, Choice (D) is the correct answer. You can reject Choice (A) because John Adams wasn't laughing with joy. He wasn't alarmed, resigned, or angry, so Choices (B) and (C) can also be eliminated.

288. **D. the Nineteenth Amendment**

The women's suffrage movement eventually resulted in the passing of the Nineteenth Amendment, giving women the right to vote, so Choice (D) is correct. Choice (A) can be eliminated because the Second Amendment refers to the right to bear arms (guns). You can eliminate Choice (B) because the Thirteenth Amendment abolished slavery. The Eighteenth Amendment concerned Prohibition, which banned the sale of alcohol in the U.S., so you can eliminate Choice (C).

289. **C. rivers**

Rivers not only provide fresh drinking water but also lead to the sea, thereby giving easy access by ship, so Choice (C) is the correct answer.

290. **B. He wanted to force an immediate Japanese surrender to bring about an end to the war.**

By 1945, World War II had been raging for almost six years, and the Japanese showed no signs of surrender. Many historians believe that the use of atomic weapons actually saved hundreds of thousands — perhaps even millions — of lives (despite killing many people) by bringing about an immediate end to the war, so Choice (B) is correct. The Japanese attack on Pearl Harbor occurred in 1941, so you can reject Choice (A). The United States had already tested its atomic weapons and knew they worked, so you can reject Choice (C). Choice (D) is also incorrect because Germany surrendered to the Allied forces in May 7, 1945, before the atomic bombs were dropped on Japan.

291. **C. Congress has 535 members, including 100 senators and 435 representatives**

You are told in the passage that Congress has 535 members, including 100 senators and 435 representatives. Hence, Choice (C) is correct.

292. **judicial branch**

The Supreme Court (part of the judicial branch) evaluates laws according to the Constitution, so it's the judicial branch's responsibility to decide whether a law such as the Affordable Care Act is constitutional.

293. **D. They wanted to ensure that there were checks and balances to prevent any one part of the government from becoming too powerful.**

The Founding Fathers wanted to make sure that no person could have too much power in the new government, so they split the powers among the three branches, each of which would be responsible for specific tasks. Therefore, Choice (D) is correct. You can reject Choice (A) because it's the opposite of what the Founding Fathers intended. Each branch has separate powers, so the branches were not intended to compete with each other, making Choice (B) wrong. Choice (C) is wrong because the new government was not based on the British monarchy.

294. **C. to ensure that no modern ideas are allowed to pollute the Supreme Court's decision-making.**

Choices (A), (B), and (D) are all true statements. The Supreme Court justices are given lifetime appointments to ensure that they're free to make decisions based on the Constitution without fear of being replaced by either the president or Congress. Because many of the same justices are present after the government changes from one party to the other, they do provide a certain level of judicial stability as the country transitions. Only Choice (C) is false, because a justice who dies or retires is replaced by a new member who will bring new ideas to the Court.

295. **A. It upheld state racial segregation laws for public facilities under the doctrine of "separate but equal."**

The passage tells you that the *Plessy v. Ferguson* decision sustained the constitutionality of Louisiana's racist Jim Crow law; hence, it allowed the states to continue their policy of racial segregation for public facilities, making Choice (A) correct.

296. **D. It led to the desegregation of the U.S. public school system.**

The passage tells you that the *Brown v. Board of Education* decision overturned the court's previous ruling. Hence, Choice (A) is incorrect. The *Brown v. Board of Education* decision applied only to public schools (not all public places), so you can reject Choice (B).

297. **B. The Court considered that segregation was traumatic and unfair to African-American children.**

The *Brown v. Board of Education* decision stated that segregation in schools makes African-American children feel inferior and can damage them permanently, so Choice (B) is a factual statement. All the other choices represent opinions, not factual statements.

298. **C. The Supreme Court can reverse its previous decisions if the justices feel that a mistake has been made.**

The passage tells you that the *Brown v. Board of Education* decision overturned the court's previous ruling, making Choice (A) incorrect and Choice (C) the best answer. Only the Supreme Court can overturn one of its previous decisions, so Choices (B) and (D) are wrong.

299. **D. freedom of life, liberty, and the pursuit of happiness.**

The excerpt tells you that the First Amendment guarantees freedom of the press, freedom of petition, and freedom of speech. However, the First Amendment does not guarantee the freedom of life, liberty, and the pursuit of happiness (which appears in the Declaration of Independence); therefore, Choice (D) is correct.

300. **D. protects the general public from the government placing restrictions on individual freedoms, such as freedom of religion, freedom of speech, and freedom of the press.**

You are told in the excerpt that the First Amendment guarantees individual freedoms (such as freedom of religion, freedom of speech, and freedom of the press) by preventing Congress from passing any laws that restrict these freedoms. Hence, Choice (D) is correct. Choice (A) is incorrect because Congress can still make new laws (just not laws that restrict these freedoms — Choice (B)). Choice (C) refers to the Second Amendment (not the First Amendment), so it can be rejected.

301. **D. a law that creates guidelines for the public to petition the government to keep a popular act that may soon be abolished**

The First Amendment guarantees the freedom of petition, so a law that creates guidelines for the public to petition the government would be allowed, making Choice (D) correct. Choice (A) would be prevented by the First Amendment's guarantee of freedom of speech. Choice (B) would be prevented by the guarantee of freedom of petition. Choice (C) would be prevented by the guarantee of freedom of religion.

302. **C. It has played an essential role in protecting individual freedoms.**

The First Amendment has played an essential role in protecting individual freedoms, making Choice (C) correct and Choice (A) false. Choice (B) is also a false statement because the Second Amendment does not overturn the First Amendment. Choice (D) is a false statement because the amendments do not undermine the Constitution — they actually make it stronger.

303. **C. Spain**

You can see from the map that Spain controlled most of South America, Central America, and a large part of North America, so Choice (C) is the correct answer.

304. **A. they wanted to help the natives of the New World.**

The passage tells you that the driving forces behind the European countries seeking settlements in the New World included the desire for increased economic wealth [Choice (D)], access to natural resources [Choice (B)], and the wish to spread Christianity to new parts of the world [Choice (C)], so you can reject all those answer choices. Nothing in the passage says that the Europeans wanted to help the natives of the New World (in fact, they ended up killing millions of them), so Choice (A) is the correct answer.

305. **D. They were forced out by rebellions, war, and revolutions.**

The areas covered in the map include North America, Central America, and South America, all of which still have plenty of natural resources, so you can reject Choice (A). Even if Choice (B) were true, it still wouldn't be a good reason to leave; there were still lots of natural resources and economic wealth to be gained by staying in the region, so you can reject Choice (B). Choice (C) may be tempting, but the European leaders didn't really care whether they were acting morally so long as they made lots of money, so you can reject Choice (C) also. The only way to get the Europeans to leave was to force them out through rebellions, war, and revolutions. Only when it became too costly to continue to control the territory did the Europeans give up control and leave; hence, Choice (D) is the correct answer.

306. **D. Spanish, English, and Portuguese**

From the map, you can see that the three countries that held the most territory in the New World were Spain, Portugal, and Great Britain, so it makes sense that the top three languages spoken in the region today would be Spanish, English, and Portuguese, making Choice (D) the correct answer.

307. **A. Canada**

From the table, you can see that Canada has the smallest value for trade deficit with the United States ($35 billion) compared to all the other countries. Hence, Choice (A) is the correct answer.

308. **A. The United States buys the most goods and services from China and sells the most goods and services to Canada**

From the table, you can see that the U.S. imports the most goods and services from China ($467 billion) and exports the most goods and services to Canada ($312 billion).

309. **D. 100%**

From the table, you can see that Japan's trade deficit is $67 billion. This is the same value (100 percent of) the value of U.S. exports to Japan ($67 billion). The correct answer is 100 percent, making Choice (D) the correct answer.

310. **C. All of the top five trading partners with the United States have negative values for their trade balances.**

From the table, you can see that the top five trading partners with the United States have negative values for their trade balances, making Choice (C) correct.

Canada buys the most goods and services from the United States ($312 billion) but has the smallest trade balance, so you can reject Choice (A). The information provided gives no indication that trade deficits will continue to increase each year, so you can also reject Choice (B). China buys the third largest amount of goods and services from the U.S. ($124 billion), so you can also eliminate Choice (D).

311. **C. The United States should impose tariffs on Chinese goods in order to reduce the large trade deficit.**

Choice (C) is an opinion rather than a factual statement; there is nothing in the passage to support it.

Each of the other answer choices is a factual statement that is supported by the given information. Of the top five partners, Germany buys the least amount of goods and services from the United States, so you can reject Choice (A). China has the largest trade deficit with the United States, so you can also reject Choice (B). Of the top five partners, Mexico has the second smallest trade deficit, so you can also eliminate Choice (D).

312. **B. the problem of racial inequality for African Americans in the United States**

Dr. King described the racial inequality that African Americans in the United States faced on a daily basis, so Choice (B) is correct. You can eliminate Choices (A) and (C) because there's no mention of sexual harassment or income inequality. You can also reject Choice (D) — the speech is called "I Have a Dream," not "I Don't Want to Have a Dream."

313. **C. they could not get good reception for their mobile phones in the large ghettos.**

When Dr. King said that "the Negro's basic mobility is from a smaller ghetto to a larger one," he wasn't referring to mobile phones (which weren't available until many decades later). He was instead referring to how difficult it was for people born in the ghetto to ever escape them; therefore, Choice (C) is the correct answer.

Dr. King mentioned that African Americans in the United States were often victims of police brutality, so you can eliminate Choice (A). Choice (B) is incorrect because many hotels did ban African Americans from staying there during the 1960s. Choice (D) is also incorrect because the speech mentions that African Americans were still being prevented from voting in Mississippi.

314. **D. He wanted to point out the hypocrisy of people who agree with the Declaration of Independence but don't agree with equal rights for African Americans.**

The quote from the Declaration of Independence states that it's obvious (self-evident) "that all men are created equal." Therefore, anyone who agrees with the Declaration of Independence but who doesn't agree with equal rights for African Americans is being hypocritical, making Choice (D) the correct answer. Choice (A) can be rejected because Dr. King's focus was gaining African American rights (rather than women's rights). Choice (B) can also be eliminated because Dr. King was fighting for equal rights, not superior rights, for African Americans. Choice (C) can be rejected because he did not think that African Americans should declare their independence from the United States.

315. **C. the rights and freedoms that ensure every citizen's ability to participate equally in social and political life**

Civil rights refers to the rights and freedoms that ensure every citizen's ability to participate equally in social and political life, making Choice (C) correct. If Choice (A) were true, there would be no need for the civil rights movement, because everyone would already be enjoying their rights. Choice (B) can be eliminated for the same reason. Civil rights are protected by federal law, so you can reject Choice (D).

316. **A. the separation of different races in public institutions and daily life**

Racial segregation describes the separation of different races in public institutions and daily life, so Choice (A) is correct. You can reject Choice (B) because although it describes a racist point of view, it doesn't describe racial segregation. Choices (C) and (D) are incorrect and can therefore be rejected.

317. **C. demographic information (such as age, ethnicity, and level of education) taken every ten years**

Every decade, the United States Census Bureau takes citizens' demographic information (such as age, ethnicity, and level of education) in order to track how the population is changing. Therefore, Choice (C) is correct. You can reject Choices (A) and (D) because the census has nothing to do with global warming and is not a tax. Choice (B) is an opinion rather than a factual statement, so you can reject it as well.

318. **A. First Amendment**

The First Amendment protects freedom of speech, so Choice (A) is the best answer. The Second Amendment protects the right to bear arms, so you can reject Choice (B). The Eighteenth Amendment banned the sale of alcohol, and the Nineteenth Amendment refers to women's suffrage, so Choices (C) and (D) are wrong.

319. **C. when the United States is at war and an individual's speech may cause a clear and present danger to national security**

According to the passage, Justice Holmes stated that the question in every case "is whether the words are used in such circumstances and are of such a nature as to create a clear and present danger," so Choice (C) is correct.

320. **C. No, because the First Amendment doesn't protect false speech that can cause panic.**

The passage says Justice Holmes stated that the First Amendment "would not protect a man in falsely shouting fire in a theatre and causing a panic," so the correct answer is Choice (C). Choices (B) and (D) can be rejected because they refer to the Second Amendment (rather than the First Amendment).

321. **A. World War I**

World War I started in 1914 and ended in 1918. The United States entered World War I in 1917, making Choice (A) the correct answer. You can reject the other answers because World War II lasted from 1939 to 1945, the U.S. Civil War was from 1861 to 1865, and the Cold War started in 1945.

322. **B. Prohibition**

The Eighteenth Amendment (Prohibition) was passed in 1917 and prohibited the sale or consumption of alcohol in the United States. It was repealed in 1933 via the Twenty-first Amendment. Hence, Choice (B) is the correct answer.

323. **C. Approximately 20 million Native Americans died during the first half of the century.**

From the graph, you can see that the population of Native Americans dropped sharply during the first half of the 16th century, making Choice (A) false and Choice (C) true. The population of Native Americans did not fall due to emigration or suicide, so you can reject Choices (B) and (D).

324. **C. Native Americans were killed off by diseases brought by the Europeans invaders.**

Although the Spanish conquistadors did kill some of the Native Americans, most of them were killed off by the new diseases that the Europeans brought to the New World. Choice (C) is the correct answer.

325. **B. Hillary Clinton**

You can see from the figure that Hillary Clinton received over 62.5 million votes, which is more than the 61 million votes that Donald Trump received, so the correct answer is Choice (B).

326. **B. 270**

The passage tells you that a candidate needs at least 270 electoral votes to become president, so the correct answer is Choice (B).

327. **B. The Electoral College system always selects the candidate who most Americans voted for.**

You can see from the figure that the outcome of the Electoral College system is not always in agreement with the outcome of the popular vote. In 2016, Donald Trump won the Electoral College vote (304 to 232), whereas Hillary Clinton won the popular vote; Choice (B) is a false statement and is therefore the correct answer. A common definition of *republic* is "a political order in which the supreme power lies in a body of citizens who are entitled to vote for officers and representatives responsible to them." A common definition of *democracy* is "government by the people, exercised either directly or through elected representatives" — hence, the United States is both a republic and a democracy, making Choice (A) a true statement. Choices (C) and (D) are stated in the passage, so you can eliminate them.

328. **B. The number of members that a state has in the U.S. House of Representatives is based on the state's population, whereas each state always has two members in the U.S. Senate.**

The information in the passage tells you that the number of members that a state has in the U.S. House of Representatives is based on the state's population, whereas each state always has two members in the U.S. Senate, making Choice (B) the correct answer.

329. **D. 6 years**

You are told in the passage that senators are elected to six-year terms. Hence, Choice (D) is correct.

330. **D. Twenty-second Amendment**

From the table, you can see that the Twenty-second Amendment sets a two-term limit on the president (which means that no person can be president for more than two terms). If the President of the United States has already been president for two terms, he cannot run for a third term, so Choice (D) is the correct answer.

331. **D. An amendment can be changed later if necessary.**

From the table, you can see that the Twenty-first Amendment repealed the Eighteenth Amendment regarding Prohibition, so Choice (D) is the correct answer. You can reject Choice (A) because amendments do change (amend) the Constitution. Once they're ratified, amendments are legally binding, so you can also eliminate Choice (B).

332. **B. to protect the people and the states from the federal government by guaranteeing their basic individual rights**

From the table, you can see that the First, Second, and Fifth Amendments all refer to protecting the rights of the individual. The Tenth Amendment also protects the rights of the states by placing limits on the federal government; hence, Choice (B) is the correct answer. You can reject Choices (A) and (C) because they describe the opposite of what the Bill of Rights accomplished. Choice (D) is untrue — amendments do not replace the Constitution; they simply change or add to it.

333. **B. Second Amendment**

From the table, you can see that the Second Amendment protects the right to bear arms (gun ownership). The NRA opposes any law that attempts to limit the right to bear arms, so Choice (B) is the correct answer.

334. **B. Fifth Amendment**

From the table, you can see that the Fifth Amendment gives you the right to avoid self-incrimination, the right to trial, and the right to due process, so Choice (B) is the correct answer.

335. **B. the total value of all the services provided and goods produced in a country in one year**

Choice (B) provides the definition of GDP and is therefore the correct answer. Choice (A) is amusing but obviously incorrect. Choices (C) and (D) are also false statements.

336. **C. the United States (US)**

You can see from the figure that the United States spends 16 percent of its GDP on healthcare services, which is higher than the healthcare spending of the other countries. Hence, Choice (C) is correct.

337. **C. the United States (US)**

You can see from the figure that the United States spends only 9 percent of its GDP on social care services, which is lower than the social care spending of the other countries. Hence, Choice (C) is correct.

338. **C. Canada spends approximately the same amount on healthcare as it does on social care.**

You can see from the figure that Canada spends approximately the same percentage on healthcare (10 percent of its GDP) as it does on social care, making Choice (B) the correct answer. Although Choice (A) may appear to be true at first glance, the U.S. spends the median *percentage* of GDP, not the actual dollar amount (which is not given). You can reject Choice (C) because the U.S. spends less than 30 percent of its GDP on its health and social care. Choice (D) is wrong because it represents an opinion rather than a fact — just because New Zealand spends a lower percentage of its GDP does not mean that it cares less for its people.

339. **C. Laissez-faire capitalism is irresponsible and should be outlawed.**

Only Choice (C) represents an opinion rather than a factual statement, making it the correct answer. The passage tells you that laissez-faire capitalism means that the government plays no major role in the economy. Choices (A) and (D) are therefore factual statements and can be rejected. Choice (B) is also a factual statement.

340. **B. Many countries rely on fossil fuels as their major source of energy.**

The question stem tells you that many countries obtain most of their energy needs by burning fossil fuels. Hence, Choice (B) is a factual statement, making it the correct answer. Each of the other answer choices is an opinion rather than a factual statement.

341. **C. the Great Depression**

The period of economic decline that lasted from 1929 until 1939 was known as the Great Depression, making Choice (C) the correct answer.

342. **A. the New Deal**

The New Deal was a series of reforms that President Franklin D. Roosevelt issued in the 1930s with the intent to improve the economy, making Choice (A) the correct answer. Choices (B) and (C) are common terms, but they don't refer to a series of reforms. Reconstruction, Choice (D), refers to the period of rebuilding that occurred shortly after the Civil War.

343. B. the start of World War II

In 1939, the start of World War II helped the United States finally recover from the Great Depression. First, the unemployment rate dropped sharply because 12 million men were sent to war. Second, America's industry was put to work producing machinery and vehicles needed for the war effort. Hence, Choice (B) is correct.

344. C. to protect essential freedoms, including the freedom of religion and the freedom to petition the government

The First Amendment protects essential freedoms, including the freedom of religion, the freedom of the press, the freedom of assembly, and the freedom to petition the government. Hence, Choice (C) is the correct answer.

345. C. a law that establishes a state-run church

You can reject Choices (A), (B), and (D) because the First Amendment protects freedom of the press, freedom of speech, freedom of assembly, and freedom to petition the government. That leaves Choice (C), which violates the Establishment Clause (freedom of religion) and therefore is the correct answer.

346. C. freedom of the press, freedom of religion, freedom of speech, freedom of petition

The excerpt tells you that the First Amendment guarantees freedom of the press, freedom of religion, freedom of speech, and freedom of petition, making Choice (C) the correct answer.

347. A. buying stock in a single startup company

The vast majority of startup companies end in failure, so investing in them is riskier than the other investments — even though startups can give very good returns on your investment when they succeed. Hence, Choice (A) is correct. Choice (C) reduces some of the risk by spreading the investment over several companies instead of putting all your eggs in one basket. Choices (B) and (D) are low-risk options.

348. C. freed slaves in Southern states.

Lincoln's Emancipation Proclamation of 1863 ended slavery in Southern states, so Choice (C) is correct.

349. **A. monopolies are too efficient.**

Monopolies are not allowed in the United States because they give too much power to one company. The company with the monopoly has no incentive to reduce its prices, because the consumer has no alternative choices. Monopolies are less efficient because there's no competition, making Choice (A) false and the correct answer.

350. **D. the largest forced migration of a group of people in world history.**

The slave trade from Africa to the New World from the mid-1500s to the mid-1800s resulted in the largest forced migration of people in world history. It's estimated that approximately 12 million slaves from Africa were forced to relocate to the New World, making Choice (D) the correct answer.

351. **B. wages and benefits**

Total worker compensation consists of wages plus benefits, making Choice (B) correct. Benefits may include healthcare, paid vacations, business lunches, use of a company car, travel expenses, and so on.

352. **B. Strikes usually shut down all production, which harms the company financially.**

A strike usually shuts down all production, which harms the company financially, putting pressure on company executives to give in to the workers' demands. Hence, Choice (B) is correct.

353. **C. the annual U.S. budget.**

Infrastructure includes the national highway system, bridges and tunnels, airports, and ports. Hence, Choice (C) is correct.

354. **C. the government encourages entrepreneurs to start, own, and operate their own companies.**

Communist economies are run by the government. Private ownership is not allowed, so Choice (C) is correct.

355. **C. Consumers reduce their spending on nonessential items.**

When high inflation occurs, one of the first things to happen is that consumers reduce their spending on nonessential items, so Choice (C) is correct. This sudden reduction in spending reduces the demand for those items, and many companies scale back production and lay off workers, leading to higher unemployment.

356. **C. It damages the company's reputation with its customers.**

Adverse publicity associated with boycotts often brings attention to company's unethical behavior, which can quickly damage the company's reputation with its customers, often forcing it to change its ways. Hence, Choice (C) is the correct answer.

357. **B. Tariffs make the imported cars more expensive, increasing the demand for American-made cars.**

Tariffs increase the demand for American-made goods by making comparable foreign goods (substitute items) more expensive. Hence, Choice (B) is the correct answer.

358. **B. NATO and the Warsaw Pact were created to work together to promote world peace.**

Choice (B) is an incorrect statement. In 1949, the United States and 11 other countries formed NATO to provide collective security against the Soviet Union. The Soviet Union established a rival alliance called the Warsaw Pact in response to the formation of NATO. Hence, NATO and the Warsaw Pact did not work together to promote world peace, making Choice (B) the correct answer. All the other answer choices are factual statements.

359. **C. Great Britain imposed tariffs on goods imported from other countries.**

During the Industrial Revolution, Great Britain quickly became the world's top producer of goods due to several factors: Great Britain had made advances in the steam train and had developed a rail network, making the transport of goods relatively easy; Great Britain had lots of coal available to power the machines needed for the mass production of goods; and Great Britain's extensive colonization gave it access to raw materials. That leaves Choice (C) as the correct answer: Great Britain didn't rise to dominance by imposing tariffs.

360. **C. filling jobs that were needed for the war effort because so many men were away fighting the war.**

More than 16 million men were sent off to fight the war. Women helped the war effort by taking over the absent men's jobs in both the private and government sectors. Hence, Choice (C) is the correct answer. Women weren't typically involved in many male-dominated industries before the war, so you can reject Choices (A) and (D).

361. **D. The generalized fear was that if one country fell to communism, all the other countries in the region would also fall to communism.**

According to the Domino Theory, once one country fell to communism, all the countries in the region would fall to communism. Hence, Choice (D) is the correct answer.

362. **C. President JFK was able to get the Soviet Union to withdraw its missiles from Cuba while the United States agreed to remove nuclear missiles from Turkey.**

The USSR removed the nuclear missiles from Cuba, and the U.S. agreed to remove its nuclear weapons from Turkey, making Choice (C) the correct answer.

363. **C. He warned that a two-party system could lead to Americans turning against each other.**

John Adams was afraid that if America divided into two political parties, the two sides would soon begin to fight against each other rather than work together, so Choice (C) is correct. You can reject Choice (A), which is from a Beastie Boys song — Adams was referring to political parties. You can reject Choice (D) because Adams does not mention a multiple-party system.

364. **D. Yes. Both Adams and Washington were against a two-party system.**

From the passage it is clear that John Adams was against the two-party system. You can therefore eliminate Choices (A) and (C). From George Washington's quote, you can see that he also opposed the two-party system (he described it as "a frightful prospect"), making Choice (D) the correct answer.

365. **C. Yes. Both Republicans and Democrats appear to detest each other and sometimes put their party's needs above the needs of the country.**

Just one look at how modern Republicans and Democrats view each other today shows that Adams and Washington were absolutely correct to be worried about the two-party system. Hence, Choice (C) is correct.

366. **B. the right of women to vote**

The goal of the suffragette movement was to gain the right of women to vote, so Choice (B) is correct.

367. **C. the U.S. exerted its force and growing influence in Latin America by "persuading" Panama to let it build the Panama Canal.**

President Teddy Roosevelt took a more aggressive approach to his foreign policy regarding the countries in Latin America by becoming the "policeman" of U.S. affairs and actions in Latin America. The U.S. exerted its force on Panama, resulting in the building of the Panama Canal.

368. **B. the students believed that America's involvement in the war in Vietnam was a necessary evil.**

Choices (A), (C), and (D) would all lend support to the student protests against the war and can therefore be eliminated. Choice (B) would be a reason to support the war, not oppose it, so Choice (B) is the correct answer.

369. **A. Tenth Amendment**

The Tenth Amendment sets up the concept of "states' rights" — that what is not delegated to the federal government is then delegated to the states. Hence, Choice (A) is the right answer. The Nineteenth Amendment refers to women's suffrage; the Twenty-fifth Amendment refers to setting the voting age at 21. There are only 27 amendments (the Thirty-second Amendment doesn't exist — yet).

370. **D. People now rely more on mainstream news than ever for reliable information about candidates and elections.**

People are relying less on mainstream news for political information and are gaining more information on cable news and Internet news sites [Choice (A)]. The recent growth of fake news websites [Choice (B)] that spread fictional information about candidates and elections was a major concern during the 2016 election, so you can reject Choice (B). Choice (C) is also a true statement. Hence, Choice (D) is the correct answer.

371. **D. a factory**

A factory is a capital resource, so Choice (D) is correct. Copper deposits are an example of raw materials, the owner of a startup company is an entrepreneur, and a skilled plumber is part of the labor force.

372. **B. Many counties are more dependent on each other for their economic growth.**

Globalization has caused the world to become a bit smaller, and each country is becoming increasingly dependent upon other countries for its economic growth and progress. Hence, Choice (B) is correct. Globalization has not reduced terrorist attacks [Choice (A)], caused human rights to decline sharply around the world [Choice (C)], or reduced the number of refugees [Choice (D)].

373. **C. an increased focus on alternative energy such as wind power and solar energy in China and the United States.**

The question stem tells you that both counties are continuing their reliance on fossil fuels, so they're unlikely to increase their focus on alternatives such as wind power and solar energy, making Choice (C) the correct answer. All the other choices describe things that are likely to happen as more fossil fuels are consumed.

374. **B. to relocate people of Japanese ancestry living in America to ten different internment camps away from the western American coastlines for the duration of the war**

Executive Order 9066 forced the relocation of 120,000 people of Japanese ancestry living in America (two-thirds of whom were U.S. citizens) to ten different military internment camps. This internment lasted until nearly the end of World War II, and the order is now considered one of the most shameful executive orders in U.S. history.

375. **C. create a monopoly by controlling nearly 90 percent of the oil production in the U.S.**

Rockefeller was able to create a huge monopoly with Standard Oil, controlling 90 percent of the petroleum production and sales in the U.S. He forced out competition and managed price controls with production, transportation, and sale of his product, so Choice (C) is the correct answer.

376. **D. The immigration rate increased steadily throughout the second half of the 20th century and then spiked in the 1990s.**

From the graph, you an see that the immigration rate increased steadily throughout the second half of the 20th century and then spiked in the 1990s, making Choice (D) correct.

377. **A. Immigration declined sharply due to World War I.**

The outbreak of World War I in 1914 greatly reduced immigration to the United State from Europe as most Europeans became caught up in the war, making Choice (A) the correct answer. You can reject the other answers because World War II lasted from 1939 to 1945, the U.S. Civil War was from 1861 to 1865, and the Cold War started in 1945.

378. **C. In 1965, the Immigration and Naturalization Act established a new immigration policy aimed at attracting skilled labor to the United States.**

Only Choice (C) would explain why the immigration rate began to rise in the second half of the 20th century. All the other choices would actually lower the immigration rate by making it harder for immigrants to move to the United States.

379. **B. Great Britain**

By issuing the Declaration of Independence on July 4, 1776, the 13 American colonies severed their political connections to Great Britain; hence, Choice (B) is the correct answer.

380. **D. he had allowed the American colonists to form a large army.**

You can see from the first excerpt that the reasons given in Choices (A), (B), and (C) were mentioned in the Declaration of Independence. Choice (D) was not mentioned and is therefore the correct answer.

381. **C. "Any reasonable, intelligent person would obviously agree with us."**

The term *self-evident* means obvious, so the phrase "we hold these truths to be self-evident" means that any reasonable, intelligent person would agree without needing explanation or proof. Hence, Choice (C) is the correct answer.

382. **C. to highlight the hypocrisy of not allowing women to vote and participate in making laws that they will be governed by**

Elizabeth Cady Stanton realized that people referring to the Declaration of Independence in support of voting rights for men should be capable of realizing that those same rights should also apply to women. It would be hypocritical to agree with the wording of the Declaration of Independence but not agree with equal rights for women, so Choice (C) is correct.

383. **A. to show that it should be obvious that men and women should have equal rights**

By adding "and women" to the original wording of the Declaration of Independence, Elizabeth Cady Stanton tied her case for equal rights for women to that document's authority and credibility. She was highlighting the hypocrisy of not allowing women to vote and participate in making the laws that governed them; therefore, Choice (A) is correct.

384. **B. Their goal was to persuade the U.S. government to allow women the right to vote.**

Elizabeth Cady Stanton and Susan B. Anthony were upset that women were not permitted to vote and participate in making laws even though those laws would be applied to them. Hence, their goal was to persuade the U.S. government to allow women to vote, making Choice (B) the correct answer.

385. **B. They wanted equal basic human rights, including the right to vote.**

From the information in the passage, you can see that the protestors simply wanted basic human rights, including the right to vote. Hence, Choice (B) is the correct answer. You're also told that the protesters were peaceful, so you can reject Choices (A) and (C). Choice (D) makes no sense because President Johnson's speech came after Bloody Sunday, not before.

386. **A. The state troopers were part of the racist establishment in Alabama who were trying to prevent African Americans from speaking out for their right to vote.**

From the passage, you can see that Alabama governor Wallace was a racist who did not want African Americans to have basic human rights. He refused to protect the marchers from the state troopers, resulting in the death of an unarmed man, making Choice (A) the correct answer. You can reject Choice (B) because the protestors didn't want to take away voting rights from white Americans. Choice (C) makes no sense and can be eliminated. Choice (D) is a false statement.

387. **C. He was the governor of Alabama.**

The passage tells you that George Wallace was the governor of Alabama in 1965, making Choice (C) the correct answer.

388. **C. to urge Congress to immediately pass the civil rights bill that would give African Americans the right to vote**

President Lyndon Johnson's administration had been working on a voting rights law before the violence of Bloody Sunday began. Because Alabama's governor refused to protect the peaceful protesters and their lives were in danger, President Johnson gave this address to Congress one week later to urge Congress to immediately pass the civil rights bill that would give African Americans the right to vote. Hence, Choice (C) is correct. You can rule out Choices (A) and (B) because President Johnson supported the protestors. Delaying the new voting laws would have led to even more protests, so you can rule out Choice (D).

389. **A. "We Shall Overcome" was a protest song that was a key anthem of the Civil Rights movement.**

You can see from the excerpt that President Johnson supported the protestors in their goal of achieving the right to vote, so you can immediately reject Choice (C). The phrase shows that President Johnson was confident that the protestors would succeed in their goals, so you can reject Choice (D). There is nothing in the passage to suggest that the president would go to Alabama himself, so you can reject Choice (B). That leaves Choice (A) as the correct answer.

390. **C. Despite the passage of the Fifteenth Amendment in 1870, many African Americans could still not vote in the South until the passage of civil rights legislation in 1965.**

The passage states: "Although the Fifteenth Amendment to the U.S. Constitution, which granted African American men the right to vote, was ratified on February 3, 1870, the promise of the law would not be fully realized for almost a century. Many Southern states continued to prevent African Americans from voting. . ." Hence, Choice (C) is correct.

391. B. Congress can overturn a presidential veto with a two-thirds majority vote in both the House of Representatives and the Senate.

The passage tells you that Congress can overturn a presidential veto with a two-thirds vote of both houses, whereupon the bill becomes law. Hence, Choice (A) is wrong and Choice (B) is correct. The Supreme Court cannot override a presidential veto, so Choice (C) is incorrect. Choice (D) is not a true statement.

392. B. The bill is automatically rejected after 10 days.

The passage tells you that a pocket veto occurs when a president doesn't sign a bill and can't return it to Congress within a 10-day period because Congress is not in session. At that point, the bill is automatically rejected.

393. C. committing perjury (lying under oath)

The only grounds for presidential impeachment are perjury (lying under oath), obstruction of justice (using barriers to hinder a criminal investigation), and abuse of power (claiming that you're above the regular reach and intent of the law). Hence, Choice (C) is the correct answer. The Constitution grants the president the authority to veto legislation passed by Congress, so you can reject Choice (A). Proposing universal healthcare coverage for the millions of uninsured Americans is certainly not an impeachable offense, so you can reject Choice (B). Choice (D) can be rejected because the law being signed is attempting to prevent improper behavior.

394. B. Natural resources have no impact on the profit margin of a business, as these costs are fixed over time.

The free market system depends on physical capital, natural resources, human capital, and trends in the marketplace. These capital resources and trends change over time. An entrepreneur often develops new technologies or methods of production and marketing to maximize profits. Hence, Choice (B) is not a true statement, making it the correct answer.

395. A. the speech helped Reagan urge Gorbachev to become more involved in European foreign affairs.

The passage tells you that Reagan took the opportunity at the Brandenburg Gate in 1987 to encourage democratic reform in Eastern Europe; within a little over two years, major democratic reform swept the region, including the dismantling of the Berlin Wall in November 1989. Hence, you can reject Choices (B), (C), and (D), making Choice (A) the correct answer.

396. **A. East Germany was communist (and impoverished), and therefore the economic and social conditions there were much worse than in capitalist West Germany.**

The passage tells you that East Germany was communist and impoverished; therefore, the economic and social conditions there were much worse than in capitalist West Germany. This explains why so many people risked their lives trying to escape from East Germany to West Germany (but not the other way around), making Choice (A) the correct answer.

397. **B. World War II**

World War II started in 1939 and ended in 1945. The United States entered World War II in 1941, shortly after the bombing of Pearl Harbor, making Choice (B) the correct answer. You can reject the other answers because World War I lasted from 1914 to 1918, the U.S. Civil War was from 1861 to 1865, and the Cold War started in 1945.

398. **D. individualism**

A free-market economy values individualism, which encourages people to become entrepreneurs. Hence, Choice (D) is the correct answer.

399. **B. the American Civil War**

The Battle of Gettysburg took place during the American Civil War (1861 to 1865), making Choice (B) the correct answer.

400. **B. The battle ended when the Union armies defeated the Confederate armies.**

The Battle of Gettysburg was fought on July 1–3, 1863, by the Union and Confederate forces, resulting in the largest number of casualties of the war. The battle ended when the Union armies defeated the Confederate armies. Hence, Choice (B) is correct.

401. **B. to bring the American people together so they could finish the work needed to rebuild the nation**

Lincoln's Gettysburg Address lasted only two minutes and was less than 300 words long. At the time, the speech didn't raise much attention, and it wasn't until 11 years after Lincoln had died that the speech became famous for its emphasis on freedom, equality, and unity. Hence, Choice (B) is the correct answer.

402. **D. so the government could gain revenue from the sales taxes on alcoholic beverages**

The question asks for the main *economic* reason that the federal government favored the repeal of Prohibition, so you can eliminate Choices (A) and (C). Although Choice (B) would save the government some money, it isn't as good as Choice (D), because the revenue from the sales taxes on alcoholic beverages would be much greater than the amount saved from investigating smuggling. Hence, Choice (D) is the correct answer.

403. **C. The number of members that a state has in the U.S. House of Representatives is based on the state's population, whereas each state always has two members in the U.S. Senate.**

The U.S. Congress consists of two chambers, the House of Representatives and the Senate. There are 100 members in the Senate. Each state elects 2 senators, no matter the size or population of the state. In the House of Representatives, there are 435 members.

404. **D. In *Texas v. Johnson* in 1989, the Supreme Court ruled to protect the right to burn the U.S. flag as a form of symbolic speech.**

Despite how many people feel about flag burning, the Supreme Court ruled that it was protected as a form of free speech in its *Texas v.* Johnson decision (1989). Choices (A) and (C) appear to restrict free speech and can therefore be rejected. Choice (B) refers to the Fifth Amendment (not the First Amendment) and can therefore be rejected.

405. **D. the main causes of inflation**

A macroeconomist focuses on the big picture of the economy, including causes of inflation. Hence, Choice (D) is the correct answer.

406. **C. Compared to residents of the United States, Japanese residents consume approximately half the amount of electricity per person.**

The graph shows you that Japanese residents consume (2,241 kWh/year), which is approximately half the amount of electricity consumed by United States residents (4,741 kWh/year), making Choice (C) the correct answer. The graph tells you the residential electricity consumption per capita (per person), so you can reject Choice (B), which talks about fossil fuel consumption, and Choice (A), which talks about total electricity consumption per country (not per person). There's no evidence in the chart to support Choice (D).

407. **A. Canada's climate is much colder than Australia's.**

Because Canada's climate is much colder than Australia's, much more electricity is needed to keep households warm in winter, making Choice (A) the correct answer. You can eliminate Choices (B) and (C) because they're both false statements. Choice (D) doesn't make sense, because a higher price wouldn't lead to a higher consumption rate.

408. **C. The government allows the free market to determine economic outcomes without interfering.**

The passage tells you that laissez-faire allows markets to operate without government interference. Hence, laissez-faire economics occurs when the government allows the free market to determine economic outcomes, making Choice (C) the correct answer.

409. **A. laissez-faire economics**

The passage says: "Before the crash, the government had done nothing to regulate banking, investments, or other basic aspects of the economy. The government had also failed to gather adequate data that could have been analyzed to highlight growing problems in stock market investing, agriculture, or other vital sectors of the economy, leading up to the crash." Hence, it appears clear that laissez-faire economics was partially responsible for the Stock Market Crash of 1929, making Choice (A) the correct answer.

410. **C. free housing.**

The passage tells you that the Social Security programs provided old-age and widows' benefits, unemployment compensation, and disability insurance, making Choice (C) the correct answer. It doesn't say anything about free housing.

411. **B. 1933**

You can see that unemployment reached its peak in 1933 at about 25 percent, making Choice (B) the correct answer.

412. **D. The unemployment rate fell steadily, although it still remained above 14 percent.**

You can see from the graph that unemployment fell steadily from its peak value of 25 percent in 1933 to about 14 percent in 1937, making Choice (D) the correct answer.

413. **A. World War II**

In 1939, the outbreak of World War II helped the United States recover from the Great Depression. First, the unemployment rate dropped sharply because 12 million men were sent to war. Second, America's industry was put to work producing machinery and vehicles needed for the war effort. Hence, Choice (A) is correct.

414. **A. freedom to place limits on the press**

The First Amendment protects freedom of religion, freedom to petition the government, freedom of speech, and the freedom of the press (not the freedom to place limits on the press). Hence, Choice (A) is the correct answer.

415. **D. It divides the power among the three branches by giving them distinctive roles to prevent any one branch from becoming too powerful.**

The system of checks and balances is an important part of the Constitution. With checks and balances, each of the three branches of government can limit the powers of the others to prevent any one branch from becoming too powerful. Hence, Choice (D) is the right answer.

416. **B. 1920**

Even though African-American men first gained the right to vote through the Fifteenth Amendment in 1870, the right to vote didn't apply to women (of any race) until the passing of the Nineteenth Amendment in 1920. Hence, the correct answer is Choice (B).

417. **A. Even though the right to vote was protected by the Constitution, many states still tried to make it almost impossible for minorities to exercise that right.**

Even though African-American men first gained the right to vote through the passing of the Fifteenth Amendment in 1870, many states still had racist policies (poll taxes, literacy tests, and so on) aimed at making it almost impossible for minorities to exercise their right to vote. The new amendment and voting laws prohibited these racist state policies, so Choice (A) is the best answer.

418. **B. The United States has not always lived up to the ideal that "all men are created equal."**

The passage notes that the second paragraph of the Declaration of Independence states that "all men are created equal." It's clear from all the constitutional amendments regarding voting rights that the United States hasn't always lived up to this ideal [reject Choice (A)]. The amendments listed in the table tried to fix this shortcoming [reject Choices (C) and (D)] by ensuring voting rights for all men and women, so Choice (B) is the best answer.

419. **A. Conscription during the Vietnam War meant than many 18- to 20-year-olds were angry that they were considered old enough to fight for their country but not old enough to vote.**

The Twenty-sixth Amendment lowered the voting age from 21 to 18. The debate about lowering the voting age was spurred by the fact that many 18- to 20-year-olds were angry that they were considered old enough to fight for their country but not old enough to vote, so Choice (A) is the best answer.

420. **C. the right to remain silent.**

The passage says, "The Sixth Amendment guarantees a citizen a speedy trial, a fair jury, an attorney if the accused person wants one, and the chance to confront the witnesses accusing the defendant of a crime." Hence, Choice (C) is the correct answer because it refers to the Fifth Amendment rather than the Sixth Amendment.

421. **A. The Fifth Amendment guarantees the criminally accused the right to remain silent, whereas the Sixth Amendment guarantees the right to a lawyer.**

The passage tells you that the Fifth Amendment guarantees that "no person shall be compelled in any criminal case to be a witness against himself" — in other words, it gives the accused the right to remain silent. The Sixth Amendment guarantees the right to an attorney. Hence, Choice (A) is correct. There is nothing to suggest that that the Fifth Amendment and the Sixth Amendment are both more important than the First Amendment, so you can reject Choice (C). Choices (B) and (D) are both false statements.

422. **C. uphold both the Fifth and Sixth Amendments**

The excerpt mentions that "detained criminal suspects, prior to police questioning, must be informed of their constitutional right to an attorney (Sixth Amendment) and against self-incrimination (Fifth Amendment)." Hence, the police must uphold both the Fifth and Sixth Amendments, making Choice (C) the correct answer.

423. **C. The president helps secure his own legacy by appointing Supreme Court justices, who will serve long after he's gone.**

All Supreme Court justices are appointed for life, so they continue to make important decisions long after the president has left the office. Even though any justices he appoints won't necessarily work to uphold whatever changes the president made while in office, the president's selections can help to shift the balance of the court in either the liberal or conservative direction that the president wants. Hence, Choice (C) is correct. All the other answer choices are false and can be rejected.

424. **A. Once a tax rate has been set, it can't be challenged or changed.**

Tax rates can be changed, making Choice (A) an incorrect statement and therefore the correct answer. All the other answer choices are true.

425. **B. A computer manufacturer finds it cheaper to outsource its customer service call center to workers in India instead of employing local workers.**

The question says that globalization can lead to the outsourcing of jobs overseas. Choice (B) fits that description nicely because the company has outsourced jobs to India. Choice (A) involves advances in technology but doesn't involve globalization. Choice (C) doesn't involve outsourcing, either, and neither does Choice (D).

426. **D. major cities tend to develop along major rivers**

You can see from the map that major cities in each state tend to develop along major rivers, making Choice (D) the correct answer. There is no indication on the map that the cities are in the mountains [reject Choice (A)] or that the Southern states have some of America's largest cities [reject Choice (B)]. Choice (C) is a false statement.

427. **B. The river provides an important connection to the sea for landlocked Midwestern states.**

You can see from the map that the river provides an important connection to the sea for landlocked Midwestern states, so Choice (B) is correct.

428. **C. Congress imposes a tax on imported Japanese cars in order to protect domestic car sales.**

A tariff is a special type of tax that the government imposes on goods imported into the United States, so Choice (C) is correct. You can reject all the other answer choices because they don't refer only to imported goods.

429. **B. 1983**

You can see from the graph that the two lines are closest together in 1983, so Choice (B) is the correct answer.

430. **C. The GDP of both regions grew at approximately the same rate during the 1970s.**

You can see from the graph that the GDP lines of both regions have approximately the same slope for the 1970s, meaning they grew at about the same rate; the lines diverge after 1983. Hence, Choice (C) is the correct answer.

431. **A. Sub-Saharan Africa no longer has the resources it needs in order to grow its GDP.**

Choice (A) is an opinion because the graph makes no indication that explains why the GDP of the region has declined since the early 1980s. All the other choices contain factual statements that are supported by the graph.

432. **D. 81%**

Fossil fuels include coal, natural gas, and petroleum. You can see from the graph that these three fossil fuels account for 81 percent of the total U.S. energy consumption, making Choice (D) the correct answer.

433. **A. 2.5%**

You can see from the graph that hydroelectric power accounts for 25 percent of renewable energy sources, which make up only 10 percent of the total U.S. energy consumption; 25 percent of 10 percent equals 2.5 percent, making Choice (A) the correct answer.

434. **B. Geothermal energy provides less than 1 percent of the total U.S. energy consumption.**

You can see from the graph that geothermal power accounts for 2 percent of renewable energy sources, which make up only 10 percent of the total U.S. energy consumption; 2 percent of 10 percent equals 0.2 percent, making Choice (B) the correct answer. The other statements are not supported by the graph.

435. **B. the Mexican-American War**

Because Texas borders Mexico, it makes sense that the United States would have gained control of Texas by winning the Mexican-American War. Hence, Choice (B) is the correct answer.

436. **D. 2028**

You can see from the graph that the world population will reach 8 billion people by approximately 2028, making Choice (D) the correct answer.

437. **C. Nigeria**

Nigeria's population is expected to more than double from 174 million in 2015 to 440 million in 2050. No other country's population is expected to grow that much, making Choice (C) the correct answer.

438. A. Most of the population growth is expected to come from less developed countries.

You can see from the graph that the line referring to the population growth of developed countries remains relatively flat, but the line referring to the less developed countries rises sharply. Hence, Choice (A) is correct.

439. C. The world population appears to be doubling in size every 40 to 60 years.

You can see from the graph that the world population was about 3 billion in 1960 but had reached 6 billion by about 2000. It then appears to double again; therefore, the world population appears to be doubling in size every 40 to 60 years, making Choice (C) a factual statement. Choice (A) is incorrect because China's population is expected to fall slightly by 2050. Choice (B) is wrong because Russia is no longer expected to be in the top 10 by 2050. Choice (D) is wrong because Russia's population could still grow slightly, but it may not be enough to keep it in the top 10.

440. B. Nigeria should encourage birth control measures to prevent its population from growing too quickly.

You can see from the tables that Choices (A), (C), and (D) are all factual statements and should therefore be rejected. China's population is expected to fall slightly from 1,357 million in 2015 to 1,314 million in 2050, making Choice (A) true. Choice (C) is also factual — the United States population is expected to grow by less than 30 percent (316 million to 400 million represents only 26.6 percent growth). Choice (D) is also a true statement. That leaves Choice (B), which is an opinion rather than a factual statement.

441. A. Los Angeles

Of the cities listed, the only one that doesn't lie along the Gulf of Mexico or along the coast of the Atlantic Ocean is Los Angeles, making Choice (A) the correct answer.

442. A. 3 years

You can see from the chart that the average person born in India lives 63.2 years, whereas a person born in Nepal lives 59.9 years. The difference is approximately 3 years, making Choice (A) the best answer.

443. C. The majority of women in Nepal do not know how to read or write properly.

You can see from the chart that the rate of illiteracy (not being able to read or write) for women in Nepal is 73.6 percent, making Choice (C) the best answer. All the other choices contain statements that aren't supported by the graph. Choice (A) is false. China has the highest life expectancy out of the three nations mentioned, but nothing in the graph suggests it has the highest life expectancy in the world, so Choice (B) is false as well. Choice (D) could be true, but it isn't supported by the graph.

444. A. Nepalese women are not given the same educational opportunities as men.

If Nepalese women were not given the same educational opportunities as men, they wouldn't be able to read or write as well as men, so Choice (A) is correct. Choice (B) is untrue (and sexist) and can be rejected. You can reject Choices (C) and (D) because they would suggest that Nepalese women should be better readers than men, not worse.

445. C. The lower the illiteracy rate, the longer the life expectancy.

The chart shows that the country with the lowest illiteracy rate (China) has the longest life expectancy. Also, the country with the highest illiteracy rate (Nepal) has the shortest life expectancy. Hence, Choice (C) is the best answer.

446. B. most Chinese women are able to read and write properly.

You can see from the chart that the illiteracy rate for women in China only is 20.4 percent, so the majority of Chinese women are able to read and write properly, making Choice (B) the correct answer. All the other choices contain opinions rather than facts.

447. A. the Louisiana Purchase

The passage tells you that the purchased territory included North Dakota, South Dakota, Arkansas, Iowa, Kansas, Oklahoma, Nebraska, Montana, Wyoming, northern Texas, and Louisiana. The only answer choice that includes all of these is Choice (A), which is the correct answer. You can reject Choices (B) and (C) because neither California nor New York is mentioned in the question stem. Choice (D) refers to the purchase of New Mexico and southern Arizona.

448. B. National Parks system

The excerpt says that President Theodore Roosevelt appreciated nature and wanted to preserve it for the next generation, so Choice (B) is correct.

449. B. conservation

The practice of preserving natural resources known as conservation. Hence, Choice (B) is correct. You can reject Choice (A) because it refers to the exaggeration of environmental damage. Similarly, Choices (C) and (D) can be rejected because they do not refer to preserving natural resources.

450. **D. EPA (Environmental Protection Agency)**

As the name suggests, the role of the Environmental Protection Agency (EPA) is to protect the environment, making Choice (D) the correct answer.

451. **C. It greatly expanded the cotton industry in the Southern states.**

The cotton gin made the cotton industry much more efficient and helped expand the industry throughout many Southern states, making Choice (C) correct.

452. **D. It allows for amendments to be made when necessary.**

The U.S. Constitution allows for amendments (changes) to its text; therefore, Choice (A) is incorrect and Choice (D) is correct. Choices (B) and (C) are false statements and should be rejected.

453. **D. American colonists should seize the land from Native Americans because doing so is part of God's plan.**

The passage says people believed that the United States should continue its westward expansion and that it was "destined by Divine Providence [God] to be peopled by one nation, speaking one language." Choice (D) is the correct answer.

454. **A. the belief that the expansion of the U.S. throughout the American continents was both justified and inevitable**

The passage says that Manifest Destiny was the belief that the United States should continue its westward expansion, as it was "destined" to do so; therefore, Choice (A) is correct.

455. **C. the forcible removal of Native Americans and the war with Mexico**

Based on the information in the passage, the attitude of Manifest Destiny helped encourage two atrocities, including the forcible removal of Native Americans and the war with Mexico. Choice (C) is correct.

456. **C. It was added to the Constitution shortly after ratification.**

Some of the Founding Fathers were concerned that the Constitution didn't go far enough in protecting the individual rights of the people, so they added the Bill of Rights to the Constitution in 1791, which was shortly after the Constitution was ratified in 1788. Hence, Choice (C) is the correct answer. The Emancipation Proclamation, not the Bill of Rights, helped end slavery in the United States, so you can reject Choice (A). Women didn't get the right to vote until the Nineteenth Amendment, so Choice (B) is also wrong.

457. D. British troops were attacked by an unruly crowd, and shots were fired during the ensuing chaos, leading to the death of several civilians.

The passage says that American colonists in Boston began throwing snowballs and rocks at British soldiers, and then several soldiers fired their weapons, resulting in the deaths of five civilians. Hence, Choice (D) is correct. Choice (A) is incorrect because the crowd provoked the British troops by throwing rocks at them. Choice (B) is incorrect because the engraving is described as *propaganda* (information, which is often false or misleading, that is meant to further a political cause). Choice (C) is a false statement because many thousands of people lost their lives during the Civil War.

458. C. several American colonists are shown lying on the floor, either dead or dying.

You're told in the passage that several civilians were killed, so Choice (C) shows an actual event that occurred during the Boston Massacre and is therefore the correct answer. All the other choices show aspects of propaganda that were intended to increase the hostility toward the occupying British troops.

459. B. They helped ignite tensions between the colonists and the British Empire, eventually leading to the American Revolution.

The passage says that Revere's engraving is considered one of the most effective pieces of war propaganda in American history, so it makes sense that it increased the colonists' tension with the occupying British troops. Hence, Choice (B) is correct. All the other choices reflect the opposite of this and can therefore be rejected.

460. D. New Supreme Court justices must be appointed by the president and confirmed by the Senate.

The passage tells you that the goal of the system of checks and balances is to prevent one branch of government from becoming too powerful. Hence, you're looking for an answer choice that shows the need for the branches to work together. Choice (D) does this nicely. All the other choices would give the president too much power over the other branches.

461. A. executive branch

The president is the head of the executive branch of the government, making Choice (A) the correct answer. The legislative branch consists of Congress (the House of Representatives and the Senate), so Choice (B) is wrong. The judicial branch is the Supreme Court and lower federal courts, making Choice (C) incorrect.

462. **B. legislative branch**

The legislative branch, which consists of Congress (the House of Representatives and the Senate), decides which laws should be passed, making Choice (B) the correct answer. Although the president can veto a bill, he can't introduce bills, making Choice (A) incorrect. The judicial branch (Supreme Court) can say whether a law is constitutional but can't introduce laws, either, making Choice (C) incorrect. Choice (D) is a false statement.

463. **D. to win first place in an official global exploration contest held in 1522**

Choice (D) is the correct answer because there was no official global exploration contest held in 1522. All the other answer choices list legitimate reasons European explorers traveled around the world during this period.

464. **D. He didn't actually step foot on the mainland of the United States during this period.**

According to the map, Christopher Columbus landed on various Caribbean islands, but he never set foot on the mainland of the United States (so much for his discovering America!); hence, Choice (D) is the correct answer.

465. **C. Magellan did not return home with his ship in 1522.**

If you look carefully at the map, you see that it was Magellan's crew who returned home in 1522 (Magellan actually died in the Philippines in 1591), making Choice (C) the correct answer. According to the map, Magellan's voyage began in 1519 and lasted until 1522, so Choice (A) is incorrect. Choice (B) is also not supported by the map because da Gama's route was different from Magellan's. There's also no evidence to support Choice (D).

466. **D. Da Gama was the first of the three explorers to reach Asia by ship.**

According to the map, da Gama landed in Asia in 1498, so Choice (D) is the correct answer. All the other answer choices are opinions rather than factual statements.

467. **B. The Japanese had launched an unprovoked attack on the United States at Pearl Harbor.**

According to the except, "The United States of America was suddenly and deliberately attacked by naval and air forces of the Empire of Japan" at Pearl Harbor in Hawaii, making Choice (B) the correct answer. Choice (A) is the opposite of what happened. There was no ongoing war between Japan and the United States; in fact, the excerpt mentions that the nations were still negotiating a peace treaty at the time of the attack, making Choice (C) incorrect. Hawaii is not part of the continental United States, so Choice (D) is false.

468. **B. The United States and Japan were in the process of discussing a peace treaty at the time of the attack.**

According to the excerpt, "the Japanese Government has deliberately sought to deceive the United States by false statements and expressions of hope for continued peace"; meanwhile, Japan had spent weeks planning the attack at Pearl Harbor, making Choice (B) the correct answer. For the same reason, you can eliminate Choice (C). Choice (A) is not true — many United States warships were stationed there. Hawaii is not close to Washington, DC, so Choice (D) is false.

469. **B. World War II**

World War II began in 1939 and continued until 1945, making Choice (B) the best answer.

470. **C. declare war on Japan**

Roosevelt said, "I ask that the Congress declare that because the unprovoked and dastardly attack by Japan on Sunday, December 7th, a state of war has existed between the United States and the Japanese Empire"; that makes Choice (C) the correct answer.

471. **A. Pearl Harbor was an important U.S. naval base.**

Roosevelt said, "The attack yesterday on the Hawaiian Islands has caused severe damage to American naval and military forces," making Choice (A) the correct answer. All the other answer choices contain false statements.

472. **C. Most countries in the world are members of the United Nations.**

The question stem tells you that the United Nations' member countries include 193 out of the 195 countries in the world, making Choice (C) a factual statement. All of the other answer choices are opinions.

473. **C. August**

You can see from the graph that Tampa experiences its greatest average temperatures during August, making Choice (C) the correct answer.

474. **C. November, January**

You can see from the graph that Tampa's driest month is November (the lowest bar), whereas its coldest month is January, making Choice (C) the correct answer.

475. **C. The highest amount of rain occurs during summer, when the average temperatures are the highest.**

The hottest temperatures coincide with the highest amount of rain. You can see from the graph that Tampa experiences its greatest rainfall during summer, making Choice (C) the correct answer.

476. **B. farming and agriculture**

An unusually long spell of dry weather would affect the farming and agriculture industry the most because crops depend on water to grow. Hence, Choice (B) is the correct answer.

477. **D. United States**

The United States has never had a king or queen, making Choice (D) the correct answer. All the other countries listed have had a monarchy in the past.

478. **A. People cannot be trusted to defend their own freedoms and liberties.**

John Adams's main point was that people tend to take their freedoms for granted and lack the political understanding necessary to protect their rights. Hence, Choice (A) is the correct answer.

479. **C. the United States' entrance into World War I**

World War I began in 1914 and lasted until 1918, but the United States only joined the war in 1917. Millions of men were sent off to fight, and industries began producing weapons and war supplies. Hence, Choice (C) is the correct answer. The abolishment of slavery occurred in 1865, so you can eliminate Choice (A). Black Tuesday occurred in 1929, so you can reject Choice (B). World War II began in 1939 and lasted until 1945, so Choice (D) can also be eliminated.

480. **B. The sharp increase in unemployment in the early 1890s was due to the actions of incompetent leaders.**

Only Choice (B) contains an opinion rather than a factual statement. All the other choices contain factual statements that are backed up by the graph.

481. **C. protect and defend the Constitution of the United States**

The excerpt tells you that a new president must say, "I do solemnly swear (or affirm) that I will faithfully execute the office of President of the United States, and will to the best of my ability, preserve, protect and defend the Constitution of the United States." Hence, Choice (C) is the correct answer.

482. **C. be a white male**

The excerpt says, "No person except a natural born citizen, or a citizen of the United States [Choice (A)], at the time of the adoption of this Constitution, shall be eligible to the office of President; neither shall any person be eligible to that office who shall not have attained to the age of thirty five years [Choice (B)], and been fourteen Years a resident within the United States" [Choice (D)]. Hence, Choice (C) is the correct answer.

483. **B. an impeachment**

The excerpt says that "the President, Vice President and all civil officers of the United States, shall be removed from office on impeachment for, and conviction of, treason, bribery, or other high crimes and misdemeanors." Hence, Choice (B) is the correct answer. A *coup* is an illegal attempt to remove a president from office, so you can reject Choice (A). *Obstructionism* is where Congress tries to prevent the president from doing his job; it doesn't result in the removal of the president from office, so you can reject Choice (C). A misdemeanor is a minor crime that can lead to impeachment, so Choice (D) is incorrect.

484. **A. the vice president**

The excerpt says, "In case of the removal of the President from office, or of his death, resignation, or inability to discharge the powers and duties of the said office, the same shall devolve on the Vice President." Hence, Choice (A) is the correct answer.

485. **D. deserts**

Areas that receive very little rainfall per year are known as deserts, so Choice (D) is correct.

486. **A. Oregon and Washington**

You can see from the map that the states that receive the most precipitation per year are Oregon and Washington, so Choice (A) is correct.

487. **A. White settlers wanted to steal the lands in the eastern states that belonged to the Indians for their own use.**

As horrific as it may appear today, in the 1830s, the U.S. government decided that it wanted to take over the lands in the eastern states that had belonged to Native Americans for generations. When the Native Americans refused to leave, they were forcibly removed so that the white settlers could steal their land and use it for themselves. Hence, Choice (A) is correct. You are told that the native American Indian tribes were forcibly moved from their tribal lands in the east, so Choice (B) is incorrect. Whites were not interested in the health or the rights of the Native Americans, so Choice (C) is incorrect. Choice (D) is untrue.

488. **A. The Trail of Tears**

The name of the forced relocation of Native Americans in the 1830s that resulted in the deaths of thousands of Native-American men, women, and children was the Trail of Tears, making Choice (B) the correct answer.

489. **C. *Brown v. Board of Education***

Brown v. Board of Education was the Supreme Court decision that overturned the doctrine of "separate but equal" and led to the desegregation of United States public schools, so Choice (C) is correct. You can reject Choice (A) because the *Plessy v. Ferguson* decision agreed with the doctrine of "separate but equal." The *Roe v. Wade* decision referred to a woman's right to an abortion, so Choice (B) is incorrect. The *Miranda v. Arizona* decision referred to the rights of the criminally accused, so you can also reject Choice (D).

490. **B. legislative branch**

The Senate (along with the House of Representatives) is part of the legislative branch of government, making Choice (B) the correct answer. You can reject Choice (A) because the executive branch refers to the president, vice president, and Cabinet. You can also reject Choice (C) because the judicial branch refers to the Supreme Court and other federal courts. Choice (D) may be tempting, but the obstructionist branch is not a real branch of government.

491. **D. It grew slowly during the 1990s and then grew rapidly after the year 2000.**

You can see from the figure that foreign direct investment inflow to Africa grew slowly during the 1990s and then grew rapidly after the year 2000, making Choice (D) correct.

492. **B. African nations provide valuable resources that the American companies need.**

African countries have many natural resources (such as minerals and precious metals) that American companies need to manufacture their goods, making Choice (B) correct.

493. **C. Foreign investments in Africa should be increased to relieve the suffering of millions of Africans.**

Choice (C) is correct because it contains an opinion rather than a factual statement. All the other choices contain factual statements supported by the figure.

494. **C. win the electoral vote**

The passage says, "To become president of the United States, a candidate must win at least 270 electoral votes," so Choice (C) is correct. Winning the televised debates [Choice (A)] may appear to be helpful but doesn't always correlate to who eventually becomes president. Choices (B) and (D) may seem reasonable, but the passage tells you that five times in history, the candidate who won the popular vote did not become president.

495. **D. The number of electors that a state has depends on the population of that state.**

The passage says, "There are a total of 538 electors, corresponding to the 435 representatives and 100 senators" and that "the number of representatives per state depends on the population of that state." Hence, the states with the most electors are the states with the biggest populations, making Choice (D) correct.

496. **C. The number of representatives per state depends on the population of that state, whereas each state is given 2 senators.**

The passage says that "the number of representatives per state depends on the population of that state" and that there are 100 senators (two for each of the 50 states). Hence, Choice (C) is correct.

497. **A. January 20 following the election**

The passage says, "Congress certifies the Electoral College vote in January, which allows the new president to takes office on January 20." Choice (A) is correct.

498. **C. Twelfth Amendment**

The passage says, "The Twelfth Amendment requires each elector to cast one vote for president," so Choice (C) is correct.

499. **A. The House of Representatives will select the president.**

The passage says, "If no person receives an absolute majority of electoral votes for president, the Twelfth Amendment provides that the House of Representatives will select the president," making Choice (A) correct.

500. **D. to explain the purpose of the Constitution**

The preamble comes before the main body of the Constitution and explains the purpose of the entire document, so Choice (D) is correct.

501. **C. eliminate all the Native Americans.**

The preamble makes no mention of eliminating all the Native Americans, so Choice (C) is correct.

502. **B. North American Free Trade Agreement**

NAFTA stands for the North American Free Trade Agreement, which was implemented on January 1, 1994 to eliminate most tariffs on trade among Mexico, Canada, and the United States. Hence, Choice (B) is correct.

503. **B. limit the rights of African Americans**

The Jim Crow laws were a set of racist laws that sought to limit the rights of African Americans, making Choice (B) correct.

504. **monopoly**

A *monopoly* is defined as a market containing a single firm that has almost total control of the market.

505. **A. Communism is associated with state-owned industries, income redistribution, and classless society, whereas capitalism is associated with private ownership, profit motive, and competitive markets.**

Communism is associated with state-owned industries, income redistribution, and classless society, whereas capitalism is associated with private ownership, profit motive, and competitive markets. Therefore, Choice (A) is correct.

Chapter 3

506. **B. lift**

The lift force [Choice (B)] keeps the plane in the air and counterbalances the weight [Choice (C)] of the plane (which tries to pull the plane downward). The thrust force [Choice (D)] from the engines drives the plane forward. The drag force [Choice (A)] always opposes the direction of motion.

507. **B. There are no unbalanced forces acting on the plane.**

Newton's first law says that an object moving at constant velocity is not acted upon by an unbalanced force, so all the forces acting on the plane must cancel each other out, making Choice (B) the correct answer. The plane isn't weightless, because the Earth's gravitational force is still acting on the plane, making Choice (A) incorrect. If the lift were bigger than the weight, the plane would rise, but the plane is moving at a constant altitude, so Choice (C) must be wrong. If the thrust were bigger than the drag, the plane would accelerate, but the plane is moving at constant speed, so Choice (D) must be wrong.

508. **potential, kinetic, sound and heat**

As an object falls from a table to the floor, it loses its stored (potential) energy and gains kinetic energy as it begins to speed up. When the object hits the ground, it loses its energy of motion, which is converted into sound and heat energy.

509. **D. chloroplasts**

Plant cells contain organelles called *chloroplasts* that contain the chlorophyll needed for photosynthesis. This is how plants produce their own food. Cell walls [Choice (A)] and vacuoles [Choice (B)] help support the plant but aren't involved in photosynthesis. Also, both plant and animal cells contain mitochondria, so Choice (C) is incorrect.

510. **C. 75%**

Because the allele for tall plants (T) is dominant, any genotype that contains it, (Tt) or (TT), will result in tall plants. The Punnett square shows that three out of four (or 75%) of the offspring have genotypes containing the dominant allele; therefore, 75% of the offspring will be tall, making Choice (C) the correct answer.

511. **heterogeneous, tall**

The genotype of both parent plants is heterogeneous, which means that both parents will be tall.

Both parent plants have the genotype Tt, which means they are heterogeneous (one allele of each type). Because they both contain a dominant T allele, which represents tall plants, both plants will be tall.

512. **A. 0%**

Because both parent plants are homogeneous for the dominant T allele, they have only dominant T alleles to pass on to their offspring. Hence, 0 percent of the offspring will be short because none of them have the genotype tt, making Choice (A) the correct answer.

513. **A. the moon passing between the Earth and the sun**

Solar eclipses occur when the moon passes between the sun and the Earth, casting the moon's shadow on the Earth's surface, making Choice A correct.

Choice (B) would never happen because the sun is much farther away from the Earth than the moon is. Choice (C) is incorrect because although clouds may partially block the sun's rays (as on a cloudy day), they do not cause solar eclipses, which involve the total blockage of the sun's rays. Choice (D) would cause a lunar eclipse (not a solar eclipse) because the Earth would cast its shadow on the moon's surface.

514. **less than, the same**

An astronaut standing on the moon weighs less than she does on Earth but has the same mass as she has on Earth.

Weight is the pull of gravity on an object. Because the moon is smaller than the Earth, gravity on the moon is much smaller that it is on Earth. This makes an object weigh less on the moon than it does on Earth.

Mass measures how much matter an object has. Because the amount of matter hasn't changed, the astronaut has the same mass on the moon as she had on Earth.

515. **D. photosynthesis**

The equation shown is photosynthesis, which requires energy from sunlight. Plants use photosynthesis to convert carbon dioxide and water into glucose and oxygen. Choices (A) and (B) are incorrect because they represent the reverse reaction, in which cells break down glucose in the presence of oxygen and convert it back into water and carbon dioxide. This produces energy and ATP. Choice (C) describes the process by which metals emit electrons when light shines on them.

516. **C. endothermic reaction**

The equation shown is photosynthesis, which requires energy from sunlight. Because this reaction absorbs (takes in) energy, it's an endothermic reaction. Exothermic reactions, Choice (B), give out energy. Choices (C) and (D) are nuclear reactions, not chemical reactions.

517. **the sun, carbon dioxide and water, oxygen and glucose**

Plants use the energy from the sun to convert carbon dioxide and water into oxygen and glucose.

518. **D. carbon**

All life on Earth is carbon-based. Note that Choices (A) and (C) are not elements — they're compounds (more than one atom joined together).

519. **B. The distant galaxies are moving away from Earth.**

Choice (B) is correct because due to the Doppler effect, redshift occurs when an object emitting light is moving away from us.

Choice (A) is incorrect because the Hubble telescope is in orbit above Earth's atmosphere. Choice (C) is incorrect because due to the Doppler effect, blueshift occurs when an object emitting light is moving toward us. Choice (D) may be tempting, but there's no reason light from distant galaxies would need to reflect off Mars's surface before reaching us.

520. **A. alpha decay**

The question stem shows an alpha particle — a helium nucleus, ${}^{4}_{2}He$ — being emitted in the nuclear reaction, making Choice (A) correct.

521. **protons, neutrons**

The nuclei of two isotopes of an element contains the same number of protons but a different number of neutrons.

522. **A. 150 million kilometers**

Convert the time taken for the light to reach the Earth into seconds by multiplying by 60:

$$8 \text{ min} \times 60 \text{ s/min} = 480 \text{ s}$$

The distance traveled is equal to the speed multiplied by the time:

$$300{,}000\text{ km/s} \times 480\text{ s} = 144{,}000{,}000\text{ km}$$

This is approximately 150 million kilometers, making Choice (A) correct.

---

523. **C. The sun's energy reaches Earth via thermal radiation in the form of electromagnetic waves.**

Thermal radiation is the only method of heat transfer that can pass through the vacuum of outer space, making Choice (C) right. Conduction can occur only when two objects are in physical contact with each other, so Choice (A) is wrong. Convection current can't occur in a vacuum, so Choice (B) is wrong. Because conduction and convection do not occur across a vacuum, Choice (D) is incorrect.

---

524. **B. The sun produces energy via nuclear fusion reactions at its core.**

These reactions involve fusing smaller nuclei like hydrogen together to make larger nuclei like helium, making Choice (B) right. Nuclear fission involves splitting up larger nuclei, not fusing them together, so Choice (A) is incorrect. Combustion requires oxygen, which is present only in trace amounts in the sun, so Choice (C) is incorrect. The sun uses nuclear reactions, not chemical reactions (which involve valence electrons), so Choice (D) is wrong.

---

525. **D. The curvature of the Earth causes the sun's rays to spread out over a larger surface area at the poles compared to at the equator.**

When the sun's rays hit the Earth's surface at an angle (like at the poles), the heat energy from them is spread out over a larger area, making the temperatures cooler there. Hence, Choice (D) is the correct answer. Choices (B) and (C) are false statements. Choice (A) confuses cause with effect. The cold temperatures at the poles cause water to freeze into snow and ice; the snow and ice don't cool the air.

---

526. **C. DNA provides information to make proteins for the cell.**

DNA provides information to make proteins that the cell needs, so Choice (C) is correct. Cell walls are made from *cellulose,* not DNA, so Choice (A) is incorrect. DNA doesn't provide the energy for the cell's activities (ATP does), so Choice (B) is wrong. DNA isn't the building block for proteins in the cell (amino acids are), so Choice (D) is wrong.

---

527. **B. Use renewable energy sources such as wind or solar power.**

One of the causes of global warming is the increased emission of carbon dioxide into the atmosphere. Renewable fuel sources such as solar or wind power don't produce carbon dioxide, so this would reduce the amount of carbon dioxide released into the atmosphere, making Choice (B) correct.

Choice (A) is hilarious but incorrect. Greenhouses have nothing to do with releasing "greenhouse gases." Trees actually remove carbon dioxide from the air during photosynthesis, so cutting down trees would make the problem worse, not better, so Choice (C) is wrong. Burning additional fossil fuels would increase the amount of carbon dioxide released, so Choice (D) is wrong.

528. **B. protons**

The number of protons in the nucleus is called the *atomic number* because it determines which element that atom belongs to. For example, an atom of carbon always contains six protons. No other element has atoms that contain six protons.

529. **A. Convection currents within the Earth's fluid mantle caused the tectonic plates floating on the mantle to move relative to each other and separate**

Continental drift is caused by convection currents within the Earth's mantle, which made the tectonic plates (that float on top of the mantle) separate. Hence, Choice (A) is right.

Although human-caused global warming is a serious problem, it has only happened quite recently (within the last two centuries), whereas continental drift began 175 million years ago, making Choice (B) incorrect. The meteorite that may have killed off the dinosaurs smashed into Earth 65 million years ago, but Pangaea began drifting apart 175 million years ago, so Choice (C) is wrong. Similarly, the Big Bang happened 15 billon years ago, so Choice (D) is incorrect.

530. **D. The Big Bang theory states that all matter in the universe expanded outward from the same point in space.**

The Big Bang theory refers to the beginning of the universe, not the breakup of Pangaea, so Choice (D) is your answer. All the other choices add support to the single supercontinent theory.

531. **D. the Doppler effect**

The Doppler effect describes how the frequency of emitted waves appears to change when there is relative motion between the source and an observer; therefore, Choice (D) is right.

The waves are not reflecting (bouncing off a surface), so Choice (A) is false. The waves are not refracting (moving from one medium to another), so Choice (B) is false. The waves are not interfering with each other, so Choice (C) is false.

532. decrease, increase

As the ambulance moves *away from* the stationary observer, the frequency of the siren appears to decrease. As the ambulance moves *toward* the stationary observer, the frequency of the siren appears to increase.

533. D. organelle, cell, tissue, organ, organ system, organism

The basic and smallest unit of life is the cell, which is made up of organelles. An organ system consists of organs, which are made of tissue (collections of specialized cells that perform a particular function). The organism is the complete plant or animal.

534. C. the number of atoms

The law of conservation of mass states that matter is always conserved. For chemical equations, this means that the number of atoms of each type of element is the same at the end of the reaction as it was before the reaction; hence, Choice (C) is correct.

Choice (A) is not true because chemical reactions can produce gases. Choice (B) is tempting but incorrect. It's the number of *atoms,* not the number of *molecules,* that stays the same. Choice (D) is incorrect because exothermic reactions give off heat, causing the temperature of the surroundings to rise, and endothermic reactions take in heat, causing the temperature of the surroundings to fall.

535. C. fish, amphibians, reptiles, birds, mammals

The fossil record begins with fish, followed by amphibians. Then, as the shallow-water ecosystems that contained amphibians began to dry up, organisms had to leave the water, and reptiles evolved. Birds are believed to have evolved from reptiles, and lastly, mammals arrived on the scene.

536. D. the Industrial Revolution, which led to a sharp increase in the rate of combustion of fossil fuels

The Industrial Revolution caused a sharp increase in the consumption of fossil fuels (which produces carbon dioxide) and has caused a sudden increase in the amount of carbon dioxide released in the atmosphere, making Choice (D) correct.

Choice (A) is wrong because using renewable fuel sources would reduce the carbon dioxide emissions, not increase them. Although human respiration does add carbon dioxide to the air, it doesn't add as much as burning fossil fuels, so Choice (B) isn't the best answer. The amount of carbon dioxide released by missions to the moon was also negligible, so Choice (C) is incorrect.

537. C. respiration by plants and animals

From the diagram, you can see that both plant respiration and animal respiration release carbon dioxide into the atmosphere, so Choice (C) is correct.

Choice (A) is wrong because photosynthesis actually removes carbon dioxide from the air and converts it into glucose. The formation of fossils and fossil fuels helps to trap carbon below Earth's surface, so Choice (B) is incorrect. Burying waste in landfills traps the carbon beneath Earth's surface, so Choice (D) is wrong.

538. 46, meiosis, 23

The normal number of chromosomes in a human body cell is 46. When the sex cells (sperm and egg) are created during meiosis, the haploid number of chromosomes, 23, results.

All regular cells divide in the process called *mitosis*, but only sex cells are produced by the process called *meiosis*. Parent cells have 46 chromosomes, but the sex cells contain only half of that, or 23 chromosomes.

539. potential energy

The higher the pendulum, the more potential energy it has. When the pendulum bob is at the top of its swing, it has maximum potential energy, whereas when the pendulum bob is at its lowest point, it has maximum kinetic energy.

540. D. 6 m/s

The formula for potential energy is $PE = mgh$, where m is the mass, g is the acceleration due to gravity (approximately 9.8 m/s^2, which you can round to 10 m/s^2). The formula for kinetic energy is $KE = \frac{1}{2}mv^2$, where m is the mass and v is the velocity.

According to the law of conservation of energy, the loss in the potential energy equals the gain in kinetic energy; therefore, you can set these equations equal to each other and solve for v:

$$mgh = \frac{1}{2}mv^2$$
$$4(10)(1.8) = \frac{1}{2}(4)v^2$$

Solving for v gives you

$$72 = 2v^2$$
$$36 = v^2$$
$$6 = v$$

Choice (D) is correct.

ANSWERS 501–600

541. **C. $2Al + 3Cl_2 \rightarrow 2AlCl_3$**

The conservation of mass tells you that the number of atoms of each element must remain the same on both sides of the equation. Choice (C) is the correct answer because it has two aluminum atoms and six chlorine atoms before and after the reaction. Choices (A), (B), and (D) do not follow this rule, so they're incorrect.

542. **A. 4**

The number of valence electrons is given by the group number. Carbon is in Group 4 and therefore has four valence electrons.

543. **B. neon, based on its Group 8 status**

When an element reacts, it tries to gain a full number of valence electrons in its outer shell. Group 8 elements already have full outer shells and are therefore very unreactive.

544. **B. Sodium has 23 neutrons.**

Choices (A), (C), and (D) are all true statements and therefore can be rejected. Sodium has an atomic number of 11, so it has 11 protons and 11 electrons. Sodium is in the third row (Period 3), so it has three electron shells. The first shell can hold a maximum of two electrons.

Sodium has a mass number of 23, which equals the sum of the number of protons (11) and the number of neutrons (12); therefore, Choice (B) is not a true statement, making it the correct answer.

545. **B. Carbon reacts with hydrogen by sharing valence electrons to form covalent bonds.**

Carbon reacts with hydrogen by sharing valence electrons to form covalent bonds, so Choice (B) is a true statement and the correct answer.

Hydrogen bonds occur only between molecules, not within a molecule itself. Within the molecule, hydrogen atoms join together via covalent bonds, not hydrogen bonds, making Choice (A) a false statement. Potassium reacts with chlorine, but because potassium is a metal, it forms ionic bonds (not covalent bonds), making Choice (C) false. Magnesium won't react with argon because argon is in Group 8 and therefore already has a full outer shell (making it unreactive), so you can reject Choice (D).

546. **D. Jupiter is about half the size of the sun.**

Mercury is the closest planet to the sun, making Choice (A) a true statement. Saturn is a giant gas planet, so Choice (C) is true. Pluto is no longer considered to be a proper planet, so Choice (C) is also a true statement. The sun is much bigger than any of the planets (more than a million Earths could fit inside the sun!), so Choice (D) is a false statement.

547. **A. 0 N**

You can calculate the unbalanced force acting on each car by multiplying the mass by the acceleration (using $F = ma$). The green car has zero acceleration; therefore, the value of the unbalanced forces acting on it must be zero. The correct answer is Choice (A).

548. **A. red**

You can calculate the unbalanced force acting on each car by multiplying the mass by the acceleration (using $F = ma$). Because all the cars have the same mass, the car with the largest acceleration must have been subjected to the largest unbalanced force, making Choice (A) the correct answer.

549. **C. All the cars have the same inertia, but the green car has the smallest final momentum.**

The inertia of an object tells you how easy or difficult it is to change the object's state of motion. Linear inertia depends only upon the mass of the object. Because each car has the same mass, they all have the same interia.

The momentum of an object is given by the mass multiplied by the velocity $\left(p = mv\right)$. The green car has a final velocity of zero, which means it has zero momentum.

550. **C. 12 m/s**

The conservation of momentum states that the total momentum before the collision is equal to the total momentum after the collision. In this case, before the collision, the red car has a momentum of 24 kg·m/s ($p = mv$, where p is momentum, m is mass, and v is velocity), whereas the green car has zero momentum. After the collision, the red car has transferred all its momentum to the green car, so the green car now has a momentum of 24 kg·m/s. Because the green car has a mass of 2 kg, that means its velocity must be 12 m/s $\left(p = mv\right)$, making Choice (C) the right answer.

551. **C. the tilt of the Earth's axis of rotation**

Many people mistakenly believe that the distance of the Earth from the sun, Choice (A), is the main factor in seasonal changes, but this is actually not as important as the tilt in the Earth, Choice (C). The Earth's tilt is responsible for the sun shining more on one hemisphere in summer and then shining more on the other hemisphere in winter, which results in the seasonal changes in temperature. Hence, Choice (C) is correct.

Global warming can make each season hotter than before, but it doesn't cause the seasons to *change* from one to another, so Choice (B) is wrong. The movement of tectonic plates causes changes to the surface of the Earth but doesn't cause the change in seasons, so you can eliminate Choice (D).

552. **C. 5 billion years old**

There's a lot of evidence that supports the theory that the Big Bang created the universe approximately 15 billion years ago. The Earth was created about 10 billion years after the Big Bang, making it about 5 billion years old, so Choice (C) is the correct answer.

Choice (A) is the estimate given by some religious leaders, but you can reject this because the question asks for a scientific estimate. Also, the 6,000-year-old estimate makes little sense considering the evidence from fossils and carbon dating, which suggest the Earth is billions of years old, not thousands of years old. Choice (B) mistakes millions for billions and can therefore be rejected. Choice (D) is the estimate for the age of the universe, not the age of the Earth.

553. **A. sedimentary rock**

Fossils are produced when a plant or animal dies and its remains become buried in mud, silt, or sand, which forms sedimentary rock as the former plant or animal becomes compacted, making Choice (A) correct.

554. **C. Each type of rock is continuously transformed into the other types.**

The rock cycle describes the processes by which the Earth recycles rocks by transforming them from one type to another, making Choice (C) the correct answer.

555. **volcano, lava**

Magma is molten rock beneath the Earth's surface. Magma is sometimes expelled via a volcano up to the surface, where it is known as lava.

556. **D. The offspring of parents that reproduce sexually inherit a mix of traits from both parents.**

The offspring of parents that reproduce sexually inherit a mix of traits from both parents. This leads to a greater level of genetic diversity for the species because the genes of the offspring aren't identical to either of the parents'; hence, Choice (D) is correct. In contrast, the offspring from asexual reproduction inherit genes that are identical to their parent's. This does not lead to increased genetic diversity.

Choice (A) is false because the offspring of parents that reproduce sexually inherit traits from both parents. You can eliminate Choice (C) because the number of offspring doesn't have anything to do with their genetic diversity. You can reject Choice (B) because the offspring of parents that reproduce sexually do *not* inherit brand-new traits entirely unlike those of either parent (the offspring inherit a mix of traits).

557. B. The human eye can see only a small fraction of the electromagnetic spectrum.

Although Choices (A) and (D) are true statements, there's no support for these statements in the diagram. X-rays have shorter wavelengths than visible light, so Choice (C) is not true. Humans are able to see only the electromagnetic waves that are in the visible light region, which is only a small fraction of the overall spectrum, so Choice (B) is correct.

558. A. red light

According to the diagram, the energy of the waves decreases as you go from left to right. Out of the answer choices given, red light is the farthest to the right, making it the lowest energy wave of the four. Hence, Choice (A) is correct.

559. short, high, long, low

Gamma rays have <u>short</u> wavelengths and <u>high</u> frequencies, whereas radio waves have <u>long</u> wavelengths and <u>low</u> frequencies.

560. C. Radio waves have long wavelengths and are low-energy waves.

Electromagnetic waves all travel at the same speed, but they differ in their wavelengths. According to the diagram, radio waves have long wavelengths, so you can eliminate Choices (A) and (B). A short wavelength makes for a high-energy wave, and this makes them more dangerous because they can penetrate the human body and cause damage to the cells. If a wave of the electromagnetic spectrum has a long wavelength, it's unlikely to have high energy, so that makes Choice (D) incorrect and Choice (C) correct.

561. A. lithosphere

The *lithosphere* includes the upper part of the mantle and the tectonic plates that make up the surface of the Earth, so Choice (A) is correct.

The *biosphere* contains all life forms on Earth; the *hydrosphere* includes all the water vapor, water, and ice present on the Earth (including the oceans, rivers, and polar ice caps); and the *atmosphere* is the layer of gas surrounding the planet. None of these include the surface of the Earth itself, making Choices (B), (C), and (D) incorrect.

562. A and D. lunar eclipses and the appearance of Haley's comet

The moon and the planets and Haley's comet have cyclic orbits (orbits that repeat themselves), making their motion predictable, so lunar eclipses and the appearance of Haley's comet can be predicted with great accuracy.

The other two choices represent events that are unpredictable because they don't take place at regular intervals.

563. B. The phytoplankton are producers, the dragonflies are primary consumers, and the snakes are tertiary consumers.

Phytoplankton are microscopic plants; they're producers because they produce their own food. Dragonflies eat the plants and are therefore primary consumers. Snakes are higher in the food chain and eat several other consumers, making them tertiary consumers.

564. B. mayflies and dragonflies

If a virus were to suddenly wipe out most of the frog population, more mayflies and dragonflies would survive because fewer frogs would be around to eat them, making Choice (B) correct.

Snakes eat frogs, so the number of these animals would decline because one of their sources of food (the frogs) would be less abundant.

565. A. When an organism is eaten, most of the energy stored in its body is transferred to the biomass (flesh) of the consumer.

Only about 10 percent of the energy stored in an organism's body is transferred to the biomass (flesh) of the consumer. The rest is used for the metabolism of the consumer, making Choice (A) a false statement and therefore the correct answer.

Primary consumers eat plants and are therefore classified as herbivores, so you can reject Choice (B). Animals can't make their own food and must consume the energy stored in plants or other animals, so they're heterotrophs. Hence, you can reject Choice (C). Plants produce their own food and are therefore autotrophs (producers), making Choice (D) a true statement and therefore not the right answer.

566. C. the carrying capacity

The maximum number of individuals of a particular species that the ecosystem can handle is known as the *carrying capacity*, so Choice (C) is correct.

Predation refers to the relationship between hunters and prey, so Choice (A) is incorrect. *Natural selection* is the way in which species adapt and evolve in order to survive and pass on their genes to the next generation, which produces greater biodiversity (variations of organisms), but this doesn't answer the question, so you can reject Choices (B) and (C).

567. **C. DNA**

Although all the answer choices are useful in explaining evolution, DNA had not been discovered in Darwin's time, so it couldn't have been part of his explanation, making Choice (C) the correct answer.

568. **D. 8.6 years**

Because Sirius is 8.6 light-years away from Earth, the light from the star takes 8.6 years to reach the Earth

569. **D. The star is moving toward Earth.**

According to the Doppler effect, the frequency of the light emitted from moving objects will shift toward either the red end of the spectrum or the blue end (depending on the direction of motion). Objects that are moving away from Earth are red-shifted. Objects that are traveling toward Earth are blue-shifted, making Choice (D) the correct answer.

Blue-shifted light doesn't tell you how hot the star is, so you can reject Choice (A). Light always travels at 300,000 km per second in a vacuum, so Choice (B) is incorrect.

570. **D. sound waves left over from the Big Bang.**

Choices (A), (B), and (C) all provide evidence supporting the Big Bang theory and can therefore be rejected. The discovery of cosmic microwave background radiation is predicted by the Big Bang theory, so Choice (A) is true. The Doppler effect showing that starlight is red-shifted supports the idea that the galaxies have all been moving away from each other since the Big Bang occurred, so Choice (B) is true. Spectral analysis of starlight showing a relative abundance of hydrogen and helium supports the Big Bang theory, which predicts that the first elements to be created would be the lightest ones (hydrogen and helium). This makes Choice (C) a true statement. Sound waves can't travel through the vacuum of space, so Choice (D) is a false statement and therefore the correct answer.

571. **C. star, solar system, galaxy, universe**

A solar system consists of at least one star and the planets that orbit it, so stars are smaller than solar systems. This makes Choices (A) and (B) incorrect. A galaxy contains millions of stars and is therefore bigger than a solar system. The universe contains all the galaxies (and everything else), so the universe is the largest and must come last in the list, making Choice (C) correct.

572. **A. Scientists believe that of all the species on Earth that have ever existed, 99 percent of them are now extinct.**

Although scientists believe that 99 percent of all species that have ever lived on Earth are now extinct, this doesn't give any support to the common ancestry theory, making Choice (A) the correct answer. Because all organisms on Earth have a large percentage of their DNA identical to that of other species, this suggests that they all evolved from a single species, which supports the common ancestry theory. Hence, Choice (C) is not the right answer. If we all have a common ancestor, it's not surprising that a lot of different animal species start out looking the same as embryos or that many different animals have similar anatomical structures. Hence, you can reject Choices (B) and (D).

573. **D. a catalyst**

A catalyst speeds up the rate of the reaction by decreasing the activation energy needed for the reactants to turn into products, making Choice (D) the correct answer. Noble gases are a group of unreactive gases with full outer shells, but they are not usually involved in speeding up reactions, so you can reject Choice (A). A compound is a group of two or more different atoms bonded together, whereas an alloy is a metallic substance made from two or more metals, so you can reject Choices (B) and (C).

574. **D. Higher global temperatures cause the polar ice caps, which reflect sunlight back into space, to melt, leading to further global warming.**

A positive feedback mechanism occurs when an initial change in one system leads to responses from other systems that amplify the initial change in the first system. Only Choice (D) is an example of this.

575. **B. The iron bar becomes magnetized.**

When the switch is closed in Circuit 1, electricity flows through the coil, which will magnetize the iron bar, turning it into an electromagnet. There is no bulb in Circuit 2, so Choice (A) is wrong. Iron is a metal, so it will conduct electricity, making Choice (C) a false statement. Iron has a very high melting point, so Choice (D) is unlikely.

576. **C. The magnets will attract each other.**

Like poles repel, and unlike poles attract. Choice (C) is correct because the student placed two unlike poles facing each other (a north pole and a south pole). Magnets don't give off electromagnetic radiation, so Choice (B) is false.

577. **B. The light bulb lights up because electricity is created.**

Moving magnets can generate electricity (this is how power stations work); hence, the light bulb in Circuit 2 will light up as the magnet moves into and out of the coil, making Choice (B) the correct answer. Choice (C) occurs when an electric current produces a magnet (not the other way around), and Choice (D) is a false statement because the magnet is unharmed.

578. **B. Away from the magnet's north pole**

Magnetic field lines come out of the north pole of a magnet and go into the south pole. The plotting compass will align itself in the direction of these magnetic field lines, so Choice (B) is correct.

579. **B. integumentary system**

The integumentary system is the protective layer of the body including the skin, hair, and nails, so Choice (B) is correct. The digestive system is involved in breaking down food into nutrients, but it isn't involved in protecting the body from the outside, so you can reject Choice (A). The circulatory system transports nutrients dissolved in the blood to all the cells of the body but doesn't protect against damage, so Choice (C) is incorrect. The muscular system is responsible for the movement of the body itself, so Choice (D) is incorrect.

580. **C. What causes the formation of stalactites in underground caverns?**

The information in the question stem tells you how stalactites are formed in underground caves; therefore, Choice (C) is the correct answer. There's nothing in the information regarding stalagmites, so you can reject Choices (A) and (D). Similarly, there's no information on how tall stalactites can become, so you can reject Choice (B).

581. **C. the two liquids mixed together.**

When a chemical reaction takes place, there is often a temperature change, a color change, or a gas given off, so you can reject Choices (A), (B), and (D). Liquids can mix together without reacting chemically, so Choice (C) is the right answer.

582. **C. 20 N**

The force due to gravity acting on the 2 kg mass is equal to the weight of the block (mg, where m is the mass and g is the acceleration due to gravity). Because g is $9.8\,m/s^2$, which is approximately equal to $10\,m/s^2$, the weight is $mg = 2 \times 10 = 20$; therefore, Choice (C) is correct.

583. A. $0\,m/s^2$

Because both the pulling force and the frictional force are the same magnitude (size) but are acting in opposite directions, they will cancel each other out. Therefore, there will be no unbalanced forces acting on the block. Because there are no unbalanced forces, there will be no acceleration, making Choice (A) the correct answer.

584. **C. The pulling force must be equal to the frictional force, and the weight of the object is equal to the normal reaction force.**

Because the block is moving with constant velocity, it isn't accelerating. Newton's laws tell you that if there are no net forces acting on the block, each pair of forces in each direction (up and down or left and right) must cancel each other out and therefore be equal to each other.

585. **B. 12 N**

Newton's second law tells you that $F = ma$, where F equals the net or unbalanced force. Because you're told that the mass is 2 kg and the acceleration is $4\,m/s^2$, you know that the net force must equal 8 N via

$$F = 2 \times 4 = 8$$

In this question, the net force equals the pulling force minus the friction:

$$\text{net force} = \text{pulling force} - \text{friction}$$

Let x equal the friction; then solve for x:

$$8 = 20 - x$$
$$x = 12$$

586. **C. 50%**

Because the trait for wrinkly seeds is recessive, only those offspring that are homozygous (rr) for the gene will have wrinkly seeds. From the Punnett square, you can see that two out of four offspring (50 percent) are homozygous for wrinkly seeds, making Choice (C) correct. Offspring that are heterozygous would have round seeds because they contain a dominant round gene (R), which is always expressed in the phenotype when present.

587. **C. One parent plant is heterozygous, and the other is homozygous.**

One parent plant has two genes for wrinkly seeds, (rr), and is therefore homozygous (same genes). The other parent plant has one gene of each type, (Rr), and is therefore heterozygous (different genes).

588. **A. 0%**

Both the parent plants have wrinkly seeds. The trait for wrinkly seeds appears only when the pea plant is homozygous (rr) for this recessive gene. There is zero possibility that their offspring will have round seeds because both parent plants will pass on an (r) gene to their offspring, making Choice (A) the correct answer.

589. **C. 75%**

Both the parent plants are heterozygous (Rr). If you draw the Punnett square, you see that the offspring have the following genotypes: (RR), (Rr), (Rr), and (rr). Because three out of the four offspring (75 percent) contain the dominant R gene, they will have round seeds. Hence, Choice (C) is the correct answer.

590. **A. microgram, milligram, gram, kilogram**

A microgram is 10^{-6} (a millionth) of a gram, so it's the smallest of the listed units. A milligram is 10^{-3} (a thousandth) of a gram. A kilogram is 10^3 (a thousand) times bigger than a gram.

591. **B. Plot B**

Plot B shows a strong positive correlation between the variables because the data points are close to the line (strong correlation) and the line is sloping upward, indicating a positive correlation.

592. **D. Plot D**

Plot D shows a strong negative correlation between the variables because the data points are close to the line (strong correlation) and the line is sloping downward, indicating a negative correlation.

593. **A. Plot A**

In Plot A, each data point appears to be randomly positioned, showing that there's no correlation between the variables. Plot C is similar but slopes downward, showing a weak negative correlation between the variables. Both Plot B and Plot D show strong correlations between the variables.

594. **C. Correlation exists between two variables that happen together and may be related.**

Choice (C) is the definition of *causation.*

Choice (A) is incorrect because even when two variables are correlated, one may increase while the other decreases.

Choice (B) is incorrect. Just because two items are correlated doesn't mean that causation exists between them.

Choice (D) is incorrect. Causation is a proven cause-and-effect relationship between two variables.

595. D. CH_4 has 1 carbon atom and 4 hydrogen atoms.

Choice (A) is incorrect because CO_2 has 1 carbon atom (not chlorine) and 2 oxygen atoms.

Choice (B) is incorrect because H_2O has 2 hydrogen atoms and 1 oxygen atom (not the other way around).

Choice (C) is incorrect because $C_6H_{12}O_6$ has 6 carbon atoms (not chlorine), 12 hydrogen atoms, and 6 oxygen atoms.

Choice (D) is correct. CH_4 has 1 carbon atom and 4 hydrogen atoms.

596. B. beta decay

The question stem shows a beta particle $\left({}^{0}_{-1}e \right)$ being emitted in the nuclear reaction, making Choice (B) correct.

597. D. protons and neutrons

There are no electrons in the nucleus of the atom, so you can reject Choices (A) and (B). Alpha particles are emitted by some radioactive elements, but they don't determine the mass number of an element, so Choice (C) is incorrect.

598. B. Arctic foxes with thinner coats did not survive because they were not well-suited to the harsh conditions of their environment.

Natural selection is the process by which individuals who are better adapted to their environment tend to survive and produce more offspring than those who are not well adapted. The foxes with the thicker coats were better adapted to the cold conditions of the Arctic than the foxes with thinner coats. Even if the statements in Choices (A), (C), and (D) were true (and they probably aren't), they would still be unrelated to natural selection.

599. C. Fur traps a layer of air next to the animal's body, which keeps it warm because air is a poor conductor of heat.

The layer of air trapped by the fur is a poor conductor of heat, so it prevents the fox's body heat from escaping, making Choice (C) the correct answer. Choice (D) would make the fox colder, not warmer. Choices (A) and (B) don't make sense because heat flows from hot objects (the fox) to cold objects (the surroundings), not the other way around.

600. **C. Black fur provides an excellent contrast with the white background of the Arctic snow.**

Choice (C) is the correct answer because the contrast of the black fur against the white environment would not be an advantage to the fox; it would make it harder for the fox to catch its prey or avoid being captured by a predator. Therefore, you can eliminate Choices (B) and (D). You can also reject Choice (A) because it explains why black fur would not be an advantage in a cold environment.

601. **C. a skydiver who has already reached terminal velocity and is falling at a constant speed toward the ground**

Because the skydiver has already reached terminal velocity, he is falling at a constant speed toward the ground, which means there are no unbalanced forces acting on him (his weight is balanced out by the air resistance), making Choice (C) correct. Choice (A) is an example of Newton's second law because there's an unbalanced force acting on the train, which slows it down. Choice (B) is an example of the conservation of momentum, not Newton's law of inertia, and Choice (D) shows that the rocket must have an unbalanced force acting on it because it's speeding up.

602. **A. Its charge would become negative.**

All atoms are neutral because they contain the same number of positively charged protons in their nucleus and negatively charged electrons in their electron shells. But if an atom gains an electron, it will no longer be neutral because the negative charge from the additional electron will change the atom into a *cation* (a negatively charged atom).

603. **C. London dispersion bonds, dipole-dipole bonds, hydrogen bonds, ionic bonds**

London dispersion bonds are the weakest of the *intermolecular bonds* (bonds between different molecules), followed by dipole-dipole interactions and then hydrogen bonds. Ionic bonds are a type of *intramolecular bond* (a bond between the atoms of a single molecule), which is stronger than intermolecular bonds.

604. **C. kilowatt**

The kilowatt is a unit of power; therefore, Choice (C) is correct.

605. **C. Group 2 was the experimental group, and Group 1 was the control group.**

The control group is the one that is not exposed to the variable that is being tested (the potential new drug); therefore, Group 1 is the control group because its members received fake pills instead.

606. **D. The drug may lower blood pressure in men.**

The drug was given only to a relatively small group of women, so you can't say with any certainty that it does not reduce blood pressure in men; hence, you can reject Choices (A) and (B).

Choice (C) may be tempting, but you can't be sure that the drug doesn't lower women's blood pressure, because you have the results of only a single experiment. (More experiments would need to be performed before you could say this for sure.)

That leaves Choice (D) as the correct answer. Notice that Choice (D) only says that the drug *may* lower blood pressure in men, not that it *does* lower blood pressure in men.

607. **D. The members of the experimental group and the control group were not similar enough.**

Ideally, the members of both the experimental group and the control group should be as similar as possible, but in this case, Group 1 consisted entirely of men while Group 2 consisted entirely of women. A drug that works well for males may not work well for females (or vice versa), so Choice (D) is correct.

You can reject Choice (A) because one of the groups has to act as the control group and therefore should not be given the drug being tested. You can reject Choice (B) because all the members should have diabetes so the pharmaceutical company can test how well the drug works. Choice (C) can be rejected because results from larger groups are more reliable than results from smaller groups.

608. **D. Swap 100 of the males from Group 1 with 100 of the females from Group 2.**

A drug can work differently for males and females, so Choice (D) would eliminate the source of error by ensuring that each group has the same number of men and women.

609. **D. It was found that the fish raised in elevated carbon dioxide levels did not avoid the sound of the predators.**

One possible reason that the fish raised in the elevated carbon dioxide levels did not avoid the sounds of the predators was that their hearing had been affected by the increased acidity of the water, making Choice (D) the correct answer.

You can reject Choice (A) because it's a claim rather than an inference from the experiment. Choices (B) and (C) simply give details of the experiment but do not give any findings that an inference could be based upon.

610. **A. An increase in ocean acidity causes a decrease in predator avoidance in fish.**

The experiment simply shows that fish raised in elevated carbon dioxide levels (increased acidity) did not avoid the sounds of the predators as much as fish raised in normal levels of acidity. Note that you cannot conclude with any certainty that this was due to a decrease in the fish's hearing (further experiments would be needed to confirm that).

611. **B. The independent variable of the experiment was the carbon dioxide level in each tank, and the dependent variable was the position of the fish in the tank.**

The *independent variable* (also known as the *manipulated variable*) is the one that is controlled and changed by the experimenter. In this case, the scientists controlled the carbon dioxide level in each tank. The *dependent variable* (also known as the *responding variable*) is the one that changes based upon changes to the independent variable. The dependent variable is the variable that is measured by the experimenters. In this case, the scientists measured the position of the fish to see how the level of the carbon dioxide in each tank affected this dependent variable.

612. **C. glucose**

The compound is glucose, so Choice (C) is correct.

613. **B. water**

The compound is water, so Choice (B) is correct.

614. **C. carbon dioxide**

The compound is carbon dioxide, so Choice (C) is correct.

615. **C. aerobic respiration**

The equation shown is aerobic respiration because oxygen is one of the reactants. Plant and animal cells use aerobic cellular respiration (when oxygen is available) to convert glucose into the energy, water, and carbon dioxide, so Choice (C) is correct.

You can reject Choice (A) because photosynthesis is the opposite reaction that plants use to create glucose. You can reject Choice (B) because anaerobic respiration occurs without the presence of oxygen. And you can reject Choice (D) because glucose is not a fossil fuel.

616. **C. $2Al + 3O_2 \rightarrow 2Al_2O_3$**

The conservation of mass tells you that the number of atoms of each element must remain the same on both sides of the equation. Choice (C) is the correct answer because it has only 2 aluminum atoms on the left-hand side of the equation but has 4 aluminum atoms on the right-hand side of the equation.

Choices (A), (B), and (D) all follow the conservation of mass.

617. **C. 15 billion years old**

There's a lot of evidence that supports the theory that the Big Bang created the universe approximately 15 billion years ago, so Choice (C) is correct.

618. **C. A blue shirt reflects blue light.**

Black is not a real color (it is merely the absence of light), so you can reject Choices (A) and (B). You can also eliminate Choice (D) because a red shirt reflects red light; it doesn't absorb it.

619. **C. The white shirt reflects more of the sun's energy, helping the person to stay cooler.**

You can reject Choice (A) because the question tells you that the shirts are made from the same material. Choice (B) can also be rejected because you're also told that wearing black (not white) makes you feel cooler. Choice (D) is funny but doesn't answer the question.

620. **A. a higher frequency and a shorter wavelength and carries more energy.**

Red light has a longer wavelength than blue light, but blue light has a higher frequency and carries more energy than red light. Hence, Choice (A) is correct.

621. **D. Do a DNA analysis.**

Choice (D) is correct because identical twins would have identical DNA.

You can reject Choice (A) because blood glucose levels vary during the day (depending upon what you eat), and they don't give any indication of whether people are related. You can reject Choice (B) because sisters can look very similar to each other, and that doesn't necessarily mean that they're identical twins. The family history will be the same for all siblings, so Choice (C) can be rejected.

622. B. The water evaporated, leaving salt behind.

Brine contains dissolved salt. When the water boils, the salt gets left behind at the bottom of the pan; the white residue is the salt, making Choice (B) the correct answer.

Rust is brown, not white, and would not occur so quickly; therefore, you can reject Choice (A). Water doesn't burn, so you can also reject Choice (C). There's no evidence that the pan was dirty, so you can reject Choice (D).

623. A. downward

According to Newton's second law, the acceleration of an object (in this case, the elevator) is always in the same direction as the unbalanced force. Because the elevator is initially accelerating downward, the unbalanced force must also be acting downward, so Choice (A) is correct.

624. D. There is no unbalanced force.

Because the elevator is traveling at a constant speed, the acceleration is zero. According to Newton's second law, when the acceleration of an object (in this case, the elevator) is zero, the unbalanced force must also be zero (there is no unbalanced force); therefore, Choice (D) is correct.

625. B. less than her usual weight.

The reading on the scale measures the mass of the object multiplied by its acceleration (mg, where g is the acceleration due to gravity). This usually equals the weight of the object, but when the object is accelerating downward, the reading becomes less than the real weight. (Think of the extreme case in which the cord of the elevator has snapped, the brakes are out, and you, the scale, and the elevator are in free-fall. Your feet would no longer be pressing down on the scale, so it would read zero.) Hence, Choice (B) is correct.

626. 750 N

Because the elevator is traveling at a constant speed, the acceleration is zero. Therefore, the reading on the scale will show Angela's correct weight, which equals 750 N (newtons).

627. C. tree

An organism is alive. The only living thing listed in the answer choices is a tree, so Choice (C) is the correct answer.

628. **A. the ball on the moon would travel farther and higher**

The acceleration due to gravity on the moon is much less, so the ball will be able to reach a greater height on the moon compared to on Earth. Hence, you can reject Choices (B) and (C).

Because the moon has no air resistance, the ball will be able to travel farther on the moon compared to on Earth. Hence, Choice (A) is correct.

629. **B. The ice was melting and was using the heat to break the bonds between its molecules.**

Ice melts at 0° Celsius. As it melts, all the heat is used to break the bonds that hold the ice molecules together as a solid. Once the bonds have been broken, the water molecules can move over each other; the ice has changed into water, so Choice (B) is correct.

You can reject Choice (A) because you were told that the ice was heated continuously throughout the experiment. Although some of the heat may escape, most of it is being used to break the bonds as the ice melts, so Choice (C) can be rejected. Water boils at 100° (not 0°) so you can reject Choice (D).

630. **C. The water was boiling.**

Water boils at 100° Celsius. As it boils, all the heat is used to break the bonds that hold the water molecules together as a liquid. Once the bonds have been broken, the water molecules can escape from the container; the water has changed into steam, so Choice (C) is correct.

631. **C. C**

During the period marked by letter C on the graph, the ice has already melted but is not yet hot enough to have turned into steam, so Choice (C) is correct.

Choice (A) represents the part of the experiment where the entire sample was still solid ice, so Choice (A) can be rejected. Choice (B) represents the part of the experiment where the ice is melting, so Choice (B) can be rejected. Choice (D) represents the part of the experiment where the water is boiling, so Choice (D) can be rejected.

632. **C. a lower density and contains molecules that are father apart.**

A gas has a lower density compared to a liquid or a solid, and gas molecules are father apart than the molecules in either liquids or solids. Hence, Choice (C) is correct.

633. **D. An extra day is added to keep the calendars accurate because the Earth actually takes 365.25 days to orbit the sun.**

The Earth actually takes 365.25 days (not 365 days) to orbit the sun, so after four years, the calendars would be off by one day if we didn't add an extra day. Hence, Choice (D) is the correct answer.

You can reject Choices (A) and (B) because they don't make any sense. Choice (C) can also be rejected because the moon takes about a month (not 365.25 days) to travel around the Earth.

634. **B. to kill bacteria**

If Jim follows the correct procedure, he'll process the jar of jelly in the pressure cooker for several minutes. The high temperature will kill bacteria that would have caused the jelly to spoil, so Choice (B) is correct.

635. **C. centripetal force**

Whenever an object moves in a circular path, the force that keeps it moving in a circle is called the *centripetal force*, so Choice (C) is correct.

636. **A. proton**

Only protons and neutrons are found in the nuclei of atoms, so you can reject Choices (C) and (D). Hydrogen is the only atom that does not contain any neutrons, so Choice (B) can be rejected. A hydrogen nucleus contains one proton, making Choice (A) the correct answer.

637. **B. biosphere**

The biosphere contains all life forms on Earth, so Choice (B) is correct.

The *lithosphere* includes the upper part of the mantle and the tectonic plates that make up the surface of the Earth; the *hydrosphere* includes all the water vapor, water, and ice present on Earth (including the oceans, rivers, and polar ice caps); and the *atmosphere* is the layer of gas surrounding the planet. None of these include the life forms, making Choices (A), (C), and (D) incorrect.

638. **C. pulley**

Only Choice (C) is a simple machine. A pulley is a simple machine that reduces the force needed to lift a heavy object and/or changes the direction of the force.

Cars and computers are complex machines; therefore, you can reject Choices (A) and (D). A tiger is a living organism, not a simple machine, so you can also reject Choice (B).

639. **D. started small, then increased rapidly before it became constant.**

You can see from the graph that the bacteria population started small, then increased rapidly, and then became constant. Hence, Choice (D) is correct.

You can reject Choice (A) because the curve shows that the population did not grow at a constant rate. You can reject Choice (B) because the population did not grow exponentially. You can reject Choice (C) because the population was not zero at the beginning.

640. **A. The population had reached the environment's carrying capacity.**

The *carrying capacity* is defined as the maximum number of organisms that an environment can support. According to the graph, the population of bacteria leveled off after a while, which suggests that the carrying capacity had been reached, making Choice (A) the correct answer.

There is nothing in the question stem to suggest that predators are present in the experiment or that the offspring had mutated, so you can reject Choices (B) and (D). You can also reject Choice (C) because additional nutrients would allow even more bacteria to grow.

641. **D. lime juice and vinegar**

The pH scale tells you whether a substance is acidic (pH value less than 7), neutral (pH value equal to 7), or basic (pH value greater than 7). Choice (D) correctly lists the two substances whose pH values are below 7, meaning they're acidic.

642. **D. 2.0 grams per liter**

On the graph, imagine drawing a horizontal line at 20 degrees until it reaches the curve for substance B. Then imagine drawing a vertical line from that point until it reaches the *x*-axis. The vertical line cuts the *x*-axis at approximately 2.0 grams per liter, making Choice (D) the correct answer.

643. **D. gases appears to decrease, but the solubility of solids appears to increase.**

You can see from the graph that the curves for the two gases (substances A and B) slope downward as the temperature of the water increases. This means that they're becoming less soluble. The curve for the solid (substance C) slopes upward as the temperature of the water increases. This means that it's becoming more soluble.

644. **Gases are more soluble in cold water than in warm water, so the air bubbles that were dissolved in the cold water began to come out of the solution as the water warmed up overnight.**

645. **B. The temperature of the water appears to have a large effect on the solubility of some substances.**

Only Choice (B) is supported by the information in the graph because the solubility of the three substances changes when the temperature changes.

Choice (A) can be rejected because the graph shows that the three substances dissolve at different rates in water. You can also reject Choice (C) because pressure isn't mentioned anywhere in the graph. Similarly, the graph gives no information as to whether water is the best solvent for any substance, so you can eliminate Choice (D).

646. **D. a hookworm that lives in the intestines of a human and drinks blood, depriving the human of nutrients**

Choice (D) describes a parasite that causes harm to its host.

You can reject Choice (A) because the flower benefits from receiving pollen from other flowers, which helps it to reproduce. Choice (B) can be rejected because the human benefits from receiving the vitamin K that the bacteria produce. Choice (C) can be rejected because the human benefits from the company of the dog.

647. **C. The products have less potential energy than the reactants.**

You can see from the graph that the reactants have more potential energy than the products, making Choice (C) the correct answer; Choice (D) is therefore wrong. The graph makes no mention of kinetic energy, so you can reject Choice (A). The amount of potential energy rises (not drops) midway through the reaction, making Choice (B) incorrect.

648. **B. exothermic reaction**

Because the reactants have more potential energy than the products and the extra energy is released, this must be an exothermic reaction, making Choice (B) the correct answer. An endothermic reaction would absorb energy (not release it), so you can reject Choice (A). You can reject Choices (C) and (D) because these refer to nuclear reactions, not chemical reactions.

649. **A. It decreases the activation energy, making it easier for the reactants to turn into products.**

A catalyst speeds up the rate of the reaction by decreasing the activation energy needed for the reactants to turn into products, making Choice (A) the correct answer.

650. **C. A 59-year-old woman with diabetes who has had six miscarriages but has five children**

According to the definition, the most evolutionarily fit individual has produced the most living offspring and has therefore made the greatest contribution to the gene pool of the next generation. Out of the individuals mentioned in the answer choices, the person in Choice (C) has produced the most living children.

651. **B. the wing of an eagle and the wing of a bee**

Choice (B) describes a pair of analogous structures because they both perform the same function (flying) yet belong to different animals that evolved separately.

Choice (A) can be rejected because it refers to where the animals live rather than the animals' body parts. Choice (C) may be tempting, but it refers to the same body part from the same species rather than different species. You can reject Choice (D) because it refers to body parts that do not perform the same function.

652. **C. 44%**

Of the components listed, only the red blood cells (42%) and white blood cells (2%) are cells. The sum of these two components gives you 44%; hence, Choice (C) is correct.

653. **D. A newly hatched goose follows a balloon that it saw shortly after it was born.**

The passage tells you that imprinting refers to a type of behavior seen in young birds when they're exposed to an object that they assume is their mother. Choice (D) correctly describes an example of imprinting and is therefore the correct answer. Choices (A) and (C) do not refer to birds and can therefore be rejected. Although Choice (B) refers to a bird, the duck isn't young enough to be imprinting, and its described behavior isn't an example of imprinting.

654. **D. It will decrease because there will not be enough food to feed the lions.**

You're told that the virus doesn't affect the lions, so you can reject Choices (B) and (C). Choice (A) can also be rejected because the lions don't compete with the zebras for food — the zebras are their food! Therefore, if the zebras are killed by the virus, the lion population will decrease because there will be less food for the lions. That means Choice (D) is correct.

655. **B. Fewer plants will be available for humans to eat because plants depend upon the bees to reproduce.**

You're told that approximately one-third of the human food supply consists of plants that bees pollinate. If the global population of bees begins to decline sharply, fewer plants will be pollinated; there will be fewer plants available for humans to eat, making Choice (B) the correct answer. Bees don't eat plants, so you can reject Choice (A). Although Choices (C) and (D) may be true, they aren't the most important consequences.

656. **B. bend towards the light**

Because the growth hormone is concentrated on the shady side of the plant, the cells there will begin to elongate and grow faster than the cells on the sunny side. As a result, the plant stem will begin to bend toward the light, making Choice (B) the correct answer.

657. **D. covalent bonding**

When carbon reacts to form methane, it shares its electrons with hydrogen. This is known as covalent bonding; hence, Choice (D) is the correct answer. Ionic bonding usually occurs when metals react with nonmetals, so you can reject Choice (A). *Carbon bonding* is a made-up term, so you can eliminate Choice (C) as well. Hydrogen bonding forms intermolecular bonds (between different molecules), not intramolecular bonds (within one molecule), so Choice (B) is wrong.

658. **B. 25%**

Because the allele for purple flowers, P, is dominant, any genotype that contains it (Pp or PP) will result in purple flowers. The Punnett square shows that three out of four (or 75 percent) of the offspring have genotypes containing the dominant allele; hence, 75 percent of the offspring will have purple flowers. That leaves only one out of four (or 25 percent) of the offspring with the recessive (pp) genotype that will result in white flowers, making Choice (B) the correct answer.

659. **C. The genotype of the offspring with white flowers is homogeneous, whereas the parent plants are heterogeneous.**

Both parent plants have the genotype Pp, which means they're heterogeneous (with one allele of each type). Because the white allele is recessive, the offspring with white flowers must contain only recessive alleles (pp), so it's homogeneous.

660. A. 0%

Both parent plants are white; therefore, they must be homogeneous for the recessive p allele and have the genotype pp. Because they have only recessive p alleles to pass on to their offspring, 0 percent of the offspring will have purple flowers — neither of the parents could pass on the dominant P. Hence, Choice (A) is the correct answer.

661. A. 0%

Because the allele for purple flowers, P, is dominant, any genotype that contains it (Pp or PP) will result in purple flowers, not pink flowers. If an offspring does not contain the dominant allele, it will have white flowers, not pink or purple flowers; hence, Choice (A) is the correct answer.

662. C. Earth's magnetic poles are at different locations than the geographic poles.

Earth's geographical poles have not changed their position, because the North Pole is always at the top of the planet and the South Pole is always at the bottom. You are told, however, that the magnetic poles have changed their locations, so they must be at different locations than the geographic poles, making Choice (C) the correct answer.

The information gives no indication that the core is shifting toward the surface or that all magnets are made of iron, so you can reject Choices (A) and (B). Choice (D) can also be eliminated because there is no reason to believe that compasses will no longer be affected by the Earth's magnetic field.

663. A. Sexual reproduction produces a greater variety of offspring.

Sexual reproduction allows for more variations in the species than asexual reproduction does because in sexual reproduction, genes from both parents are combined to produce the offspring. Hence, Choice (A) is correct and Choice (B) can be rejected. You can also eliminate Choices (C) and (D) because sexual reproduction results in fewer offspring and is generally harder to accomplish.

664. C. a telescope

A telescope is an optical instrument that allows you to see objects that are very far away, so Choice (C) is correct. Electron microscopes are useful for viewing very small objects (like the structure of proteins) but are not useful for looking at the moon, so you can reject Choice (A). A lens with a short focal length might make a good magnifying glass for small objects that are nearby but would not be useful for viewing the moon, so you can reject Choice (B). Although the naked eye can be used to view the moon, it is not as good as a telescope, so Choice (D) can be rejected.

665. **B. steel**

The car with the largest mass will be the heaviest because weight equals the mass multiplied by the acceleration due to gravity. You can see from the table that the heaviest car belongs to Contestant 2, who built his car from steel. Hence, Choice (B) is correct.

666. **D. Each contestant began with the same potential energy.**

Each contestant has the same combined mass (60 kg) when you add the mass of the car and the mass of the driver. The contestants also all start from the same height on the hill (20 m), so you get the same answer when you substitute the given values into the equation for the potential energy ($PE = mgh$), making Choice (D) the correct answer.

667. **D. Contestant 2 has the greatest ratio of car mass to driver mass, and Contestant 3 has the smallest ratio of car mass to driver mass.**

The ratio of the car mass to driver mass for each contestant is as follows:

Contestant 1: $\frac{20}{40} = \frac{1}{2}$

Contestant 2: $\frac{25}{35} = \frac{5}{7}$

Contestant 3: $\frac{15}{45} = \frac{1}{3}$

Therefore, Choice (D) is correct.

668. **D. 12,000 J**

The combined mass of the car and driver is 60 kg, and the final velocity reached was 20 m/s. Substitute the given values into the equation for kinetic energy:

$$\begin{aligned} KE &= \frac{1}{2}mv^2 \\ &= \frac{1}{2}(60\text{ kg})(20\text{ m/s})^2 \\ &= 12{,}000\text{ J} \end{aligned}$$

Choice (D) is the correct answer.

669. **B. The car driven by Contestant 1 was the most efficient because it converted more of its potential energy into kinetic energy.**

Because each contestant has the same total mass (car plus driver) and started at the same height above the finish line, each began with the same potential energy. Contestant 1 had the fastest speed (velocity), so he finished first. His higher velocity suggests he converted more potential energy into kinetic energy than the other contestants did.

ANSWERS 601–700

670. **Some of the stored potential energy was used up in order to overcome the forces of friction and air resistance that were acting on the cars. Hence, some of the potential energy was converted into heat or sound energy instead of kinetic energy, which accounts for the "missing energy."**

671. **17**

Because the mean of the five life spans is 15, you can calculate the total by multiplying 15 by 5 to get 75. The sum of the four life spans in the table is 58, so the missing value must have been 17.

672. **A. 9**

The atomic number of an atom is equal to the number of its protons. From the table, you can see that fluorine has 9 protons, so the correct answer is Choice (A).

673. **C. 23**

The atomic mass number of an atom is equal to the sum of the number of its protons and neutrons. From the table, you can see that sodium has 11 protons and 12 neutrons, for a total of 23, so the correct answer is Choice (C).

674. **D. fluorine, because the atom contains 9 protons**

The number of protons in the nucleus is called the *atomic number* because it determines which element that atom belongs to. The number of neutrons in the atom can vary, but the number of protons is always the same for a particular element (atoms of the same element that contain different numbers of neutrons are called *isotopes*). Because the unknown atom contains 9 protons, it must be fluorine, so Choice (D) is correct.

675. **B. hydrogen**

The atomic number of an atom is the number of protons in the nucleus, whereas the atomic mass number is equal to the sum of the number of protons and neutrons. From the table, you can see that hydrogen has 1 proton and 0 neutrons; therefore, the value of hydrogen's atomic number (1) is the same as its atomic mass number (1+0), so Choice (B) is correct.

676. **A. Sodium contains 1 valence electron, whereas fluorine contains 7 valence electrons.**

You're told that the number of electrons found in the outermost shell is the number of valence electrons. You're also told that the first energy shell holds a maximum of 2 electrons and that the second energy shell holds a maximum of 8 electrons.

Sodium has 11 electrons in total, so the first 2 go in the first energy shell and the next 8 go in the second energy shell, leaving 1 valence electron in the outermost shell. Similarly, fluorine has 9 electrons in total, so the first 2 go in the first energy shell, leaving 7 valence electrons in the outermost shell. Therefore, Choice (A) is correct.

677. **B. Its charge would become positive.**

Because sodium has 11 electrons (which are negatively charged) and 11 protons (which are positively charged), the atom has zero charge. If sodium loses an electron, it will now have only 10 electrons but will still have 11 protons; therefore, the overall charge will now be positive 1 (because $11 - 10 = 1$). Hence, Choice (B) is correct.

678. **C. Comets are much more interesting than other celestial bodies.**

Choice (A), (B), and (D) are all factual statements from the information in the question stem. Choice (C) is an opinion, not a factual statement, making Choice (C) the correct answer.

679. **D. They are decomposers.**

Earthworms help to break down or decompose the bodies of larger dead organisms, such as leaves, making Choice (D) the correct answer. Earthworms do not produce their own food, so you can reject Choice (A). Choices (B) and (C) refer to organisms that eat fresh plants or animals.

680. **C. a meteorologist who is studying weather patterns to predict the weather**

Weather patterns involve the interactions between the atmosphere and the hydrosphere, so a meteorologist would need to have a good understanding of these two systems in order to predict the weather, making Choice (C) the correct answer. The moon doesn't have any water or an atmosphere, so you can reject Choice (A). You can also reject Choice (B) because a zoologist would need a strong understanding of genetics (rather than of Earth's systems) to study the hereditary patterns of primates. Choice (D) may be tempting, but you can reject it because the chemist is studying reactions in the laboratory rather than in the atmosphere or hydrosphere.

681. **C. The planet nearest the sun is called Mercury. The planet that is the third closest to the sun is called Earth. The largest planet in the solar system is called Jupiter.**

The order of the planets is Mercury, Venus, Earth, Mars, Jupiter, Saturn, Uranus, Neptune. Jupiter is the largest planet in the solar system.

682. D. Big Bang > formation of planet Earth > life first appeared on Earth > extinction of the dinosaurs > *Homo sapiens* (modern humans) first appeared

The universe was created 15 billion years ago in an event known as the Big Bang. About 5 billion years later, the sun and the Earth began to form. Then, about 4 billion years ago, the first life appeared on Earth. Dinosaurs didn't appear until about 250 million years ago and died off 65 million years ago, long before *Homo sapiens* (modern humans) first appeared (only 200,000 years ago). Hence, Choice (D) is correct.

683. D. 78%

The air in the atmosphere is approximately 78 percent nitrogen, 21 percent oxygen, and 1 percent water vapor, carbon dioxide, and other gases. Hence, Choice (D) is correct.

684. A. use compost made from animal and plant waste matter

You're told that the farmer grows organic produce, so he or she would need to use a more natural way to restore the nitrogen content of the soil. Choice (A) is correct.

685. B. Legumes contain nitrogen-fixing bacteria that return nitrogen to the soil.

You can see from the figure that legumes contain nitrogen-fixing bacteria that return nitrogen to the soil. Hence, Choice (A) is wrong and Choice (B) is correct. Choice (C) is unlikely because you're told that the farmers grow organic produce, so they wouldn't use artificial fertilizers. You can also reject Choice (D) because the problem that the farmer is trying to solve involves the lack of nitrogen in the soil; it has nothing to do with cows eating the corn.

686. C. +2

An alpha particle is a helium nucleus that contains two protons and two neutrons. Because protons are positively charged and neutrons are neutral, the charge of an alpha particle must be +2, making Choice (C) the correct answer.

687. B. positive

You're told that alpha particles are positively charged and also that some of them bounced back from the gold atoms. Because you're also told that an atom consists mostly of empty space but has a dense nucleus at the center, you can reasonably assume that the alpha particles that bounced back were repelled by the nucleus of the atom. Because like repels like, the nucleus must be positively charged, so Choice (B) is correct.

688. **C. Gold is more malleable and can be beaten into a foil that is only a few atoms thick, which reduces the chance of multiple collisions with the alpha particles.**

Gold is an extremely malleable metal that can be beaten into a foil that's only a few atoms thick. That reduces the chance of multiple collisions with the alpha particles, which is important for the experiment to be valid; hence, Choice (C) is the right answer. You can reject Choice (A), which is amusing but clearly not the right answer. You can also eliminate Choice (B) because gold was still expensive in 1911. Choice (D) can also be rejected because it's a false statement; all atoms consist mainly of empty space.

689. **B. Some alpha particles bounced straight back off the gold foil.**

Because a few of the alpha particles bounced back, Rutherford concluded that an atom contains a nucleus that has most of the atom's mass and all of its positive charge; Choice (B) provides evidence for this conclusion. Choice (A) suggests that the atom is mainly empty space but doesn't provide evidence that the nucleus is dense and positively charged. You can also reject Choice (C) because this has nothing to do with atomic structure. Choice (D) is wrong because it focuses on the alpha particle, not the structure of the gold atoms.

690. **C. freezing and condensing**

When a substance freezes or condenses, it releases heat to its surroundings, making Choice (C) the correct answer. You can eliminate Choice (A) because evaporation requires the addition of heat energy. Similarly, both melting and boiling need heat energy, so Choices (B) and (D) can also be rejected.

691. **B. chemical energy to kinetic energy to gravitational potential energy**

When Alex works out at the gym, he sometimes lifts weights. As he lifts the barbell, the chemical energy stored in his body is converted into kinetic energy as the barbell moves, which is then converted into potential energy, which reaches its maximum value as the barbell reaches its highest point.

692. **B. Copper is a good conductor.**

Copper is a good conductor of electricity, which makes it an excellent material for electrical wiring; Choice (B) is correct. Choices (A), (C), and (D) are all false.

693. D. The magnets will move apart because the two south poles will repel each other.

You should remember that in magnetism, like poles repel and unlike poles attract. Because the two poles are south poles, they will repel each other, causing the magnets to move apart. Choice (D) is correct.

694. A. The current will be halved.

You're told that the current is inversely proportional to the resistance within the circuit if the voltage remains constant. Therefore, as the resistance gets bigger, the current will get smaller. Only Choice (A) shows a smaller current, so it's the correct answer.

695. A. troposphere

Most humans live close to the Earth's surface, so they live in the layer that has the smallest altitude (the troposphere), making Choice (A) correct.

696. C. mesosphere and ionosphere

From the table, you can see that the temperature of the mesosphere and ionosphere can be as low as −212 degrees, which is colder that any of the other layers, making Choice (C) the correct answer.

697. D. Neptune

From the table, you can see that Neptune is 2.8 billion miles away from the sun, making Choice (D) the correct answer.

698. A. Venus

From the table, you can see that Venus is only 26 million miles away from Earth (93 million miles minus 67 million miles), whereas Mars is 49 million miles from Earth (142 million miles minus 93 million miles). All the other planets are farther away, so Venus is the closest, making Choice (A) the right answer.

699. Mars

From the table, you can see that a day on Mars (24 hours, 37 minutes) takes approximately the same amount of time as a day on Earth (23 hours, 56 minutes, 4.1 seconds).

700. **C. The planet with the shortest day is Jupiter, and the planet with the longest year is Neptune.**

From the table, you can see that Jupiter has the shortest day (9 hours, 51 minutes) and Neptune has the longest year (165 Earth years).

701. **A. A day on Venus takes longer than a year on Venus.**

From the table, you can see that a day on Venus takes 243 Earth days, whereas a year on Venus takes 225 Earth days. Hence, a year on Venus takes less time than a day on Venus, making Choice (A) the correct answer.

All the other statements are false: Mercury does not have a moon [making Choice (B) false], each planet takes a different amount of time to orbit the sun [making Choice (C) false], and the sun contains 99 percent of the mass in the solar system [making Choice (D) false].

702. **C. Although heart disease is still the leading cause of death, the number of deaths due to cancer has increased steadily since 1950.**

Although the curve that represents deaths via cancer has risen sharply since 1950, it's still below the curve that represents deaths via heart disease; therefore, Choice (A) is wrong and (C) is correct. You can reject Choice (B) because the deaths due to heart disease have risen only slightly since 1950. Choice (D) is also wrong because deaths via cancer have tripled since 1950.

703. **D. 200%**

From the graph, you can see that the number of deaths via cancer has tripled since 1950. This is an *increase* of 200 percent:

$$\frac{(600{,}000 - 200{,}000)}{200{,}000} \times \frac{100}{1} = 200\%$$

Therefore, Choice (D) is correct.

704. **A. hummingbird**

From the graph, you can see that the hummingbird has the fastest metabolic rate. It's higher up the curve than the other animals, so Choice (A) is correct.

705. **C. rabbit**

From the graph, you can see that the out of the seven animals listed, the animal with the fourth largest body weight is the rabbit, so Choice (C) is correct.

706. **C. The more the animal weighs, the slower its metabolic rate, whereas the less the animal weighs, the faster its metabolic rate.**

From the table, you can see that the larger animals, such as the horse and the elephant, have much slower metabolic rates than the smaller animals, such as the hummingbird and the mouse.

707. **A. The new average is greater than the old average.**

From the graph, you can see that the elephant has the slowest metabolic rate. Removing the lowest value from the group will cause the average of the remaining values to increase.

708. **D. producers, primary consumers**

Plants are producers because they produce their own food. Rabbits eat the plants and are therefore primary consumers.

709. **B. The population of rabbits and birds would increase.**

If a virus were to suddenly wipe out most of the fox population, more rabbits and birds would survive because fewer foxes would be around to eat them, making Choice (A) incorrect and Choice (B) the right answer. The number of snakes would also increase, making Choice (C) incorrect. You can also reject Choice (D) because an increase in the rabbit and bird populations would mean more plants would be eaten.

710. **C. 10%**

When a plant is eaten, only 10 percent of its stored energy is transferred to the primary consumer's biomass (flesh), making Choice (C) the correct answer. The rest of the plant's energy is used by the consumer's metabolism for movement or heat generation. Also, some parts of the plant may be indigestible, adding further to the inefficiency in the energy transferred to the consumer's biomass.

711. **C. the sun**

The given info tells you that plants are called producers because they produce their own food using the energy of the sun; therefore, the ultimate source of energy in a food web is the sun, making Choice (C) the correct answer.

712. **C. changes in the Earth's crust**

The theory of plate tectonics explains that the outer rigid layer of the Earth (the lithosphere) is divided into several plates that move relative to each other, like slabs of ice on a lake. As the plates move, they can produce volcanoes, earthquakes, ocean ridges, and other changes in the Earth's crust, making Choice (C) the correct answer.

713. **B. About 200 million years ago, all the continents were joined in a single landmass known as Pangaea.**

Choice (A), (C), and (D) are all scientific facts that can be verified via observations. Although Choice (B) has a lot of evidence to support it, it is still a theory because there is no way to verify it through direct observation. Hence, Choice (B) is the correct answer.

714. **D. A student sitting at the back of class breaks wind. The unpleasant odor quickly spreads through the room, forcing the teacher to open all the windows.**

The question asks you to give an example of the diffusion of a gas, so you can reject Choices (A), (B), and (C); they don't refer to gases. That leaves Choice (D) as the correct answer. It describes the spreading of a gas (an unpleasant one!) until it occupies the entire room.

715. **C. They produce antibodies that help protect the body from infectious diseases.**

The passage tells you that white blood cells produce antibodies that help protect the body from infectious diseases, making Choice (C) the correct answer.

716. **B. They carry oxygen to all the cells of the body, where it is used during cellular respiration.**

The passage tells you that red blood cells carry oxygen from the lungs to all the cells of the body, where it is used during cellular respiration, making Choice (C) the correct answer. Although Choice (D) is a true statement, it can still be rejected because making the blood appear red is not the main function of red blood cells.

717. **D. plasma carries dissolved oxygen around the body.**

The passage tells you that plasma consists mainly of water and surrounds the blood cells. It helps maintain blood pressure and body temperature and helps transport nutrients around the body and remove waste products. Choices (A), (B), and (C) are true statements and can therefore be rejected. That leaves Choice (D), which is not a true statement because the red blood cells, not the plasma, carry oxygen.

718. **C. 45%**

The table tells you that red blood cells make up 44 percent of the blood and white blood cells make up an additional 1 percent of the blood. Therefore, 45 percent of the blood consists of cells, making Choice (C) the correct answer.

719. **D. The isotope with the longest half-life is uranium-238, and the isotope with the shortest half-life is carbon-11.**

You can see from the table that uranium-238 has the longest half-life by far compared to the other isotopes (4.5×10^9 years). Also, you can see from the table that carbon-11 has the shortest half-life (only 20 minutes), so the correct answer is Choice (D).

720. **C. The half-life of carbon-14 is too long, so the radiation it emits could be harmful to the patient if it remained in the body.**

You can see from the table that carbon-14 has a much longer half-life than carbon-11 (5,750 years compared to only 20 minutes). For biomedical imaging, carbon-11 is injected as a radioactive tracer that allows medical images to be viewed (rather like those from an X-ray). However, you need a radioactive isotope that has a relatively short half-life so it doesn't harm the patient if it remains in the body, making Choice (C) the correct answer. Choices (A), (B), and (D) are all untrue statements and can therefore be rejected.

721. **D. Carbon-14 contains 8 neutrons, whereas carbon-11 contains only 5 neutrons.**

The number of protons in the nucleus of an atom determines which element the atom belongs to. Because the question refers to the element carbon (which contains 6 protons), you can reject Choices (A) and (C). The number in the name of the isotope tells you the mass number (the protons plus the neutrons) of the isotope. Carbon-14 has a mass number of 14 (6 protons and 8 neutrons), and carbon 11 has a mass number of 11 (6 protons and 5 neutrons), making Choice (D) the correct answer.

722. **D. 250 grams**

The passage tells you that the *half-life* is the time taken for half of the sample to decay. From the table, you can see that the half-life of carbon-11 is 20 minutes. The researcher left for an hour, which is 60 minutes, or three 20-minute blocks. The researcher started with 2,000 grams, so after the first 20 minutes, only 1,000 grams would be left. Then after another 20 minutes, only 500 grams would be left. After another 20 minutes, only 250 grams would be left, so the correct answer is Choice (D).

723. **C. circulatory system.**

The circulatory system transports nutrients dissolved in the blood to all the cells of the body, so Choice (C) is correct. The digestive system is involved in breaking down food into nutrients, so you can reject Choice (A). The integumentary system is the protective layer of the body, including the skin, hair, and nails, so Choice (B) is incorrect. The muscular system is responsible for the movement of the body itself, so Choice (D) is incorrect.

724. **C. The gunpowder in a cannon explodes, sending a cannonball high into the air.**

In chemical reactions, the reactants change into completely different products. Signs of a chemical reaction include a change in temperature, the production of a gas, or a color change. Choice (C) describes an explosion, which is a chemical change.

725. **B. Sydney**

You can see from the chart that Sydney's record temperature rose the least (from about 39 degrees to about 42 degrees), making Choice (B) the correct answer.

726. **B. This year's record temperatures were higher than the previous record temperatures in all four cities.**

You can see from the chart that this year's record temperatures were higher than the previous record temperatures in all four cities, making Choice (B) the correct answer. The chart doesn't predict what next year's temperatures will be, so you can reject Choice (A). Choice (C) is false because Adelaide's temperature rose by about 10 degrees. There is no indication that any of the cities experienced a major drought this year, so you can reject Choice (D).

727. **C. 33%**

You can see from the chart that Adelaide's record temperature rose from about 30 degrees to about 40 degrees. To find the percent increase, divide the change in temperature by the previous high and multiply by 100:

$$\frac{(40-30)}{30} \times \frac{100}{1} = 33\%$$

Choice (C) is the correct answer.

728. **D. An attractive force acts on each mass, pulling the masses together.**

The passage tells you that a gravitational force of attraction acts on each mass, so you can rule out Choices (A) and (C). The force of attraction will pull the two masses together, making Choice (D) the correct answer.

729. **B. Increasing the masses increases the gravitational force acting on them, whereas increasing the distance decreases the gravitational force acting on the objects.**

The passage tells you that the force is directly proportional to the product of the mass; therefore, increasing the masses will increase the force. You're also told that the force is inversely proportional to the square of the distance r between the masses, so increasing r will decrease the force. Hence, Choice (B) is correct.

730. A. The force will be decreased by a factor of 4.

The passage tells you that the force is inversely proportional to the square of the distance r between the objects. Because the distance is squared, doubling r (to $2r$) will decrease the force by a factor of 4:

$$\frac{1}{(2r)^2} = \frac{1}{4r^2}$$

Chapter 4

731. B. He hates Christmas.

You can see from the passage that Scrooge hates Christmas: "Every idiot who goes about with 'Merry Christmas' on his lips," he says, "should be boiled with his own pudding, and buried with a stake of holly through his heart. He should!" Hence, Choice (B) is the correct answer. Choice (A) is what Scrooge's nephew (not Scrooge) believes. Choice (C) is also contradicted by the passage because Scrooge rejects his nephew's offer to spend Christmas with him. You can also reject Choice (D) because Scrooge is using the word "humbug" as a curse word rather than as a description of his favorite candy.

732. A. Scrooge is miserable and wealthy, whereas Scrooge's nephew is amicable and forgiving.

Based on the passage, Scrooge could be described as miserable and wealthy. Scrooge's nephew could be described as amicable and forgiving. Hence, Choice (A) is correct.

733. D. Scrooge is threatening to sack his employee if he says another word.

Scrooge is angry that his employee applauded at the end of his nephew's speech, so Scrooge threatens to sack (fire) his employee if he says another word. Hence, Choice (D) is correct. There is no evidence to support any of the other answers.

734. C. Scrooge is being sarcastic.

Scrooge is clearly angry with his nephew and does not agree with his speech. Scrooge is therefore being sarcastic when he praises the speech, making Choice (C) the correct answer.

735. B. Scrooge wants to end the conversation.

Toward the end of the excerpt, you can see that Scrooge is becoming impatient with his nephew's cheerful wishes and simply wants to end the conversation. "Good afternoon" is a clear dismissal, so Choice (B) is correct. You can reject Choices (A) and (D) because nothing in the passage suggests that Scrooge's nephew has a hearing problem or that Scrooge is getting old and often repeats himself. Choice (C) is clearly wrong because Scrooge isn't full of the Christmas spirit.

736. B. poisonous hatred

The poem's main message is that if you if don't communicate your anger, it will grow into poisonous hatred, making Choice (B) the correct answer.

737. D. anger, revenge, and death

The poem's main themes are anger, revenge, and death, as shown by phrases such as "I was angry with my foe" and "In the morning glad I see; My foe outstretched beneath the tree." Hence, Choice (D) is the correct answer.

738. B. Tell your friend why you are angry, and your anger will fade away.

The poem's main message is that if you express your anger by communicating it to your friend, your anger will subside [Choice (B)], but if you don't communicate your anger, it will grow into poisonous hatred, so you can reject Choice (A). The goal of the poem is to teach people how to communicate their anger, not how to eliminate their friends, so Choices (C) and (D) can be rejected.

739. D. frustrating.

The excerpt says, "Cooking is fun and interesting and can be relaxing, exciting, and even therapeutic." Only Choice (D), frustrating, isn't mentioned.

740. A. how much a meal at your favorite restaurant costs.

The excerpt says that with cooking, "you control the ingredients, flavors, and health profile of your food" — Choices (B), (C), and (D), respectively. Although the passage says, "You can eat for less money than you'd spend ordering take-out or dining in a restaurant every night," that isn't the same as controlling how much a meal at your favorite restaurant costs, so Choice (A) is the correct answer.

741. B. The ideal kitchen is a comfortable environment with a/an efficient working space.

Based on the passage, the ideal kitchen is a comfortable environment with a/an efficient working space. Hence, Choice (B) is correct.

742. C. to show how important it is to set up an efficient working space

The passage states: "If you want to spend the day running, join a health club. If you want to enjoy an efficient and pleasurable cooking experience, consider where your main appliances are located and where you store the equipment and ingredients you use the most. Do you have to walk 10 feet from the stove to get the salt? That's not efficient." Hence, the working space. should be efficient so you don't need to run around while cooking, making Choice (C) correct.

743. kitchen triangle

The excerpt says that "the working space actually has a name: the *kitchen triangle*."

744. A. the sink, the stove, and the refrigerator

You are told in the excerpt that "you should be able to move from your working counter space to the stove/oven, refrigerator, and sink in a smooth, unobstructed fashion." Hence, Choice (A) is correct.

745. B. a short, wide kitchen

The excerpt says the kitchen triangle works "whether you have a long narrow kitchen, a U-shaped kitchen, or an L-shaped kitchen" — Choices (A), (C), and (D), respectively. Therefore, Choice (B) is the correct answer.

746. B. informative

The entire passage appears to contain information that will help the reader learn to cook. Therefore, Choice (B) is the best answer. The author is not being sarcastic (joking in a nasty way) or belligerent (trying to start a fight), so you can reject Choices (A) and (D). *Ambivalent* means having mixed feelings about something, so you can also eliminate Choice (C).

747. B. what you intend to use the drone for

The passage says, "Before you buy a drone, you need to know how you will use it," making Choice (B) the correct answer. The other answer choices are important but apply only after you've decided what you'll use the drone for.

748. C. an airplane or other fixed-wing drone

The passage says, "If you want to fly fast in a straight line, an airplane or other fixed-wing drone may be the right fit," so Choice (C) is the correct answer.

749. D. motor power and battery life

The passage says, "If you intend to fly for extended periods of time, you want to make sure that you have the right balance of motor power and battery life."

750. D. The passage does not specify.

The passage says, "Pricing in this range is for drones that are intended for more than hobby, personal, or small business uses" — Choices (A), (B), and (C), respectively. Hence, Choice (D) is the correct answer.

751. C. the cost of replacement parts and repairs

The passage says, "When contemplating budget, take into consideration how much money you can spend on replacement parts and repairs." Hence, Choice (C) is the correct answer.

752. D. long list

The phrase in the passage that uses the word is "this opens up a litany of additional questions." It suggests that there are a lot more questions to consider, making Choice (D) the correct answer.

753. B. Nanotechnology is much younger than the other sciences.

The passage says, "Nanotechnology has been around as a recognized branch of science for only about fifty years, so it's a baby compared to physics or biology." Hence, Choice (B) is the correct answer.

754. D. nanotechnology is still evolving, so its definition keeps changing.

The passages states: "*Nanotechnology* is still evolving, and there doesn't seem to be one definition that everybody agrees on," making Choice (D) the correct answer.

755. **C. 10^9.**

The passage says that *nano* means "on a very small scale: larger than atoms but smaller than a breadcrumb," Choice (D). You're also told that "*nano* is a scientific prefix that stands for 10^{-9} or 1 billionth [Choice (B)]; the word itself comes from the Greek word *nanos*, meaning dwarf [Choice (A)]." Choice (C) is the correct answer because *nano* means 10^{-9}, not 10^9."

756. **D. 80,000 nanometers**

The passage says that "you can fit about 80,000 nanometers in the width of a single human hair." Hence, Choice (D) is the correct answer.

757. **D. providing jobs.**

The passage says, "The promise that nanotechnology holds for the human race ranges from extending our lives by centuries to providing cheap energy and cleaning our air and water" — Choices (A), (B), and (C), respectively. Hence, Choice (D) is the correct answer.

758. **C. billions of euros**

The passage says, "Products based on nanotechnology are already in use and analysts expect markets to grow by hundreds of billions of euros during this decade," so Choice (C) is the correct answer.

759. **B. 100 nanometers**

The passage mentions that "nanotechnology is the understanding and control of matter at dimensions between approximately 1 and 100 nanometers." Hence, Choice (C) is the correct answer.

760. **D. It focuses on the potential impact on the way we live.**

The definition states: "Nanotechnology is an upcoming economic, business, and social phenomenon. Nano-advocates argue it will revolutionize the way we live, work, and communicate." Hence, it appears to focus on the potential impact on the way we live, making Choice (D) the correct answer. The other definitions in the passage focus more on scientific terms, including the physical and chemical properties and the scale of the particles involved.

761. **B. The animals rebelled and took over the farm.**

The passage says, "Jones and all his men, with half a dozen others from Foxwood and Pinchfield . . . were going to attempt the recapture of the farm," so it appears that the animals have rebelled and taken over the farm. Hence, Choice (B) is correct.

762. B. Snowball

The passage says, "Snowball, who had studied an old book of Julius Caesar's campaigns which he had found in the farmhouse, was in charge of the defensive operations." Hence, Choice (B) is correct.

763. B. The pigeons fly over the men's heads while the geese peck at the men's legs.

The passage says that "as the human beings approached the farm buildings, Snowball launched his first attack." This consists of the pigeons flying to and fro over the men's heads while the geese rush out and peck viciously at the calves of their legs. Hence, Choice (B) is correct.

764. A. The animals pretend to retreat but then cut the men off from the rear when they enter the yard.

The passage says that the men "rushed after them in disorder. This was just what Snowball had intended. As soon as they were well inside the yard, the three horses, the three cows, and the rest of the pigs, who had been lying in ambush in the cowshed, suddenly emerged in their rear, cutting them off." Hence, Choice (A) is correct.

765. C. shameful

The passage says that "within five minutes of their invasion they were in ignominious retreat by the same way as they had come," so it appears that the men left in shame at losing the battle. Choice (C) is the correct answer.

766. D. a horse

The passage says that "the most terrifying spectacle of all was Boxer, rearing up on his hind legs and striking out with his great iron-shod hoofs like a stallion." Even if the other animals could rear up "like a stallion," they wouldn't be wearing horseshoes, so Choice (D) is the correct answer.

767. C. Snowball shows no remorse, but Boxer is upset.

In the passage, Boxer sorrowfully says, "He is dead . . . I had no intention of doing that," whereas Snowball says, "The only good human being is a dead one." Hence, Choice (C) is the correct answer.

768. **D. cunning, resourceful, brave**

The passage says that Snowball studied an old book of Julius Caesar's campaigns, which he had found in the farmhouse (this shows he is being resourceful). Snowball was also cunning because he planned the retreat of the animals in order to trap the men who chased after them. Snowball showed his bravery when he dashed straight for Jones even as Jones raised his gun and fired. Hence, Choice (D) is correct.

769. **C. 10**

The passage states that "if you are in a room with three *other* adult U.S. citizens, one of you will probably have prediabetes." That means that one out of every four people (or 10 out of 40 people) have prediabetes. (If you are in a room with 39 other people, the room contains 40 people — including you.) Hence, Choice (C) is the correct answer.

770. **C. to convince the reader to read the rest of the book**

The first paragraph of the passage contains the statement "Anyone who reads this book will know whether he or she has prediabetes. Anyone who follows the recommendations in this book will not proceed to diabetes and will probably return to normal health." So the author is clearly trying to encourage the reader to finish reading his book, making Choice (C) the correct answer. Choice (A) is tempting but can be eliminated because it's really the focus of the entire book rather than the first paragraph. You can also reject Choice (C) because the first paragraph doesn't give a definition of prediabetes. Choice (D) involves diabetes, not prediabetes.

771. **D. He is suggesting that reading this book could prevent you from dying of diabetes.**

The author uses this phrase to show the reader that diabetes and prediabetes are serious illnesses that can lead to an early death. He's suggesting that the reader can avoid dying young by reading his book, making Choice (D) the correct answer.

772. **D. postdiabetes**

The passage says, "In this chapter, you discover how to differentiate among three physical states: normal health, prediabetes, and diabetes" — Choices (A), (B), and (C), respectively. Therefore, Choice (D) is the correct answer.

773. **B. AIDS**

The passage says that "prediabetes is a recent phenomenon, which parallels the epidemic of obesity and lack of exercise in the United States" — Choices (D), (A), and (C), respectively. Choice (B) is the correct answer.

774. C. a brief, revealing account of an individual person's experience

The anecdote is a short story that describes how Jane Johnson discovered that she had prediabetes. Hence, Choice (C) is the correct answer. Choice (A) describes an antidote, not an anecdote. Choice (B) is wrong because *anecdote* refers to the story itself, not the method of diagnosing prediabetes. Anecdotes are often amusing, but Jane's story wasn't, so you can eliminate Choice (D).

775. A. The author wants to emphasize that prediabetes is caused by too much blood sugar.

The anecdote describes how Jane Johnson discovered that she had prediabetes, so Choice (A) is the correct answer. You can eliminate Choices (B) and (C) because the doctor's name contains the word *sugar,* which would be a big coincidence. Choice (D) is a false statement.

776. B. by measuring the fasting blood glucose level

The passage says, "One of the blood tests the doctor orders is called a *fasting blood glucose*, and it discovers the level of sugar in someone's blood in the morning after that person has fasted through the night," making Choice (B) the correct answer. Although people with prediabetes should avoid sugary foods, the disease is not diagnosed by measuring sugar intake, so Choice (A) is wrong. Many people with prediabetes have no symptoms, so you can eliminate Choice (C). Choice (D) is a false statement.

777. B. The author knows the reader will probably answer yes to these questions and will be interested in learning more.

Because the passage comes from a book on stress management, it makes sense that the reader would be interested in learning how to manage stress. The author is asking questions such as "Are you worrying more? Enjoying life less?" because he knows the reader will probably answer yes to these questions and want to continue reading. Hence, Choice (B) is correct.

778. C. having too much money.

The passage says that "your stress may come from your job [Choice (A)] or lack thereof [Choice (B)], your money worries, your personal life [Choice (D)], or simply not having enough time to do everything you have to do — or want to do." Although money worries are mentioned, they don't usually refer to having too much money, so Choice (C) is the right answer.

779. D. the Bible story in which God confronts Adam in the Garden of Eden about eating from the Tree of Knowledge

The author is making a funny allusion (reference) to the classic Bible story in which God confronts Adam in the Garden of Eden about eating from the Tree of Knowledge; hence, Choice (C) is the correct answer. Even if you're unfamiliar with the referenced work, you can still reach the correct answer by eliminating the other answers. You're told that the author's name is Allen, not Adam, so Choice (A) is incorrect. Choice (B) doesn't even refer to a person called Adam, so you can eliminate it. There's no indication that the author has a nephew named Adam, so you can eliminate Choice (C).

780. B. having suicidal thoughts.

The passage begins by listing some of the symptoms of stress: "Are you feeling more tired lately than you used to?" eliminates Choice (D), "Is your fuse a little shorter than normal?" eliminates Choice (A), and "Are you worrying more?" eliminates Choice (C). Only Choice (B) is unmentioned and therefore the right answer.

781. A. We still need about the same amount of time to do what has to be done at home.

All those "time-saving" inventions haven't really saved us time. According to the passage, "Juliet Schor points out that, in spite of all the new innovations and contraptions that could make our lives easier, we still need about the same amount of time to do what has to be done at home." Hence, Choice (A) is the right answer. You can eliminate Choices (C) and (D) because they contradict the information in the passage. There's no evidence in the passage to support Choice (B).

782. C. money

According to the passage, "Americans report that money (76 percent) and the economy (65 percent) are their most common sources of stress." Hence, Choice (C) is the right answer.

783. B. office politics, traveling to and from work, and unpleasant bosses

The passage says, "Concerns about job security, killer hours, long commutes, unrealistic deadlines, bosses from hell, office politics, toxic coworkers, and testy clients are just a few of the many job-related stresses people experience." Only Choice (B) mentions some of these sources of stress and hence is the correct answer.

784. C. People now spend more time at work to deal with today's larger workloads

According to the passage, "Workloads are heavier today than they were in the past, leaving less and less time for family and the rest of your life." Hence, Choice (C) is the right answer. All of the other answer choices would explain why work today should be less stressful (not more stressful) and can be rejected.

785. D. read his book

The passage states, "Thankfully, you can eliminate or at least minimize much of the stress in your life and better manage the stress that remains. This chapter helps you get started." Hence, Choice (D) is the right answer.

786. C. playful but informative

The passage is certainly playful because the author makes several jocular statements, but it's also informative, as he gives information about the causes and symptoms of stress; therefore, Choice (C) is the right answer. You can eliminate Choice (A) because the author isn't belligerent (hostile and aggressive). Although he's talking about a serious topic, the author's tone is playful, so Choice (B) is wrong. The purpose of the book is to give the reader practical advice about how to reduce stress; he is not being capricious (unpredictable), so Choice (D) is wrong.

787. D. a large number of trades that generate small profits.

The passage states that day traders "make quick decisions because their ability to make money depends on successfully executing a large number of trades that generate small profits." Hence, Choice (D) is the right answer.

788. A. by closing out their positions at the end of each day

The passage states that day traders "close out their positions in the stocks, options, and futures contracts they own at the end of the day, which limits some of the risks." Hence, Choice (A) is the right answer. You can eliminate Choice (B) because it describes an investor, not a day trader. Choice (C) is wrong because nobody knows with certainty which stocks will go up or down, and you can eliminate Choice (D) because if you aren't trading at all, you aren't a day trader.

789. C. they are charged cheaper fees for each trade they perform

The passage states that "the individual human-being day trader is up against a tough opponent: high-frequency algorithms programmed and operated by brokerage firms and hedge funds [Choice (D)] that have no emotion [Choice (A)] and can make trades in less time than it takes to blink your eye [Choice (B)]." Hence, Choice (C) is the right answer.

790. **C. The rules that may have helped the investor pick good long-term investments do not apply to day trading.**

The passage states, "When you take up day trading, the rules that may have helped you pick good stocks or find great mutual funds over the years no longer apply. Day trading is a different game with different rules." Hence, Choice (C) is the right answer. Choice (A) is a false statement because the passage states that day trading involves zero-sum markets. Choice (B) would actually be useful for day trading, which relies on making many trades per day. Choice (D) is silly and should be rejected.

791. **C. A mobile phone provider takes market share away from its main rival.**

The passage states that "a zero-sum game has exactly as many winners as losers. . . . There's no net gain or net loss in the market as a whole." Choice (C) gives an example of a winning company taking market share away from a losing company and is therefore the right answer. You can reject Choices (A) and (D) because there are no losers in either scenario. Choice (B) can be rejected because there are no winners in this scenario.

792. **B. *Day traders* hold their securities for only one day, *swing traders* hold securities for days and sometimes even months, and *investors* sometimes hold securities for years.**

The passage states that "day traders hold their securities for only one day," while "*swing traders* hold securities for days and sometimes even months" and "*investors* sometimes hold for years." Hence, Choice (B) is correct.

793. **A. Speculators try to profit from price changes, whereas hedgers try to protect themselves from price changes.**

The passage states, "*Speculators* look to make a profit from price changes. *Hedgers* look to protect against a price change." Hence, Choice (A) is the correct answer. Both speculators and hedgers are professional traders, so you can reject Choices (C) and (D).

794. **C. a patient, quick-thinking risk-taker who possesses self-discipline**

The passage states that day traders need both patience and the ability to make quick decisions. There are risks involved, but a disciplined day trader reduces those risks by closing his or her position every day, making Choice (C) the right answer.

The passage states that day trading is not for everyone, which rules out Choice (D), and that the rules of day trading are different from those of

ANSWERS 701–800

long-term investing, which rules out Choice (B). Although day trading has risks associated with it, it isn't the same as gambling, which rules out Choice (A).

795. **B. Writing a business plan is one of the most important steps in shaping an idea and putting it to its first test.**

You can reject Choices (A) and (C) because they both incorrectly use the contraction *it's* (which means it is) instead of the possessive adjective *its* (which means belonging to it). Choice (D) can also be rejected because the plural pronoun *them* is supposed to refer to the singular *idea*. Hence, Choice (B) is the correct answer.

796. **D. Apple did too, when the company decided to build a touch screen device big enough to read, draw, and write on.**

You can reject Choices (A) and (B) because they both incorrectly use the word *right* (which means correct) rather than the word *write* (which means to compose). Choices (A) and (C) can be rejected because they use the present tense of the verb *decides* rather than the past tense *decided*. Hence, Choice (D) is the correct answer.

797. **A. The young couple who decides to open a doggy day care in a town where a lot of people commute to work may have a great idea, too.**

You can reject Choices (B) and (C) because they both incorrectly use the preposition *to* rather than the word *too* (which means as well). Choice (D) can also be rejected because the relative pronoun *who*, not *which* or *that*, should be used when referring to people. Hence, Choice (A) is the correct answer.

798. **D. Putting your business idea into words is a no-brainer if you're starting a new company.**

You can reject Choices (A) and (B) because they both confuse the contraction *you're* (which means you are) with the possessive adjective *your* (which means belonging to you). Choice (C) can be eliminated because it mistakenly uses the wrong tense of the verb by using "put" rather than "putting." Hence, Choice (D) is the correct answer.

799. **C. The emphasis of your plan will differ depending on your goal, of course.**

You can reject Choice (A) because it uses the word *differing* rather than the word *differ*. Similarly, you can reject Choice (C) because it confuses the word *coarse* (which means rough) with the phrase *of course* (which means obviously). You can also reject Choice (D) because it uses the wrong verb tense *depending* rather than *depend*. Hence, Choice (C) is the correct answer.

800. **D. As you develop the essential idea behind the new direction, compare it to the idea that launched your business in the first place.**

You can reject Choice (A) because it uses the plural pronoun *them* rather than singular pronoun *it* when referring to *the essential idea.* Similarly, you can reject Choice (C) because it incorrectly uses the wrong verb tense *developing* instead of *as you develop,* which leaves the sentence grammatically incorrect. You can also reject Choice (C) because it leaves out the comma after the word *direction;* the comma is required to separate the two ideas within the sentence. Hence, Choice (D) is the correct answer.

801. **C. Being excited about what you want to do is no guarantee of success.**

You can reject Choice (A) because it confuses the verb form *been* (past participle form of *to be*) with *being* (present participle form of *to be*). You can reject Choice (B) because *guarantee* is misspelled. You can also reject Choice (D) because the phrase *not guaranteed of success* is awkward. Hence, Choice (C) is the correct answer.

802. **C. If you're hoping to turn a personal passion into a successful business, you need to ask yourself a simple question: Can it make a profit?**

You can reject Choices (A) and (B) because they both confuse the plural noun *personnel* (which means employees) with the adjective *personal* (which means belonging to you). You can reject Choice (D) because it omits the comma after the word *business,* which is needed to separate the two ideas in the sentence. Hence, Choice (C) is the correct answer.

803. **C. No chess gene decides who can and can't play; take my word for it.**

You can reject Choice (A) because it confuses the noun *jeans* (denim pants) with the noun *gene* (genetic makeup). Choices (B) and (D) are also wrong because they both incorrectly use the word *whom* (the object of a verb) rather than *who* (the subject of the verb). Here, *who* is the subject of the clause "who can and can't play." Hence, Choice (C) is the correct answer.

804. **D. Chess, simply stated, is a board game for two**

You can reject Choices (A) and (B) because they both incorrectly use the word *too* (which means as well) rather than the number *two.* You can also reject Choices (B) and (C) because they confuse the adjective *bored* with the noun *board.* Hence, Choice (D) is the correct answer.

805. **B. if you already know how to play but want to hone your prowess, you'll find plenty of information to help you do just that.**

You can reject Choices (A) and (D) because they both incorrectly use the pronoun *one* rather than the pronoun *you.* Note that if the sentence begins in the second person *(you)*, it should stay in the second person and not switch to the third person *(one)* midway through. You can also reject Choice (C) because it incorrectly uses the pronoun *you* rather than the contraction *you'll* (which means you will). Hence, Choice (B) is the correct answer.

806. **A. If one player deploys more force more quickly than the other player, it may be impossible for the latter player to defend against a subsequent invasion.**

You can reject Choices (B) and (C) because they both incorrectly use the adjective *quick* rather than the adverb *quickly*. You can also reject Choices (B) and (D) because they confuse the adverb *later* (which relates to time) with the adjective *latter* (which mean the second of the two things mentioned). Hence, Choice (A) is the correct answer.

807. **D. One thing to note, however, is that placing your opponent in check doesn't necessarily mean you'll win**

You can reject Choices (A) and (B) because they both incorrectly omit the commas before and after the word *however*. You can also reject Choice (B) because it confuses the noun *proponent* (a person who supports a theory) with the noun *opponent* (the person you're trying to beat). Choice (C) can be eliminated because it contains a double negative: *doesn't not*. Hence, Choice (D) is the correct answer.

808. **B. Besides, unlike real warfare, the worst you'll suffer in your chess career is a bruised ego.**

You can reject Choices (A) and (C) because they incorrectly use the preposition *beside* (which means next to) rather than *besides* (which is a way of adding new supporting information to a previously stated point). Choice (D) can be rejected because it incorrectly uses the contraction *you're* (which means you are) rather than *you'll* (which means you will). Hence, Choice (B) is correct.

809. **B. uneasy and lonely**

The opening paragraph states, "There is something so strange about this place and all in it that I cannot but feel uneasy." The narrator also complains about having no one to talk to, so he's feeling lonely. Therefore, Choice (B) is the correct answer.

810. **A. clear and direct**

The passage states, "Let me be prosaic so far as facts can be; it will help me to bear up, and imagination must not run riot with me. If it does I am lost." The narrator is trying to get his thoughts together in a clear and direct way, so Choice (A) is the correct answer. Choice (B) is wrong because the narrator is trying to avoid letting his imagination run away with him. He isn't being *capricious* (unpredictable) or *vague* (unclear), so you can eliminate Choices (C) and (D).

811. D. The Count's reflection did not appear in the mirror that the narrator was looking at.

The passage states, "Suddenly I felt a hand on my shoulder, and heard the Count's voice saying to me, 'Good-morning.' I started, for it amazed me that I had not seen him, because the reflection of the glass covered the whole room behind me." The Count does not appear to have a reflection in the mirror, making Choice (D) the correct answer. Nothing in the passage supports any of the other answer choices.

812. B. greeting

Salutation means greeting, so Choice (B) is the correct answer.

813. B. He becomes furious and tries to grab the narrator by the throat.

The passage states, "When the Count saw my face, his eyes blazed with a sort of demoniac fury, and he suddenly made a grab at my throat," making Choice (B) the correct answer. There's no evidence in the passage to support any of the other answer choices.

814. D. The crucifix makes him withdraw immediately and become calm again.

The passage states, "I drew away, and his hand touched the string of beads which held the crucifix. It made an instant change in him, for the fury passed so quickly that I could hardly believe that it was ever there," making Choice (D) the correct answer. No evidence in the passage supports any of the other answer choices.

815. C. on a cliff overlooking a beautiful forest

The passage states, "The castle is on the very edge of a terrible precipice [cliff]. . . . As far as the eye can reach is a sea of green tree tops, with occasionally a deep rift where there is a chasm"; the narrator also calls the view "magnificent," making Choice (C) the correct answer. There is no evidence in the passage to support any of the other answer choices.

816. D. he would not survive the fall

The passage states, "A stone falling from the window would fall a thousand feet without touching anything!" making Choice (D) the correct answer. There is no evidence in the passage to support any of the other answer choices.

817. **A. actual**

The word *veritable* means genuine or actual, making Choice (A) the correct answer. All the other answer choices mean the same thing as each other and can therefore be eliminated.

818. **D. enthusiastic and informative**

The author's tone in the passage can best be described as enthusiastic and informative, making Choice (D) the best answer. He is not grim or sardonic (cynical), so you can reject Choice (A). He is not being sarcastic (mocking with contempt), so Choice (B) can be rejected. He is not being disingenuous (pretending to know less about the subject than he actually does), so Choice (C) is incorrect.

819. **C. chemistry is a branch of physics.**

The passage states that chemistry "seemed so interesting [Choice (B)], so logical [Choice (A)]. I think it's fascinating to watch chemical changes take place, to figure out unknowns, to use instruments, to extend my senses, and to make predictions [Choice (D)] and figure out why we're right or wrong." Although the author was a physics major, he doesn't claim that chemistry is a branch of physics, so Choice (C) is the best answer.

820. **D. changes in matter and energy**

The passage states, "*Chemistry* is the study of the composition and properties of matter and the changes it undergoes, including energy changes." Therefore, Choice (D) is the best answer. You can eliminate the other answer choices because the passage also states, "If it was alive, it was biology [Choice (B)]. If it was a rock, it was geology [Choice (A)]. If it smelled, it was chemistry. If it didn't work, it was physics [Choice (C)]."

821. **A. There is more of an overlap among the sciences now.**

The passage states, "Science used to be divided into very clearly defined areas. . . . In today's world, however, those clear divisions are no longer present." Therefore, Choices (B) and (D) are untrue and Choice (A) is the best answer. Choice (C) is too extreme because the definitions have been changed, not completely discarded.

822. **B. The foul smell of the cadaver may make you want to vomit.**

Dissection involves cutting up *cadavers* (dead bodies), and many people find the smell of the chemicals used to preserve the body so unpleasant that they actually vomit. The nose plug helps prevent this, making Choice (C) the best answer. Choices (A) and (B) are both untrue statements, and Choice (D) is amusing but also incorrect.

823. **C. the existence of gravity**

The passage states that "being testable is what makes science different from faith." Choices (A), (B), and (D) are all related to faith and are therefore unsuitable to be tested by science. Choice (C) can be tested by science because you can show that gravity exists (by dropping an apple, for example), making Choice (C) the best answer.

824. **A. doubtful**

The passage states that scientists are skeptical and "simply won't take another person's word for a phenomenon — it must be testable." Choice (A) is therefore the best answer. Choices (B) and (D) both mean the opposite of doubtful and can be rejected. Although scientists are often highly intelligent, that isn't the same as being skeptical, so you can eliminate Choice (C).

825. **D. They keep asking *why*.**

The passage states, "Scientists wonder, they question, they strive to find out *why*, and they experiment — they have exactly the same attitudes that most small children have before they grow up." Choice (D) is therefore the best answer.

826. **B. chance**

The passage states, "It wasn't until the 17th century that experimentation replaced serendipity." This eliminates Choice (D) and suggests that serendipity is the opposite of carefully planned investigation, making Choice (B) the correct answer.

827. **C. People are curious about nature and seek scientific knowledge.**

The passage says, "I don't think this newfound interest in all things forensic stems from some macabre fascination with death [Choice (A)] or a guilty enchantment with the criminal world [Choice (B)]. If you ask me, people simply are curious by nature and have a strong appetite for scientific knowledge." Hence, Choice (C) is the correct answer.

828. **B. identifying the motive behind the criminal act.**

The passage says, "The cool tools and magical feats of forensic science, such as making fingerprints appear from nowhere [Choice (A)], identifying suspects by their shoe-prints, sniffing out a forger by the unique signature of a laser printer [Choice (C)], and finding even the most obscure poisons [Choice (D)] are proving equally fascinating." Hence, Choice (B) is the correct answer.

829. **C. fascination**

The passage says that people watch TV shows about forensic science because they have a "guilty enchantment with the criminal world." In other words, they find it fascinating, making Choice (B) the correct answer.

830. **D. He wants to explain the origin of the word *forensic*.**

The author brings up Ancient Rome in the passage in order to explain how the word *forum* is related to the word forensic. The passage says, "The term *forensic* stems from the Latin word *forum* and applies to anything that relates to law." Hence, Choice (D) is the correct answer.

831. **C. Serology is the study of the blood, pathology is the study of human diseases, and toxicology is the study of drugs and poisons.**

Serology is the study of the blood, *pathology* is the study of human diseases, and *toxicology* is the study of drugs and poisons.

832. **C. What did the suspect have to gain by killing the victim?**

The passage tells you that forensic sciences help "resolve legal issues and answer questions like: When and how did the victim die [Choice (D)]? Does the suspect's blood match the blood found at the crime scene [Choice (B)]? Was a suspect's unusual behavior caused by drug use [Choice (A)]?" Hence, Choice (C) is the correct answer.

833. **A. eyewitnesses and confessions**

The passage says, "Not long ago identifying, capturing, and convicting criminals depended primarily upon eyewitnesses and confessions." Hence, Choice (A) is the correct answer. All the other choices describe forensic science techniques.

834. **C. It made eyewitness accounts less reliable.**

The passage says that in the past, "whenever anyone witnessed a crime, he likely knew the perpetrator." But "trains, planes, and automobiles changed all that. Criminals can now rapidly travel far and wide, and with this newfound mobility they are less and less likely to be recognized by an eyewitness. Besides, eyewitness evidence these days frequently is proven to be unreliable." Therefore, Choice (C) is the correct answer. Although Choice (A) is a true statement, it isn't the best answer. Choices (B) and (D) are untrue statements and can therefore be eliminated.

835. **D. People are often suspicious of scientific breakthroughs.**

The passage says, "Many scientific breakthroughs are viewed with suspicion, if not downright hostility. . . . And before a science can ever enter the courtroom, it must be widely accepted." Hence, Choice (D) is the correct answer. Choices (A) and (C) are untrue. Fingerprint analysis is a forensic technique, so Choice (B) is incorrect.

836. **B. 40 million**

The passage says that "the population of the United States was stabilized at forty-million souls." Hence, Choice (B) is the correct answer.

837. **D. Not many people are born each day anymore.**

The passage says that Mr. Wehling is the only man waiting at the maternity ward of the hospital because "not many people were born a day any more." Hence, Choice (D) is the correct answer. Even though Choices (A) and (C) are true statements, they wouldn't explain why Mr. Wehling is the only person at the maternity ward (which specializes in births).

838. **B. The average age of the population is 129.**

The passage says that the average age of the population is "one hundred and twenty-nine." Hence, Choice (B) is correct.

839. **C. a man who had volunteered to die**

Although the faces in the mural are "to be filled with portraits of important people on either the hospital staff or from the Chicago Office of the Federal Bureau of Termination" and Dr. Hitz's portrait is already on the wall, the passage tells you that the room "was being redecorated as a memorial to a man who had volunteered to die." Hence, Choice (C) is the correct answer. Dr. Benjamin Hitz *is* the hospital's chief obstetrician, so Choices (A) and (D) can be eliminated. Nothing in the passage supports Choice (B).

840. **D. cynical**

The passage states, "A sardonic old man, about two hundred years old, sat on a stepladder, painting a mural he did not like." The man's attitude is cynical because he clearly does not believe in the supposed meaning of the painting, making Choice (D) the correct answer.

841. B. to disguise the true purpose of the Bureau

You are told in the passage that the Federal Bureau of Termination kills people who have outlived their purpose. The cheerful nicknames are used to disguise the true purpose of the Bureau by giving it harmless-sounding names. Hence, Choice (B) is correct.

842. A. humans who have outgrown their useful purpose in life.

The passage says that the mural depicts "a very neat garden" in which "men and women in purple uniforms pulled up weeds, cut down plants that were old and sickly, raked leaves, carried refuse to trash-burners." The weeds and refuse are a metaphor for members of society who are considered useless, and their removal is a metaphor for killing them, making Choice (A) the correct answer.

843. D. He believes that the mural is dishonest and does not represent real life.

The passage states, "The painter's face curdled with scorn. 'You think I'm proud of this daub?' he said. 'You think this is my idea of what life really looks like?'" The man's attitude is cynical, as he clearly doesn't believe in the supposed meaning of the painting, making Choice (D) the correct answer.

844. B. anxiety

The narrator admits to being "dreadfully nervous," so Choice (B) is correct. He denies being insane, Choice (A). He also states that the disease had "sharpened my senses—not destroyed—not dulled them"; hence, Choice (D) is incorrect. Choice (C) is incorrect because it refers to the old man, not the narrator.

845. D. cunning, unbalanced, and compulsive.

The narrator sees the old man's eye and says he was "haunted" by it "day and night." This shows he is compulsive. He carefully planned the murder, showing his cunning, and he is clearly unbalanced. Hence, Choice (D) is correct.

846. A. by pointing out his ability to tell the story calmly and clearly

The narrator invites the reader to observe "how healthily—how calmly" he can tell you the whole story, making Choice (A) the correct answer.

847. **B. so he would never have to look at the old man's diseased eye ever again**

The passage states, "I loved the old man. He had never wronged me. He had never given me insult [reject Choice (A)]. For his gold I had no desire [reject Choice (C)]. I think it was his eye! yes, it was this! He had the eye of a vulture [reject Choice (D)]. . . . I made up my mind to take the life of the old man, and thus rid myself of the eye forever." Choice (B) is the correct answer.

848. **B. The old man was asleep, so the narrator could not see the "Evil Eye" that he wanted to get rid of.**

The passage states, "And this I did for seven long nights—every night just at midnight—but I found the eye always closed; and so it was impossible to do the work; for it was not the old man who vexed me, but his Evil Eye." Hence, Choice (B) is the correct answer.

849. **C. casually asking him where he kept his gold.**

The passages states, "And every morning, when the day broke, I went boldly into the chamber, and spoke courageously to him, calling him by name in a hearty tone, and inquiring how he has passed the night." Therefore, Choice (C) is the correct answer.

850. **A. perception**

The passage says the narrator is slowly opening the old man's door and listening carefully to make sure he is still asleep, making Choice (A) the correct answer. You can reject the other choices because the narrator is not passionate or impulsive and makes no mention of his physical strength.

851. **B. He stands perfectly still for over an hour.**

The passage says, "I kept quite still and said nothing. For a whole hour I did not move a muscle, and in the meantime I did not hear him lie down," making Choice (B) the correct answer.

852. **D. You want your brain to work at its best, whether you want to stay sharp to keep up with your children or to excel at your work.**

You can reject Choices (A) and (B) because they both incorrectly use the contraction *you're* (which means you are) rather than the possessive adjective *your* (which means belonging to you). Choice (C) can also be rejected because it uses the plural noun *brains* instead of the singular *brain*. Choices (B) and (C) are also incorrect because they replace the verb *excel* with the noun *Excel*. Hence, Choice (D) is the correct answer.

853. **A. The brain weighs a mere three pounds, yet it's responsible for the smooth running of your whole body.**

You can reject Choices (B) and (C) because they both incorrectly use the possessive adjective *its* (which means belonging to it) instead of the contraction *it's* (which means it is). You can also reject Choices (C) and (D) because they incorrectly use the noun *hole* instead of the adjective *whole*. Hence, Choice (A) is the correct answer.

854. **C. This understanding gives you the foundation for knowing how to best train your brain.**

Choices (A) and (D) can be rejected because they use the wrong verb tense, *know,* instead of *knowing*. You can reject Choices (B) and (D) because they use the wrong verb tense, *training,* instead of *train*. Hence, Choice (C) is the correct answer.

855. **B. People who use their brains more efficiently tend to have better jobs, better relationships, and more happy and fulfilling lives.**

You can reject Choices (C) and (D) because they use the singular noun *brain* instead of the plural noun *brains* (lots of people don't share one brain!). You can reject Choices (A) and (C) because they both incorrectly use the word *whom* (the object of a verb) rather than *who* (the subject of the verb). Hence, Choice (B) is the correct answer.

856. **D. The different parts of the brain don't work in isolation; they work together as a team.**

You can reject Choices (A) and (B) because they omit the semicolon needed to separate the two independent clauses (sentences). You can reject Choice (C) because it incorrectly uses the singular noun *part* rather than the plural noun *parts*. Hence, Choice (D) is the correct answer.

857. **C. Doing so can make the difference between living a fulfilled life and living a frustrated one.**

You can reject Choice (A) because it incorrectly replaces the verb *doing* with *do*. You can reject Choices (B) and (D) because they incorrectly replace the preposition *between* with the prepositions *among* and *amongst,* respectively (these prepositions are used when referring to more than two items). Hence, Choice (C) is the correct answer.

858. **A. Whether you're a music lover, a budding writer, or a person with dozens of other interests, you can choose from a range of activities to help your brain.**

You can reject Choices (B) and (D) because they incorrectly replace the conjugation *whether* (which means if) with the noun *weather*. Choices (B) and (C) can be rejected because they incorrectly use the past-tense verb *chose* rather than the present-tense verb *choose*. Hence, Choice (A) is the correct answer.

859. **C. tall, burly, beady-eyed, and red-cheeked.**

The passage says that Sergeant-Major Morris is a "tall, burly man, beady of eye and rubicund of visage (red-cheeked)." Hence, Choice (C) is correct.

860. **B. The son is informing the father that their game is over.**

In the passage, the father and son are playing chess. The son has just won the game and is saying "mate" as an abbreviation of "checkmate." Hence, Choice (B) is the right answer.

861. **C. She has realized that the real reason he is upset is that he has just lost the game.**

According to the passage, the father has just lost a game of chess and is upset. He is letting off some steam by redirecting his anger. His wife realizes this and addresses the real reason he's upset. Hence, Choice (C) is the right answer.

862. **B. India**

The passage implies that Sergeant-Major Morris has been living in India. During the discussion of the past twenty years, Mr. White replies, "I'd like to go to India myself,. . . just to look round a bit, you know." Hence, Choice (B) is correct.

863. **C. wild monkeys**

In the passage, Mr. White says, "I should like to see those old temples and fakirs and jugglers." Hence, Choice (C) is correct.

864. **C. It has had a magic spell placed on it.**

Sergeant-Major Morris describes the monkey's paw as "an ordinary little paw, dried to a mummy." But then he adds, "It had a spell put on it by an old fakir." Hence, Choice (C) is the right answer. Although Choice (B) is a true statement, it is not as special as having a magic spell placed on it.

865. **A. He wanted to show that people who interfere with fate do so to their sorrow.**

The passage states, "He wanted to show that fate ruled people's lives, and that those who interfered with it did so to their sorrow." Hence, Choice (A) is correct.

866. **C. The author wanted to display the boy's character to the reader by spelling the words in the manner in which the boy says them.**

The passage says, "'It's a-movin',' he said to me as he passed; 'a-screwin' and a-screwin' out. I don't like it. I'm a-goin' 'ome, I am.'" By spelling the words as the boy would have said them, the author displays some of the boy's character to the reader. Hence, Choice (C) is the correct answer.

867. **B. Ogilvy**

The passage states, "'I say!' said Ogilvy; 'help keep these idiots back. We don't know what's in the confounded thing, you know!'" This suggests that Ogilvy is in a position of authority, so Choice (B) is the correct answer.

868. **D. excitement and anticipation to horror and panic**

As the occupants of the cylinder begin to emerge, the mood of the spectators changes swiftly from excitement and anticipation to horror and panic.

869. **A. The cylinder is being unscrewed from within.**

The passage states, "The end of the cylinder was being screwed out from within," which means that someone or something must have been inside it.

870. **D. a creature that resembled a human**

The passage states that "everyone expected to see a man emerge — possibly something a little unlike us terrestrial men, but in all essentials a man." Hence, Choice (D) is correct.

871. **C. the alien's eyes**

The narrator states that above all, "the extraordinary intensity of the immense eyes—were at once vital, intense, inhuman, crippled and monstrous." Hence, Choice (C) is the correct answer. Even though all the other answer choices are mentioned, the narrator finds the inhuman eyes to be the most disturbing feature.

872. **B. Mars**

The passage refers to the aliens as "Martians," so Choice (B) is the correct answer.

873. **A. The narrator becomes firm friends with the aliens.**

The passage states that the narrator was "overcome with disgust and dread" and found the aliens "inhuman and monstrous." Hence, it's very unlikely that he'll become firm friends with them, making Choice (A) the correct answer.

874. **C. In any situation, first thoroughly review the pros and cons of putting a complaint in writing at all.**

You can reject Choices (A) and (D) because they both omit the commas before the word *first.* Choices (B) and (D) can also be eliminated because they mistakenly use the wrong tense of the verb *(reviewing)* rather than *review*. Hence, Choice (C) is the correct answer.

875. **D. Bringing up the problem in a telephone or in-person conversation may be a smart way to deal with the complaint, depending on the situation and whether you can keep your cool.**

You can reject Choices (A) and (C) because they incorrectly use the word *bring* rather than the word *bringing.* Similarly, you can reject Choices (A) and (B) because they confuse the noun *weather* with the conjunction *whether* (which expresses doubt). Hence, Choice (D) is the correct answer.

876. **A. Your goal in a complaint letter is never – no matter how you feel – to let off steam.**

You can reject Choice (B) because it omits the dashes needed to separate the phrase "no matter how you feel." Similarly, you can reject Choice (C) because it incorrectly uses the wrong verb form *feeling* instead of *feel.* You can also reject Choice (D) because it uses the double negative phrase "not never." Hence, Choice (A) is the correct answer.

Technical Stuff: If the dashes look shorter than usual, that's because the excerpt is from a British book. British publishers use the shorter en dash (–), whereas most American publishers prefer the longer em dash (—).

877. **B. Controlling your *tone* also helps you achieve your purpose.**

You can reject Choices (A) and (C) because they use the wrong verb form *control* instead of *controlling.* You can also reject Choice (D) because it uses the verb *propose* rather than the noun *purpose.* Hence, Choice (B) is the correct answer.

878. **A. I looked into several complaints from three of my departments last week, and the records show that service on our network has been slow.**

Only Choice (A) uses *looked*, the past-tense verb that the sentence requires. Choice (B) uses the pluperfect tense *(had looked)* incorrectly. Choices (C) and (D) use the future tense, even though the incident they refer to happened in the past.

879. **D. Of course, this is not the service level we signed on for or experienced in the prior year.**

You can reject Choices (A) and (C) because they both confuse the adjective *coarse* (which means rough) with the phrase *of course* (which means obviously). You can reject Choice (B) because it omits the comma after the word *course*, which is needed to separate the two ideas in the sentence. Hence, Choice (D) is the correct answer.

880. **C. Note how using specific facts supports the goal and provides the best shot at remedying the situation.**

You can reject Choice (A) because it uses the plural verb conjugations for *support* and *provide*, which do not match the singular subject ("using specific facts"). Choice (B) is incorrect because it confuses the noun *shot* with the verb *shoot*. Choice (D) incorrect because it swaps the word *note* for *noting*. Therefore, Choice (C) is correct.

881. **C. your budget.**

The beginning of the passage tells you that "choosing a varied diet of healthful foods supports any healthy mind and body, but which healthful foods you choose says much about your personal tastes [Choice (D)] as well as the culture [Choice (B)] from which you come." The culture you live in is strongly affected by the country in which you live, so Choice (A) can also be rejected. Your budget is not mentioned in the passage, so Choice (C) is the correct answer.

882. **D. necessary to live a happy life.**

The passage says, "Technically speaking, nutrition is the science of how the body uses food [Choice (A)]. In fact, nutrition is life [Choice (B)]. All living things, including you, need food and water to live. Beyond that, you need good food, meaning food with the proper nutrients, to live well [Choice (C)]." Hence, Choice (D) is the correct answer.

883. D. nickel

The passage says, "If you don't eat and drink nutritious food and beverages: Your bones may bend or break (not enough calcium) [Choice (A)]. Your gums may bleed (not enough vitamin C) [Choice (B)]. Your blood may not carry oxygen to every cell (not enough iron) [Choice (C)]." Hence, Choice (D) is the correct answer.

884. Energy, Food

The passage says, "Energy is defined as the ability to do work" and "Food is the fuel on which your body runs."

885. A. heat

The passage says, "The amount of heat produced when food is burned (metabolized) in your body cells." Hence, Choice (A) is correct.

886. D. vitamins and minerals, amino acids, and fatty acids.

The passage says, "Essential nutrients for human beings include many well-known vitamins and minerals, several amino acids (the so-called building blocks of proteins), and at least two fatty acids." Hence, Choice (D) is the correct answer.

887. C. She is strongly in favor of it.

The passage says that although some people see the term *food processing* as a nutritional dirty word, "They're wrong. Without food processing and preservatives, you and I would still be forced to gather (or kill) our food each morning and down it fast before it spoiled." Hence, Choice (C) is correct.

888. B. spoil

The text is talking about trying to preserve food (or stop it from spoiling). To degrade means to spoil, so Choice (B) is the correct answer.

889. C. It is sustainable and personally customizable.

The opening paragraph of the passage states that additive manufacturing will transform the industry into a "sustainable and personally customized environment." Hence, Choice (C) is the correct answer. There is no mention of additive manufacturing being cheaper than traditional methods, so you can reject the other answer choices.

890. **D. They want to show how much additive manufacturing will revolutionize our lives.**

The passage states the advent of additive manufacturing "is not the slow change of progress from one generation of iPhone to the next but instead a true revolution, mirroring the changes that introduced the world to the Industrial Age and then brought light and electricity to our homes and businesses," making Choice (D) the correct answer. Choice (A) is the opposite of this, so you can eliminate it. Choices (B) and (C) both contain false statements.

891. **A. It will be disruptive as it brings swift changes to all aspects of the economy.**

The passage states, "This will not be a 'bloodless coup' by any means; any truly fundamental change that spans all aspects of the global economy will, by its nature, be disruptive." Hence, Choice (A) is the correct answer. There is no evidence in the passage to support any of the other answer choices.

892. **C. so easy to use and make, you can build one yourself.**

The passage states that you can get involved in this amazing transformation by "building and using a 3D printer at home," making Choice (C) the correct answer. There is no evidence in the passage to support any of the other answer choices.

893. **B. to provide a clear example of a similar device that the reader may be familiar with**

The passage tells you that although 3D printers are not quite there yet, they work on the same principal as the replicators in *Star Trek,* which the reader may be familiar with. Hence, Choice (B) is the correct answer. Choice (A) is amusing but incorrect since there is no evidence in the passage to suggest that 3D printers will be used to make replicators. Replicators don't actually exist, so Choice (C) must be incorrect. Choice (D) is not a true statement and can therefore be rejected.

894. **C. the inventor of the printing press**

The passage tells you that Johannes created "multiple printed documents" that "brought literacy to the world." Hence, Choice (C) is the correct answer.

895. **B. A 3D printer stores an object in a computer, translating it into a series of very thin slices, and then builds the object one layer at a time.**

According to the passage, a 3D printer stores an object in a computer, translating it into a series of very thin slices, and then builds the object one layer a time. Hence, Choice (B) is correct.

896. D. to show how amazed Gutenberg would be to see how far printing has progressed since his time

The passage states, "3D printing does the exact same thing for objects: Designs and virtual 3D models for physical objects can be shared, downloaded, and then printed out into physical form. It's hard to imagine what Johannes Gutenberg would have made of that." The authors are trying to show how far printing has progressed since Guttenberg's original invention; therefore, Choice (D) is the best answer. There is no evidence in the passage to support any of the other answer choices.

897. B. can make choosing wines a lot easier.

The passage states, "Knowing a lot of information about wine definitely isn't a prerequisite to enjoying it [so Choice (A) can be rejected]. But familiarity with certain aspects of wine can make choosing wines a lot easier, enhance your enjoyment of wine, and increase your comfort level." Hence, Choice (B) is correct. There's no evidence in the passage to support any of the other answer choices.

898. A. sugar

The passage states that yeasts convert that sugar into alcohol, Choice (B). Yeasts also produce carbon dioxide, Choice (C), and convert your grape juice into wine, Choice (D). The yeasts consume the sugar that's in the juice — they don't produce it — making Choice (A) the best answer.

899. B. milk left at room temperature.

The passage states that milk "contains a different sort of sugar than grapes" that "develops a small amount of alcohol if left on the kitchen table all day long." Hence, Choice (B) is correct. There is no evidence in the passage to support any of the other answer choices.

900. A. He discovered fermentation.

The passage states, "Louis Pasteur is the man credited with discovering fermentation in the 19th century." Choice (A) is therefore the best answer.

901. D. They're attempting to be humorous.

The authors are joking that the Garden of Eden (paradise) could not have been perfect if it didn't have wine available. Hence, Choice (D) is the correct answer. There's no evidence in the passage to support any of the other answer choices.

902. **C. the type of grapes used.**

Note that the question stem asks how the brewer controls the flavor of the wine *after* all the ingredients have been collected and prepared, making Choice (C) the correct answer.

903. **A. by letting the wine mature for a particular amount of time**

The passage says, "After fermentation, winemakers can choose how long to let the wine *mature* (a stage when the wine sort of gets its act together) and in what kind of container." Hence, Choice (A) is the correct answer. Note that the question asks about affecting the flavor *after* fermentation is complete, making Choices (C) and (D) incorrect.

904. **D. the variety of grapes used**

The last paragraph of the passage tells you that the type of grape used to make the wine determines the type of wine produced; hence, Choice (D) is the correct answer.

905. **C. Signing uses your hands, body, and face to convey meaning.**

The first paragraph says, "Signing isn't difficult, although moving your hands, body, and face to convey meaning instead of just using your voice may seem odd at first." Hence, Choice (C) is correct.

906. **C. an action sign that looks like what it means**

The passage says, "*Iconic* or *natural* signs look like what they mean," so Choice (C) is the correct answer.

907. **C. slapping your forehead and shouting, "Speak up, fool!"**

The passage says, "If you have trouble reading someone's signs, check the context and then ask yourself, 'What could this person mean?' [Choice (D)]. Remember that it's okay to ask someone to repeat something [Choice (A)]. You can show a signer you're 'listening' by nodding your head. If at any time someone is signing something to you and you begin not to understand, stop the person and let her know what you did understand and where you stopped understanding [Choice (B)]." Therefore, Choice (C) is the correct answer.

908. **B. American Sign Language**

The passage says, "This chapter illustrates the manual alphabet in American Sign Language and talks about hand and body movements." Therefore, Choice (B) is the correct answer.

909. **D. You should watch the signer's abdomen on up to the signer's head in order to understand the message.**

The passage says, "Remember not to watch the signer's hands primarily. You want to watch the signer's hands through your peripheral vision. Keep your eyes on the whole picture, from the signer's abdomen on up to her head. The eyes, face, hands, and body movements tell the whole story." Hence, Choice (D) is correct.

910. **B. signing the individual letters with your fingers**

The passage says, "Signers use the manual alphabet all the time, especially beginners. Signers *fingerspell* — spell using the manual alphabet." Therefore, Choice (B) is the correct answer.

911. **A. pause for just a second between each pair of words**

The passage says, "If you want to fingerspell two or more words in a row, such as a title or someone's first and last name, pause for just a second between each word." Hence, Choice (A) is the correct answer.

912. **C. to communicate with a whole new group of people**

According to the passage, "Your goal and reward is being able to meet and communicate with a whole new group of people." Hence, Choice (C) is the correct answer. Nothing in the passage supports any of the other answer choices.

913. **A. ironic**

The tone of the poem is ironic [Choice (A)] rather than sincere [Choice (B)] because throughout the poem, the author uses phrases that seem to reassure the reader that war is glorious and the wounded soldiers will be fine, but then he immediately follows these phrases with detailed descriptions of the mental scars that war creates. The tone is certainly not jovial [Choice (C)] or proud [Choice (D)].

914. **B. the horrors of war**

Both poems are clearly anti-war because since they both describe the horrific effect that war has on young soldiers. Only Choice (B) conveys that message properly.

915. **C. the soldiers are so old that they have forgotten how to walk properly.**

The poem focuses on the horrific physical effects [Choice (A)] and mental effects [Choices (B) and (D)] that war has on young soldiers. There is no indication that the soldiers are old (only that these boys have old faces), so Choice (C) is the correct answer.

916. **A. He was an injured war veteran and wrote the poem while recovering from his injuries in the hospital.**

From the anger and power presented in the poem and the date (1917), it is reasonable to conclude that the author was an injured war veteran who wrote the poem while recovering from his injuries in the hospital. You are also told in the passage information that the author is a WWI veteran. There is no evidence to suggest any of the other answer choices.

917. **C. He has utter contempt for them.**

Toward the end of the second poem, the author refers to the war supporters as "smug-faced" and suggests that they should "sneak home and pray you'll never know / The hell where youth and laughter go." He clearly has contempt for them, making Choice (C) the best answer. Choice (A) is wrong because the author does not respect their opinion. Choice (D) is wrong because the author does not see both sides of the situation.

918. **B. The soldiers went to war as men but came back broken and almost insane.**

The last two lines of the poem show that the soldiers who went to war glad to fight for their country returned home reduced to the level of helpless children, making Choice (B) the correct answer. The term "children" refers to the soldiers themselves (not their offspring), so you can reject the other answer choices.

919. **B. war**

The poem refers to the horrors of war, and the last sentence describes war itself as hell, making Choice (B) the correct answer. Although losing the war [Choice (A)] and coming home from the war [Choice (C)] may be unpleasant, "hell" refers to the war itself.

920. **C. He would be totally against it.**

Only Choice (C) matches the author's hatred of war and its supporters. Choice (A) is the opposite of what the author believes. He would not be ambivalent [Choice (B)] because he would not agree that there is any positive aspect of the parade. There is no evidence to suggest that he would secretly wish to attend the parade, so you can reject Choice (D).

921. **C. they demand too much money for their books.**

The passage states, "Writing a really good children's book is *hard* [Choice (A)]" but "getting it published is even harder. If you don't know the conventions and styles [Choice (B)], if you don't speak the lingo

[Choice (D)], if you don't have someone to advocate for your work, or if you or your manuscript doesn't come across as professional [also Choice (D)], you'll be hard pressed to get your manuscript read and considered, much less published." Hence, Choice (C) is the correct answer.

922. **C. keep trying until you find a publisher who is willing to take a chance on you**

The passage tells you that many of today's most successful writers were rejected time after time until they finally found someone who decided to take a chance on them. Hence, Choice (C) is the correct answer. Nothing in the passage supports any of the other answer choices.

923. **A. decide what type of children's book you want to write**

The passage says, "Before you do anything else, figure out what kind of children's book you're writing (or want to write)," making Choice (A) the correct answer. Having a child, Choice (B), is not a requirement for writing a children's book. Although Choices (C) and (D) are necessary, neither of them is the first step.

924. **physical, trim size, hardcover or softcover**

Formats involve the physical characteristics of a book, including page count, *trim size* (width and height), and the cover type (hardcover or softcover).

925. **C. making a writing schedule and stick to it**

The passage tells you about the importance of making a writing schedule and sticking to it. Hence, Choice (C) is the correct answer.

926. **D. when a writer cannot think of anything to write**

The passage tells you that "coming up with an interesting idea for a story isn't necessarily as easy as you may think" and "there are ways to get you unstuck if you find yourself with a mysterious case of writer's block." Hence, Choice (D) is the correct answer.

927. **B. do research to make sure your idea fits your target audience**

The passage says, "As soon as you have your good idea, it's time to get out there and research to make sure the idea fits your target audience." Hence, Choice (B) is the correct answer.

928. **D. realistic but encouraging**

The passage focuses on encouraging would-be writers to pursue their dreams but gives realistic advice on how they can achieve their goal. Hence, Choice (D) is correct.

929. **C. He eats a secret dish each night.**

The passage says that the king had a strange custom: "Every day after dinner, when the table was cleared, and no one else was present, a trusty servant had to bring him one more dish. It was covered, however, and even the servant did not know what was in it, neither did anyone know, for the king never took off the cover to eat of it until he was quite alone." Hence, Choice (C) is the right answer.

930. **C. He is overcome by curiosity.**

The passage says, "One day the servant, who took away the dish, was overcome with such curiosity that he could not help carrying the dish into his room." Hence, Choice (C) is the right answer.

931. **D. He hears a strange whispering of little voices outside his window.**

The passage says, "No sooner had it touched his tongue than he heard a strange whispering of little voices outside his window." Hence, Choice (D) is correct. Nothing in the passage supports any of the other answer choices.

932. **B. He has access to everywhere in the castle.**

The passage states that when the queen lost her most beautiful ring, "suspicion of having stolen it fell upon this trusty servant, who was allowed to go everywhere." Hence, Choice (B) is correct. Nothing in the passage supports any of the other answer choices.

933. **A. He overhears a conversation between some ducks.**

The passage states that the servant overhears a conversation between some ducks in which one of them says, "Something lies heavy on my stomach; as I was eating in haste I swallowed a ring which lay under the queen's window." Hence, Choice (A) is the right answer. He does hear sparrows chattering, but they tell him nothing about the ring, so Choice (C) is wrong. Nothing in the passage supports the other answer choices.

934. **B. He orders the cook to kill and prepare the duck for dinner.**

According to the passage, the servant "seized [the duck] by the neck, carried her to the kitchen, and said to the cook: 'Here is a fine duck; pray, kill her.'" As the cook prepares to cook the duck, he finds the queen's ring in her. Hence, Choice (B) is the right answer. The passage doesn't support any of the other answer choices.

935. **C. a horse and some money for traveling**

The passage says, "The king, to make amends for the wrong, allowed him to ask a favor, and promised him the best place in the court that he could wish for. The servant refused everything, and only asked for a horse and some money for travelling." Hence, Choice (C) is the right answer. The passage doesn't support any of the other answer choices.

936. **C. He saves their lives.**

According to the passage, "One day the servant saw three fishes caught in the reeds and gasping for water. As he had a kind heart, he got off his horse and put the three prisoners back into the water." Hence, Choice (C) is the right answer. The passage doesn't support any of the other answer choices.

937. **A. One good deed deserves another.**

The passage describes the servant as kind-hearted, and he seems to help the animals he encounters (with the exception of the duck!). Hence, Choice (A) is the best answer.

938. **B. "Diatoms: Flying Wonders of Nature."**

The passage states that diatoms are amazing little structures that can fly huge distances when they're taken up by the wind, so Choice (B) is the best answer. Choice (C) is not bad but doesn't mention that they fly, and Choice (A) is too general — it doesn't mention diatoms at all. Choice (D) is wrong because Professor Ram is not the main topic of the passage; the diatoms are.

939. **A. living or dead algae transported through the air.**

The opening paragraph of the passage mentions that diatoms are glass-shelled algae that are transported through the air, so you can reject Choices (C) and (D). The last paragraph discusses living diatoms, so the correct answer must be Choice (A), not Choice (B).

940. **D. He wants to give his listeners a familiar example of a large object that can fly long distances.**

You're seeking an answer that explains how mentioning Frisbees can help the reader understand why diatoms are able to fly, even though they're relatively large. Choice (D) is correct because the audience can easily visualize a Frisbee, which is an example of a large object that can fly long distances. Choices (A), (B), and (C) all contain false statements.

941. **B. where diatoms spend most of their brief lives.**

The opening paragraph of the passage says that diatoms "raise interesting questions. They seem to defy the size limit for far-flying dust, for one thing. And they may sometimes fly with a purpose." Hence, Choices (D) and (A) are true statements and can therefore be rejected. The last paragraph mentions Choice (C), leaving you with Choice (B) as the correct answer.

942. **C. extracting.**

The passage uses the word *teasing* in the second paragraph to describe how professor Ram removes or *extracts* the diatoms from their ice core; hence, the best answer is Choice (C).

943. **A. their geometric perfection**

The third paragraph says that diatoms' "geometric perfection" makes them stand out when they're viewed under a microscope, so Choice (A) is correct. Choice (B) is wrong because although diatoms can fly as well as Frisbees, there is no evidence to suggest that they are the same shape as Frisbees. There's no mention of their color, so you can reject Choice (C). Choice (D) refers to desert dust particles, not diatoms.

944. **shallow lake, sediment**

The passage states, "The ideal source of diatom dust is a shallow lake that shrinks in the dry season, exposing the sediment at its edges to the wind."

945. **B. She wants to reinforce the idea that heavy objects can be lifted and transported by strong winds.**

She is giving examples of heavy items that have been carried by the wind, so Choice (B) is correct.

946. **D. Of course, when television began, we humans had more toes than the TV had channels.**

You can reject Choices (A) and (C) because they both incorrectly use the pronoun *us* (which is the object of the verb) rather than the pronoun *we* (which is the subject of the verb). Choices (B) and (C) can also be rejected because they omit the commas needed to separate the phrase "when television began." Hence, Choice (D) is the correct answer.

947. **B. That makes running a successful YouTube channel seem a bit more daunting.**

You can reject Choices (A) and (C) because they both incorrectly use *make* rather than *makes*. Choices (C) and (D) can also be rejected because they incorrectly use *seemed* rather than *seem*. Hence, Choice (B) is the correct answer.

948. **A. Yet, regardless of the steep increase in competition, the intention has always been the same — getting people to watch your channel.**

You can reject Choices (B) and (C) because they both incorrectly use the word *irregardless* (which doesn't exist!) rather than the word *regardless* (which means nevertheless). Choices (B) and (D) can also be rejected because they both incorrectly use the noun *intension* (which means inner meaning) rather than *intention* (which means purpose). Hence, Choice (A) is the correct answer.

949. **C. Back then, it took a great deal of capital to get started on television.**

You can reject Choices (B) and (D) because they both incorrectly use the noun *Capitol* (which is a government building in Washington, DC) rather than the noun *capital* (which means money). Choice (A) can also be rejected because it incorrectly uses the present tense of the verb *takes* rather than the past tense *took*. Similarly, Choice (B) can be rejected because it incorrectly uses the future tense of the verb, *will take*. Hence, Choice (C) is the correct answer.

950. **D. Saying that your channel needs to host solid content that people actually want to see seems as glaringly obvious as saying a hamburger joint must make a good burger in order to survive.**

You can reject Choices (A) and (B) because they incorrectly use the wrong tense of the verb *say* rather than *saying*. Choices (A) and (C) can also be eliminated because they incorrectly use the wrong tense of the verb *surviving* rather than *survive*. Hence, Choice (D) is the correct answer.

951. **C. — and it should come as no surprise that the more viewers you can attract, the greater your potential to generate advertising revenue.**

You can reject Choices (A) and (D) because they both incorrectly use the past-tense verb *came* instead of *should come*. You can also reject Choices (B) and (D) because they incorrectly use the adverb *potentially* (which means with the capacity of happening in the future) instead of the noun *potential* (which means unrealized ability). Hence, Choice (C) is the correct answer.

952. **C. But before you start worrying about all that money you're going to make, let's take a look at what it takes to get started on a YouTube channel for you or your business.**

You can reject Choices (A) and (B) because they confuse the contraction *let's* (which means let us) for the third-person singular form of the verb *lets* (which suggests a request). You can reject Choices (A) and (D) because they incorrectly use the third-person pronoun *one* instead of the second-person pronoun *you* (which is used in the rest of the sentence). Hence, Choice (C) is the correct answer.

953. **D. And since you already love making videos and most likely exhibit some expertise or viewpoint to share with the world, YouTube may be your best creative outlet.**

You can reject Choices (A) and (C) because they confuse the phrase *all ready* (which means completely prepared for) with the adverb *already* (which means happened previously). You can reject Choice (B) because it incorrectly uses the verb *exhibiting* instead of *exhibit*. Hence, Choice (D) is the correct answer.

954. **B. "How many?" you ask.**

You can reject all the answer choices except Choice (B) because the question mark must appear within the quotation marks.

955. **B. Then you have performers who regard the video hosting site as their personal stage**

You can reject Choices (A) and (C) because they confuse the pronoun *whom* (the object of the verb) with the pronoun *who* (subject of the verb). Choices (A) and (D) are also wrong because they both incorrectly use the singular possessive adjective *his* (belonging to him) rather than the plural possessive adjective *their* (belonging to them). Hence, Choice (B) is the correct answer.

956. **B. Twitter is basically a powerful social network that allows you to keep up with the people, businesses, and organizations you're interested in**

You can reject Choices (C) and (D) because they incorrectly use the third person pronoun *one* instead of the second person pronoun *you* (which is used in the rest of the sentence). Choices (A) and (C) are also wrong because they both incorrectly use the adjective *basic* (which means simple) rather than the adverb *basically* (which means essentially). Hence, Choice (B) is the correct answer.

957. **D. You'll have to bear with us to find out why you would want to do that.**

You can reject Choices (A) and (B) because they both incorrectly use the adjective *bare* (which means naked) rather than the verb *bear* (which means to carry a burden). You can also reject Choice (C) because it incorrectly uses *you have* rather than the contraction *you'll* (which means you will). The positioning of this sentence in the passage requires the future tense. Hence, Choice (D) is the correct answer.

958. **B. That's a whole lot of tweeting!**

You can reject Choices (C) and (D) because they both incorrectly use the noun *hole* rather than the adjective *whole*. You can also reject Choices (A) and (D) because they replace the exclamation mark with a question mark, even though the statement is not supposed to be a question. Hence, Choice (B) is the correct answer.

959. **A. Twitter is a fast-evolving, surprisingly powerful new way to exchange ideas and information and to stay in touch with people, businesses, and organizations that you care about.**

You can reject Choices (B) and (D) because they both incorrectly omit the hyphen in the compound modifier *fast-evolving*. You can also reject Choices (B) and (C) because they confuse the adjective *surprising* with the adverb *surprisingly*. Hence, Choice (A) is the correct answer.

960. **B. Twitter has one central feature: It lets users instantly post entries of 140 characters or less, known as *Tweets***

You can reject Choices (A) and (C) because they both incorrectly use a comma instead of a semicolon, which is needed to separate the two connected sentences, or independent clauses. You can also reject Choice (D) because it confuses the contraction *let's* (which means let us) with the verb *lets* (permits). Hence, Choice (B) is the correct answer.

961. **D. But writing headlines and very short advertising copy is famously hard to do really well, and the right words can be quite powerful.**

You can reject Choices (A) and (B) because they both incorrectly use the adjective *real* rather than the adverb *really*. You can also reject Choices (A) and (C) because they both incorrectly use the adjective *good* rather than the adverb *well*. Hence, Choice (D) is the correct answer.

962. **C. Twitter sounds simple — deceptively simple.**

You can reject Choices (A) and (D) because they both incorrectly use the plural form of the verb *sound* rather than the singular form *sounds*.

Choice (A) also incorrectly uses the adjective *deceptive* rather than the adverb *deceptively*. You can also reject Choices (B) and (D) because they both incorrectly use the adverb *simply* rather than the adjective *simple*. Hence, Choice (C) is the correct answer.

963. **A. In tech-speak, Twitter is a microblogging tool; however, you can more easily think of Twitter as a giant cocktail party with dozens of conversations you can join (or start) at any moment.**

You can reject Choices (B) and (C) because they both incorrectly omit the semicolon before the word *however* (the semicolon is needed to separate the two independent clauses). Choice (B) also omits the comma following the word *however*. You can also reject Choices (C) and (D) because they both incorrectly use the adjective *easy* rather than the adverb *easily*. Hence, Choice (A) is the correct answer.

964. **C. If you're familiar with blogs, instant messaging, and web-based journals, you can start to understand what makes Twitter unique.**

The word *unique* is an absolute modifier, which means that it makes no sense to place a comparative modifier — such as *very* or *most* — before it. Either something is unique, or it isn't. There's also no such word as *uniquest*. Hence, Choice (C) is the correct answer.

965. **B. dominating**

The sentence is referring to the Appalachian Mountains, which rise above the surrounding countryside and dominate it due to their height. Hence, Choice (B) is the correct answer.

966. **D. The passage does not say.**

The opening sentence of the passage tells you, "Whoever has made a voyage up the Hudson must remember the Catskill Mountains." Therefore, you can reject Choice (A) because the Hudson is a river and reject Choice (B) because the Catskills are a mountain range. Fort Christina was the site of a siege, not the name of Rip's village, so Choice (D) is the correct answer.

967. **C. downtrodden**

The passage tells you that Rip's wife is constantly henpecking (nagging) her husband to do chores around the house. Rip is therefore henpecked (downtrodden or bullied) by his wife, making Choice (C) the correct answer.

968. **C. Rip's wife**

The passage states, "Certain it is that he was a great favorite among all the goodwives of the village, who took his part in all family squabbles; and never failed, whenever they talked those matters over in their evening gossipings, to lay all the blame on Dame Van Winkle." Therefore, Choice (C) is the correct answer. Nothing in the passage supports any of the other answer choices.

969. **B. They're much too large for him.**

The passage states that Rips son "was generally seen trooping like a colt at his mother's heels, equipped in a pair of his father's cast-off breeches [pants], which he had much ado to hold up with one hand, as a fine lady does her train in bad weather." The pants are so big on him that he has to hold them up, so Choice (B) is the correct answer.

970. **B. He has a strong dislike of all kinds of profitable labor.**

The passage states, "The great error in Rip's composition was a strong dislike of all kinds of profitable labor," making Choice (B) the correct answer. There is no evidence in the passage to support any of the other answer choices.

971. **C. simple, good-natured, kind, and obedient**

The passage describes Rip as "a simple, good-natured man; he was, moreover, a kind neighbor and an obedient, henpecked husband." Hence, Choice (C) is correct.

972. **D. Don't worry; be happy.**

The passage states that Rip "would have whistled life away in perfect contentment." Hence, Choice (D) is the best answer.

973. **C. The victim was an important person.**

The phrase "high position of the victim" suggests the victim was famous and important, making Choice (C) correct.

974. **C. shortly after 11 p.m.**

According to the passage, the maid went to her bedroom around 11 p.m. and witnessed the murder shortly after that time, making Choice (C) correct. Choice (A) is when she woke up and told the police about the murder.

975. A. Sir Danvers Carew

The victim is revealed to be Sir Danvers Carew, making Choice (A) the correct answer. Mr. Hyde, Choice (D), was the murderer, not the victim. Mr. Utterson, Choice (B), was the lawyer. Dr. Jekyll, Choice (C), was the doctor to whom Mr. Utterson had given the walking stick to many years before.

976. C. The motive for the murder was probably not robbery.

The fact that the victim's purse and gold watch were found at the scene of the crime makes it clear that the motive for the murder was probably not robbery, so Choice (C) is correct.

977. C. He gave it to Dr. Jekyll many years ago.

The passage states that the lawyer gave the murder weapon to Dr. Jekyll many years ago, making Choice (C) correct.

978. A. white-haired.

The passage describes Mr. Hyde as a person of small stature, wicked-looking, and ill-tempered, so you can reject Choices (B), (C), and (D). It's the victim, not Mr. Hyde, who has white hair, making Choice (A) the correct answer.

979. C. The officer realized that solving such a high-profile crime would help his career.

The officer's eye lights up "with professional ambition" because he realizes that solving the murder of such an important person would be very good for his career, making Choice (C) the correct answer. Nothing in the passage supports any of the other answer choices.

980. D. She thinks he's handsome.

The passage states that the maid initially pays more attention to the "aged and beautiful gentleman" in the alley, which suggests she thinks he's handsome, so Choice (D) is correct. Choices (A), (B), and (C) all refer to Mr. Hyde, not the older gentleman, so you can reject them.

981. A. freezing

The passage lists several ways of preserving foods: "You can freeze them, can them, dry them for storage, or ferment them." The question asks how people preserved foods *before* the days of refrigerators, so Choice (A) is the correct answer.

982. **D. The authors love them.**

The passage describes bacteria, yeasts, and molds as "healthy living microbes" and suggests that the reader will fall in love with them upon learning more about them. Hence, Choice (D) is the correct answer. Nothing in the passage supports any of the other answer choices.

983. **B. natural and ancient**

According to the passage, fermentation is a natural and ancient way to preserve your food, making Choice (B) the correct answer.

984. **B. freshly squeezed apple juice.**

The passage tells you that fermented foods include sourdough bread [Choice (D)], soy sauce, tofu, yogurt, cheese, cider and wine [Choice (A)], pickles [Choice (C)], and sauerkraut. Hence, Choice (B) is the correct answer.

985. **B. a process involving yeast and bacteria that does not require oxygen**

The passage says that fermentation requires yeast and bacteria. The passage also states that anaerobic conditions are those in which there's no oxygen present. Hence, Choice (B) is the correct answer. All the other answer choices contain oxygen, which would lead to *aerobic* conditions rather than *anaerobic* conditions.

986. **C. The changes caused by fermentation can be either good or bad, or they can be both good and bad, depending on the conditions.**

The passage says, "The changes caused by fermentation can be both good and bad . . . but when you control the fermentation process, you can actually have some incredible results! When you execute fermentation processes properly, something that could have turned rotten instead turns into a consumable product." Hence, Choice (C) is the correct answer. Nothing in the passage supports any of the other answer choices.

987. **C. increased alcohol content.**

The passage says that controlling mold and promoting good bacteria maximizes the shelf life of the foods, enhances flavors, and increases health benefits. Hence, Choice (C) is the correct answer. Nothing in the passage supports any of the other answer choices.

988. **A. it takes only one day to complete.**

The passage says that fermenting is "a low-cost [Choice (D)], highly efficient [Choice (C)] way of preserving foods." The passage also suggests the fermenting is enjoyable, Choice (B). Hence, Choice (A) is the correct answer.

989. **D. He was transformed into a giant cockroach.**

The first few lines of the passage suggest that Gregor Samsa has turned into a giant cockroach: "His many legs, pitifully thin compared with the size of the rest of him, waved about helplessly as he looked." Hence, Choice (D) is the correct answer.

990. **D. Gregor Samsa is a traveling salesman who hates his job.**

The passage says that "Samsa was a travelling salesman," and Samsa says, "Oh, God,. . . what a strenuous career it is that I've chosen!"

991. **D. He is lonely and wishes he were in a relationship.**

The second paragraph tells you that "a collection of textile samples lay spread out on the table — Samsa was a travelling salesman — and above it there hung a picture that he had recently cut out of an illustrated magazine and housed in a nice, gilded frame." Hence, Samsa does not know the lady, so you can reject Choices (A) and (B). Samsa appears to sell textiles, so you can reject Choice (C). Hence, Choice (D) is the correct answer.

992. **C. He doesn't want to have to look at his floundering legs.**

The passage states, "He must have tried it a hundred times, shut his eyes so that he wouldn't have to look at the floundering legs, and only stopped when he began to feel a mild, dull pain there that he had never felt before." Hence, Choice (C) is correct. It's raining outside, so Choice (A) is incorrect. He also knows he isn't dreaming, making Choice (B) wrong.

993. **B. carrying heavy luggage.**

The passage says that the curse of traveling includes "worries about making train connections [Choice (D)], bad and irregular food [Choice (A)], contact with different people all the time so that you can never get to know anyone or become friendly with them [Choice (C)]." Hence, Choice (B) is correct.

994. **C. He likes to appear superior.**

The passage says that Gregor considers it to be "a funny sort of business to be sitting up there at your desk, talking down at your subordinates from up there"; hence, Choice (C) is correct. Nothing in the passage supports any of the other answer choices.

995. **A. He wants to end the conversation quickly before his mother realizes how strange his voice sounds.**

The passage says that "Gregor was shocked when he heard his own voice answering, it could hardly be recognized as the voice he had had before." Gregor wants to give a full answer and explain everything, but in the circumstances decides to end the conversation quickly, making Choice (A) the correct answer. Nothing in the passage supports any of the other answer choices.

996. **A. his relationship with his wife.**

The passage mentions that all the factors in Choices (B), (C), and (D) add to Gregor's overall feeling of despair, so you can reject those answer choices. There is no mention of Gregor's wife or even whether he's married; therefore, Choice (A) is a false statement, making it the correct answer.

997. **C. He needs to pay off his parents' debt to his boss.**

The passage says that Gregor longs to quit his job, but he can't do so until he has paid off his parents' debt to his boss, making Choice (C) the correct answer.

998. **B. employees**

In the passage, you're told that Gregor's boss likes "talking down" at his "subordinates" (employees); hence, Choice (B) is the correct answer.

999.

When reviewing your essay, ask yourself the following questions:

- Have I responded to the prompt?
- Is my point of view clearly stated?
- Do my ideas flow in a logical order?
- Have I provided enough evidence to support my point of view?

» Are there any errors in punctuation (commas, periods, semicolons, apostrophes, and so on)?

» Are there any misspelled words?

» Does my essay consist of 4 to 7 paragraphs with 3 to 7 sentences each?

» Is my essay 300 to 500 words of writing?

A well-written essay that addresses these questions will score well on the GED. A sample essay is shown here. What does the writer do well? How could the essay be improved?

In the discussion as to whether the minimum driving age should be raised to 18 years old, both authors made several claims to support his point of view, however the author of Passage 2 did a much better job of supporting his claims with clear, documented facts, and testimony from leading experts. In contrast, many of the claims by the author of Passage 1 were not supported by any evidence whatsoever and appear to be based more in opinion rather than in fact.

The author of Passage 1 begins by stating that, "Scientific evidence shows that the brain of an average teen operates very differently from that of an average adult," but he fails to provide this "scientific evidence." If the evidence exists then the author should show it — he can't simply refer to such evidence and hope that we will take him at his word.

The author of Passage 1 then claims that, "technological distractions appear to be much more important to younger teenagers," and that, "By the age of 18, however, there has been an adjustment in the teenager's brain that makes this technology appear not so important." Once again the author offer no supporting evidence to these statements so an intelligent reader is forced to take them with a pinch of salt.

The author of Passage 1 also claims that, teenagers have a 'need for speed' and that "drinking and driving is a problem at all ages but it is more so for younger teens."

Yet again, the author does not offer a single shred of evidence to support these rather dubious claims. He also appears to be unaware that the minimum drinking age is 21 which would actually mean that teenagers are less likely to drink and drive compared to older drivers.

In contrast, the author of Passage 2 offers a variety of evidence for his more balanced statements and he correctly gets to the heart of the issue by focusing more on the inexperience of the driver rather than the driver's age.

He cites evidence from the data collected by the Insurance Institute for Highway Safety to show that raising the driving age does not actually prevent teen driver crashes — it simply just delays them. This data compared two states with different driving ages and clearly showed that 17 year-old drivers were no safer on the road than 16 year-old drivers.

The author of Passage 2 also points out that raising the minimum driving age to 18 may actually make the problem worse by preventing teenagers from getting the expert training and driving education they need to become safe, reliable drivers. He supports this claim with a very logical argument by pointing out that if a teenager cannot legally start learning to drive until the age when he or she may have already left home, there may not be anyone nearby to teach him or her to drive safely. He also quotes from leading experts in the field such as Kate Willette of Seattle's SWERVE Driving School to back up his claim that "It's careful and extensive training, more than age, that prepares teenagers to be safe drivers."

Both authors may have had the same goal in mind — to reduce fatal road accidents — but only the author of Passage 2 used real evidence to support his argument. Also, by applying a logical, fact-based argument to the problem, the author of Passage 2 appears to have 'hit the nail on the head' by focusing on the driver's inexperience rather than the age of the driver. After all, "Teens have to get their driving experience somehow and the only place they can do that is behind the wheel."

1,000.

When reviewing your essay, ask yourself the following questions:

- » Have I responded to the prompt?
- » Is my point of view clearly stated?
- » Do my ideas flow in a logical order?
- » Have I provided enough evidence to support my point of view?
- » Are there any errors in punctuation (commas, periods, semicolons, apostrophes, and so on)?
- » Are there any misspelled words?
- » Does my essay consist of 4 to 7 paragraphs with 3 to 7 sentences each?
- » Is my essay 300 to 500 words of writing?

A well-written essay that addresses these questions will score well on the GED. A sample essay is shown here. What does the writer do well? How could the essay be improved?

Both authors have strong opinions about whether school uniforms should be mandatory for all students, but the author of Passage 1 does a much better job arguing his case and supporting his point of view with evidence and expert opinions. In contrast, the author of Passage 2 comes across as a spoilt brat who is only interested in her own selfish point of view.

The author of Passage 1 cites the study by education expert, Virginia Draa, to support his statement that educators and experts who support school uniforms agree that uniforms contribute positively to the behavior of students.

The author of Passage 1 also stated that many experts who support the school uniform policy also believe that wearing uniforms decreased bullying and teasing related to clothing. He supported this opinion with direct evidence from the school district in North Jersey that recently reported a reduction in bullying after it had implemented a mandatory school uniform policy.

In his essay, the author of Passage 1 considered the beneficial affect that a mandatory school policy would have on the whole community. This is in direct contrast to the self-centered focus of Passage 2.

The author of Passage 2 makes several inflammatory comments such as, "they are idiots who don't know what they are talking about," and "imposing school uniforms on students is immoral, stupid, and should obviously be illegal!" Neither of these opinions is supported by any evidence, studies, or expert opinion and hence, the reader cannot take them too seriously.

Furthermore, her entire argument against mandatory school uniforms appears to be based around the fact that she would no longer be able to look down at other students who cannot afford the latest designer clothing. "What's the point of being able to afford the latest Mui Mui shoes and Gucci tops if I can't flaunt them in front of everyone at school each day?", she says.

The author of Passage 2 also seems to be more concerned about how she will be able to continue to discriminate against other students if school uniform policies are imposed. Statements like, "How am I supposed to judge whether a new girl in my class is worthy of my company if I can't immediately dismiss her based on her lack of fashion sense (or her lack of ability to afford designer clothes)?" display the author's rather unpleasant attitude. This is also exactly the sort of behavior that can lead to the bullying of less privileged students — and the sort of behavior that school uniforms would help to minimize.

The author of Passage 1 presented a clear, well-reasoned argument that he supported with expert testimony and evidence. In contrast, rather than successfully making her case, the author of Passage 2 ironically adds support to the opposite point of view by displaying an odious attitude that mandatory school uniforms would help to stamp out.

1,001.

When reviewing your essay, ask yourself the following questions:

- Have I responded to the prompt?
- Is my point of view clearly stated?
- Do my ideas flow in a logical order?
- Have I provided enough evidence to support my point of view?
- Are there any errors in punctuation (commas, periods, semicolons, apostrophes, and so on)?
- Are there any misspelled words?
- Does my essay consist of 4 to 7 paragraphs with 3 to 7 sentences each?
- Is my essay 300 to 500 words of writing?

A well-written essay that addresses these questions will score well on the GED. A sample essay is shown here. What does the writer do well? How could the essay be improved?

Passage 2 does a good job in relating how Justice Harlan's enduring truth, that "all citizens are equal before the law," can be applied to the arguments for and against affirmative action. According to the passage, affirmative action was intended to uphold Justice Harlan's sentiments, but the passage later describes how these new laws may have unintentionally discriminated against non-minority citizens and how recent court cases are trying to restore the balance.

Passage 2 begins by showing that Justice Harlan's profound ideals have not always been applied throughout the history of the United States, and how this disparity led to the need for affirmative action to protect the rights of underprivileged minorities.

According to Passage 2, when affirmative action first began in the 1960's, it was intended as "positive action through programs initiated by governmental entities that benefit certain groups." Executive Order 10925, signed by President Kennedy, and the Civil Rights Act of 1964 are examples of government policies that benefit certain disadvantaged groups (who had been treated unfairly in the past) in an attempt to restore the balance of equal rights for all citizens. In this respect, the passage successfully argues that affirmative action appears to uphold Justice Harlan's enduing truths. This makes sense, because, as President Lyndon Johnson said in 1965, "You do not take a person who, for years, has been hobbled by chains and liberate him, bring him up to the starting line of a race and then say you are free to compete with all the others, and still just believe that you have been completely fair."

However, Passage 2 also mentions that not everyone agreed with the ideas of affirmative action and that some non-minority citizens soon began to view the new laws in a very different way. The passage suggests that some white Americans believe that affirmative action actually undermines Justice Harlan's enduring truth by discrimination against non-minority citizens. The subsequent lawsuits filed by these 'underprivileged' whites led to "a decisive turning point in judicial thought," which stopped focusing on "the rights of minorities to protection of the rights of all citizens, including White Americans."

Although one may argue that the views of the opponents of affirmative action may not be based in reality (since white men make up less than 50% of the college-educated workforce but account for the vast majority of high-paying jobs, including CEO positions, law firm partnerships, and tenured college faculty positions!) the passage still does a good job linking their viewpoint back to Judge Harlan's original point.

Passage 2 does not appear to take one side in the debate and retains a neutral tone that simply informs the reader about the reasoning behind the two points of view. Hence, the passage is able to successfully examine how Justice Harlan's truth can be used by both the proponents and opponents of affirmative action to argue the pros and cons of the new laws that were intended to make the Constitution "color-blind" and ensure that "all citizens are equal before the law."

Index

D

E

F

G

H

I

J

K

L

M

N

O

P

R

S

T

U

V

W

Y

About the Author

Dr. Stuart Donnelly has prepared students for the GED and the TASC, both academically and emotionally, for the past two decades. After he was awarded his PhD in mathematics from Oxford University at the age of 25, Dr. Donnelly moved to Hong Kong, where he established the territory's most successful tutoring service. Upon his return to the United States in 1998, he founded Tutors of Oxford NYC and Doctor MCAT, which specialize in providing the finest quality one-on-one tutoring available in New York City. With over 20 years of private tutoring and teaching experience at all levels, including teaching at both George Washington University and Western Connecticut State University, Dr. Donnelly is considered by many leading educators to be one of the most experienced and qualified private tutors in the country. Many of his students have been admitted to the world's leading schools and universities. Stuart lives on the Upper West Side of Manhattan with his wife and young son.

Publisher's Acknowledgments

Executive Editor: Lindsay Sandman Lefevere

Project Editor: Tim Gallan

Copy Editor: Danielle Voirol

Technical Reviewer: Cindy Kaplan

Production Editor: Siddique Shaik

Cover Image: © Skip ODonnell/iStockphoto